John — I think these are
fascinating
I hope yo...

D0705531

100 Reasons
Shake-speare
was the
Earl of Oxford

With New Introduction
By the Author

Hank Whittemore

GMJ Global Media
2021

Second Edition
Errata Corrections, Text Emendations
And New Introduction
Published in 2021 by
GMJ Global Media
Nyack, NY

First Edition
Published in 2016 by
Forever Press
Somerville, MA

Copyright © 2016, 2021
Copyright © Hank Whittemore
All rights reserved

Third Printing
December 2021

LCCN: 2021917425

ISBN 978-1-7373832-1-5

Cover by William Boyle
Cover image from the title page of
Minerva Britanna by Henry Peacham (1612)
Discussed in Reason 95

Images used in this publication are all courtesy of
Wikimedia Commons, Wikipedia, various literary websites
around the web, or were derived from pre-1930 print sources.
All images in the public domain.

Printed in the USA

Once again, to Glo

With Love Always

"While mainstream academia largely dismisses questions of authorship in studying the works of Shakespeare, Whittemore strongly champions the Oxfordian argument in this tour de force defense while remaining a highly entertaining writer. A breezy but very intelligent tone is maintained throughout the book; the reader is neither patronized nor boggled by minutiae and jargon. Instead, there is a magnetic sense of history, art, politics, and human nature injected into a smooth and eminently readable storytelling style. It is obvious that the author's research has been painstaking, but the resulting document is more than painless -- it's downright pleasurable."
– *Kirkus Reviews* – 2016 *(Full Review Below)*

"Each reason, masterfully combining logical thought and solid historical support, is powerful in itself. Combined into *100 Reasons Shake-speare was the Earl of Oxford*, and read one after another, their effect is overwhelming. This book is an entertaining journey into the heart of the Shakespeare mystery and shows why Oxford's authorship is the key that unravels it."
– James A. Warren, *Shakespeare Revolutionized*, 2021

"An exceptionally lucid and thorough exploration of the arguments supporting J.T. Looney's controversial theory that the true Shakespeare was the Earl of Oxford. Masterfully organized, the book takes the reader through 100 primary reasons supporting the theory. Whittemore's long experience studying and writing about the authorship question, and keen eye for problematic fact or surprising but enlightening perspective, is evident throughout."
– Roger Stritmatter, Ph.D., associate Professor of Humanities at Coppin State University and general editor of *Brief Chronicles: An Interdisciplinary Journal of Authorship Studies*

"If Stratfordians could assemble even a handful of arguments this powerful and this persuasive for Will Shakspere of Stratford as the author of the Bard's plays and poems, they'd say, 'Game over. We've proved our case.' But either they can't, or they haven't. Or maybe it's both. Whatever the case, they should buy this book. Hank Whittemore's brilliant *100 Reasons* shows how it's done."
– Mark Anderson, author of *"Shakespeare" by Another Name*

"Hank Whittemore is a superb and enlightened scholar whose historical accounts are consistently entertaining, accessible and accurate; his *100 Reasons* unlocks the door to a rich garden of truth about William Shakespeare from whence no serious lover of his poems and plays will ever wish to return."
– Alexander Waugh, author, scholar, critic, composer; Chairman of the De Vere Society of London and Honorary President of the Shakespeare Authorship Coalition

"Whittemore has compiled the reasons why Oxford wrote the Shakespeare canon in the most comprehensive and articulate way possible. I've learned things I didn't know even after decades of research in the Shakespeare Authorship Question, and it clarified some things I thought I knew."
– Bonner Miller Cutting, author of *Necessary Mischief: Exploring the Shakespeare Authorship Question*

"Written with wit, humor, erudition and the instincts of a real working actor, Hank Whittemore's *100 Reasons* bristles with humanity as it seeks to convince readers that the name Shakespeare was simply a pseudonym. Begun as a search by the author for the roots of Shakespeare's titanic creativity, this extraordinary document becomes a personal narrative of the life of the wild and witty Edward de Vere, the most erudite aristocrat in the court of Queen Elizabeth I. And Whittemore does ultimately convince us that de Vere was the real Shakespeare. A truly original approach to academic research, this forensic examination of centuries-old evidence is well worth the attention of academics and non-academics alike
-- Don Rubin, editor of Routledge's six-volume *World Encyclopedia of Contemporary Theatre* and former chair of the Department of Theatre at York University, Toronto

"I watched for several years as Hank Whittemore clearly, concisely, and completely enumerated and elucidated the Oxfordian case for the Shakespeare authorship online. I eagerly awaited each essay as this clear and engaging writer explained the case for Edward DeVere as Shakespeare with indisputable data, and disarming charm. Whittemore's masterwork is now available in book form as *100 Reasons Shake-speare Was the Earl of Oxford*.
"The erudition and specificity of this amazing commentary makes Whittemore's compilation of historical information about Oxford's life and its relationship to the Shakespeare canon an

indispensable trove of information on the authorship question. We now have an indisputable claimant for the answer to the question: What is the first book to read about the Shakespeare authorship question? Answer: Hank Whittemore's *100 Reasons Shake-speare Was the Earl of Oxford.*

– Linda Theil, editor of the *Oberon Shakespeare Study Group* weblog

"Read this book before you decide who wrote Shakespeare. Challenges to the traditional authorship theory are often ignored or dismissed by impugning unworthy motives to authorship skeptics. The mountain of evidence against the legendary author is dealt with by selecting a single pebble and rejecting it as only circumstantial evidence. Hank Whittemore, by contrast, closely examines 100 important features of this mountain, leaving the reader convinced there is more to the authorship debate than she had suspected.

"Traditionalists insist the real author knew the world of the theater from the inside. Whittemore begins presenting far more evidence of Edward de Vere's close associations with the theater than the skimpy evidence of the traditional author's theatrical involvement (which may have been primarily as a money lender).

"Whittemore remains closely attuned to his reader's reactions along the way, serving as a sympathetic, knowledgeable guide on this exciting journey. Those who claim it makes no difference who wrote Shakespeare will think twice about that assumption when they discover new pleasure in watching a Shakespeare play, or reading a Shakespeare sonnet, now that we know so much more about the true author."

– Richard M. Waugaman, M.D., Clinical Professor of Psychiatry, Georgetown University School of Medicine; Training and Supervising Analyst, Emeritus, Washington Psychoanalytic Institute. Oxfordian of the Year, 2021.

Kirkus Review
2016

100 Reasons makes a progressively stronger case for the Earl of Oxford as the sole author of the works of Shakespeare. Beginning in the book's introduction by questioning how such a seemingly unremarkable man as Shakespeare could demonstrate such near-miraculous genius, Whittemore takes the reader on an intricate journey in scholarship regarding the theater and the Renaissance period. He touches on the first Oxfordian supporter—John Thomas Looney—and builds profiles of the various players in Shakespeare's world, from Queen Elizabeth I's chief adviser, Lord Burghley, to her spymaster, Francis Walsingham. During this odyssey, an image of de Vere himself emerges: a brilliant, controversial man and an intimate of Elizabeth's court with poetry and theater in his blood—an ideal alternative to Shakespeare for reasons ranging from creativity to insight into statecraft.

While mainstream academia largely dismisses questions of authorship in studying the works of Shakespeare, Whittemore strongly champions the Oxfordian argument in this tour de force defense while remaining a highly entertaining writer. A breezy but very intelligent tone is maintained throughout the book; the reader is neither patronized nor boggled by minutiae and jargon. Instead, there is a magnetic sense of history, art, politics, and human nature injected into a smooth and eminently readable storytelling style. It is obvious that the author's research has been painstaking, but the resulting document is more than painless— it's downright pleasurable. The text itself is immaculate, as one would expect from such a seasoned nonfiction writer and scholar.

One may or may not accept the Oxfordian argument, but Whittemore ensures that the reader will never again lightly dismiss it. An engrossing and thoughtful literary examination.

Foreward/Clarion Review
2021

"Probing, provocative, and absorbing ... Captivating passion and scholarship."

Hank Whittemore works to reclaim the literary works attributed to Shakespeare for Edward de Vere, the seventeenth Earl of Oxford. The idea that "Shakespeare" was a pen name for a talented nobleman who fell in and out of favor with the royal court has been around for more than a century, and this book presents one hundred reasons to believe it. In this revised interpretation of the texts and the available history, Will

Shakespeare, also referred to as William of Stratford, was an actor and businessman who didn't have the education, experiences, or inclination to write all the works attributed to him. But Edward De Vere did.

Whether one cheers, howls in disagreement, or falls somewhere in between over such assaults on the literary reputation of William of Stratford, Whittemore's argument is fascinating. He summarizes over a century's worth of investigation into the possibility that the Earl of Oxford was the primary writer behind most of the works we consider to be Shakespeare's, while Shakespeare's plays and poems are analyzed in detail for indications that support Oxford as their author.

Some of the book's findings are, if not incontrovertible, interesting, and quite convincing. Making the case for *Hamlet* as the Earl of Oxford's most autobiographical, personal play, Whittemore argues that Hamlet's family tree much resembles the court of De Vere's day, with Queen Elizabeth I as inspiring Queen Gertrude; Polonius based on Sir William Cecil, the writer of his own set of precepts to guide his son; and Ophelia modeled on Cecil's daughter Anne, who married Edward De Vere.

Though the book favors Oxford as the rightful recipient of credit for Shakespeare's canon, previous scholarship is cited both for and against Oxford's authorship. Much of the evidence for Oxford might seem circumstantial, yet it accumulates in side-by-side examples of De Vere's documented work and Shakespeare's, or sometimes, in the absences of documentation of Shakespeare's earliest literary attempts and De Vere's later ones.

But even when a conclusion is reached by several measures of informed speculation, the result is titillating, and the incidental information engrossing. A book that Hamlet carries in the 1603 version of the play is identified as *De Consolatione*, a work whose first English translation was financed by De Vere, a dedicated patron of the arts. This leads to comparisons of similar ideas and phrasing between Hamlet's definitive "To be or not to be" soliloquy and passages in the book he carries. The origins and inspirations of *Romeo and Juliet*, *The Merchant of Venice*, and many other works are investigated with the same captivating passion and scholarship. A multi-page bibliography and comprehensive index aid in Whittemore's analysis and illuminate avenues for further reading.

100 Reasons Shake-speare was the Earl of Oxford is a probing, provocative, and absorbing alternative look at some of the most famous works in the English language — and the man responsible for them.

"I have taught annual classes on the Shakespeare attribution at the Osher Lifelong Learning Institute of Southern Oregon University for the past dozen years. While I often assign readings from internet sources and books, no other titles match the utility of Hank Whittemore's collection of essays in *100 Reasons Shake-speare was the Earl of Oxford* to introduce students to the wide spectrum of historical and literary evidence that challenges tradition and elevates Edward de Vere's claim to the authorship.

"Topically organized and carefully indexed for ease of searches, Whittemore's *100 Reasons* provide an avalanche of circumstantial evidence regarding Oxford's education, travels, patronage, and literary reputation, and how these biographical details are reflected through Shakespeare's specialized knowledge of foreign languages, the Classics, Law, Medicine, Music, and the natural worlds of plants, the sea, and the stars.

"My personal top 10 *Reasons* upon which I planned to base my last class expanded seamlessly to my top 25! There is no better collection of reasoned Oxfordian discourse than Whittemore's *100.*"

- Earl Showerman, MD, an emergency medicine physician in Oregon for more than thirty years, has delivered many ground-breaking papers on a range of Oxfordian topics that have included Shakespeare's detailed knowledge of medicine and his previously unrecognized use of Greek sources.

TABLE OF CONTENTS

INTRODUCTION

The idea that the works of Shakespeare weren't written by William Shakspere of Stratford-upon-Avon is often met with disbelief and ridicule from the so-called experts in the field. Those who believe that "William Shakespeare" was a pen name for a high-ranking, multitalented, somewhat eccentric member of the aristocracy of Elizabethan England are derided as conspiracy theorists, elitists, or as emotionally and mentally unbalanced. Such persons, the thinking goes, cannot accept that the great poet-dramatist could have come from a lowly background and pulled himself up by his bootstraps. They cannot accept that Shakespeare was simply a "genius" capable of using his imagination to create his masterpieces. They ignore the "facts" that the man from Stratford-upon-Avon was a working actor and an active member of London's theatrical world. Why must the author of *As You Like It* and *King Lear* have been some aristocrat? How could an earl, a member of the House of Lords, have written masterworks that appealed to all segments of the public, including the groundlings who crowded onto the dirt-covered floor in front of the stage at the Globe?

That the world could be deceived about Shakespeare's identity—for more than four centuries, no less—must seem, at first, to be impossible. How could anyone have gotten away with such a deception? How could Ben Jonson write his great eulogy for Shakespeare without having known the man? How could he write such a passionate, thrilling tribute to him, in the First Folio of Shakespeare plays in 1623, without believing wholeheartedly in every word he was setting down for all time?

I, too, scoffed at the idea, when it was first brought to my attention in the summer of 1987. The bearer of this heretical notion was Charles Boyle, an actor-writer in Boston performing the lead role in a one-act play I had written during a workshop at the Playwrights Platform. At the time I was living in Portland, Maine, and Charles asked me what I'd been reading. I told him I had just plowed through five biographies of William Shakespeare, which I had bought cheaply at some local used bookstores. When Charles asked why, I told him I had gone looking for the Bard's "creative process," seeking clues to the secrets of his greatness. How did he work? Specifically, how could he transport himself out of his own background and into the great halls of power—the palaces, the royal courts, the battlefields, the foreign lands—and write dialogue for his characters with such power and authenticity, such confidence and boldness?

Charles nodded and asked what I had found out. I shook my head and told him: "Absolutely nothing." Reading those biographies had been a numbing expeience. It seems that Mr. Shakespeare was not at all a man like his most autobiographical-seeming protagonist, Hamlet, but instead had been a steady, well-balanced businessman who, near the end of his life, actually set down his pen, returned to his hometown and busied himself with gardening and putting his financial affairs in order. As I had read this basic story line, which varied little from book to book, I had begun to realize that the only answer to my questions was that the man was a genius. It was pure magic; it was a life and career of miracles, which, by definition, could not be explained.

In addition, while reading through the biographies I realized that the authors were setting down all kinds of interesting information—about London, the playhouses, and so on—without providing a picture of the man himself. He seemed to be invisible. No letters from him; in relation to theatrical activity or writing, no believable anecdotes about him; no information about his looks, his voice, how he worked, where he stored his manuscripts, how he had access to all the books he needed, where he bought the pens and inks and paper, how he could write so much and yet still be an actor, rehearsing when not performing, memorizing lines. No, I had learned virtually nothing about the flesh-and-blood man who, by all accounts, was a towering figure in that relatively small town, where *Venus and Adonis* was going through ten editions and crowds were packing the public theaters to attend his plays! I wasn't doubting anything at this point, though I was feeling disappointed by the emptiness at the core of those books. In college I had acted in both *Hamlet* and *Othello*, and even then I had wondered about Shakespeare and his life. That there was no information was a letdown, but it was more than that. The real disappointment was realizing that Shakespeare was virtually alone among writers in leaving us with a life that cannot be related to his works. I had been an avid reader of works about the lives of Hemingway, Fitzgerald and others; here, in the case of the one who was probably the greatest of all, there was no correspondence between the man's known life and what he wrote. For me this was not (yet) an authorship question; it was just disappointment.

In the mail a few days later a large envelope from Boyle arrived with copies of pages from *The Mysterious William Shakespeare: The Myth and the Reality* by Charlton Ogburn, Jr., published three years earlier. This book put forward the theory (first proposed by J. Thomas Looney in *"Shakespeare" Identified*, 1920) that the true author was a high-ranking nobleman, a well educated, well-traveled, sophisticated courtier named

Edward de Vere, 17th Earl of Oxford (1550-1604), who wrote poetry and plays while patronizing troupes of players and musicians—a great lord whose standing at the court of Queen Elizabeth of England was virtually the same as that of Prince Hamlet at the court of King Claudius of Denmark. Oxford, like Hamlet, was both an insider and a man apart; he was eccentric, witty, secretive, misunderstood, a passionate student, generous and proud—yet entirely human and flawed, "with more offenses at my beck than I have thoughts to put them in, imagination to give them shape, or time to act them in," as Hamlet tells his bewildered young fiancée, the daughter of the king's chief minister and the mirror image of Oxford's real-life young fiancée, the daughter of Queen Elizabeth's chief minister.

It was amazing to learn that in sixteenth-century England there had been a real-life figure very much like Hamlet, a man who had been deeply involved as a patron and guide for writers whose works comprised the contemporary sources upon which "Shakespeare" would draw. Those works were created in the decades immediately preceding the 1590s, when the Bard's poems and plays began to be printed; as Oxford was still very much alive in that decade, it would seem at the least that he and "Shakespeare" must have known each other—unless, of course, they were one and the same man.

I was shocked to realize that this extraordinary nobleman had been so neglected by historians, literary scholars and Shakespeare biographers. One reason for the neglect was that de Vere had been largely expunged from the official record of his own time, and, too, had suffered from vicious criticisms of his character and actions based on what had been deliberately left on that record. It also became clear to me that other theories of the authorship (mainly involving Francis Bacon and, to a lesser degree, Christopher Marlowe) had been passionately explored and expounded only to be proved woefully inadequate and downright wrong. The Bacon authorship theory, mostly taken up by well-meaning folks who seriously doubted the Stratford man's authorship, had become a "red herring" that prevented any genuine look at Oxford as a serious candidate. "Oh, no," came the cry, "here we go again! What's the matter with these conspiracy theorists? With these snobs? Won't they ever quit?"

Of course, another reason for the neglect of Oxford was—and continues to be—not only the iconic stature of "Shakespeare" as a British national hero, but also the powerful image of the Stratford man as a Horatio Alger figure who "pulled himself up by his bootstraps" to become the greatest writer of the English language. His magnificent achievement is seen as the result of an extraordinary imagination combined with outsized genius; there is no need to explain exactly how he actually acquired the knowledge and wisdom exhibited in his works—"genius" explains everything.

But no one is born with knowledge about astronomy or anatomy or the supposedly nonexistent waterways of inland Italy (which did, in fact, exist). Logic requires that the extensive knowledge exhibited by "Shakespeare" could not have come by way of sheer fantasy. The great works had to come from an imaginative mixing together of elements gained as a result of the author's own observations and experience.

We owe a large debt to the Oxfordian pioneers during the past century, some of whose names can be found in this book's bibliography—J.T. Looney, Percy Allen, Eva Turner Clark, Ruth Loyd Miller, Charlton and Dorothy Ogburn, their son Charlton Ogburn Jr., William Plumer Fowler, and many others, not to mention more recent Oxfordian scholars and authors. Now it's time for new generations to take a much deeper and more complete look at the character and life of de Vere in relation to the English literary and dramatic renaissance of the sixteenth century, and for a more detailed reconstruction of the path that led to the phenomenon known as Shakespeare.

Why are high schools, colleges and universities choosing to phase out or drop their Shakespeare courses? One reason is that there has been no way to inspire students by linking the creation of those works with the personal experience and intentions of their creator; without that dynamic connection to an author's lived life, it is difficult for those students to see how the poems and plays relate to their own lives. The entranceway to fully comprehending and appreciating Shakespeare has been blocked.

This book presents a hundred reasons for concluding that "William Shakespeare" was the pen name of Edward de Vere. Each focuses on one aspect of the circumstantial evidence. My intention is to set forth information in a way that makes it easy and even entertaining to read. I invite you to take the journey on your own terms, using your own judgment, and to come to your own conclusions.

The project began in early 2011 when I made an offhand remark on my blogsite that there "must be at least a hundred reasons to conclude that Oxford was Shakespeare." Having made such a claim, I started to compile a list of whatever came to mind. Then I began to think seriously about fulfilling this prediction. My initial idea was to write a paragraph for each "reason" and no more. I figured the whole project might take three or four months at most. Once I began, however, each new item drew me to look through mounds of old printed material and notes I had collected over a quarter-century, and soon it became obvious that the subject matter demanded fuller treatment. The first reason was posted on 23 February 2011: "Oxford, like Hamlet, was involved with Plays and Play Companies at the Royal Court." Running about 430 words, it turned out to be the shortest entry of them all. Each time I thought of a new reason, the process of researching and writing became that of producing an original essay. I kept notes on new ideas, but deliberately avoided compiling anything like an entire list. The thought of knowing every reason beforehand was stultifying; searching for the next one, and getting to work on it, was much more exciting—and rewarding, since it often led to "new" information and original ways of seeing how pieces of evidence fit together. As a result, the blog project itself took more than three and a half years, until the late summer of 2014. Then it took a while to think about shaping the material into book form.

I received much input and encouragement from visitors to the site who made comments, and want them to know my gratitude. In particular I am grateful to Brian Bechtold, who contributed editorial assistance; Alex McNeil, who served as the main editor, focusing his incomparable skills on every aspect of the text; and publisher William Boyle, who has guided this book through Forever Press.

Hank Whittemore
Nyack, NY
Septermber 2016

This new issuance of *100 Reasons* cleans up a few errors and typos from the original, adds some front matter, and appears under a different imprint with the present new introduction.

INTRODUCTION
(2021)

J. Thomas Looney identified the seventeenth Earl of Oxford as "Shakespeare" over a century ago, but even now the Oxfordian movement to gain acceptance of him as the great author is still in its infancy. At the same time, it appears we are on the brink of a new kind of gold rush to mine his life and work for previously untapped riches. Now, five years after the original publication of this book, I'm gratified to see it being used as an "entrance way" into the theory that Edward de Vere – on the brink of his full maturity as an artist, at age forty-three in 1593 – adopted "Shakespeare" as his ultimate pen name.

Does it "matter" who wrote *Hamlet* or the *Sonnets*? The following pages answer "yes" in a hundred different ways. Do they supply "proof" that Oxford was Shakespeare? This book lays out numerous strands of circumstantial evidence; my hope is that the cumulative weight of all these strands will lead the reader to certainty that Oxford was indeed Shakespeare. The juncture at which such a "tipping point" occurs (if it occurs at all), will, of course, vary from reader to reader. I urge students and other newcomers to look at the evidence without feeling compelled to arrive at a final judgment; there is great pleasure to be had in the journey itself.

Searching for the author of the greatest works of the English language might be helped by asking first who is "more likely" to have written them. For example, few would disagree that Ernest Hemingway is more likely than F. Scott Fitzgerald to have written *A Farewell to Arms*. We know that Hemingway drew upon his own experiences in the Italian campaigns of the First World War; that the character of Catherine Barkley is based on a nurse who cared for him in a Milan hospital; many other known links to the author's life can add to and deepen our appreciation of the novel.

Does it matter to know that Tennessee Williams wrote *The Glass Menagerie*? Yes – it adds to our understanding of this "memory play" to recognize the character of Tom as the author himself in relation to his histrionic mother and mentally fragile sister. The tragic personal past that Williams suffered becomes a pervasive undercurrent of this early masterpiece.

It also helps to know that Arthur Miller wrote his drama *The Crucible*, set amid the Salem "witch trials" of the 1690s, as an allegory for McCarthyism and its own "witch hunts" against American communists in the 1950s. It is further enlightening that Miller himself was convicted in 1956 of contempt of Congress, after he had refused to name others with whom he had attended meetings of the American Communist Party. Miller's personal frustration and anger toward McCarthy's exaggerated allegations and the resulting hysteria can bring *The Crucible* into even sharper focus as a warning that, if we are not careful, the same unfounded fire and fury can flare up again.

Great works of art spring from the soul of the artist; under the traditional view of Shakespeare, however, he alone stands at arm's length from his work; only he, the master, writes without intimate connection to his material and without drawing upon his personal experience. Students are taught, directly or indirectly, that Shakespeare weaves his imagination with a kind of magic wand attuned to the box office; they are led to believe that this poet-dramatist, who towers above all others, never had to spend time in Italy or France, or learn very much of anything firsthand; the miracle of innate "genius" spared him from the need to work hard and long at his craft, and even from the need to rewrite and revise, as put forth to "the great Variety of Readers" of the First Folio of Shakespeare plays in 1623:

"His mind and hand went together: And what he thought, he uttered with [such] easiness that we have scarce received from him a blot in his papers."

This dangerously false lesson was supposedly written for the Folio by two members of Shakespeare's acting company, but it was more likely penned by Ben Jonson, whose great tribute "To the memory of my beloved, the AUTHOR, Mr. William Shakespeare" in the same volume contains the exact opposite (but true) information:

"And that he/ Who casts to write a living line must sweat/ (Such as thine are) and strike the second heat/ Upon the Muse's anvil: turn the same/ (And himself with it) that he thinks to frame:/ Or for the laurel he may gain a scorn, / For a good Poet's made as well as born, / And such wert thou."

All important literature must emanate from a personal core of dearly acquired experience, knowledge, and skill. This bond, common to all writers, must also apply to "Shakespeare," whether he was writing a history or a comedy or a tragedy, whether he was writing a play or a poem. The power of these works comes from within the author, from the heat of an inner furnace drawing upon the full range of the "slings and arrows" he has faced, along with the craftsmanship he has learned through tireless trial and error – by striking "the second heat" upon the anvil, as Jonson reports. The key to the author's creations is to be found in his deep involvement in life itself, in his ability to weep or laugh in the full measure that his spirit allows, along with the constant, careful labor to more accurately "hold as 'twere the mirror up to nature," to borrow from Hamlet's advice to the actors. Our inability to know this great artist of the written word as thoroughly and deeply as possible renders us unable to fully comprehend and empathize with the characters, stories, themes, true meanings, and original intentions of the work itself.

In *"Shakespeare" Identified*, the book that launched the Oxfordian movement in 1920, J. Thomas Looney described his process of looking for the true author as relying "very largely upon what is called circumstantial evidence." Such evidence "may at first be of the most shadowy description, but as we proceed in the work of gathering together facts … we find that the case at last either breaks down or becomes confirmed by such an accumulation of support that doubt is no longer possible."

The predominating element of circumstantial evidence is "that of coincidences," Looney wrote, adding that "a few coincidences we may treat as simply interesting; a number of coincidences we regard as remarkable; a vast accumulation of extraordinary coincidences we accept as conclusive proof."

Many years ago, when I initially looked over the circumstantial case, three items quickly impressed me:

Arthur Golding: All scholars agree that the Roman poet Ovid's *Metamorphoses* was Shakespeare's favorite classical source, in both its original Latin and in Golding's 1567 English translation. Golding was Edward de Vere's maternal uncle. When Oxford was a teenager in the mid-1560s, the puritanical Golding lived under the same roof with him at Cecil House while supposedly creating the rollicking English translation of *Metamorphoses* that would be credited to him. (In more recent years, many Oxfordians have concluded that the young earl himself must have created the youthful, zesty translations.)

John Lyly: Known for his novels and plays written during the late 1570s and 1580s, he is regarded as a major contemporary influence upon Shakespeare, whose works began to be appear in print in the 1590s. Lyly was Oxford's personal secretary all during those previous years, when he was supposedly writing works for the private theater and the royal court (such as *Endymion*, about Oxford and Queen Elizabeth, performed for the monarch herself). The record shows Lyly's career as a playwright abruptly stopped just when de Vere disappeared from public life and the name "William Shakespeare" appeared on the dedication of *Venus and Adonis* to nineteen-year-old Henry Wriothesley, the 3rd Earl of Southampton. Lyly should correctly be understood not as someone who influenced Shakespeare, but rather as one who was directly influenced by the great author.

Hamlet: Oxford was the highest-ranking earl of England's royal court and stood in much the same relationship to Queen Elizabeth as the Prince of Denmark stands in relation to the King of Denmark. Hamlet brings players to court and inserts lines for them to "catch the conscience of the king," just the way Oxford brought actors to court to grab the queen's attention; that is, he used plays with seemingly innocuous characters and plots to indirectly "speak truth to power."

The King: Have you heard the argument? Is there no offence in it?
Hamlet: No, no, they do but jest, poison in jest; no offence in the world. (3.2.214-215)

We in the audience know that the prince himself is the anonymous playwright who has written a scene reenacting the fatal poisoning of his father by his uncle, Claudius, who has married his mother and installed himself on the throne, from which King Claudius watches the scene of his own murderous deed with growing horror. The new King, now fully aware that Hamlet is dangerous, swiftly orders his murder – much as Oxford, having revealed too many secrets of the English court, was regarded as politically dangerous.

Since 2015 the Shakespeare Oxford Fellowship has been running a series of essays on its website by individuals describing "How I Became an Oxfordian." These short pieces, edited by current SOF president Bob Meyers, recount personal journeys along different pathways to arrive at similar "aha" moments of transformative thinking:

Diane Elliott, a freelance copy editor and artist, sees the Oxford story as "tied to truth by a thousand fine threads, adding complexity and resonance." Attending Shakespeare's plays and reading his poetry with de Vere's life in mind "feels like I'm looking at a familiar photograph that has suddenly become three-dimensional."

Paul N. Arnold, approaching the authorship question as a scientist, relied on "the sense that derives from many inputs, from the head and heart." These data points "are based on intuition, probability – not on certainty." After reading, researching, and contemplating, "the point eventually comes when we must decide; and we say, not with scientific certainty, but with intellectual integrity," that Oxford "most probably" wrote the works of Shakespeare.

Karen Calderone, with clinical experience in developmental psychology, writes that the traditional Stratfordian story "defies basic truths of human development," while Oxford's personal odyssey "courses through the works as lifeblood and finally makes sense of it all."

Clare Davis, an optometrist, read numerous books about the poems and plays as well as the history, only to find that virtually all the writers and patrons (and anyone else linked to "Shakespeare") appeared to have "some connection to Edward de Vere." She now realizes that "no one piece of evidence" convinced her, but rather that "many, many pieces of circumstantial evidence, far too numerous to put into a concise argument," moved her to become an Oxfordian. She realizes that truth is not to be found "in having one big piece of evidence," but emerges when "we begin to make sense of the whole picture."

University of Winnipeg librarian Michael Dudley has made an in-depth study based on fifty of the "How I Became an Oxfordian" essays. He found that a common experience is that of reaching "a threshold point" when "the previously unsatisfying, dissonant state is irreversibly abandoned as these essayists find a rewarding, transcendent experience." The most significant finding is that "the coherence and sense-making" afforded by the model of de Vere "unleashes a level of empathy unavailable to the reader wedded to the Stratfordian mythology." In place of "the remote, god-like paragon" of "natural genius," the new Oxfordian "comes to know, understand and profoundly empathize with the author."

100 Reasons Shake-speare was the Earl of Oxford owes its positive reception and continually expanding readership to dozens of Oxfordian scholars whose works are cited in these pages. I am grateful to every one of them, including those who have been my friends and colleagues over many years.

One who has made invaluable contributions is James A. Warren, who recorded in his monumental work *Shakespeare Revolutionized* (2021) how researchers over the past century have worked to recover what appears to have been a deliberately buried history. In other words, Oxford's central role in the renaissance of English literature and drama resulting in "Shakespeare" must have been erased by officials of the government.

Warren first advanced this conclusion in the 2015 issue of the Oxfordian journal *Brief Chronicles*, arguing that those who controlled the Elizabethan state must have used their power "not only to destroy evidence of the Earl of Oxford's literary activities, but also to airbrush him from much of the historical record." Among the missing evidence of de Vere's literary and theatrical life are government records, private papers of important officials, records of theatrical performances, personal documents (such as letters to or from Oxford mentioning any of his literary activities) and his own dramatic works, papers, and books (as well as his will, which has never been found).

A few Oxfordians had suggested this conclusion in the past, such as Charles and William Boyle; but apparently, they could not persuade others to believe that a cleansing of the record of this critically important individual could have been carried out. Warren reports in *Revolutionized* that Charlton Ogburn Jr. argued in *The Mysterious William Shakespeare* (1984) that virtually all records of Oxford's literary work must have been removed and destroyed; but he adds that Ogburn also forecast that most Oxfordians would view such a far-reaching sweep of evidence as "highly improbable."

Warren writes that it's "truly astounding" that no "direct" evidence exists in support of *either* leading candidate for the authorship. *Neither William Shakspere of Stratford-upon-Avon nor Edward de Vere, Earl of Oxford, is connected directly to the Shakespearean works.* The only support for Shakspere cited by traditional scholars is an assumption that the name "Shakespeare" on printed publications must refer to him, even while they are unable to cite any specific link between him and the writings. The logical conclusion, which those scholars cannot entertain, is that "Shakespeare" was a pen name.

"Those who controlled state power believed it was necessary to separate the plays from the royal court in the public mind," Warren writes, "and the best way they found to do that was by cutting the connection between the plays and the author."

Just four years prior to the sudden appearance of the heretofore unknown poet "Shakespeare" on the dedication of *Venus and Adonis* in 1593, the reading public was reminded by the anonymous author of *The Arte of English Poesie* (1589) that Oxford stood high (or highest) on the list of courtier poets: "And in her Majesty's time that now is are sprung up another crew of Courtly makers, Noble men and Gentlemen of her Majesty's own servants, who have written excellently well as it would appear if their doings could be found out and made public with the rest, of which number is first that noble Gentleman Edward Earle of Oxford..."

In fact, as the following pages demonstrate, de Vere had been well known as a poet and champion of literary arts, supported by Queen Elizabeth's personal encouragement and royal patronage. From at least his early thirties, Oxford was bursting forth to proclaim her Majesty's enthusiastic support for a new English renaissance of literature and drama. In effect, Edward de Vere was a contemporary superstar; and while working on this additional introduction, it struck me with new certainty that the 100 "reasons" relating to this one man should have given him equal prominence in subsequent history. The fact that Oxford seldom appears at all, or that when he does it's usually in negative ways, demands an explanation.

It further struck me that the very absence of de Vere's activities from so much of the record is yet another reason to conclude he must have been the great author. How could this quintessential "renaissance man" be missing from every place in the record where we know, thanks to a century of Oxfordian digging, that he was the guiding force behind it?

From a young age, de Vere had used many psuedonyms as well as names of living individuals. In the end, he must have had no choice but to publish his supreme works behind the mask of his new Shakespeare pen name. He also must have submitted to official pressure to accept, in advance, his own posthumous oblivion, just as the poet of the *Sonnets* testifies that his Shakespearean identity and true contributions to England will not survive after his death:

"My name be buried where my body is" – Sonnet 72

"I, once gone, to all the world must die" – Sonnet 81

Exactly why the state would have felt the need to use its pervasive power to obliterate him from the record is not for this book to explore (see *The Monument*, 2005; and *The Living Record*, forthcoming in 2022), but it's logical to conclude he posed a political danger to those in charge. Officials with the most at stake, and with the most ability to destroy files relating to Oxford's literary and dramatic work, were chief minister William Cecil Lord Burghley (1520-1598) and his son Robert Cecil (1563-1612), principal secretary, who engineered the succession of James Stuart as King James I of England in 1603 and thereby retained his own power behind the throne. The deliberate elimination of Oxford from the "records" or "registers" of his leading role in the Elizabethan Age appears to be reflected by the poet of the *Sonnets* when he cries against the false testimony of Time and its chronicles, that is, against the history already being determined and written by the winners:

> No! Time, thou shalt not boast that I do change...
> Thy registers and thee I both defy...
> For thy records and what we see doth lie   Sonnet 123, 1, 9, 11

It turns out that the near-total elimination of Oxford from the historical record may be the most important reason of all to conclude he wrote the "Shakespeare" poems and plays. Without the massive "airbrushing" of his many exploits and accomplishments, along with his enormous contributions to English literature and drama, there would have been no "Shakespeare mystery" in the first place. I hope the following pages adequately demonstrate the magnitude of Edward de Vere's life and his mastery of the myriad fields in which "Shakespeare" is an acknowledged expert. When the breadth and depth of this single individual's greatness is weighed against the paltry record of him in the traditional history, these two contradictory realities sound an alarm bell to which Shakespeare lovers are increasingly responding with reinvigorated passion for the truth.

CHAPTER ONE

A MAN OF THEATER

Reason 1 – The Patron-Playwright

Fig. 1 - Edward de Vere, 17th Earl of Oxford (circa 1575-76).

Edward de Vere, 17th Earl of Oxford, began his theatrical life as a child. His father, John de Vere, the sixteenth earl, sponsored an acting company known as Oxford's Men. Edward spent much of his boyhood in the 1550s at the home of his tutor, the great Cambridge scholar Thomas Smith, but his family residence was Castle Hedingham in Essex. Oxford's Men came there to put on plays during the Christmas season and at other times. Young Oxford would have mingled with the players, watching them rehearse and learning their craft.

Queen Elizabeth and her court visited Hedingham for five days in August 1561, when Edward was eleven, and Oxford's Men contributed to the royal entertainment. The boy had a close-up view of her responses and witnessed the power of the stage to gain her attention, stir her emotions and even affect her policies. Court members also watched her reactions, to see how to please the queen and avoid offending her.

These early experiences set young Edward on the very course he took; eventually, he brought his own players and plays to perform for the queen.

When John de Vere died in 1562, under feudal law Edward became a ward of the Crown. He went to London in the custody of the queen's chief minister, William Cecil, the future Lord Burghley. The year before, Elizabeth had appointed Richard Edwards as Master of the Chapel Royal. The privilege of entertaining Her Majesty with plays was mostly that of the Choir Boys of the Chapel Royal, but it also belonged to the

1

separate child acting companies of Paul's, Westminster and Windsor. Much later, the *Arte of English Poesie* of 1589 would record Oxford and Edwards as fellow playwrights, citing "the Earl of Oxford and Master Edwards of Her Majesty's Chapel" as deserving of "the highest praise" for "Comedy and Enterlude."

De Vere joined Elizabeth on her 1564 progress to Cambridge, where she attended performances of *Aulularia* by Plautus, *Dido* by Edward Haliwell and *Ezechia* by Nicholas Udall. That fall *Damon and Pythias*, credited to Edwards, was performed at court. At Oxford in 1566, the queen attended *Palaemon and Arcyte*, a "lost" play also credited to Edwards and thought to be a source for *The Two Noble Kinsmen*, attributed to Shakespeare. Most likely young Oxford co-wrote both plays with Edwards, who died in the fall of 1566, or he wrote them himself. In any case, theatrical events were part of his world and the productions were usually connected to the queen, who clearly loved plays and had an insatiable demand for them. To communicate with Her Majesty, there was no better means than the stage.

In 1567 Oxford was admitted to Gray's Inn, where George Gascoigne was studying for the bar and writing plays acted by the Gentlemen of the Inn. One of these works was *The Supposes*, translated from the Italian of Ariosto and said to be the first "prose play" in English (and a source for *The Taming of the Shrew*); another was *Jocasta*, from Euripides, the first adaptation of a Greek play to the English stage. Stephanie Caruana and Elisabeth Sears argue that it was Oxford who wrote *The Supposes*, which contained seeds of his own Euphuist movement of the 1580s while anticipating aspects of *The Comedy of Errors* as performed in the 1590s.

In Italy during 1575-76, Oxford became familiar with the *Commedia dell'arte*, a theatrical form begun in that century and responsible for the advent of improvised performances with masked "types" based on sketches or scenarios. The *Commedia* troupes, which included female actors, would greatly influence the Shakespearean plays. Meanwhile the first successful public playhouse in England, the Theatre, opened soon after Oxford's return in 1576. Among the new plays listed as performed for the queen in January 1577 was "The historie of Error," possibly an early version of *The Comedy of Errors*. In February at Whitehall the Lord Chamberlain's Men performed "The historie of the Solitaire knight," possibly an early version of *Timon of Athens*. The Lord Chamberlain of Her Majesty's Household, responsible for court lodgings and dining as well as entertainment for the queen, was Thomas Radcliffe, Earl of Sussex, who was a generation older than Oxford and his chief supporter among the nobility. Oxford had served under him in the 1570 military campaign against the rebellion of Catholic earls; also they were allied in their strong antipathy toward Robert Dudley, Earl of Leicester, who had been Elizabeth's lover in the 1560s.

By 1579 Oxford was employing John Lyly, Anthony Munday and many others (some were members of the writing group later called the University Wits, who are also identified as influencing Shakespeare). The Earl of Warwick's actors moved to Oxford's service, with Lyly as manager, and the amalgamated company performed at court in January 1580. In April two of Oxford's actors were temporarily jailed for "frays committed upon certain Gentlemen of the Inns of Court" at the Theatre. In June that year a plague outbreak forced Cambridge and Oxford to cancel highly anticipated productions by Oxford's Men.

Oxford was now financing an adult acting company, a boy's acting company and a troupe of musicians. In 1583 he saved the private Blackfriars playhouse by purchasing the sublease and transferring it to Lyly, so the choirboys could continue rehearsing there before performing at court. Sir William More recovered possession of the property in 1584, however, shutting down Blackfriars as a playhouse. Oxford had sold forty-seven pieces of land between 1576 and 1584, thirteen of them in 1580; by 1583 his household had been reduced to four servants.

Sussex died in June 1583. A new company, the Queen's Men, was quickly formed by Francis Walsingham, head of England's growing network of paid spies and informants who made up England's first full-fledged secret service. Actors were valuable informants and plays served as powerful vehicles for propaganda, as war with Spain was looming. The Queen's Company was formed with twelve of the best actors from all companies, including Oxford's; the evidence points to Lyly, whom Oxford still employed, serving as its stage manager and acting coach.

Several of the comedies performed at court are credited to Lyly, but it is far more likely that Oxford actually wrote them. No ordinary playwright would have dared to present *Sapho and Phao*, a thinly veiled allegory representing the love affair of Elizabeth and the French duke of Alençon; given Oxford's well-known love of music and personal association with contemporary composers such as William Byrd and John Farmer, logic dictates that the song lyrics in these plays were also his. All the quartos were published anonymously, and the lyrics were never printed during Lyly's lifetime, further indicating he could not claim them as his own. The play *Endymion*, credited to Lyly, is acknowledged by orthodox scholars such as David Bevington as focusing allegorically on Oxford and Elizabeth.

A number of anonymous plays performed by the Queen's Men in the 1580s would be revised in the 1590s, under similar titles, as by "Shakespeare." These include *The Famous Victories of Henry V, The Troublesome Reign of King John, The True Tragedy of Richard III* and *The True Chronicle History of King Leir*. It is more logical to assume that in all these cases "Shakespeare" is revising his own works, rather than reworking plays written by others. Some of the plays helped to rouse national unity, contributing to the defeat of the Spanish Armada in the summer of 1588. After that, the

Fig. 2 - Queen Elizabeth (Ermine Portrait, 1585)

Queen's Company became less important and de Vere went underground, so to speak, becoming a reclusive figure who stayed away from court and out of the public eye for the rest of his life. With the publication of the 1,200-line poem *Venus and Adonis*, "Shakespeare" arrived in 1593, instantly becoming England's most popular poet; in 1598, when his name began appearing on play quartos, he became known as the top playwright of the new Lord Chamberlain's Men, which had been formed in 1594.

Beneath the surface of these facts is an enormous, largely unseen theatrical life. An "aerial view" of Oxford's connections to the stage reveals one major thoroughfare running through the landscape—an unbroken line connecting the life spans of the three major acting companies, linked one to another in three successive stages of development:

THE LORD CHAMBERLAIN'S MEN (1573-1583)

From the 1570s until 1583 the Lord Chamberlain's Men, under the Earl of Sussex, brought play after play to the royal court, as indicated by the keepers of the records. Many of these are identified by Eva Turner Clark as early versions of dramatic works destined to be revised and issued, under new titles, as works of "Shakespeare" in the 1590s. Clark believes that early versions of *all* the Shakespeare plays may have been penned before 1589. Her list includes: "The historye of Titus and Gisippus" (possibly an early *Titus Andronicus*, performed by the Paul's

Boys in February 1577 at Whitehall); "An history of the crueltie of A Stepmother" (possibly an early *Cymbeline*, performed by the Lord Chamberlain's Men in December 1578 at Richmond); "A Morrall of the marryage of Mynde and Measure" (possibly an early *The Taming of the Shrew*, performed by Paul's Boys in January 1579 at Richmond); "The historie of the Rape of the Second Helene" (possibly an early *All's Well That Ends Well*, performed in January 1579 at Richmond). She also notes possible early versions of *Love's Labour's Lost* and *The Two Gentlemen of Verona* in 1579.

Clark supports her identifications with extraordinary scholarship, linking events of contemporary history to characters and scenes in the Shakespeare plays. She often notices the different stages of revision within a given play, just as archaeologists can "read history" from fossils or rings within a tree trunk. Given de Vere's intense involvement with writers and play companies, along with his great friendship with Sussex, I believe that Clark was largely correct: many of the earliest versions of future "Shakespeare" plays were performed for Elizabeth at the royal court by the Lord Chamberlain's Men under Sussex.

THE QUEEN'S MEN (1583-1593)

The Queen's Men, often with two separate troupes, traveled around the countryside, usually performing plays of royal history, geared to rousing patriotic fervor as England prepared for invasion by Philip of Spain and his Armada. Now that scholars are becoming more aware that early versions of Shakespearean history plays were performed by this company in the 1580s, with titles that would remain quite similar, the next logical inference is that de Vere, while remaining involved in companies under his own name, was writing for the Lord Chamberlain's Men and then for the Queen's Men. Oxford's extraordinary annual grant of £1,000, begun in June 1586, was drawn from the government treasury with the same formula used for the secret service, bringing him into close alignment with the Queen's Men from that angle as well.

THE LORD CHAMBERLAIN'S MEN (1594-1603)

The new Lord Chamberlain's company gave its first performances at court during the Christmas season of 1594. It would become known to us as "Shakespeare's Company," because it became the exclusive stage producer of the Shakespearean plays. In government records for March 1595, actors Richard Burbage and Will Kemp along with "William Shakespeare" are listed as payees of the newly formed Chamberlain's Men, collecting payment for the previous December's court performances. The inclusion of "Shakespeare" in that record is highly suspicious, however, since the name had just been introduced as a poet in the dedications of *Venus and Adonis* (1593) and *Lucrece* (1594) to Henry Wriothesley, 3rd Earl of Southampton, and because the name would never again be listed a payee for the Chamberlain's Men. (After the succession of King James of Scotland in 1603 and the creation of the King's Men, with Principal Secretary Robert Cecil retaining and even increasing his power behind the throne, the government made a feeble attempt to indicate "Shakespeare" as an actor with the company.)

The Lord Chamberlain in 1594 was Henry Carey, Lord Hunsdon, who was followed by his son George Carey, the next Lord Hunsdon. But they were nominal figures when it came to the running of the company. The logical conclusion is that Oxford himself was the guiding hand of "Shakespeare's Company"—not because of his similar title—Lord Great Chamberlain—but, rather, because this new group was an extension of the previous companies which Oxford had used as the primary vehicles for presenting his plays on public stages.

This perspective on the history requires taking an aerial view to see the larger picture of de Vere as the major force behind the three great acting companies of the Elizabethan reign. All three are linked in history to produce the renaissance of English literature and drama in the 1570s and 1580s, followed by the Shakespeare works in the 1590s.

Shakespeare's company, the Chamberlain's Men, put on some of the most dangerously political plays of the reign, yet it never got in trouble with officialdom. Obviously, it was receiving protection from on high. In the 1590s the government was moving rapidly to take control of the theater, limiting the playing companies in London to two, restricting the number of playhouses used for drama to two, and exercising increasingly heavy censorship that led, for example, to the Bishops' Bonfire of books in 1599.

(It was Shakespeare's company, also, that performed *Richard II* at the Globe on 7 February 1601, at the behest of the conspirators of the Essex Rebellion, which erupted the following morning; yet the actors were let go after cursory questioning and the author of the play was never summoned.) Meanwhile Oxford had withdrawn entirely from court life after 1590. Remarrying in 1591, he and his new countess (Elizabeth Trentham) moved to the village of Stoke Newington, just north of Shoreditch—the center of the London theater scene, where the Curtain playhouse would become the premier venue of Shakespeare's Company prior to the 1599 construction of the Globe.

"Thus we see him moving quite close to the 'Shakespeare' work, but never in it," J. Thomas Looney writes, describing a man who had become virtually invisible—and yet who, in my view, was singularly responsible for the outpouring of Shakespearean plays in public performance, igniting the explosion of theatrical activity that remains perhaps the grandest chapter in the history of the stage.

De Vere emerged briefly from his retirement to serve as highest ranking earl on the tribunal at the one-day trial of Essex and Southampton on 19 February 1601 for their leading roles in the so-called Essex Rebellion. He had no choice but to join the other twenty-four peers in finding both earls guilty of high treason and condemning them to death. Essex was beheaded six days later; but Southampton, the "fair youth" of the Shakespeare sonnets, unofficially had his sentence reduced to life in prison. Two years later, in April 1603, King James granted him his freedom with a royal pardon. Meanwhile the adult acting troupe under Oxford's own name, which was mainly a touring group, had merged with Worcester's Company in 1602. Even the aging Queen Elizabeth became involved in this new, expanded company, ordering the Lord Mayor of London to allow them to play at their favorite Boar's Head tavern. "In August of that year the united company was acting at the Rose under Henslowe," B.M. Ward writes, "and among the actors we find the names of William Kemp and Thomas Haywood, the playwright."

Will Kemp! This was the same man listed back in 1595 as a payee of the new Lord Chamberlain's Men, along with Richard Burbage and "William Shakespeare." Now, as the Elizabethan reign draws to its close, Kemp is acting in the company patronized by the earls of Worcester and Oxford. All along, just beneath the surface or standing in the wings, we find the figure of Edward de Vere, a man of the theater throughout his life.

Reason 2 – The Allowed Fool

"Give a man a mask, and he will tell you the truth." – Oscar Wilde

The Shakespeare plays are populated by many truth-tellers wearing the masks of fools or jesters. Fools had existed from ancient history all the way up to the contemporary jesters of European royal courts in the Elizabethan age. In our own time, Jon Stewart of *The Daily Show* may be the closest analogue, with the job of running spears of truth through the guts of our politicians, making them squirm while the rest of us howl with laughter—a function even the most powerful officials must allow, however grudgingly. What many of Shakespeare's fools have in common is their ability, within the dangerous setting of the court, to speak truth to power. Touchstone in *As You Like It* and Feste in *Twelfth Night* are the best-known court jesters or Fools who have that authorization. (*King Lear*'s nameless fool is "all-licensed," as Goneril puts it.)

In *A Poet's Rage*, collected and edited by William Boyle, a chapter on the Shakespearean Fools, written twenty years ago by Charles Boyle, remains just as important to the Oxfordian case as it was back then. Discussing Troilus and Hamlet as characters, Charles Boyle emphasizes that Shakespeare's world revolved around the royal court and that his audacious political satire was made possible only by the clever use of thinly disguised allegory. Oxford enjoyed the protection of "a great patron" (Queen Elizabeth) and was "the most amazing court jester who lived;" perhaps, he adds, there is no character called "The Fool" in the play featuring Prince Hamlet, his most autobiographical portrait, precisely because Hamlet himself is the Fool.

The Prince of Denmark is an expert at using allegory, the accepted Elizabethan literary device for commenting on the current political scene. He warns Polonius, chief counselor to King Claudius and Queen Gertrude, that the players "are the abstract and brief chronicles of the time" (2.2)—i.e., the actors and their "harmless" plays are actually pointing to prominent and powerful persons and important issues of the day. As Hamlet tells Ophelia, Polonius's daughter, the players "cannot keep counsel" but will "tell all" (3.2).

"Have you heard the argument?" the wary King asks as the play in front of the royal court begins. "Is there no offence in't?"

"No, no," Hamlet replies with the proverbial straight face, "they do but jest, poison in jest. No offence i'th'world" (3.2).

A famous example of Elizabeth's recognition that plays often reflected contemporary matters occurred in 1601, several months after the performance by Shakespeare's company of *Richard II*, including a scene showing the deposition of Richard. The hastily scheduled performance helped trigger the failed Essex rebellion against Robert Cecil and other counselors the following day. Recalling the staging of that play, the queen reportedly blurted out to her antiquary: "I am Richard the Second, know ye not that!?"

Traditional scholars, believing the author to be the Stratford fellow, have been forced to shy away from seeing Polonius as a satirical portrait of William Cecil Lord Burghley. The reason, of course, is that for William of Stratford to satirize Elizabeth's powerful chief minister in any way—not to mention in such a bold, ruthless manner—would have been suicidal. He would have lost more than his writing hand.

The notion that Shakspere was the author "has stymied all reasonable inquiry into Shakespeare's relationship to the world he lived in and his favorite setting, the court," Charles Boyle writes, because the author of the Shakespeare works clearly *did* live in the world of the court and, not surprisingly, *did* write about the intrigues of that world. Equally clearly, that same author was being protected by the monarch herself—as expressed by none other than Polonius, who urges Gertrude to severely reprove her son the prince: "Tell him his pranks have been too broad to bear with, and that your Grace hath screened and stood between much heat and him" (3.4).

Polonius is referring partly to the play-within-the-play, by which Hamlet has been able to "catch the conscience of the King" by means of allegory—presenting one story that seems harmless while, in fact, revealing the dangerous truth that Claudius murdered Hamlet's father, the previous king. The play at court, into which the prince inserted the crucial lines, is but the latest of his "pranks" that have pushed the chief minister beyond his limits. But Polonius is even angrier at the queen. Unable to accuse her directly, he exhorts Gertrude to tell Hamlet that his antics will be no longer tolerated; more to the point, the queen should confess to him that she herself is the reason he gets away with his madcap behavior. She has "screened" her son from the fury of others; she has "stood between" the prince and the wrath of other members of the court.

With Oxford as the author, it becomes clear that Hamlet is his most self-revealing character and that the court of Denmark represents the English court. There can be no more doubt that Polonius is a caricature of Burghley, who was Oxford's father-in-law, nor any question that Gertrude represents Elizabeth. From there it's a very short step to the recognition that, in fact, the Queen of England had protected de Vere in the same way, having "screened and stood between much heat and him" primarily because of his satirical comedies and other truth-telling plays, performed at her court from as early as the 1560s.

Elizabeth demanded such entertainment. The female monarch who loved the cruel spectacle of bear baiting also feasted upon stinging portrayals of members of her court, and on various characters in which she could recognize herself, usually in the form of a flattering portrait. She enabled Oxford to function as her "allowed fool," as Olivia calls Feste the clown in *Twelfth Night*. Telling Malvolio to shake off Feste's barbs, she reminds him that the jester uses his biting wit because she allows him to do so: "There is no slander in an allowed fool, though he do nothing but rail" (1.5). Olivia has given Feste permission to slander others; because her command is law, it follows that Feste's slander cannot be slanderous.

When Malvolio has gone, Olivia turns to Feste and pretends to scold him: "Now you see, sir, how your fooling grows old, and people dislike it" (1.5). Eva Turner Clark observes that "although Olivia likes his nonsense, she makes a mild protest for the sake of the victims who do not." In Clark's opinion, Olivia's term "allowed fool" is "an expression Elizabeth probably applied to Oxford, for he would never have dared to include the many personal allusions in his plays had not the queen permitted, even encouraged, him to do it."

Hamlet is a prankster, jester, clown; he is a court fool with permission to say what he likes, even to put on plays that tell the truth about royal crimes. Gertrude has given him the freedom to criticize or make fun of high-ranking persons, right up to the king himself, without suffering repercussions. The prince—and by extension his creator, Oxford—is a political satirist who displays far more daring than that displayed by the comedy writers and performers of *Saturday Night Live*, given the harsh punishments of the Elizabethan age. Having easily led Polonius into revealing his hypocrisy, Hamlet exclaims in an aside: "They fool me to the top of my bent!" (3.2)—a statement translated by the Riverside Shakespeare editors as: "They make me play the fool to the limit of my ability!"

Thus, the character who speaks with the playwright's most authorial voice describes himself as the court fool—a role that de Vere is known to have played, from his high-step dancing for the queen, to his early signed poetry, to his reputation as "best for comedy" for the court stage, to his playing of the lute and his singing for Elizabeth, and so on, not to mention the many escapades for which he would otherwise have been punished (e.g., planning in 1571 to rescue the Duke of Norfolk from the Tower; racing off to the Continent in 1574 without authorization; twice refusing the queen's command in 1579 to dance for the French delegates who had come to England to negotiate the marriage alliance of Elizabeth and the Duke of Alençon.) In *As You Like It* Jaques speaks of himself as a fool and comes close to how Oxford would describe himself:

I must have liberty
Withal, as large a charter as the wind,
To blow on whom I please, for so fools have...
Invest me in my motley, give me leave
To speak my mind, and I will through and through

Cleanse the foul body of th'infected world,
If they will patiently receive my medicine. (2.7)

Reason 3 – The Director-Actor

If "Shakespeare" lived in our own time, he would likely have been not only a poet, playwright and novelist, but also a screenwriter and director on a grand scale, similar to modern greats such as David Lean or Steven Spielberg. He would have seized the chance to make the most of advances in the technology and art of filmmaking. When Oxford emerges from the shadows of history, the curtain will rise not only on the hidden genius who adopted the pen name "Shakespeare" at age forty-three in 1593, but also on the great impresario who, unknown to the public, was the primary force behind the extraordinary pageant of entertainments for Queen Elizabeth and her royal court.

In the summer of 1572 at Warwick Castle, an elaborate "show" was presented in the form of a mock military battle between two armies, one under Oxford's command, according to a contemporary chronicler: "Be it remembered that in the year of our Lord 1572, and in the fourteenth year of our Sovereign Lady Queen Elizabeth, the twelfth day of August in the said year, it pleased our said Sovereign Lady to visit this borough of Warwick in person...."

On her royal progress with the court, she arrived in great splendor as all the chief citizens knelt outside the town to greet her: "Her Majesty in her coach, accompanied with the Lady of Warwick in the same coach ... the Lord Burghley, lately made Lord Treasurer of England, the Earl of Sussex, lately made Lord Chamberlain to Her Majesty, the Lord Howard of Effingham, lately made Lord Privy Seal, the Earl of Oxford Lord Great Chamberlain of England...." By now Oxford's close friends Sussex and Charles Howard, Earl of Effingham, were in charge of ensuring that plays were brought to court, a duty they would carry out until Sussex's death in 1583.

The queen spent a week in the Warwick area and on Sunday the 18th of August "it pleased her to have the country people resorting to see her dance in the Court of the Castle ... which thing, as it pleased well the country people, so it seemed Her Majesty was much delighted and made very merry." In the evening after supper came the mock battle, which, among other things, was an exercise in theatrical realism. Elizabeth and the court first saw a fort, commanded by Fulke Greville, "made of slender timber covered with canvas." Inside were "divers persons to serve the soldiers; and therefore, so many harnesses as might be gotten within the town … wherewith men were armed and appointed to cast out fireworks, [such as] squibs and balls of fire.

"Against that fort was another castle-wise prepared of like strength, whereof was governor the Earl of Oxford, a lusty gentleman, with a lusty band of gentlemen. Between these forts, or against them, were placed certain battering pieces, to the number of twelve or fourteen, brought from London, and twelve fair chambers, or mortar pieces, brought also from the Tower … These pieces and chambers were by trains fired, and so made a great noise, as though it had been a sore assault.…

"The Earl of Oxford and his soldiers, to the number of two hundred, with calivers and arquebuses [muskets] likewise gave divers assaults; they in the fort shooting again, and casting out divers fires, terrible to those that have not been in like experiences, valiant to such as delighted therein, and indeed strange to them that understood it not. For the wild fire falling into the river Avon would for a time lie still, and then again rise and fly abroad, casting forth many flashes and flames, whereat the Queen's Majesty took great pleasure.…

"At the last, when it was appointed that the overthrowing of the fort should be, a dragon flying, casting out huge flames and squibs, lighted up the fort, and so set fire thereon, to the subversion thereof; but whether by negligence or otherwise, it happened that a ball of fire fell on a house at the end of the bridge … And no small marvel it was that so little harm was done, for the fire balls and squibs cast up did fly quite over the Castle, and into the midst of the town; falling down some on the houses, some in courts … and some in the street … Four houses in the town and suburbs were on fire at once, whereof one had a ball come through both sides, and made a hole as big as a man's head, and did no more harm."

A man and his wife were sleeping in the house hit by the fireball, so Oxford and Greville ran over to help. After some difficulty, they rescued the couple; the next morning the queen and her courtiers gave the man more than £25 to cover the damage.

Such high drama is exactly what we might expect to find "Shakespeare" creating as a young man, more than two decades before his adoption of that pen name. We might well expect to find that, in addition to becoming the greatest writer of the English language, the poet-dramatist was also a master showman.

Reason 4 – Performance in the Tiltyard

Whitehall Palace, 22 January 1581: An overflow crowd at the Whitehall Tiltyard watches thirty-year-old Oxford as he once again proves himself a master showman. The spectators gasp as he emerges from his magnificent tent, appearing as the Knight of the Tree of the Sunne. His boy page approaches Queen Elizabeth and, facing her, delivers a "Sweet Speech" (written, no doubt, by the earl himself). Now, after an exchange with his delighted queen, Oxford mounts his horse and rides to defend his title against the challenger. At the end he is still champion of the tilt; and members of the cheering, frenzied crowd race to tear both the tent and the tree into pieces.

This dramatic episode of the Elizabethan reign will be described eleven years later, in 1592, in a book published by Cuthbert Burby (who will also issue three quartos of the "Shakespeare" plays, including *Romeo and Juliet* in 1599 as "newly corrected, augmented and amended" by the author himself). The description of Oxford's 1581 production (rendered in more modern English) in the tiltyard (without the page's speech) follows:

> By the tilt stood a stately Tent of Orange tawny Taffeta, curiously embroidered with Silver & pendants on the Pinnacles very slightly to behold. From forth this Tent came the noble Earl of Oxenford in rich gilt Armor, and sat down under a great high Bay-tree, the whole stock, branches and leaves whereof were all gilded over, that nothing but Gold could be discerned.

> By the Tree stood twelve tilting staves, all which likewise were gilded clean over. After a solemn sound of most sweet Music, he mounted on his Courser, very richly caparisoned, when his page ascending the stairs where her Highness stood in the window, delivered to her by speech this Oration:
> [A SWEET SPEECH SPOKEN AT THE TRYUMPH BEFORE THE QUEEN'S MOST EXCELLENT MAJESTIE, BY THE PAGE TO THE RIGHT NOBLE CHAMPION, THE EARL OF OXENFORD]
> The speech being ended, with great honor he ran, and valiantly broke all the twelve staves. And after the finishing of the sports: both the rich Baytree, and the beautiful Tent, were by the standers-by torn and rent in more pieces than can be numbered.

When J. Thomas Looney identified Oxford as "Shakespeare" in 1920, he was probably unaware of this "show" that the earl produced, directed and starred in. But let us imagine Looney making observations and gathering evidence, which would come together as an initial theory of Shakespearean authorship, and then coming upon the above account of an event in Oxford's life. Isn't it just the kind of thing he had expected and hoped to find?

There is a clear link between Oxford's appearance in 1581 before Queen Elizabeth as "the Knight of the Tree of the Sunne" and the allegorical elegy *The Phoenix and Turtle*, printed in 1601 as by "William Shake-speare" in a compilation of verses called *Love's Martyr or Rosalins Complaint*. In his 1581 tiltyard performance Oxford had depicted Elizabeth as the Phoenix, the mythical bird that consumes itself in flames ignited by the sun and is reborn from its own ashes; even earlier, the queen herself had used the Phoenix as a symbol of her chastity and of the rebirth (through succession to the throne) of her Tudor dynasty.

Oxford depicted himself as the queen's loyal knight devoted to protecting "the Tree of the Sunne"—the single (or sole) Arabian tree in which the Phoenix had her nest, symbolic of the English throne and Elizabeth's dynastic seat. The earl's page delivered an oration to the queen describing how the earl had made "a solemn vow to incorporate his heart into that Tree," adding that "as there is but one Sun to shine over it, one root to give life unto it, one top to maintain Majesty, so there should be but one Knight, either to live or die for the defense thereof." Oxford was symbolically merging with Elizabeth, as if they were a single entity, and pledging to protect the queen and her dynasty with his "constant loyalty" as well as with his life.

CHAPTER TWO

HAMLET & OXFORD

Reason 5 – Plays for the Court

"You are welcome, masters! Welcome, all! – I am glad to see thee well – Welcome, good friends – O, old friend! ... Masters, you are all welcome! We'll e'en to't like French falconers, fly at anything we see. We'll have a speech straight. Come give us a taste of your quality, come a passionate speech!"- Hamlet to the Actors (2.2)

Hamlet loves the players; he is the first to greet them as they arrive to perform at Denmark's royal court. The prince is overjoyed to see these actors, who are old friends, many of whom he has known since he was a boy. It's a given that the author who wrote those lines for the prince was himself a man of the theater. The stage was in his blood and bones. He was at home with plays and players in their magical world. He made it his business to learn everything he could about the theater, down to the details of entrances, exits, costume changes, musical interludes, sound effects, laughter, tears, fact, fiction—a mix of talent and skill and hard work in service of the powerful art of bringing stories to life on stage through actions, and, above all, through the power of words.

But what was the nature of "Shakespeare's" involvement in the theater? Was he, as the orthodox scholar tells us, in the same position as the actors who arrive at the court? Was his love of the stage, as we are told, from the perspective of the common players who receive Hamlet's greeting? If the writer of this play was one of those actors, as orthodox biography would have it, would he express his love for his colleagues from the point of view of the prince? Isn't it far more likely that the author himself was of high rank, and that Hamlet's greeting to the players is a mirror of the author's own relationship to them? Doesn't it seem that the author wrote Hamlet's lines to the players based on his own experience, using his own sophisticated voice, to express his dual attitude of affection and condescension?

"Shakespeare" and de Vere both lived in the world of the theater; but unlike the conjectural flights of Stratfordian biography, the earl's connection to the stage is a documented fact; for Oxford, it began when he was a young boy and his father's company of players arrived at the castle for the winter season to provide entertainment during the long cold evenings.

In the graveyard Hamlet believes that the skull he holds in his hands was that of the king's jester, Yorick, whom the prince had known during his boyhood. The jester had given him rollicking piggyback rides filled with laughter, a memory engraved in Hamlet's mind and heart: "Alas, poor Yorick! I knew him, Horatio—a fellow of infinite jest, of most excellent fancy! He hath borne me on his back a thousand times!" (5.1).

De Vere most certainly recalled the evenings warmed by flames in the great stone fireplace, while the guests of the castle sat around the long table, all keeling over with laughter, much as the prince recalls when speaking to Yorick while holding the jester's skull: "Where be your gibes now, your gambols, your songs, your flashes of merriment that were wont to set the table on a roar?"

After greeting the players, Hamlet turns to Polonius, chief minister to the king: "Good my lord, will you see the players well bestowed? Do you hear? Let them be well used; for they are the abstract and brief chronicles of the time. After your death you were better have a bad epitaph than their ill report while you live."

To the leading player: "Dost thou hear me, old friend? Can you play 'The Murder of Gonzago' . . . We'll have it tomorrow night. You could, for a need, study a speech of some dozen or sixteen lines which I would set down and insert in it?"

In other words, the prince himself is also a playwright and a director, instructing the actors in their own art: "... the purpose of playing, whose end, both at the first and now, was and is, to hold, as 'twere, the mirror up to nature; to show virtue her own feature, scorn her own image, and the very age and body of the time his form and pressure."

The turning point of *Hamlet* begins when the prince composes lines for the players to speak, so that he might "catch the conscience of the King." Edward de Vere also brought plays to court and for much the same reason. In 1583, at age thirty-three, he acquired the sublease of the Blackfriars playhouse; his company of child actors, known as Oxford's Boys, joined up with Paul's Boys to form a composite troupe. The earl then transferred the lease of Blackfriars to Lyly, who rehearsed there with the children in front of private aristocratic audiences before performing at court for the queen. Oxford was also an active patron of an adult acting company.

If William of Stratford held high rank at court while bringing acting companies to perform before the monarch, who would doubt that he also created Shakespeare's most multi-dimensional, fully realized protagonist? Who would doubt he had captured those wonderful interactions between the prince and the actors? But it was in fact Oxford, hereditary Lord Great Chamberlain and highest ranking earl of the realm, virtually the Prince of England, who brought play companies to the royal court. It was Oxford who stood in the same relation to the players as Hamlet. Not the least of his own motives was to "catch the conscience" of his own sovereign mistress, the Queen of England.

Reason 6 – "Lights! Lights! Lights!"

When Oxford was barely into his teens, he witnessed a real-life event that was virtually the same as the one "Shakespeare" would create many years later for the dramatic turning point of *Hamlet*, when the prince puts on a play to "catch the conscience of the King." At fourteen, Oxford was on the 1564 summer progress when Queen Elizabeth paid her historic visit to Cambridge for five thrilling days and nights. Chancellor William Cecil (later Lord Burghley) was in charge while his arch political enemy, High Steward Robert Dudley (later the Earl of Leicester), acted as master of ceremonies.

Although in his early teens, Oxford was already a well-tutored scholar whose Renaissance outlook had drawn him to literature and history among a myriad of fields, and Elizabeth, thirty-one, had displayed her own Renaissance spirit and love for learning when she and her retinue entered Cambridge that summer. The chapel of King's College had been transformed into a "great stage" and she spent three of the five nights feasting on "comedies and tragedies."

Elizabeth was set to leave on Thursday, 10 August, for a ten-mile ride to the home of Sir Henry Cromwell at Hinchingbrooke, where she was to spend the night, and Her Majesty was eager to get going. According to Guzman de Silva, the Spanish ambassador, Elizabeth made a speech praising all the plays or "comedies" and disputations, but some of the anti-Catholic students "wished to give her another representation, which she refused in order to be no longer delayed." The students were so anxious for her to hear their play, however, that they "followed her [to Hinchingbrooke] and so importuned her that at last she consented." That evening, in a courtyard, an exhausted queen gathered with members of her court by torchlight for the student production.

It turned out to be a distasteful burlesque intended to mock those Catholic leaders who were then imprisoned in the Tower of London. The university atmosphere had become charged with the rapidly developing Protestant radicalism known as the Puritan movement. But the queen and Cecil were ending hostilities with France while trying to maintain good relations with Catholic Spain, so Elizabeth was in no mood for anti-papal displays that de Silva would (and did) dutifully report back to King Philip:

"The actors came in dressed as some of the imprisoned bishops. First came the Bishop of London carrying a lamb in his hands as if he were eating it as he walked along, and then others with devices, one being in the figure of a dog with the Host in his mouth ... The Queen was so angry that she at once entered her chamber, using strong language; and the men who held the torches, it being night, left them in the dark."

Imagine how this scene must have struck young Oxford! Here was vivid proof that a dramatic representation could directly alter the emotions of the monarch; here was spontaneous evidence of the power of a play to affect Elizabeth's attitude and even her decisions.

Her Majesty swept away using "strong language" as the torchbearers followed, leaving all "in the dark," and the author of *Hamlet* would write:

Ophelia:	The King rises.
Hamlet:	What, frighted with false fire?
Gertrude:	How fares my lord? (to King Claudius)
Polonius:	Give o'er the play!
King:	Give me some light! Away!
All:	Lights! Lights! Lights!

Did the mature dramatist "Shakespeare" later recall this event when he came to write the "Mousetrap" scene of *Hamlet*, setting it at night with the King's guards carrying torches? When, in 1564, the queen rose in anger and rushed off, did chief minister Cecil call to stop the burlesque, as chief minister Polonius would do in *Hamlet*? Did Elizabeth call for light as Claudius does in the play?

Reason 7 – "The Courtier"

"O what a noble mind is here o'erthrown! The courtier's, soldier's, scholar's eye, tongue, sword, the expectancy and rose of the fair state, the glass of fashion and the mold of form!"— Ophelia, speaking of Prince Hamlet (3.1)

When Shakespeare created his most self-revealing character through the words and actions of Hamlet, he drew upon his own intimate knowledge and obvious love for Baldesar Castiglione's *Il Cortegiano* or *The Book of the Courtier*, one of the great volumes of the High Renaissance. That book portrays a group of real-life thinkers, politicians, soldiers, clerics, diplomats and wits who gather at the Palace of Urbino in 1507 to play a game, over four evenings, trying to piece together a portrait of the most perfect courtier. The topics of their conversations, John Lotherington writes in his introduction to a 2005 edition, range "from chivalry to humanist debates about language, literature, painting and sculpture, to the art of conversation and the telling of jokes, the role and dignity of women, the delicate job of guiding willful princes, and finally to love and its transcendent form in pure spirit."

Originally published at Venice in 1528, Castiglione's book attempts "to refashion the medieval ideal of the chivalrous knight and to fuse it with the Renaissance virtues of learning and grace," Oscar Campbell writes, adding that Shakespeare "may have derived the 'merry war' of Beatrice and Benedick in *Much Ado About Nothing* from a similar battle in *The Courtier*." "Shakespeare may have read Castiglione in Italian," Charles Boyce suggests—an amazing statement if one believes the author was William of Stratford, who, by all reckoning, was unable to read Italian.

First translated into English in 1561 by Thomas Hoby, *The Courtier* exerted a strong influence on the courtly ideals of the reign of Elizabeth. A little more than a decade later, in January 1571/2, having just come of age at twenty-one as a courtier, Oxford "commanded" the publication of a new Latin translation by one of his former tutors, Bartholomew Clerke; to give it the biggest possible sendoff he wrote an eloquent introduction, also in Latin. Oxford had been captivated by literature from his earliest days; studying with the best tutors, he went on to receive honorary degrees at Cambridge and Oxford at ages fourteen and sixteen; before age twenty his personal library included works of Chaucer, Plutarch, Cicero and Plato, the Geneva Bible and more. In 1571 his uncle, Arthur Golding, noted that he knew from personal experience how his nephew had taken a keen interest in "the present estate of things in our days, and that not without a certain pregnancy of wit and ripeness of understanding."

By the following year Oxford was enjoying the highest royal favor at court. The apparent intimacy of his relationship with Queen Elizabeth was the subject of scandalous gossip; in December 1571 he married Anne Cecil, the Ophelia-like daughter of Burghley, the Polonius-like chief minister to the queen. Although he had grown up in the household and custody of his father-in-law, the architect of the Protestant reformation, Oxford leaned away from the Puritan movement in favor of the classical languages and old feudal values of knighthood and chivalry. In his early twenties, he was the latest descendant of a line of noble earls stretching back 500 years to William the Conqueror; in every way, he became the man whom Walt Whitman would describe as one of the "wolfish earls" who must have written the Shakespeare plays:

> Conceived out of the fullest heat and pulse of European feudalism—personifying in unparalleled ways the medieval aristocracy, its towering spirit of ruthless and gigantic caste, its own peculiar air and arrogance (no mere imitation)—only one of the 'wolfish earls' so plenteous in the plays themselves, or some born descendent and knower, might seem to be the true author of those amazing works—works in some respects greater than anything else in recorded history.

The young earl wrote enthusiastically of Castiglione in his preface:

> For who has spoken of Princes with greater gravity? Who has discoursed of illustrious women with a more ample dignity? No one has written of military affairs more eloquently, more aptly about horse-racing, and more clearly and admirably about encounters under arms on the field of battle. I will say nothing of the fitness and the excellence with which he has depicted the beauty of chivalry in the noblest persons.

"Without Castiglione we should not have Hamlet," Drayton Henderson writes. "The ideal of the courtier, scholar, soldier, developed first in Italy, and perfected in the narrative of *Il Cortegiano*, was Castiglione's gift to the world. Prince Hamlet is the high exemplar of it in our literature. But it is not only Shakespeare's Hamlet that seems to follow Castiglione—Shakespeare himself does."

Reason 8 – "Hamlet's Book"

Polonius: *What do you read, my lord?*
Hamlet: *Words, words, words.* (2.2)

The book Hamlet carries on stage and reads during the play has been identified by scholars as *De Consolatione*, by the Italian mathematician and physician Girolamo Cardano, or Jerome Cardan (1501-1576). Its first English translation was published upon the orders of the passionate, enthusiastic de Vere, who, at twenty-three, financed its printing. The title page of the first London edition read in part:

Cardanus Comforte translated into English and published by commandment of the right honorable the Earl of Oxenford, Anno Domini 1573.

Signaling his intention to henceforth devote himself primarily to literature, Oxford contributed both a prefatory letter and a poem in honor of the translator, his friend Thomas Bedingfield.

The earliest identification of *Cardanus' Comforte* with the character of Prince Hamlet was made in 1839 by Francis Douce, who writes, "Whoever will take the trouble of reading the whole of *Cardanus* as translated by Bedingfield will soon be convinced that it had been perused by Shakspeare." (Many scholars of the nineteenth century used the "Shakspeare" spelling instead of "Shakespeare," reflecting the spelling that was used most often in Stratford.)

"This seems to be the book which Shakespeare placed in the hands of Hamlet," Joseph Hunter writes of *Comforte* in 1845, citing passages that "seem to approach so near to the thoughts of Hamlet that we can hardly doubt that they were in the Poet's mind when he put certain speeches into the mouth of his hero."

In the first quarto of *Hamlet* in 1603, just before the prince launches into his "To be or not to be" soliloquy, the king sees him "poring upon a book" (scene 7) —suggesting that originally Hamlet was to be holding it while delivering that famous soliloquy, which is virtually a poetical paraphrase of Cardan's words:

Cardan: "In holy scripture, death is not accounted other than sleep, and to die is said to sleep ... better to follow the counsel of Agathius, who right well commended death, saying that it did not only remove sickness and all other grief, but also, when all other discommodities of life did happen to man often, it never would come more than once.... Seeing, therefore, with such ease men die, what should we account of death to be resembled to anything better than sleep.... Most assured it is that such sleep be most sweet as be most sound, for those are the best wherein like unto dead men we dream nothing. The broken sleeps, the slumber, the dreams full of visions, are commonly in them that have weak and sickly bodies."

Hamlet: "To die, to sleep—no more; and by a sleep to say we end the heartache and the thousand natural shocks that flesh is heir to: 'tis a consummation devoutly to be wished. To die, to sleep—to sleep, perchance to dream; ay, there's the rub; for in that sleep of death what dreams may come when we have shuffled off this mortal coil must give us pause."

The resemblances, Hardin Craig writes in 1934, are "more numerous and of a more fundamental character than even Hunter seems to have realized." Indeed, he continues, it may be said "without exaggeration that *Cardanus' Comforte* is pre-eminently 'Hamlet's book,' since the philosophy of Hamlet agrees to a remarkable degree with that of Cardan." Craig cited "even more striking agreements" between them:

> Cardan: "For there is nothing that doth better or more truly prophecy the end of life, than when a man dreams that he doth travel and wander into far countries ... and that he travels in countries unknown without hope of return...."
>
> Hamlet: "But that the dread of something after death, the undiscovered country, from whose bourn no traveler returns...."

Craig finds not only parallels to Hamlet's speeches but clarifications of their meaning:

> Cardan: "Only honesty and virtue of mind doth make a man happy, and only a coward and corrupt conscience do cause thine unhappiness."
>
> Hamlet: "Thus conscience does make cowards of us all, and thus the native hue of resolution is sicklied o'er with the pale cast of thought...."

Most scholars mistakenly interpret Hamlet's use of "conscience" as a "sense of right and wrong," but Craig's reading of Bedingfield's translation reveals that Hamlet is referring not to moral scruples about suicide, but, rather, to lack of virtue. In speaking of "virtue" both Cardan and Hamlet mean the power to find remedies for our ills within ourselves, that is, to use our innate capacity to exercise fortitude and act in response to the calamities of life.

Cardan strongly emphasized the virtues of giving comfort and consolation to others. In that regard, Charles Wisner Barrell writes in 1946: "It speaks well for the character and mental proclivities of the young Earl of Oxford that he had encouraged or 'commanded' Bedingfield to the accomplishment of this work of permanent, cosmopolitan interest. The situation, however, is all of a piece with Oxford's recorded career as an inspiring leader and generous supporter of so many of the scholars and literary innovators whose works are clearly reflected in the deep well of Shakespeare's knowledge."

Reason 9 – The Polonius-Hamlet Family

An obvious link in the chain of evidence connecting Edward de Vere to "Shakespeare" is the similarity of his and Hamlet's family relationships:

- Gertrude is the mother of Hamlet, while Elizabeth was the legal mother of Oxford, when he was her ward.

- Polonius is chief advisor to Gertrude, while Burghley (William Cecil) was chief advisor to Elizabeth.

- Hamlet is engaged to young Ophelia, daughter of Polonius, while Oxford became engaged to young Anne Cecil, daughter of Burghley.

- Ophelia's older brother, Laertes, goes off to Paris, his behavior causing great distress to his father, who recites the famous "precepts" to him as guidance. Anne's eldest brother, Thomas Cecil, went off to Paris, his behavior causing great distress to his father, who wrote him long letters full of wise "precepts" as guidance. Later he would also write his famous precepts to son Robert Cecil.

Claudius, who fatally poisons Hamlet's father and marries the prince's mother, the queen, thereby becoming king, reflects Elizabeth's

lover Robert Dudley, Earl of Leicester, who was suspected of many poisonings. Oxford may have concluded that Leicester had caused the death by poisoning of his own father, John de Vere, 16th Earl of Oxford.

In *Hamlet*, the Shakespeare play carrying the most autobiographical tone of them all, we find the main character in virtually the same web of family relationships at court as Edward de Vere. Traditional scholars might ask rhetorically, "Well, now, you're not claiming this as proof that Oxford wrote *Hamlet*, are you?" We might reply, "No, of course not, but doesn't this give you a little queasy feeling in the gut? Don't you

Fig. 3 - William Cecil, Lord Burghley

have the slightest tremor of doubt that Will of Stratford could have, or would have, written such a play? Do you think this mirror image of family relationships can be mere coincidence?"

James Shapiro of Columbia University argues that "such claims about representing on the public stage some of the most powerful figures in the realm betray a shallow grasp of Elizabethan dramatic censorship." He adds that Edmund Tilney, Master of the Revels, "whose job it was to read and approve all dramatic scripts before they were publicly performed, would have lost his job—and most likely his nose and ears, if not his head, had he approved a play that so transparently ridiculed privy councilors past and present."

Perhaps it is Shapiro who betrays a shallow grasp of what is really happening on the public stage. The author himself supplies a further clue to this when an exasperated Polonius, speaking of Hamlet, tells Gertrude: "He will come straight. Look you lay home to him. Tell him his pranks have been too broad to bear with, and that your Grace hath screened and stood between much heat and him." Hamlet-Oxford *has* taken too many liberties, unbearably so, but nonetheless the queen has protected him from "much heat" and/or reprisals by government officials (such as Tilney) and his enemies at court (see Reason 2).

Otherwise, Shapiro is right: not only Tilney but also the playwright surely *would* have lost his head . . . if he had been Shakspere of Stratford!

Reason 10 – "These Few Precepts"

Mention "precepts" to an Oxfordian and you will undoubtedly hear about Polonius delivering *"these few precepts"* to Laertes in *Hamlet*. Then you'll hear how de Vere, as a royal ward living at Cecil House, would have known Burghley's real-life *Certain Precepts,* which were not printed until 1616, the year that Shakespere died and long after the play had been written.

In 1869 the scholar George French observed in *Shakspeareana Genealogica* that Lord Chamberlain Polonius, his son Laertes and his daughter Ophelia "are supposed to stand for Queen Elizabeth's celebrated Lord High Treasurer Sir William Cecil, Lord Burghley, his second son Robert Cecil and his daughter Anne Cecil." In other words, long before the "authorship debate" got rolling it was hardly controversial to suggest that Polonius was modeled after Burghley and that Laertes and Ophelia were "supposed" to be modeled after Robert (and/or Thomas) Cecil and their sister Anne.

William Cecil was elevated in 1571 to the peerage as Lord Burghley so that Oxford could enter an arranged marriage with his fifteen-year-old daughter, who would then become a member of the nobility. When Burghley's younger son, Robert, was setting forth on his travels in 1584 (the year when many Oxfordians believe the earl wrote the first draft of *Hamlet*), Burghley wrote out "certain precepts" for him as guides to behavior —"and in some of these," French notes, "the identity of language with that of Polonius is so close that SHAKSPEARE [sic] could not have hit upon it unless he had been acquainted with

Burghley's parental advice to Robert Cecil."

In the decades after Looney first proposed Oxford as the author in 1920, orthodox scholars began to back away from seeing Polonius as Lord Burghley. They even tried to suggest that the two sets

Fig. 4 - William Cecil and his son Robert

of precepts are not necessarily similar; but here are some comparisons:

> Burghley: Be not scurrilous in conversation, or satirical in thy jests...

> Polonius: Give thy thoughts no tongue, nor any un-proportioned thought his act . . . be thou familiar, but by no means vulgar.

> Burghley: Let thy kindred and allies be welcome to thy house and table. Grace them with thy countenance ... But shake off those glow-worms, I mean parasites and sycophants, who will feed and fawn upon thee in the summer of prosperity.

> Polonius: Those friends thou hast, and their adoption tried, grapple them to thy soul with hoops of steel; but do not dull thy palm with entertainment of each new-hatched unfledged comrade.

> Burghley: Neither borrow of a neighbor or of a friend, but of a stranger, whose paying for it thou shalt hear no more of it . . . Trust not any man with thy life credit, or estate.

> Polonius: Neither a borrower nor a lender be; for loan oft loses both itself and friend, and borrowing dulls the edge of husbandry.

It is evident that the author of *Hamlet* needed to be—and was—familiar with Burghley's maxims, the better to mirror them and simultaneously satirize them. He had heard them firsthand (probably on numerous occasions) at Cecil House, where he had lived until age twenty-one. In fact, such is the argument made by none other than Michael Cecil, the 18th Baron Burghley and a direct descendant of the first baron, William Cecil.

Reason 11 – Pirates in the Channel

Does Oxford have a stronger claim as the author of *Hamlet* because, like the prince, he was actually captured by pirates? That depends on one's point of view. If William of Stratford had been stopped by pirates in real life, we would have books with titles like *Shakespeare's Encounter with Pirates: A Turning Point for His Life & Work.*

The earl's capture and release by Dutch pirates in the English Channel is just one example of something in his life resembling what we find in the Shakespearean plays. The similar episode in *Hamlet* does not originate from any of the play's recognized sources, so it seems to have come from the author's own experience. The pirates intercepted and boarded Oxford's ship in 1576, as he was returning to England from his sixteen-month tour of France, Germany and Italy. They stripped the ship clean.

"De Vere's luggage was ransacked, and the pirates even took the clothes from the earl's back," Mark Anderson writes. Oxford was left virtually "naked," as the French ambassador reported, and he would have lost his life had not one of the pirates, a Scotsman, recognized him. Nathaniel Baxter, a member of Oxford's entourage, recalled the pirate episode in a poem published in 1606, two years after the earl's death:

Naked we landed out of Italy
Enthralled by pirates, men of no regard
Horror and death assailed nobility

Hamlet writes to King Claudius in virtually the same language: "I am set naked on your kingdom."

Hamlet writes to Horatio: "'Ere we were two days old at sea, a pirate of very warlike appointment gave us chase. Finding ourselves too slow of sail, we put on a compelled valor, and in the grapple I boarded them. On the instant, they got clear of our ship, so I alone became their prisoner. They have dealt with me like thieves of mercy, but they knew what they did; I am to do a good turn for them."

The prince, like the earl, had been bound for England; now he turns back to Denmark while Rosencrantz and Guildenstern "hold their course for England"—where, because Hamlet has craftily switched the written orders, they will be killed instead of him. Of course, *Hamlet* is not strict autobiography; the point is that the vast majority of the world's best novelists and dramatists draw upon their personal experiences and transmute them, through imagination and skill, into fictional art forms. It is not a matter of having to choose between reality and invention; all great art is a blend of both.

Shapiro concedes, as he must, that "we know almost nothing about [the Stratford man's] personal experiences" and, therefore, "those moments in his work which build upon what he may have felt remain invisible to us." Moreover, since scholars must face this vacuum in the orthodox biography, he boldly declares that all attempts to link the author's life with his works should hereby cease! Traditional efforts at such linkage have failed; therefore, as the authorship question continues to catch fire and spread, such failures will become increasingly obvious. Thus, as Shapiro would have it, virtually every writer deserves to be the subject of literary biography except the greatest writer of all.

Oxford was again targeted by pirates in the Channel in 1585, when he returned from Holland after his brief command of 4,000 foot soldiers and 400 horse. He was summoned home, and, according to one report, a ship carrying his "money, apparel, wine and venison" was "captured off Dunkirk by the Spaniards." Among his confiscated belongings was the original letter from Burghley with orders for the Horse command.

"*Hamlet* contains not only an encounter with pirates," Mark Anderson writes, "but, also, an analogous plot twist involving suborned letters at sea."

Reason 12 – The Kingdom of the Mind

"O God, I could be bounded in a nutshell and count myself a king of infinite space, were it not that I have bad dreams" – the prince in *Hamlet* (2.2)

The prince's point is that we humans have the potential to deal with terrible suffering by retreating from the world—into a nutshell, as he puts it—and by ruling over the vast kingdom of the mind. Hamlet does have the ability to endure "the slings and arrows of outrageous fortune" by using his sovereign power of thought. In the circumstances of the play, of course, he has been deprived of the crown by his uncle; therefore, while he cannot be the King of Denmark, he can always be the king of his limitless mind.

This theme appears elsewhere in writings attributed to both "Shakespeare" and de Vere, with frequent appearances of similar words such as "king" or "kingdom" and "mind" and "content" or "contented." In *Henry VI, Pt.3* (3.1), for example, the king is in disguise when he meets up with two Keepers who wonder why he talks like a monarch:

Keeper:	Say, what art thou that talk'st of kings and queens?
Henry VI:	More than I seem, and less than I was born to: A man at least, for less I should not be; And men may talk of kings, and why not I?
Keeper:	Ay, but thou talk'st as if thou wert a king.
Henry:	Why, so I am—in mind; and that's enough.

Keeper: But, if thou be a king, where is thy crown?

Henry: My crown is in my heart, not on my head;
              Not decked with diamonds and Indian stones,
              Nor to be seen: my crown is called content:
              A crown it is that seldom kings enjoy.

Oxford expresses the same basic ideas in similar ways. The earl stopped putting his own name on his writings at age twenty-six in 1576, the year *The Paradise of Dainty Devices* was first published (probably by his doing); but even by then his poems (or song lyrics) often reflect Hamlet's outlook. One such poem (actually lyrics to a song), "My mind to me a kingdom is," is often attributed to Edward Dyer; but in the Rawlinson MSS it's subscribed *Earle of Oxenforde*. The words were set to music under the title "In praise of a contented mind" by the Elizabethan composer William Byrd, with whom Oxford was closely associated. Steven May, always cautious, cites this work as "possibly" by Oxford:

My mind to me a kingdom is,
Such perfect joy therein I find,
That it excels all other bliss
That world affords or grows by kind;
Though much I want which most men have,
Yet still my mind forbids to crave …
Content I live, this is my state,
I seek no more than may suffice …
Lo thus I triumph like a king,
Content with that my mind doth bring …

That verse-song might as well have been penned by Hamlet himself! It comes from the same sensibility, with the same note of defiance. May assigns the following verse to Oxford without qualification:

Were I a king I could command content,
Were I obscure unknown should be my cares,
And were I dead no thought should me torment,
Nor words, nor wrongs, nor loves, nor hopes, nor fears;
A doubtful choice of these things one to crave,
A kingdom or a cottage or a grave.

Here is the same preoccupation with the lack of kingship, echoing lines spoken by the king in *Richard II*:

What must the king do now? Must he submit?
The king shall do it. Must he be deposed?
The king shall be contented…

And my large kingdom for a little grave,
A little little grave, an obscure grave … (3.3)

Oxford began signing his letters with a "crown signature" (i.e., its overall shape resembling a king's crown) in November 1569 when he was nineteen; he stopped using it after the funeral of Queen Elizabeth on 28 April 1603, when the Tudor dynasty was officially ended. Did he think of himself as a rightful king deprived of his

Fig. 5 - Edward de Vere's "Crown signature"

crown? Such a provocative signature could get a nobleman in big trouble; Oxford's uncle, Surrey, had been imprisoned and executed by Henry VIII for provocatively altering his coat of arms. How Oxford got away with using this highly suggestive signature is unknown.

Sonnet 114 by "Shakespeare" has these lines:

Or whether doth my mind, being crown'd with you,
Drink up the monarch's plague, this flattery …
And my great mind most kingly drinks it up …

The anonymous verse publication *Willobie His Avisa* (1594) ends with a long poem, "The Praise of a Contented Mind," signed *Ever or Never*, one of de Vere's early pen names, concluding with:

Of all the brave resounding words, which God to man hath lent,
This soundeth sweetest in mine ear, to say: "I am content."

Oxford was a member of the House of Lords, where "Content" or "Not Content" were the formal expressions of assent or dissent (equivalent to "Aye" or "No" in the Commons); but in *Willobie*, as in works attributed to both Oxford and "Shakespeare," the phrase "I am content" is an expression of inner peace despite the experience of painful loss. Returning to *Hamlet*, we can say that Hamlet has learned to travel "out of body" to some other dimension, one that may actually be the realm of madness, as he tells Laertes:

Hamlet: What I have done
That might your nature, honor and exception
Roughly awake, I here proclaim was madness.
Was't Hamlet wronged Laertes? Never Hamlet.
If Hamlet from himself be ta'en away,
And when he's not himself does wrong Laertes,
Then Hamlet does it not. Hamlet denies it.
Who does it then? His madness. (5.2)

In effect, he has split himself in two, resulting in an appearance on the surface that's very different from what is actually going on inside him:

Oxford: I am not as I seem to be,
            Nor when I smile I am not glad...

Reason 13 – "Hamlet's Castle"

"Travel up to Hamlet's Castle in the city of Elsinore, where you will see the outer walls and towers of this historic fortress immortalized by Shakespeare..."—A tourism advertisement

Travelers to Denmark are encouraged to visit Kronborg Castle, known as Hamlet's Castle, but the advertisers are not quite sure why "Shakespeare" chose Elsinore (rather than Copenhagen) as the setting for his great play about the Danish royal court. Given the usual view, which dates the play's composition *circa* 1600, they point to the Elsinore castle's strategic location at Sound Øresund (three miles across the water from Sweden). However, when tourism promoters finally realize that *Hamlet* was actually written by Oxford, they will find a far more obvious reason.

In the summer of 1582, Queen Elizabeth sent Oxford's brother-in-law, Peregrine Bertie, Lord Willoughby de Eresby, on a special mission to the court at Kronborg Castle in Elsinore. Under the rule of King Frederick II, Denmark had become one of the great powers on the Continent and claimed the right to levy duties on all foreign merchant ships passing through its sea lanes. Willoughby's task was to invest Frederick as a Knight of the Garter while trying to persuade him that English ships trading with Russia should be exempt from such levies.

Willoughby remained at the Elsinore castle from July to September, soaking up the atmosphere of the great fortification. He and the king became drinking and hunting buddies; although the mission itself was not entirely successful, he wrote a colorful and detailed chronicle of it when he returned home, which was circulated at the English court and is preserved at the British Museum: *"Relation of my Lord Willoughby's embassy into Denmark, in his own hand."*

In it he describes daily hunting expeditions and nightly revels, with drinking bouts that prompted "many affectionate and loving speeches to Her Majesty and all of the Order." These grand toasts were "performed after a whole volley of all the great shot of the castle discharged, a royal feast, and a most artificial and cunning fireworks."

Ogburn Jr. points to the January 1896 issue of *Contemporary Review,* in which the scholar Jan Steffanson observes that the author of *Hamlet* manifests a "correct knowledge of Danish names, words, and customs of his time," along with "a local knowledge of the royal Castle of Elsinore, which he could not have derived from books." The dramatist shows a detailed knowledge of one particular room in the castle, plus a familiarity with the strictly Danish custom of drinking "cannon healths," where those mighty guns were fired every time the king drank:

King: No jocund health that Denmark drinks today. But the great cannon to the clouds shall tell... (1.2)

A flourish of trumpets and ordnance shot off, within.

Hamlet: The king doth wake tonight and takes his rouse, keeps wassail and the swaggering up-spring reels; and, as he drinks his draughts of Rhenish down, the kettle-drum and trumpet thus bray out the triumph of his pledge... (1.4)

King: Give me the cups; and let the kettle to the trumpet speak, the trumpet to the cannoneer without, the cannons to the heavens, the heavens to earth: "Now the king drinks to Hamlet!" (5.2)

Willoughby also wrote of a state dinner at the castle with twenty-four noblemen, of whom two—Jorgen Rosencrantz and Alex Gyldenstjerne—had names that would be matched by the names of the famous spies Rosencrantz and Guildenstern to appear in *Hamlet.*

Willoughby was married to Oxford's sister, Lady Mary Vere, a former Maid of Honor to Queen Elizabeth. At family gatherings he would have regaled them with hilarious tales of King Frederick at the Court of Denmark in the castle at Elsinore. That is just one reason why many Oxfordians have concluded that Oxford wrote the first version of *Hamlet, Prince of Denmark* in 1583 or 1584, nearly two decades before the traditional dating of that great play, and that he revised it right up until his reported death on 24 June 1604.

Reason 14 – *Beowulf* and *Hamlet*

Whenever scholars begin to suspect that "Shakespeare" was influenced in his writing of *Hamlet* by the ancient narrative poem *Beowulf,* they usually make a sharp turn away from that idea. *Beowulf,* as generations of students can attest, is the earliest surviving Old English poem, dated between the eighth and eleventh centuries, its author unknown. Set in Scandinavia and told in 3,182 alliterative lines, it's one of the most important works of AngloSaxon literature, as well as one of the earliest European epics written not in Latin, but, rather, in the vernacular or native language.

Beowulf, a hero of the Geats, comes to the aid of Hrothgar, King of the Danes, whose mead-hall (great royal feasting hall, where warriors could sleep at night) has been under attack by the monster Grendel. Beowulf slays Grendel; when Grendel's mother attacks, he kills her, too; he then returns home to Geatland in Sweden, where he becomes King of the Geats. Fifty years pass until the third and final battle, when Beowulf's friend Wiglaf helps him slay the Dragon; after being mortally wounded in the fight, Beowulf delivers his dying words to his friend (as rendered below in the 1963 translation by Burton Raffel), with its striking similarities to Hamlet's dying words to Horatio:

Beowulf: Take what I leave, Wiglaf, lead my people,
                Help them; my time is gone…

Hamlet: O, I die, Horatio,
                The potent poison quite o'er-crows my spirit…

Beowulf: Have the brave Geats build me a tomb …
                And build it here, at the water's edge, high
                On this spit of land, so sailors can see
                This tower and remember my name.

Hamlet: O God, Horatio, what a wounded name,
                Things standing thus unknown, shall I leave behind me!
                If thou didst ever hold me in thy heart,
                Absent thee from felicity awhile,
                And in this harsh world draw thy breath in pain
                To tell my story.

There is only one known manuscript copy of *Beowulf*. It's a fragile document, possibly the anonymous author's working copy, the result of two scribes taking down the words as he spoke them. Although the poem is set in Scandinavia, it was written in England; the earliest known owner of the manuscript was the scholar Laurence Nowell, an expert collector of AngloSaxon documents, who received it while he lived at the London house of his patron, William Cecil. After coming into possession of a volume of handwritten manuscripts which included the *Beowulf* text, he signed his name in pencil on the back of it along with the year, 1563. The manuscript volume is bound in what is still known as the "Nowell Codex" at the British Library. Only a few other highly placed individuals had access to *Beowulf* until well after the sixteenth century. The man from Stratford-upon-Avon could not have seen it; therefore, orthodox scholars noticing the influence of *Beowulf* in *Hamlet* struggle to find some explanation for the similarities or else ignore them—just one example of the losses suffered from being unable to identify the correct author.

Laurence Nowel—antiquarian, cartographer, Anglo-Saxon scholar—was summoned by Cecil to act as a special tutor to young Edward de Vere, who arrived at Cecil House in September of 1562. In 1563 Nowell acquired the manuscript; it is easy to imagine young Oxford in the same room when the Anglo-Saxon scholar shared his excitement about having this precious ancient text in his possession.

Oxfordians have been finding such surprising information ever since Looney published *"Shakespeare" Identified* in 1920. This specific link has been known at least since 1990, when it was treated in depth by Dr. Andrew Hannas. As Dr. T.K. Kenyon writes more recently: "Consider, if you will, the obvious plot and character parallels between *Hamlet* and *Beowulf.* The author of *Hamlet* clearly had read *Beowulf.* (Any other explanation is like denying the literary relationship between *The Heart of Darkness* and *Apocalypse Now.*) Because of his tutor, de Vere was one of very few people in England or elsewhere with access to *Beowulf.*"

B.M. Ward writes that "in June 1563 Laurence Nowell wrote a Latin letter to Cecil, drawing his attention to the slip-shod manner in which the cartographers and geographers of England were doing their work. He goes on to ask Cecil that to him may be entrusted the task of compiling an accurate map, because 'I clearly see that my work for the Earl of Oxford cannot be much longer required.' That a scholar of Nowell's attainments should speak thus of his pupil, then age thirteen-and-a-half, argues a precocity quite out of the ordinary."

Here is a selection from Hannas's groundbreaking 1990 report:

But what was *Beowulf* to 'Shake-speare'? Conventional scholarship on the play most likely to show such a link, *Hamlet,* is silent on any connection to *Beowulf.* The Stratford fellow couldn't possibly have known of the Old English manuscript of a poem that didn't 'surface' to literati until a librarian noticed it over a century later, the wisdom holds … But scholars also realize that the play *Hamlet* abandons the obvious Saxo/Belleforest 'source' after the revengeful killing of the uncle. That is, what happens after Amleth kills Feng in Saxo is not found in *Hamlet,* nor is any of the motif of Hamlet's death found in Saxo or Belleforest. Enter *Beowulf…*

I would like to suggest that in the dying words of Hamlet we see a refiguring of the poignant exchange between the dying Beowulf and his faithful (and lone follower) Wiglaf—who also is a relative, a cousin, of his lord [the military hero Horatio Vere was Oxford's cousin]. Not insignificantly, both Beowulf and Hamlet are concerned not just about their own names and stories—which Wiglaf and Horatio will report—but also over the fate of the kingdom, the succession to the throne. Both lands either are, or soon will be, overrun by foreign power. And oddly, the puzzling slipping of time, the aging of Beowulf, bears a curious resemblance to the passage of time in which Hamlet appears in Act Five to have aged from a prince in early manhood to an ostensible thirty years of age...

As for the youthful Oxford ever seeing the Beowulf story, I cannot imagine a tutor such as Nowell not at some juncture showing his pupil that poem— and telling the story—written in a hand from the days of the first Earls of Oxford.

And many years later, I believe, Edward de Vere translated "I am Beowulf the Great" into a famous line attributed to Shakespeare: "This is I, Hamlet the Dane!"

More from the Burton Raffel translation, near the end of the story, with a few parting words from the Prince of Denmark and his friend Horatio:

Beowulf: You're the last of all our far-flung family.
Fate has swept our race away,
Taken warriors in their strength and led them
To the death that was waiting.
And now I follow them.

The old man's mouth was silent, spoke
No more, had said as much as it could;
He would sleep in the fire, soon. His soul
Left his flesh, flew to glory...

Hamlet: The rest is silence.

Horatio: Now cracks a noble heart.
Good night, sweet Prince,
And flights of angels sing thee to thy rest!

CHAPTER THREE

FOOTPRINTS

Reason 15 – The Earl of Surrey

If Shakspere of Stratford-upon-Avon could have boasted that one of his uncles had introduced into England the sonnet form later made famous by "Shakespeare," who would question his authorship of SHAKE-SPEARES SONNETS? Of course, he had no such uncle; but Edward de Vere's uncle Henry Howard, earl of Surrey (1517-1547), was one of the founders of English Renaissance poetry.

One of Oxford's aunts, Frances de Vere (a sister of his father, the sixteenth earl), had married Surrey, the nobleman-poet who, with his friend Sir Thomas Wyatt (1503-1542), had pioneered the writing of English sonnets. Wyatt and Surrey are known as the "Fathers of the English Sonnet." Surrey created the rhyming meter and quatrain divisions of the "Elizabethan" or "Shakespearean" form of sonnet.

Surrey was beheaded in January 1547 by the dying Henry VIII, who had become increasingly paranoid as illness overwhelmed him. The king had

Fig. 6 - Henry Howard, Earl of Surrey

accused the poet-earl of treason, charging him with planning to usurp the crown from his nine-year-old son, the future Edward VI of England. There was no evidence in support of the charge.

In 1557, ten years after Surrey's death and when Oxford was seven, the publisher Richard Tottel issued *Songes and Sonettes written by the right honorable Lorde Henry Haward, late Earle of Surrey and other*, known later and more famously as *Tottel's Miscellany*. (It was the custom for noblemen's poetry to be printed posthumously.) This was the first printed anthology of English poetry and the most important verse collection of the sixteenth century, running into many editions during Elizabeth's reign of nearly forty-five years.

With his translations of two books of Virgil's *Aeneid*, Surrey was the first English poet to publish blank verse; in this, too, Oxford's uncle prepared the way for Shakespeare. Well before his death Surrey's poetry (inspired by the Italians) had been circulated in manuscript, so a young de Vere would have seen copies owned by his relatives. Aunt Frances, his father's sister and Surrey's widow, herself a versifier, lived until 1577, when Oxford was twenty-seven.

As a young man Oxford was close to his cousins, Surrey's son Thomas Howard, 4th Duke of Norfolk (1536-1572), and the duke's younger brother Henry Howard, the future 1st Earl of Northampton (1540-1614). Norfolk was executed in 1572 for taking part in the Ridolfi plot to put the Catholic Mary Stuart, Queen of Scots on the throne; and Henry Howard was one of those responsible for turning Oxford against his wife Anne Cecil in 1576. This younger son of Surrey was extremely well-educated and intelligent, which drew Oxford to him, but he also had a "stupendous want of principle," as Sir Sidney Lee writes in the *Dictionary of National Biography* (DNB). Oxford would accuse Howard in 1580 of plotting a Catholic overthrow of Queen Elizabeth on behalf of the still captive Mary Stuart.

Oxford's relatives and their friends had been actively involved in the rise of English poetry that would flourish in the Elizabethan age and reach its extraordinary heights in the poems, plays and sonnets of "William Shakespeare." These poets had included not only Wyatt and Surrey, but others:

- **Thomas Lord Vaux (1509-1556),** inventor of the six-line stanza used for verses by both Oxford and "Shakespeare." Lord Vaux contributed some verse posthumously to *The Paradise of Dainty Devices* (1576), in which seven of Oxford's poems appeared under the initials *E.O.*; Vaux had also composed a song adapted by "Shakespeare" into the Gravedigger's song in *Hamlet*.

- **Edmund Baron Sheffield (1521-1549),** another of Oxford's poet-uncles, was the husband of the sixteenth Earl of Oxford's sister Anne de Vere. Sheffield has been linked with Surrey as an upholder of "chivalric poetry." He was reported to have had great "skill in music" and to have written "a book of sonnets in the Italian fashion," but all these have been lost. Sheffield had little time; he died at twenty-eight, in the act of helping to suppress a rebellion.

- **Thomas Churchyard (1520-1604),** a soldier-poet who was also an indefatigable "miscellaneous" writer. The DNB records he was "attached in his youth to the household of the famous Earl of Surrey, whose memory he fondly cherished throughout his long life." After serving militarily against Spain in the Low Countries on behalf of Prince William of Orange, the Protestant champion, Churchyard returned to England in 1567 and a year later entered the employ of eighteen-year-old de Vere. He soon embarked on an intelligence mission abroad, probably for William Cecil.

In 1580, according to Steven May, Churchyard proposed dedicating two works to "the most worthiest (and towards noble man), the Erle of Oxford," who was spending his own money (and draining his purse) on patronizing many men of letters. Among them was Churchyard, who must have captured Oxford's full attention while recalling his youthful service to Surrey.

Reason 16 – Arthur Golding

"The influence of Ovid was apparent throughout Shakespeare's earliest literary work, poetic and dramatic. His closest adaptations of Ovid's Metamorphoses often reflect the phraseology of the popular English version by Arthur Golding issued between 1565 and 1567."—Sidney Lee, *A Life of William Shakespeare*, 1898

"Ovid, the love of Shakespeare's life among Latin poets, made an overwhelming impression upon him, which he carried with him all his days: subjects, themes, characters and phrases haunted his imagination. The bulk of his classical mythology came from the Metamorphoses, which he used in the original as well as in Golding's translation."—A.L. Rowse, *Shakespeare, the Man*, 1973

All scholars agree that the favorite classical source of "Shakespeare" was the literary work of the ancient Roman poet Publius Ovidius Naso, known as Ovid (43 BCE – 18 CE). He drew upon the stories, rhythms and language of Ovid, from the original Latin text and, heavily so, from the English translation of the *Metamorphoses* by Arthur Golding, published in 1567; Golding was young Oxford's uncle, living at various times under the same roof with him at Cecil House in the 1560s, just when the translating of Ovid's fifteen-book masterpiece was being carried out.

Often these "coincidences" are startling because of the way we come upon them. In this case, the British schoolmaster Looney suggested in 1920 that Oxford wrote the Shakespeare works, which happen to be filled with material drawn from Ovid's *Metamorphoses*; only afterward did Looney learn that young de Vere had been physically present at Cecil House in London when Golding acted as the receiver for de Vere's financial affairs and was supposedly translating the Ovid work for which he has been credited. I use the word "supposedly" because it is far more likely that the actual translation was done by Golding's young nephew, the future earl. Golding was a puritanical sort who translated Calvin's *Psalms of David* (dedicating it to Oxford) and would not have been interested in translating Ovid's tales of passion, seduction and lovemaking as well as incestuous activity by pagan gods and goddesses. In terms of his character and outlook, Oxford's uncle was in every way unsuited to the task.

Looney used the phrase "long foreground" for Shakespeare's formative years, a period of necessary artistic growth and development that has always been missing from the Stratford man's biography. Unless he had miraculous powers, the sophisticated English poet who wrote *Venus and Adonis* (the first work to carry Shakespeare's name) must have gone through much trial and error, creating a substantial body of apprenticeship work before its publication in 1593. By all logic this "new" poet had already been writing for decades. "Shakespeare" must have begun translating Ovid in his teenage years, becoming thoroughly grounded in it. He would have labored over the original Latin texts and "tried on" various nouns, verbs, adjectives and adverbs, inventing new ones along the way; in the process he would have acquired his vocabulary of some 25,000 words, more than twice the size of the one possessed by John Milton.

Reason 17 – "Romeus and Juliet"

> *"Arthur Brooke's sole claim to fame is his long poem* 'The Tragicall History of Romeus and Juliet' *(1562), a metrical version of a story in Boaistuau's* 'Histories Tragiques' *(1559) and the main source of Shakespeare's tragedy of* 'Romeo and Juliet'.... *Brooke adds a number of features not in the French version, which Shakespeare adopted, including the comic garrulity of the nurse and the notion of Fortune as the controller of the lovers' fates."*—O. J. Campbell, *The Reader's Encyclopedia of Shakespeare*, 1966

Arthur Brooke died at nineteen in the wreck of the queen's ship *The Greyhound* in March 1563, only months after the narrative poem attributed to him had been published. Oxfordian researcher and author Nina Green has shown that Brooke was a close relative of William Brooke Lord Cobham and that in December 1561 he had been admitted to the Middle Temple for the study of law. When the 3,000-line *Romeus and Juliet* by "Ar. Br." was published in 1562, twelve-year-old de Vere was a royal ward in the custody of William Cecil, a close friend of Cobham; Green writes of the likelihood "that Lord Cobham would have been a visitor at Cecil House in the Strand," where Oxford was living. Based on further connections, Green believes that "the likelihood is strong that Oxford was personally acquainted with Arthur Brooke."

Given young de Vere's demonstrable interest in literature, he was surely familiar with *Romeus and Juliet*, the acknowledged principal source of one of Shakespeare's best-known plays.

Brooke's long poem offers one more reason to conclude that Oxford grew up to become "Shakespeare." Imagine the fuss that orthodox scholars would make if Will of Stratford had been connected even remotely to Shakespeare's main source for *Romeo and Juliet*! But the possibility exists that Oxford himself had composed that narrative poem by age twelve, and caused it to be published under "Ar. Br."—an abbreviated form of "Arthur Brooke." Dorothy and Charlton Ogburn quote from a 1944 essay by Professor Ned B. Allen, citing "parallels between the old poem and the Shakespeare stage work, passage for passage, demonstrating that, in many respects, the play *Romeo and Juliet* is a highly finished, more mature version of the poem." Aware that young Oxford wrote in French and that many of his early poems (or song lyrics) in *The Paradise of Dainty Devices* may have been written before he was sixteen, the Ogburns conclude that *Romeus and Juliet* could be his earliest printed poem.

Ogburn Jr. agrees, writing of the poem attributed to Brooke: "If the narrator seems childish, he does so, I submit, for the best possible reason: he was little more than a child. If 'Shakespeare' was not put off by its childish clumsiness ... and would accept a story wholeheartedly from such a source ... the only reasonable explanation I can think of is that he had written it himself in his boyhood and, probably touched by it, regarded it with parental indulgence." He adds that the mature author would have turned "the awkward effort into the undying drama of the star-crossed lovers as we know it" by way of "repaying a debt to the earnest, striving boy" he had been in 1562.

More recently, Paul Altrocchi has made the most convincing case for de Vere's youthful authorship. Altrocchi first points out that in 1563 was published *The Agreement of Sondry* [Sundry] *Places of Scripture* by the same Arthur Brooke, who died at nineteen that year, and that this book is a series of translations from French of contradictory biblical quotations, such as "Eye for eye and tooth for tooth" versus "If any man strike thee on the right cheek give him the other also."

"Brooke's remarkably dreary, verbatim translation of *Sundry Places* must raise a strong suspicion that he was not the author of the clever, imaginative *Tragicall Historye of Romeus and Juliet*," Altrocchi writes. "The marked stylistic discrepancy between the two works is striking and compels further investigation, not mere submissive acceptance of Brooke's authorship of both because his name is on both title pages." By contrast he quotes various lines from *Romeus and Juliet*, for example:

> But when she should have slept, as wont she was, in bed,
> Not half a wink of quiet sleep could harbor in her head.
> For lo, an hugy heap of divers thoughts arise,
> That rest have banished from her heart, and slumber from her eyes.
> And now from side to side she tosseth and she turns,
> And now for fear she shivereth, and now for love she burns.
> And now she likes her choice, and now her choice she blames,
> And now each hour within her head a thousand fancies frames.

"Who can deny that these lovely verses remind one of Shakespeare, albeit a young Shakespeare?" Altrocchi asks, offering a sample of Brooke's translational style in *Sondry Places* for comparison: "When the apostle to that Debra sayeth that the first ordinance ceased signifying that the law and the office of Priesthood were at an end because this law was weak and unprofitable, he showeth evidently that he speaketh in respect of ceremonies forasmuch as he addeth threreunto the office of sacrificing."

The writing in *Sondry Places* "bears not a scintilla of similarity to the imaginative, verbal beauty" of *Romeus and Juliet*, writes Altrocchi. "On linguistic evidence alone, especially since the two works were written in consecutive years, logic suggests that Brooke should be expunged from any serious consideration as the author of the captivating *Tragicall Historye*."

Moreover, the author of the play *Romeo and Juliet* followed the story line of *Romeus and Juliet* so closely, using similar passages and word clusters, Altrocchi writes, "that Shakespeare would have been an outright plagiarist were he not the author of both works. . . . The idea that the Western World's greatest literary genius was guilty of plagiarizing a teen-aged poet named Arthur Brooke, or anyone else, is discordantly jarring."

Altrocchi poses this rhetorical question: "What writing genius in England was alive and could have written both the narrative poem *Tragicall Historye of Romeus and Juliet* in 1561-1562 and the great play

Romeo and Juliet?" He concludes: "If the 1562 edition of *Tragicall Historye* is indeed an early publication of William Shakespeare, this makes it impossible for Shaksper of Stratford-upon-Avon to be the great playwright and poet, since Shaksper was not born until two years later, in 1564."

Reason 18 – Richard Edwards

> "*For Tragedy, Lord Buckhurst and Master Edward Ferrys do deserve the highest praise: the Earl of Oxford and Master Edwards of Her Majesty's Chapel, for Comedy and Enterlude.*"— *The Arte of English Poesie*, 1589 [anon.]

Elizabethan musician and poet Richard Edwards was thirty-eight in 1561 when he became Master of the Children of the Chapel Royal, the choirboys who entertained the queen with plays and concerts. In the following year, de Vere arrived in London as the first of Elizabeth's royal wards. During the rest of his life he would actively patronize the Chapel Children and the Children of St. Paul's (later known in the countryside as Oxford's Boys), and an adult acting company as well.

In the Christmas season of 1564-65 a play attributed to Edwards was performed by the Chapel Children for Elizabeth and the court at Whitehall. The play, *Damon and Pithias*, was the first "tragicomedy" in England and the high watermark of English drama up to then. It was set in the royal Greek court of Dionysius, but its closing songs expressed loyalty to the queen by name, revealing that the court of Elizabeth had been intended all along—an early example of what would become Shakespeare's habit of using foreign settings to reflect England itself.

The prologue of *Damon and Pythias* (printed in 1571), referring to its author, stated that "to some he seemed too much in young desires to range." Then it switched to the plural "Authors" of the play, adding, "I speak for our defense." Did de Vere collaborate on *Damon and Pythias* with Master Edwards, as the *The Arte of English Poesie* suggests? Or was he the sole author of this youthful, highly spirited play?

The closing song evoked Oxford's motto "*Nothing Truer than Truth*":

True friends talk truly, they gloss for no gain...
True friends for their true prince refuseth not their death.
The Lord grant her such friends, most noble Queen Elizabeth!

Sonnet 82 by "Shake-speare" will echo those lines:

Thou, truly fair, wert truly sympathized
In true plain words by thy true-telling friend

In August 1566 the queen visited Oxford University and presented de Vere with an honorary Master of Arts degree. (The young earl had studied mainly with private tutors.) During Her Majesty's historic visit she arrived at Christ Church Hall for the student performance of *Palamon and Arcyte*, a new play attributed to Edwards, dramatizing Chaucer's *Knight's Tale*; and this performance on two separate nights became a major chapter of campus lore. Word of mouth from rehearsals and previews had served to build up tremendous excitement and anticipation. After Elizabeth and her court were seated, the incoming crowd swelled to the point that a wall beside the stairs ripped away, crushing three persons to death and injuring five others. Elizabeth sent for her own doctors to help; after all the hurt and the dead had been carried off, the show went on as scheduled.

Palamon and Arcyte is now a "lost" play, but is often cited as a source of *The Two Noble Kinsmen*, printed nearly seventy years later in 1634 as by (according to the title page) "the memorable Worthies of their times, Mr. John Fletcher and Mr. William Shakespeare," both cited as "Gent." Scholars have identified the "Shakespearean" sections as well as the "lesser" contributions by Fletcher; but they are baffled as to why the Bard, near the end of his illustrious career, would decide to collaborate with an inferior writer. The logical answer is that he did nothing of the sort—on the contrary, the "young Shakespeare" wrote *Palamon and Arcyte* by age sixteen in 1566, with some of his text surviving into the next century, when Fletcher filled in the missing parts, with his own inferior writing, to create the play known as *The Two Noble Kinsmen*.

During the 1566 performance, with Oxford in attendance, the queen was thrilled by the staging of a "cry of hounds" for Theseus, Duke of Athens. Reacting to the realism of the scene, students began "hallooing" and Elizabeth is reported to have shouted, "O excellent! Those boys are ready to leap out at windows to follow the hounds!"

Perhaps the author of *Hamlet* recalled Her Majesty's delight at the naturalness of it all when writing the prince's statement about "the purpose of playing, whose end both at the first, and now, was and is, to hold as 'twere the mirror up to nature...."

In the future, *A Midsummer Night's Dream* by "Shakespeare" would also present Theseus, Duke of Athens, who says: "My love shall hear the music of my hounds ... My hounds are bred out of the Spartan kind ... A cry more tuneable was never holloo'd to, nor cheered with horn." When the queen attended the latter play at court, did she recall the earlier play from 1566? Did she realize Oxford must have inserted the hounds as a private, shared recollection of those earlier hounds at the university?

The alleged playwriting career of Richard Edwards lasted just two years. His death on 31 October 1566 occurred only weeks after *Palamon and Arcyte* had been staged for the queen at Oxford. A decade later in 1576 came publication of *The Paradise of Dainty Devices*, a collection of ninety-nine poems (and song lyrics) that Edwards had compiled "for his private use" before he died, according to the printer Henry Disle. Ten of the verses were attributed to "M. Edwardes," with eight signed "E.O." for Edward Oxenford, as he often signed his name.

If in fact Edwards had compiled the poems ten years earlier, Oxford would have composed his contributions by age sixteen; but if the earl himself had done the compiling for the 1576 edition, he might have written his own poems at any time up to then. Of the nine contributors whose names or initials appear on the title page, only Oxford and Lord Vaux were noblemen, and the latter was deceased.

There are many unanswered questions about *The Paradise*, not least of which is how many other verses in the volume might have come from Oxford's pen. Alexander B. Grosart in the *Fuller Worthies' Library* of 1872 identified twenty-two poems by de Vere, remarking that "an unlifted shadow lies across his memory."

"Shakespeare" would later use part of a song, attributed in *The Paradise* to Edwards, entitled *In Commendation of Music* ("Where griping grief the heart would wound," etc.). The excerpt appears in *Romeo and Juliet*:

When griping grief the heart doth wound,
And doleful dumps the mind oppress,
Then music with her silver sound... (4.5)

Hyder Rollins in his edition of 1927 reports that *Paradise* was "the most popular miscellany printed during the reign of Queen Elizabeth" and that by 1606 it had "reached at least a tenth edition." Additional poems were included with many of the new printings.

So we find the teenage de Vere and the Master of the Chapel Children with intensely shared interests in music, lyrics, poetry, players and plays, strands of which are all intertwined with, and connected to, the future "Shakespeare" works.

Reason 19 – Oxford's Bible

A great irony of the authorship movement is that Henry Clay Folger, founder of the Folger Shakespeare Library, that bastion of Stratfordian tradition in Washington, D.C., was very likely an Oxfordian sympathizer. He took such keen interest in Looney's 1920 identification of Oxford that, in 1925, he bought the Geneva Bible that the earl himself had purchased three and a half centuries earlier in 1570. De Vere's copy was quietly ensconced in the Library when it opened in 1932, two years after Folger's death. There it remained, unheralded, until 1992, when two Oxfordian researchers, Dr. Paul Nelson and Isabel Holden, learned it was being guarded by folks with powerful reasons to keep its contents under wraps. Those contents were explosive: more than a thousand marked and/or underlined verses, apparently in Oxford's own hand, with plenty of links to the Shakespeare works.

Enter Roger Stritmatter, who would pore over the handwritten annotations in Oxford's bible (often in partnership with Mark Anderson) for the next eight years, eventually earning his Ph.D. in Comparative Literature at the University of Massachusetts Amherst.

Stritmatter's 2000 dissertation, *The Marginalia of Edward de Vere's Geneva Bible*, stands as both a remarkable achievement in scholarship and a landmark event in the history of Shakespearean authorship studies. It is also a powerful demonstration of insights and connections that become possible when the correct biography of "Shakespeare" is brought into alignment with historical documents.

When de Vere obtained his Geneva Bible he was still a ward of Queen Elizabeth in William Cecil's custody. In his documentary life of Oxford in 1928, Ward reports finding an account book with *"Payments made by John Hart, Chester Herald, on behalf of the Earl of Oxford"* during 1570, with entries such as: "To William Seres, stationer, for a Geneva Bible gilt, a Chaucer, Plutarch's works in French, with other books and papers . . . Tully's and Plato's works in folio, with other books . . . ."

"The first edition of that bible was published in 1560 in Geneva," Stritmatter reports. "Due to its incendiary implied criticisms of Catholicism, it remained a popular unauthorized translation throughout the reign of Elizabeth I ... Over a hundred years of scholarship has made it clear that the Geneva Bible was the translation most familiar to Shakespeare."

Among the approximately 1,043 underlined or marked verses in Oxford's bible, 147 are cited by previous scholars as having influenced Shakespeare. Twenty marked verses contain language "at least as close" to other language already identified as Shakespearean influences—and so on, not to mention cases where Stritmatter found connections to the works of Shakespeare that previously had gone unnoticed. The earl's copy also contains some thirty-two short notes that have been verified through independent forensic paleography to be in his handwriting. Many themes reflected in the marked passages "can be traced directly to known biographical facts of Oxford's life," Stritmatter writes, confirming that "not only was Oxford the original owner of the book," which had his de Vere crest on the cover, "but it was he who made the annotations."

Stritmatter began to perceive a series of "patterned relations" narrating a "spiritual story," one that we can begin to see once de Vere is perceived as Shakespeare. It is a story about "secret works" by an annotator whose name is removed from the historical record but who, nonetheless, re-emerges as the man who gave the world the greatest works of the English language. For example, Oxford marked and partially underlined Micah 9.7:

> I will bear the wrath of the Lord, because I have sinned against him, until he plead my cause and execute judgment for me; then will he bring me forth to the light....

"Shakespeare" wrote in *Lucrece:*

> Time's glory is to calm contending Kings,
> To unmask falsehood, and bring truth to light.

And Oxford wrote under his own name to Robert Cecil in 1602:

> "Now time and truth have unmasked all difficulties."

Reason 20 – Gad's Hill

In the early 1570s the young nobleman Gilbert Talbot wrote from court to his father the Earl of Shrewsbury that Oxford, twenty-three, had "lately grown into great credit, for the Queen's Majesty delighteth more in his personage and his dancing and his valiantness than any other," adding, "If it were not for his fickle head he would pass any of them shortly." By "fickle" Talbot meant Oxford was unpredictable, changeable, volatile, all of which was "probably the symptom of high spirits bursting the seams of restraint," as Ogburn Jr. suggests. De Vere was much like Berowne, the "merry madcap lord" of *Love's Labour's Lost*, of whom Maria says: "Not a word with him but a jest" (2.1) and another comparison would be to Henry V back in his riotous days as Prince Hal.

On 20-21 May 1573, three of Oxford's servants helped him carry out an elaborate prank involving the robbery of two of the earl's former employees. After lying in wait for them at Gad's Hill, by the highway between Rochester and Gravesend, they jumped out of hiding; apparently the robbers were led by Oxford himself, since the two men later described his "raging demeanor" as he led the mock assault. The two former employees were traveling on state business for Oxford's father-in-law, Burghley, who was Lord Treasurer of England, and were carrying money that would have been intended for the royal Exchequer.

John Stow reported in the first edition of his *Chronicles of England* (1580) that Prince Hal "would wait in disguised array for his own receivers and distress them of their money; and sometimes at such enterprises both he and his company were surely beaten; and when his receivers made to him their complaints, how they were robbed in their coming unto him, he would give them discharge of so much money as they had lost, and besides that, they should not depart from him without great rewards for their trouble and vexation."

Oxford may have heard this tale of the young heir apparent, given that many stories of the monarchs were handed down by his ancestors. Was he trying to imitate Hal's notion of a fun time? Did he manage to return the money with "great rewards" as the prince had done?

During the 1580s the Queen's Men performed *The Famous Victories of Henry the Fifth*, an anonymous stage work which may have been written much earlier. In this spirited and often raucously comical play, a forerunner of Shakespeare's royal histories, Hal and his friends carry out the same elaborate prank in the same exact place: the highway near Gad's Hill between Rochester and Gravesend, and the money is also intended for the Exchequer. Also in *Famous Victories* the Clerk at the Court of the King's Bench says the robbery took place on "the 20th day of May last past, in the fourteenth year of the reign of our sovereign lord King Henry the Fourth"—in the same month (and perhaps on the exact same day) as Oxford's caper in 1573. As the earl was reported in the 1580s as "best for comedy," isn't it logical to suggest that he himself wrote that anonymous play? This would explain how and why *Famous Victories* indicates the robbery took place in the month of May in the fourteenth year in the reign of Hal's father (Henry IV), when, in fact, there was no May in that regnal year. The king had died in March, two months short of May. But if Oxford wrote the play it means he deliberately erred, that is, he actually wanted to link it to his own experience in May 1573 (which was actually during the *fifteenth* regnal year of Queen Elizabeth, a slight discrepancy he could not have avoided.) At the time, young Oxford probably figured that only members of the court would realize his authorship of *Famous Victories*; later, revising the play into *1 Henry IV* as by "Shakespeare," he would have protected his identity by eliminating any date; to be sure, the date is gone in the later play.

The Famous Victories serves as a veritable template for the Shakespearean trilogy of *1 Henry IV*, *2 Henry IV* and *Henry V*. "Without doubt a very intimate connection of some kind exists between Shakespeare's three plays and this old text," writes John Dover Wilson, "though what the connection is has never been established."

"Shakespeare" supposedly lifted (i.e., stole) the Gad's Hill episode in *Famous Victories* for one of the most beloved scenes of *1 Henry IV*. Falstaff and three of Hal's other companions from the Boar's Head Tavern hold up and rob some travelers bearing "money of the king's ... on the way to the king's Exchequer" on the highway near Gad's Hill between Rochester and Gravesend—just as in *Famous Victories* and just as in the real-life episode involving Oxford and his men.

The two former employees of Oxford who were robbed, William Faunt and John Wotton, submitted a complaint to Burghley endorsed "May 1573 from Gravesend." They recall "riding peacefully by the highway from Gravesend to Rochester" when "three calivers charged with bullets discharged at us by three of my Lord of Oxford's men ... who lay privily in a ditch awaiting our coming with full intent to murder us; yet (notwithstanding they were all discharging upon us so near that my saddle, having the girths broken, fell with myself from the horse and a bullet within half a foot of me) it pleased God to deliver us from that determined mischief; whereupon they mounted on horseback and fled towards London with all possible speed."

"We can imagine the elation of the Stratfordians if they were able to come up with as dramatic a correlation between Shakspere's life and one of the plays as proof of his authorship," Ogburn Jr. writes.

CHAPTER FOUR

OXFORD THE WRITER

Reason 21 – Youthful Verse

Some who cling to the traditional Shakespearean biography sneer at Oxford's poetry, declaring it too inferior to be written by the great author; what these critics may not realize, however, is that many (if not most) of the earl's signed poems were actually songs. Moreover, most were published in *The Paradise of Dainty Devices* of 1576, when he was twenty-six, but he may have written them much earlier. Much later, in *The Arte of English Poesie* of 1589, he would be cited first among "noblemen and gentlemen of Her Majesty's own servants, who have written excellently well as it would appear if their doings could be found out and made public with the rest." Dr. Louis Benezet of Dartmouth College (1876-1961), a pioneer in educational reform, created a string of lines attributed to "Shakespeare" and mixed them with lines attributed to Oxford; then he challenged his colleagues in the English Department to guess which lines were from which author. If they failed to guess correctly (as usually happened), the next question was, "Well, do you think it's possible that all those lines came from the same poet?"

Following is a section of that test, using some of Benezet's examples with some new ones I've thrown in; this is followed by a section with the same lines plus the name of the author—Oxford or Shakespeare—to whom they are attributed. It's not scientific and "proves" nothing; but before looking at the answers, try guessing which lines come from "Shakespeare" and which from Oxford:

> Who taught thee how to make me love thee more
> The more I hear and see just cause of hate?
>
> In constant truth to bide so firm and sure
>
> Oaths of thy love, thy truth, thy constancy
>
> In true plain words by thy true telling friend
>
> To scorn the world regarding but thy friends
> Who taught thee first to sigh, alas, my heart?

48

Who taught thy tongue the woeful words of plaint?

If women would be fair, and yet not fond
Or that their love were firm and not fickle still

For if I should despair, I should go mad

And shall I live on th'earth to be her thrall?

A torment thrice threefold thus to be crossed

And since my mind, my wit, my head, my voice, and tongue are weak

My love is strengthened, though more weak in seeming

If care or skill could conquer vain desire
Or reason's reins my strong affection stay

Past cure I am, now reason is past care

My death delayed to keep from life the harm of hapless days

Desire is death, which physic did except

I saw a fair young lady come, her secret fears to wail
A plaintful story from a sistering vale

Here are the answers:

Who taught thee how to make me love thee more,
The more I hear and see just cause of hate?
Shakespeare, Sonnet 150

In constant truth to bide so firm and sure
Oxford, Rawlinson MS

Oaths of thy love, thy truth, thy constancy
Shakespeare, Sonnet 152

In true plain words by thy true telling friend
Shakespeare, Sonnet 82

To scorn the world regarding but thy friends
Who taught thee first to sigh, alas, my heart?
Who taught thy tongue the woeful words of plaint?
Oxford, Rawlinson MS

If women would be fair, and yet not fond
Or that their love were firm and not fickle still
Oxford, Britton's Bower of Delights

For if I should despair, I should go mad
Shakespeare, Sonnet 140

And shall I live on th'earth to be her thrall?
> Oxford, *Paradise of Dainty Devices, 1576*

A torment thrice threefold thus to be crossed
> Shakespeare, *Sonnet 133*

And since my mind, my wit, my head, my voice, and tongue are weak
> Oxford, *Paradise, 1576*

My love is strengthened, though more weak in seeming
> Shakespeare, *Sonnet 102*

If care or skill could conquer vain desire
Or reason's reins my strong affection stay
> Oxford, *Paradise, 1577*

Past cure I am, now reason is past care
> Shakespeare, *Sonnet 147*

My death delayed to keep from life the harm of hapless days
> Oxford, *Paradise, 1576*

Desire is death, which physic did except
> Shakespeare, *Sonnet 147*

I saw a fair young lady come, her secret fears to wail
> Oxford, *Rawlinson MS*

A plaintful story from a sistering vale
> Shakespeare, *A Lover's Complaint*

There are hundreds of similarities between writings attributed to Oxford and to "Shakespeare," for example:

Shakespeare, *Sonnet 66:*

> Tired with all these, for restful death I cry:
> As, to behold desert a beggar born

Oxford:

> Experience of my youth, made think humble truth
> In deserts born

Shakespeare, *Sonnet 89*:

> As I'll myself disgrace; knowing thy will,
> I will acquaintance strangle and look strange,
> Be absent from thy walks, and in my tongue
> Thy sweet beloved name no more shall dwell.

Oxford:

> Thus farewell, friend: I will continue strange,
> Thou shalt not hear by word or writing aught.
> Let it suffice, my vow shall never change;
> As for the rest, I leave it to thy thought.

Shakespeare, *Sonnet 114:*

> And my great mind most kingly drinks it up.

Oxford:

> My mind to me a kingdom is.

Can it be that the poetry Oxford wrote during his youth is the missing early work—the all-important apprenticeship—of the young Shakespeare? If we went looking for evidence of Shakespeare's early poetry, the verses attributed to de Vere when he was young are exactly what we should expect to find. The other side of that coin seems true as well: that the more mature poems and sonnets attributed to "Shakespeare" are exactly what we should expect to find from the pen of the older, more experienced de Vere; and that, of course, leads to the conclusion that, in fact, Oxford's mature poetry was published under the "Shakespeare" pen name.

Reason 22 – *"Love Thy Choice"*

Poetry was part of Edward de Vere's family heritage. He was a boy when the lyrical verses of his late uncle, Henry Howard, Earl of Surrey (see Reason 15) were published, which included the first English sonnets in the form that would later be known as the "Shakespearean" form. About the time Oxford turned twenty-one in 1571 and began his steep rise in royal favor, he composed one of the first "Shakespearean" sonnets of the Elizabethan reign. It consists of a series of rhetorical questions to himself about the extraordinary female sovereign who was the center of his universe. The answer to each question was Queen Elizabeth, who "above the rest in Court" was the one who gave him "grace." (Only a monarch had royal grace to give to anyone.) All his loyalty and devotion were directed to his sovereign mistress. The earl's verse was later given the title "Love Thy Choice," taken from its ending couplet.

> Who taught thee first to sigh, alas, my heart?
> Who taught thy tongue the woeful words of plaint?
> Who filled your eyes with tears of bitter smart?
> Who gave thee grief and made thy joys to faint?

Who first did paint with colors pale thy face?
Who first did break thy sleeps of quiet rest?
Above the rest in Court who gave thee grace?
Who made thee strive in honor to be best?
In constant truth to bide so firm and sure,
To scorn the world regarding but thy friends?
With patient mind each passion to endure,
In one desire to settle to the end?
   Love then thy choice wherein such choice thou bind,
   As nought but death may ever change thy mind.

Although this sonnet is an early work by a young poet still developing his craft, many of its key words and themes would reappear in the private verses published in 1609, five years after Oxford's death, as SHAKE-SPEARES SONNETS:

• "Who taught thee first to sigh alas, my heart" will be echoed in Shakespeare's Sonnet 150: "Who taught thee how to make me love thee more."
• "Above the rest" will appear in Sonnet 91: "Wherein it finds a joy above the rest."
• "In constant truth to bide so firm and sure" will find similar expression in Sonnet 152: "Oaths of thy love, thy truth, thy constancy."

These abundant similarities are another link in the chain of evidence that, over a period of time, Edward de Vere developed into the author of the more mature and powerful works attributed to Shakespeare.

Oxford's early sonnet would reappear in 1593 with some different words as No. 60 in the sixty verses of *Tears of Fancy* attributed to Thomas Watson, an Oxford protégé, who had died the year before.

Reason 23 – Hawks and Women

When Looney was still searching for the true author in early years of the twentieth century, he opened an anthology of sixteenth-century verse and looked for poems in the stanza form that Shakespeare employed in *Venus and Adonis*. Looney thought it likely that "Shakespeare," whoever he was, had previously written poetry in that form, with six lines, each of ten syllables, using the rhyme scheme of a quatrain followed by a couplet [*ababcc*].

Poems in that form were "much fewer than I had anticipated," Looney recalled; he found just two that could have come from the same hand that wrote the Shakespearean verse. One was anonymous; the other was a poem about *"Women"* by de Vere, with this opening stanza:

If women would be fair and yet not fond,
Or that their love were firm not fickle still,
I would not marvel that they make men bond,
By service long to purchase their good will:
But when I see how frail these creatures are,
I muse that men forget themselves so far.

Oxford's verse stood out, conveying "a sense of its harmony with Shakespeare's work," in terms of "diction, succinctness, cohesion and unity." What then caught Looney's attention was the earl's use of "haggard"—a wild or imperfectly trained hawk or falcon—as a metaphor for "fickle" women in the second stanza:

To mark the choice they make and how they change,
How oft from Phoebus do they cleave to Pan,
Unsettled still like haggards wild they range,
These gentle birds that fly from man to man:
Who would not scorn and shake them from his fist
And let them fly (fair fools) which way they list?

In the several places where Shakespeare uses "haggards" (or the singular form) he almost always employs it as a figure of speech referring to wild, untamed, fickle women. In Oxford's poem the word refers to women who "fly from man to man," a sentiment identical to Shakespeare's use of it in *Othello*: "If I do prove her haggard, though that her jesses were my dear heart strings, I'd whistle her off and let her down the wind to play at fortune." (3.3)

Ren Draya and Richard F. Whalen report in their Oxfordian edition of *Othello* that the Moor's speech is "an extended metaphor from falconry, the sport of aristocrats."

(*Haggard* = a female hawk captured after getting its adult plumage, hence still wild and untamed; *Jesses* = leather straps tied to the legs of a hawk and attached to a leash; *Whistle her off . . . down the wind* = send her off the way a hawk is turned loose when not performing well and sent downwind.)

Further striking parallels in Shakespeare are to be found in the third and final stanza of Oxford's poem, which refers to the "lure" or decoy bird:

Yet for disport we fawn and flatter both,
To pass the time when nothing else can please,
And train them to our lure with subtle oath,
Till, weary of their wiles, ourselves we ease;
And then we say, when we their fancy try,
To play with fools, O what a fool was I!

The same idea is expressed in *The Taming of the Shrew* when Petruchio speaks of himself as a falconer training his wife, Kate, as a falcon who needs to be kept hungry (or less than "fullgorged") so she'll continue to follow his lure: "My falcon now is sharp and passing empty, and till she stoop she must not be full-gorged, for then she never looks upon her lure. Another way I have to man my haggard, to make her come and know her keeper's call, that is, to watch her, as we watch these kites that bate and beat and will not be obedient." (4.1) (*Kites* = birds of prey, such as the falcon; *bate* = beat down and weaken a female bird who still won't obey.)

Just as Oxford writes of men who use a "subtle oath" as a lure or bait to "train" women to their wills, Hero in *Much Ado About Nothing* speaks of "the false sweet bait that we lay" for Beatrice, of whom she says, "I know her spirits are as coy and wild as haggards of the rock." (3.1)

Coming back full circle, in *Venus and Adonis* the poet writes of the Goddess of Love and Beauty: "As falcons to the lure, away she flies...." (1027)

"What we have in this instance, as a matter of fact," Looney writes, "is a complete accordance at all points in the use of an unusual word and figure of speech. Indeed, if we make a piece of patchwork of all the passages in Shakespeare in which the word 'haggard' occurs, we can reconstruct de Vere's single poem on *'Women.'* Such an agreement not only supports us in seeking to establish the general harmony of de Vere's work with Shakespeare's, but carries us beyond the immediate needs of our argument—for it constrains us to claim that either both sets of expression are actually from the same pen, or 'Shakespeare' pressed that license to borrow (which was prevalent in his day) far beyond its legitimate limits. In our days we should not hesitate to describe such passages as glaring plagiarism, unless they happen to come from the same pen."

Sonnet 91 speaks of hawks, hounds and horses; if the Sonnets are autobiographical, as they appear to be, then we are hearing the voice of a nobleman spontaneously referring to various aspects of his everyday world:

Some glory in their birth, some in their skill,
Some in their wealth, some in their body's force,
Some in their garments, though new-fangled ill,
Some in their hawks and hounds, some in their horse . . .

Prince Hamlet exclaims to the players: "Masters, you are all welcome," adding spontaneously: "We'll e'en to't like French falconers, fly at anything we see!" (2.2)

Juliet calls out: "Hsst, Romeo, hist! O for a falconer's voice to lure this tassel-gentle back again!" (2.2)

A terrifying stanza in *The Rape of Lucrece* portrays the rapist Tarquin as a falcon circling above his helpless prey:

This said, he shakes aloft his Roman blade,
Which, like a falcon towering in the skies,
Coucheth the fowl below with his wings' shade,
Whose crooked beak threats if he mount he dies;
So under his insulting falchion lies
Harmless Lucretia, marking what he tells
With trembling fear, as fowl hear falcons' bells (505-511)

(*Coucheth the fowl* = causing the bird to hug the ground; *Falchion* = sword; *Marking* = listening to; *Falcons' bells* = bells were attached to the hawks or falcons.)

Oxford was an expert falconer; so, too, was the author known as Shakespeare.

Reason 24 – "A New Glory of Language" (*The Courtier*)

Imagine looking through records from the sixteenth century and suddenly coming upon an essay written in Latin by Shakespeare when he was just twenty-one. Think of the exhilaration upon discovering that the great author had crafted this early piece of writing to proclaim "a new glory of language" while championing "all the glory of literature"—a document in which the young genius predicts the quality of the works of language and literature that he himself is destined to produce.

I suggest that, in fact, we *do* have such an essay written by "Shakespeare" as a young man, although he was still using his real name. In effect this was his "manifesto" as a young writer, publicly championing the humanistic side of the Renaissance with its medieval traditions of chivalry and at the same time expressing values and intentions regarding literature that he would carry with him throughout his life.

This manifesto was presented in the form of an eloquent, 1,100-word Latin preface to Clerke's translation of Castiglione's *The Courtier* (see also Reason 7) from Italian into Latin under the full panoply of his titles: *Edward de Vere, Earl of Oxford, Lord Great Chamberlain of England, Viscount Bulbeck and Baron Scales and Badlesmere to the Reader - Greeting.* English readers had never before been addressed in such terms by a high-born lord, Ogburn Jr. observes, adding that the subscription to the preface "could well have been intended to make doubly plain the standing the lord was claiming for letters— *'Given at the Royal Court.'*"

"It is not only remarkable as an eloquent piece of Latin prose," writes B.M. Ward. "It seems to indicate a determination on the part of its author to do something more for literature than merely to accept dedications from authors. For the first time in our annals we find a nobleman taking immense trouble to recommend a book in which he is interested." Oxford's early Cambridge friend Gabriel Harvey would allude to the preface as an example of the earl's literary eminence: "Let that courtly epistle, more polished even than the writings of Castiglione

Fig. 7 - Baldassare Castiglione

himself, witness how greatly thou dost excel in letters!" In that preface, as translated into English, the earl praises the Italian author of *The Courtier*:

> For what more difficult, more noble, or more magnificent task has anyone ever undertaken than our author Castiglione, who has drawn for us the figure and model of a courtier, a work to which nothing can be added, in which there is no redundant word, a portrait which we shall recognize as that of the highest and most perfect type of man. And so, although nature herself has made nothing perfect in every detail, yet the manners of men exceed in dignity that with which nature has endowed them; and he who surpasses others has here surpassed himself, and has even outdone nature which by no one has ever been surpassed.

Oxford goes on to say of Castiglione that no matter how "elaborate the ceremonial, whatever the magnificence of the court, the splendor of the courtiers, and the multitude of spectators, he has been able to lay down principles for the guidance of the very Monarch himself." At the same time, "Whatever is heard in the mouths of men in casual talk and in society, whether apt and candid, or villainous and shameful, that he has set down in so natural a manner that it seems to be acted before our very eyes."

One is reminded of Hamlet's advice to the players: "Suit the action to the word, the word to the action; with this special observance, that you o'er-step not the modesty of nature: for anything so overdone is from the purpose of playing, whose end, both at the first and now, was and is, to hold, as 'twere, the mirror up to nature...."

Oxford continues:

> Again to the credit of the translator of so great a work, a writer too who is no mean orator, must be added a new glory of language.... For who is clearer in his use of words? Or richer in the dignity of his sentences? Or who can conform to the variety of circumstances with greater art? If weighty matters are under consideration, he unfolds his theme in a solemn and majestic rhythm; if the subject is familiar and facetious, he makes use of words that are witty and amusing. When therefore he writes with precise and well-chosen words, with skillfully constructed and crystal-clear sentences, and with every art of dignified rhetoric, it cannot be but that some noble quality should be felt to proceed from his work....

Oxford left no doubt Her Majesty had encouraged him in this enthusiastic praise of literature, saying he had "the protection of that authority" and that she had offered "to mark it with the superscription of her name." To Elizabeth alone "is due all the praise of all the Muses and all the glory of literature," he added, signing off, "Given at the Royal Court 5 January 1571 [1572]." Here is yet another example in Oxford's life of the "long foreground" of writing and ideas that we should expect to find during the apprenticeship of the young Shakespeare.

Reason 25 – A Public Letter (To *Cardanus' Comforte*)

Fig. 8 - Gerolamo Cardano

When John Thomas Looney hypothesized that Oxford was "Shakespeare," he found the earl's prefatory letter that accompanies Thomas Bedingfield's 1573 translation of *Cardanus Comforte* (see also Reason 8); and we can imagine his amazement upon discovering such self-evident support for his thesis, in the form of a public letter that might well have come from "Shakespeare" as a young man. Oxford's letter "gives us a glimpse into the nature of the man himself as he was in these early years," the schoolmaster wrote, "and bears ample testimony to the generosity and largeness of his disposition, the clearness and sobriety of his judgment, and the essential manliness of his actions and bearing towards literary men whom he considered worthy of encouragement.... As a letter it is, of course, prose, but it is the prose of a genuine poet: its terse ingenuity, wealth of figurative speech, and even its musical quality...."

Looney hoped his readers would "familiarize themselves thoroughly with the diction" of Oxford's letter and then read over "Shakespeare's" dedication of *Venus and Adonis* to Southampton, written twenty years later. "So similar is the style," he wrote, "that it is hardly necessary to make any allowance for the intervening years."

Oxford wrote his public letter to "my loving friend Thomas Bedingfield Esquire, one of Her Majesty's gentlemen pensioners":

> After I had perused your letters, good Master Bedingfield, finding in them your request far differing from the desert of your labor, I could not choose but greatly doubt whether it were better for me to yield you your desire, or execute mine own intention towards the publishing of your book. For I do confess the affections that I have always borne towards you could move me not a little. But when I had thoroughly considered in my mind of sundry and divers arguments, whether it were best to obey mine affections or the merits of your studies, at the length I determined it better to deny your unlawful request than to grant or condescend to the concealment of so worthy a work...
>
> What doth avail the tree unless it yield fruit unto another? What doth avail the vine unless another delighteth in the grape? What doth avail the rose unless another took pleasure in the smell? Why should this tree be accounted better than that tree, but for the goodness of his fruit? Why should this vine be better than that vine, unless it brought forth a better grape than the other? Why should this rose be better esteemed than that rose, unless in pleasantness of smell it far surpassed the other rose...
>
> Wherefore considering the small harm I do to you, the great good I do to others, I prefer mine own intention to discover your volume before your request to secret the same; wherein I may seem to you to play the part of the cunning and expert mediciner or physician, who, although his patient in the extremity of his burning fever is desirous of cold liquor or drink to qualify his sore thirst, or rather kill his languishing body, yet for the danger he doth evidently know by his science to ensue, denieth him the same. So you being sick of too much doubt in your own proceedings, through which infirmity you are desirous to bury and insevill your works in the grave of oblivion, yet I, knowing the discommodities that shall redound to yourself thereby (and which is more, unto your countrymen) as one that is willing to salve so great an inconvenience, am nothing dainty to deny your request.
>
> Again, we see if our friends be dead, we cannot show or declare our affection more than by erecting them of tombs; whereby when they be dead indeed, yet make we them live as it were again through their monument; but with me, behold, it happeneth far better, for in your lifetime I shall erect you such a monument, that as I say [in] your lifetime you shall see how noble a

shadow of your virtuous life shall hereafter remain when you are dead and gone. And in your lifetime, again I say, I shall give you that monument and remembrance of your life.... By your loving and assured friend, E. Oxenford.

Compare Shakespeare's Sonnet 81 ("Your monument shall be my gentle verse") and Sonnet 107 ("And thou in this shalt find thy monument").

Here is Shakespeare's dedication of *Venus and Adonis* to Southampton:

> Right Honourable, I know not how I shall offend in dedicating my unpolished lines to your Lordship, nor how the world will censure me for choosing so strong a prop to support so weak a burden. Only, if your Honour seem but pleased, I account myself highly praised, and vow to take advantage of all idle hours, till I have honoured you with some graver labour. But if the first heir of my invention prove deformed, I shall be sorry it had so noble a godfather: and never after ear so barren a land, for fear it yield me still so bad a harvest. I leave it to your Honourable survey, and your Honour to your heart's content, which I wish may always answer your own wish, and the world's hopeful expectation. Your Honor's in all duty, William Shakespeare.

Oxford and "Shakespeare" write personally and publicly from the same vantage point. They both speak in the voice of one who knows the art of sophisticated, humble flattery that can be slightly humorous, but, nonetheless, sincere.

Reason 26 – Private Letters

Attorney William Plumer Fowler served as president of the solidly orthodox Shakespeare Club of Boston in 1960, but eventually came to doubt the traditional belief. After assuming the presidency of the club for the second time in 1972, he spent an additional year of investigation before finally becoming "convinced beyond any doubt" that Edward de Vere had written the great works. It "came as a shock to me," he wrote, "after over half a century spent in the mistaken traditional belief, to at last realize that the true author was not the Stratfordian William Shakespeare, but someone else."

Fowler completed his 900-page masterwork *Shakespeare Revealed in Oxford's Letters* in 1986. He had chosen thirty-seven of some fifty surviving letters written by the earl between 1563 and 1603, to demonstrate how they contain "consistent correspondences (averaging over two to a line) in nearly every phrase to the thought and phraseology of Shakespeare's plays and poems."

"The letters speak for themselves," Fowler writes, adding that they "offer convincing documentary evidence of their being those of the true poet Shakespeare, as distinct from the Stratford William Shaksper of similar name. They are far more than just Oxford's letters," he concluded. "They are Shakespeare's." Among hundreds of examples is a statement from Oxford to Burghley in July 1581, shortly after the earl's release from the Tower. He had accused his Catholic cousins Henry Howard and Charles Arundel of engaging in treasonable correspondence with Spain, and they had retaliated with vicious countercharges. It appears they also had revealed his affair with Anne Vavasour, a Queen's Maid of Honor, who gave birth in March 1581 to his illegitimate son (Edward Vere). She and the baby as well as Oxford were committed to the Tower for two months; now in July he wrote to Burghley: "But the world is so cunning, as of a shadow they can make a substance, and of a likelihood a truth."

"This shadow-substance antithesis harks back to Plato's Socratic dialogue in the Seventh book of *The Republic*, about the shadows cast by a candle in a cave," Fowler writes, "and is a favorite of Shakespeare's. It is unfolded again and again, in the repeated portrayal of what Dr. Herbert R. Coursen Jr. terms 'Shakespeare's great theme—the discrepancy between appearance and reality.'"

In *Richard II*, for example, Bushy tries to calm the queen's anxiety over Richard's departure for Ireland: "Each substance of a grief hath twenty shadows, which show like grief itself, but are not so . . . So your sweet Majesty, looking awry upon your lord's departure, finds shapes of grief more than himself to wail, which, look'd on as it is, is naught but shadows of what it is not" (2.2). The metaphor is intensified after Richard surrenders his crown to Bolingbroke:

Bolingbroke:	The shadow of your sorrow hath destroyed the shadow of your face.
King Richard:	Say that again. The shadow of my sorrow! Ha! Let's see. 'Tis very true, my grief lies all within. And these external manners of laments are merely shadows to the unseen grief that swells with silence in the tortured soul. There lies the substance.... (4.1).

"So then I am not lame, poor, nor despised / Whilst that this shadow doth such substance give," the poet Shakespeare writes in Sonnet 37, and he begins number 53: "What is your substance, whereof are you made,/ That millions of strange shadows on you tend?"

Oxford's statement that "the world is so cunning as of a shadow they can make a substance and of a likelihood a truth" appears in reverse order in *The Merchant of Venice* when Bassanio talks about "the seeming truth which cunning times put on to entrap the wisest" (3.2)—and is put more simply in *The Phoenix and Turtle*: "Truth may seem, but cannot be." Oxford wrote to Robert Cecil on 7 May 1603, several weeks after the death of Elizabeth, echoing his motto *Vero Nihil Verius* ("Nothing Truer than Truth") in this striking passage: "But I hope truth is subject to no prescription, for truth is truth though never so old, and time cannot make that false which was once true." These ringing words "are mirrored many times by the dramatist Shakespeare," Fowler writes, "most notably in *Measure for Measure*, where the entire thought is duplicated by Isabella: 'For truth is truth to the end of reckoning'" (5.1); and, for example, in *Troilus and Cressida*: "What truth can speak truest, not truer than Troilus" (3.2).

De Vere was twenty-two in 1572 when news of the St. Bartholomew's Day Massacre in France shocked the Elizabethan court as tens of thousands of Protestant Huguenots were slain. In an emotional letter he told Burghley: "This estate hath depended on you a great while as all the world doth judge"—a statement, Fowler notes, anticipating with arresting closeness both Shakespeare's words and thought in two scenes from *Hamlet*:

> Laertes, warning his sister Ophelia against getting too involved with Prince Hamlet because of his high position, tells her: "He may not, as unvalued persons do, carve for himself, for on his choice depends the safety and health of this whole state" (1.3.20).

> Claudius gives Rosencrantz and Guildenstern their commission to escort Hamlet to England, telling them, "The terms of our estate may not endure hazard so near us," and Rosencrantz remarks: "The single and peculiar life is bound . . . to keep itself from noyance; but much more that spirit upon whose weal depends and rests and lives of many" (3.3).

The nearly fifty surviving letters from Oxford to William Cecil and/or his son Robert are mostly about business matters, but in every line he spontaneously reveals himself as the most likely author of Shakespeare's poems, plays and sonnets. Take, for example, the same letter of September 1572, after the Elizabethan court had received the shocking and frightening news of the massacre, in which the Protestant hero Admiral Coligny had also been slain; Oxford, in a highly emotional state, wrote to Burghley:

> I would to God your Lordship would let me understand some of your news which here doth ring dolefully in the ears of every man, of the murder of the Admiral of France, and a great number of noble men and worthy gentlemen, and such as greatly in their lifetimes honoured the Queen's majesty our mistress, on whose tragedies we have an number of French Aeneases in this city, that tell of their own overthrows with tears falling from their eyes, a piteous thing to hear but a cruel and far more grievous thing we must deem it them to see. All rumours here are but confused, of those troops that are escaped from Paris, and Rouen, where Monsieur [Alençon] hath also been; and like a *vesper Sicilianus*, as they say, that cruelty spreads all over France....
>
> And since the world is so full of treasons and vile instruments, daily to attempt new and unlooked-for things, good my Lord, I shall affectionately and heartily desire your Lordship to be careful both of yourself and of her Majesty....
>
> And think if the Admiral in France was an eyesore or beam in the eyes of the papists, that the Lord Treasurer of England is a block and a crossbar in their way, whose remove they will never stick to attempt, seeing they have prevailed so well in others. This estate hath depended on you a great while as all the world doth judge, and now all men's eyes, not being occupied any more on those lost lords, are as it were on a sudden bent and fixed on you, as a singular hope and pillar whereto the religion hath to lean.

The above passages, spilled from de Vere's pen in the heat of the moment, are Shakespearean in dozens of ways.

Ken Kaplan, a colleague in the authorship field, points out Oxford's use of hendiadys (expressing a single idea using two words connected by "and") when he refers to the Lord Treasurer as the "hope and pillar" of the state; and how Shakespeare uses literally hundreds of hendiadys, such as when Hamlet, in his "to be or not to be" soliloquy, refers to the "whips and scorns" of time. Roger Stritmatter notes that in Oxford's account of the massacre there are many hendiadys such as "noble men and worthy gentlemen," "a cruel and far more grievous thing," "treasons and vile instruments," "new and unlooked-for things," "an eyesore or a beam," "a block or a crossbar," "bent and fixed," etc. The earl's emotionally charged letter "reads like a sketch for a Shakespeare history play," Stritmatter writes:

> Envisioning the St. Bartholomew's Day massacre as a contemporary tragedy, shadowed by the allegorical precedent of Aeneas' tragic exile from burning Troy, it paints a picture of the *mise en scene* in which the tragedy unfolds. Appealing in alternating schema to senses of both sight and sound,

it supplies a potent witness to Oxford's powers of *demonstratio*, the literary figure by which "we apprehend [things] as though before our eyes." The iterated appeal to sight, and the organs of sight, could not be more 'Shake-spearean': like the audience listening to Ophelia's superlative portrait of the mad Hamlet (2.1.85-99), we are made to "see" the "French Aeneases that tell of their overthrows with tears falling from their eyes." De Vere's technique is precisely the same as that of "Shakespeare"....

The earl "slips into his tragic Shakespearean metaphor of *'French Aeneases'* with remarkable ease," Fowler writes, adding that Aeneas, the hero of Virgil's great epic, is mentioned twenty-eight times by Shakespeare. Oxford's description of the cruelty that "like a *vesper Sicilianus* ... spreads all over France" refers to the murder of 8,000 French in Sicily three centuries earlier, a massacre that also started during a pageant. "It is noteworthy that Shakespeare too shows the same familiarity as Oxford with the *vesper Sicilianus* and its pageant," Fowler observes, citing Antony's warning in *Antony and Cleopatra* that "Thou has seen these signs; they are black vesper's pageants" (4.14), with "black" meaning ominous.

When Oxford laments that "the world is so full of treasons and vile instruments," he appears to coin a phrase that Shakespeare will use in *Cymbeline* when Pisanio cries out, "Hence, vile instrument!" (3.4). His characterization of Coligny as "an eyesore or beam in the eyes of the papists" will be echoed in *The Taming of the Shrew* when Baptista refers to "an eyesore to our solemn festival" (3.2) and when Tarquin in *The Rape of Lucrece* says, "Yea, though I die, the scandal will survive, and be an eye-sore in my golden coat" (205).

Even this single early specimen of Oxford's letters, Fowler writes, "serves to corroborate that the earl, rather than the man from Stratford, was the true 'Shakespeare,' and that these letters of Oxford are really 'Shakespeare's,' the name by which the talented dramatist will always be known. Coincidence in the use of common phrases of speech can explain some parallelisms, but not any such tidal wave of them."

CHAPTER FIVE

TRIBUTES & ALLUSIONS

Reason 27 – Gabriel Harvey

The scholar Gabriel Harvey addressed de Vere in Latin during Queen Elizabeth's visit to Audley End near Cambridge in July 1578, in a speech that included a provocative statement as translated from Latin to English by B. M. Ward: "Thy countenance shakes a spear!" (See the Latin context with Ward's translation, which should have been "Thy countenance shakes spears.") Oxford had met the eccentric scholar a decade or so earlier. According to Harvey the earl had been "in the prime of his gallantest youth" when he "bestowed Angels [funds] upon me in Christ's College in Cambridge, and otherwise vouchsafed me many gracious favors."

"It is evident that a genuine friendship between the earl and Harvey sprang up as a result of their early acquaintance," Ward notes, "and it is equally evident that literature must have been the common ground on which they met." It appears that early on, at the university, Harvey understood Oxford was a literary genius and became obsessed with the earl from then on. On the 1578 visit Elizabeth was accompanied by the entire membership of the royal court, including de Vere as Lord Great Chamberlain; William Cecil, Lord Treasurer Burghley; Robert Dudley, Earl of Leicester; Sir Christopher Hatton; and Sir Philip Sidney. Harvey delivered Latin speeches to each of these dignitaries, but his address to Oxford was startling. For example, he urged him to "throw away the insignificant pen" and, instead, honor his noble heritage by becoming a military leader in the nation's preparation for its inevitable war against Spain. Here is part of Ward's translation of the Latin speech, printed later that year in his *Gratulationis Valdinensis Liber Quartus* or "The Fourth Book of Walden Rejoicing":

> O great-hearted one, strong in thy mind and thy fiery will, thou wilt conquer thyself, thou wilt conquer others; thy glory will spread out in all directions beyond the Arctic Ocean; and England will put thee to the test and prove thee to be a native-born Achilles. Do thou but go forward boldly and without hesitation: Mars will obey thee, Hermes will be thy messenger,

Pallas striking her shield with her spear shaft will attend thee, thine own breast and courageous heart will instruct thee.

For a long time past Phoebus Apollo has cultivated thy mind in the arts! English poetical measures have been sung by thee long enough! Let that Courtly Epistle—more polished even than the writings of Castiglione himself—witness how greatly thou dost excel in letters. I have seen many Latin verses of thine, yea, even more English verses are extant; thou hast drunk deep draughts not only of the Muses of France and Italy, but has learned the manners of many men, and the arts of foreign countries....

O thou hero worthy of renown, throw away the insignificant pen, throw away the bloodless books, and writings that serve no useful purpose; now must the sword be brought into play, now is the time for thee to sharpen the spear and to handle great engines of war.... In thy breast is noble blood, Courage animates thy brow, Mars lives in thy tongue, Minerva strengthens thy right hand, Bellona reigns in thy body, within thee burns the fire of Mars. Thine eyes flash fire, thy countenance shakes a spear! Who would not swear that Achilles had come to life again?

Harvey was taking it for granted that most court members knew de Vere had written many poems in Latin and English. Fifteen years later the "Shakespeare" name would appear for the first time, on the dedication of *Venus and Adonis* to Southampton. Isn't Harvey's address to Oxford exactly how we should expect the young Shakespeare to be described? Harvey's Latin lines related to spear-shaking:

Virtus fronte habitat: Mars occupat ora; Minerva
In dextra latitat: Bellona in corpore regnat:
Martius ardor inest; scintillant lumina: *vultus*
Tela vibrat: quis non redivivum iuret Achillem?
O age, magne Comes, spes est virtutis alenda Ista tibi;

Ward's translation:

Courage animates thy brow, Mars lives in thy tongue, Minerva strengthens thy right hand, Bellona reigns in thy body, within thee burns the fire of Mars. Thine eyes flash fire, thy countenance shakes a* spear; who would not swear that Achilles had come to life again?
[* It should be the plural "shakes spears"]

Reason 28 – "A Pleasant Conceit of Vere"

In 1732 the antiquary Francis Peck published Volume I of a book called *Desiderata Curiosa or a Collection of divers Scarce and Curious Pieces relating chiefly to matters of English History, consisting of*

Choice Tracts, Memoirs ... The book ended with a list of items to be included in a planned second volume, among them an intriguing manuscript described as "A pleasant Conceit of Vere Earl of Oxford, discontented at the Rising of a mean Gentleman in the English Court, circa 1580."

By 1580 de Vere had served for a decade as the highest ranking earl at the court of Elizabeth, by virtue of his hereditary title Lord Great Chamberlain of England, as well as the longevity (five centuries) of his earldom. He had enjoyed Her Majesty's continuous royal favor; there was gossip in the early 1570s that he was the queen's lover. During that decade, however, he had been increasingly "discontented" at the "rising" in fortune of his rival Sir Christopher Hatton, Captain of the Queen's Bodyguard, whom he regarded with disdain as "mean"—inferior by birth as a commoner, but also in terms of his conniving and duplicitous character as well as his mawkish personality.

Fig. 9 - Christopher Hatton

Peck further noted that the manuscript of Oxford's "pleasant conceit" had belonged to Abraham Fleming, one of the earl's secretaries and literary protégés. Was it in de Vere's own hand, or had Fleming copied it from his master's original manuscript or from dictation? As Oxford was cited in 1598 as "best for comedy," it is likely that this work was one of his plays and that he was making fun of Hatton, strictly for the merriment of the queen and insiders at the court. Alas, however, Peck never published his second volume and those papers from Fleming's folders (if they ever existed) are missing.

Only after 1920, when Looney identified de Vere as "Shakespeare," would anyone have wondered about the relationship of the earl's "pleasant conceit" to any of the Shakespeare plays. Only then would anyone have realized, surely with sudden excitement, that the earl's "pleasant conceit" must have been an early version of *Twelfth Night, Or What You Will*, and that the character of Malvolio is no less than a blistering, hilarious caricature of Hatton.

One of the amazing aspects of the authorship question is that within each play is an entire world which remains invisible until seen in its true context of time and circumstance. In this case, as the curtain opens on *Twelfth Night* we see the world of the English royal court in the 1570s and 1580s. We can see Malvolio-Hatton in relation to Olivia, who represents Queen Elizabeth, and de Vere portraying himself as Feste, the jester or clown in service to Olivia-Elizabeth, who calls him her "allowed fool"—an expression, Clark writes, that "Elizabeth probably applied to Oxford, for he would never have dared to include the many personal allusions in his plays had not the queen permitted, even encouraged, him to do it."

Traditional scholars believe the comedy was written *circa* 1600, with a performance at the Middle Temple in 1602 recorded as "a play called *Twelve night or what you will*." It was never published in quarto, however, and appeared in print only as part of the Folio of plays in 1623; this suggests that it was one of Oxford's "comedies" that originated as a private entertainment at court. As such it would have contained material that, if printed too soon, would have been embarrassing to either Elizabeth or King James and to various noble families whose relatives had been satirized.

The performances during the 1570s and 1580s within those Elizabethan palaces—Whitehall, Richmond, Greenwich, Nonsuch, Windsor Castle, Hampton Court, and so on—were staged for a small but powerful group of "cousins" who, by way of analogy, might well have been stranded together by a snowstorm for several days. In that context, Oxford was providing much needed entertainment by mercilessly "roasting" many of these same well-known individuals, among them Hatton, the queen and himself; much later he would have revised these political satires, adding new layers of material for public consumption.

"I may command where I adore,'' Malvolio reads in a fabricated letter in *Twelfth Night*. He assumes it is addressed to him by the rich countess Olivia, whom he slavishly serves as both steward and hopeful lover. "Why," he exclaims, "she may command me: I serve her; she is my lady." Now the self-infatuated steward glances at what appears to be a coded name in the letter and says to himself, "If I could make that resemble something in me! Softly: 'M.O.A.I.'... M—Malvolio. M— Why, that begins my name!... 'In my stars I am above thee, but be not afraid of greatness,'" he reads aloud. "'Some are born great, some achieve greatness, and some have greatness thrust upon 'em ....'" (2.5)

The letter is signed "The Fortunate Unhappy"—echoing the Latin pen name *Fortunatus Infoelix* apparently used by Hatton. Tall and handsome, he had attracted the queen's attention in 1572 with his dancing. His ambition to become her lover may well have been realized, at least for a time; now his path was being blocked by twenty-two-year-old de Vere, himself a superb dancer but also a victor of the tilt, a gifted poet and musician, and a scholar. Moreover, Oxford was a madcap earl who could not help but make fun of competitive climbers at the royal court. "There is no man of life and agility in every respect in Court but the Earl of Oxford," George Delves had written to the earl of Rutland on 24 June 1571.

In October 1572 the courtier and poet Edward Dyer wrote to Hatton with advice about competing for the queen's most intimate favors against "my Lord Ctm"—apparently referring to Oxford with an abbreviation of "Lord Great Chamberlain" of England. Dyer's letter must stand as a gross example of the cynical maneuverings of men at court seeking Her Majesty's favor:

> First of all, you must consider with whom you have to deal, and, what we be towards her; who though she do descend very much in her sex as a woman, yet we may not forget her place, and the nature of it as our Sovereign.... But the best and soundest way in mine opinion is to put on another mind; to use your suits towards her Majesty in words, behavior and deeds; to acknowledge your duty, declaring the reverence which in heart you bear, and never seem deeply to condemn her frailties, but rather joyfully to commend such things as should be in her, as though they were in her indeed; hating my Lord Ctm [probably referring to Oxford] in the Queen's understanding for affection's sake, and blaming him openly for seeking the Queen's favour.

> For though in the beginning when her Majesty sought you (after her good manner), she did bear with rugged dealing of yours, until she had what she fancied, yet now, after satiety and fullness, it will rather hurt than help you; whereas, behaving yourself as I said before, your place shall keep you in worship, your presence in favour.... Marry thus much I would advise you to remember, that you use no words of disgrace or reproach towards him [Oxford] to any; that he [Oxford], being the less provoked, may sleep, thinking all safe, while you do awake and attend your advantages.

Dyer's display of cold calculation about how to gain advantage over Oxford is remarkable. So is his blunt description of Elizabeth's sexual appetite and behavior.

Hatton was infatuated with the queen, whose nickname for him was "mutton" or "sheep," whereas Oxford's was the "boar" because of the boar on his coat of arms. During the summer of 1573, when Hatton became ill, Elizabeth sent him to Spa in Liege (Belgium); he wrote back to her using those nicknames to express his jealousy over Oxford, who now had Her Majesty all to himself:

Your mutton is black ... so much hath this disease dashed me ... I love yourself. I cannot lack you. I am taught to prove it by the wish and desire I find to be with you.... You are the true felicity that in this world I know or find. God bless you forever. The branch of the sweetest bush I will wear and bear to my life's end. God doth witness I feign not. It is a gracious favour, most dear and welcome to me. Reserve it to the sheep [Hatton himself]. He hath no tooth to bite, where the boar's [Oxford's] tusk may both raze and tear.

While Oxford enjoyed his intimacy with the queen, she would have shown him these letters to arouse his jealousy as well as to feed her own vanity; and when Hatton returned in October 1573, after five months of convalescence, he discovered that in fact "the boar" had done some razing and tearing in his absence.

Oxford had edited and published a book called *A Hundredth Sundrie Flowres*, much (if not all) of which he had written himself. Tucker Brooke of Yale calls it "the richest collection of early Elizabethan poetry." *Flowres* opens with a 25,000-word novel (perhaps the first prose narrative in English) entitled *The Adventures of Master F.I.* (the initials of Hatton's Latin pen name) about a man in love with a mistress (whom the court would view as Elizabeth), followed by sixteen poems signed *Si fortunatus infoelix*—again linking to "F.I." and now specifically identifying Hatton, who had had nothing to do with the writing of them and was probably not even the subject of the novel.

The prank was so scandalizing that in 1575, while Oxford was traveling in Italy, *A Hundredth Sundrie Flowres* was republished in a radically altered fashion as *The Poesies of George Gascoigne*, obscuring the embarrassing connection to Hatton while claiming that Gascoigne wrote the entire anthology. But the original text of *Flowres*, which has been preserved, represents an early stage of the English literary renaissance that was already begun: thirteen poems signed with Hatton's pen name (but surely written by Oxford) are actually sonnets composed in the form later known as the Shakespearean form.

Hatton continued his rise during the rest of the decade. In 1577 he was appointed Vice Chamberlain of the Royal Household, joined the Privy Council and was knighted. The following year the queen formally granted him the Bishop of Ely's house in Holborn; such appointments, along with valuable grants which Elizabeth showered on him, prompted rumors that he was her lover. No wonder we have a later reference to "A Pleasant Conceit of Vere, Earl of Oxford, Discontented at the Rising of a Mean Gentleman in the English Court, circa 1580."

This brings us back to the allusion to Hatton's pen name as "The

Fortunate Unhappy" that appears in the letter Malvolio reads in *Twelfth Night*, believing it was written to him by Olivia-Elizabeth. In the same Shakespeare play Olivia's uncle, Sir Toby Belch, refers to Malvolio as a "niggardly rascally sheep-biter"—echoing Hatton's 1573 letter to the queen, when he referred to himself as Queen Elizabeth's sheep in contrast to Oxford as the boar. It appears Oxford put himself into the character of Feste, the clown, who serves Olivia but is permitted to take great liberties of speech. Feste is Olivia's "allowed fool" and Malvolio dislikes him just as the jealous Hatton disliked Oxford.

"I marvel your ladyship takes delight in such a barren rascal," Malvolio tells Olivia, referring to Feste, but she defends her clown to him just as Elizabeth must have defended Oxford to Hatton: "O, you are sick of self-love, Malvolio, and taste with a distempered appetite. To be generous, and of free disposition, is to take those things for bird-bolts that you deem cannon-bullets. There is no slander in an allowed fool...." (1.5)

This is another example of how knowing the true author of a literary or dramatic work opens a door to insights from which, otherwise, we are blocked—as scholars of "Shakespeare" have been—for centuries.

Reason 29 – "The Art of Poetry"

Edward de Vere received a prominent place in an anonymous work *The Arte of English Poesie* (1589), regarded as the central text of Elizabethan courtly politics. His position in the world of letters had already been stated unequivocally in 1586, when William Webbe declared in *A Discourse of English Poetry*: "I may not omit the deserved commendations of many honourable and noble Lords and Gentlemen in Her Majesty's Court, which, in the rare devices of poetry have been, and yet are, most skillful; among whom the Right Honourable Earl of Oxford may challenge to himself the title of the most excellent among the rest." Now, three years later, another overview, this one by an unnamed author, is published by Richard Field, formerly of Stratford-upon-Avon and a Protestant printer close to Burghley. Field will issue *Venus and Adonis* in 1593 and *Lucrece* in 1594, both dedicated by "William Shakespeare" to Henry Wriothesley, Earl of Southampton. Most modern scholars have attributed the *Arte* to George Puttenham, but others believe the author was Oxford's friend Lord John Lumley; Richard M. Waugaman has set forth a case for Oxford's own authorship. The publication, dedicated by Field to Lord Burghley, is addressed to Elizabeth herself. It emphasizes the importance of deception, disguise and anonymity. The author says many members of the nobility or gentry "have no courage to write & if they have, yet are they loath to be known of their skill," and continues: "So as I know very many notable Gentlemen in the Court that have written commendably, and suppressed it again, or else suffered it to be published without their own names to it: as if it were a discredit for a Gentleman to seem learned and to show himself amorous of any good Art."

He proceeds to name names: "And in her Majesty's time that now is are sprung up another crew of Courtly makers, Noble men and Gentlemen of her Majesty's own servants, who have written excellently well as it would appear if their doings could be found out and made public with the rest, of which number is first that noble Gentleman Edward Earle of Oxford, Thomas Lord of Buckhurst, when he was young, Henry Lord Paget, Sir Philip Sidney, Sir Walter Raleigh, Master Edward Dyer, Master Fulke Greville, Gascoigne, Britton, Turberville and a great many other learned Gentlemen, whose names I do not omit for envy, but to avoid tediousness, and who have deserved no little commendation."

The author of *Arte* knew he was putting a spotlight on Oxford and his literary work. Moreover, on the very next page he names just a few playwrights: "For Tragedy Lord Buckhurst and Master Edward Ferrys do deserve the highest praise: the Earl of Oxford and Master Edwards of Her Majesty's Chapel for Comedy and Enterlude. "

An excerpt of one of Oxford's poems from *The Paradise of Dainty Devices* was reprinted in *Arte* of 1589, wherein the anonymous author wrote: "Edward Earl of Oxford, a most noble and learned gentleman, made in this figure of response an emblem of Desire, otherwise called Cupid, which for excellency and wit I set down some of the verses" – using the following example of an Oxford poem, in the form of a dialogue:

When wert thou born desire?
In pomp and prime of May.
By whom sweet boy wert thou begot?
By good conceit men say.
Tell me who was thy nurse?
Fresh youth in sugared joy.
What was thy meat and daily food?
Sad sighes with great annoy.
What hadst thou then to drink?
Unfeigned lovers' tears.
What cradle wert thou rocked in?
In hope devoid of fears.

Arte speaks of a poet as a "dissembler" motivated by "a secret intent not appearing by the words." He offers the example of four lines referring to Queen Elizabeth—not by name, but in words that "any simple judgment might easily perceive" to be referring to her:

> When Princes serve, and Realms obey,
> And greatest of Britain kings begot:
> She came abroad even yesterday,
> When such as saw her knew her not.

It was common practice to write on two levels at once:

> And the rest followeth, meaning her Majesty's person, which we would seem to hide leaving her name unspoken, to the intent the reader should guess at it: nevertheless upon the matter did so manifestly disclose it, as any simple judgment might easily perceive by whom it was meant, that is by Lady Elizabeth, Queen of England and daughter to King Henry the Eighth, and therein resteth the dissimulation.

In that same year of 1589, Field would also publish the second edition of the English translation of Ovid's *Metamorphoses,* credited in 1567 to Oxford's uncle Golding. Here at the end of the tumultuous wartime decade of the 1580s, Oxford was about to leave public life and become something of a recluse. Was he using Field's press to make a final appearance as an identified poet? Was he withdrawing from the world while preparing to use the same publisher-printer under the name of "Shakespeare" just four years later?

Reason 30 – "Our Pleasant Willy"

Edmund Spenser published the first books of *The Fairie Queene* in 1590; in the following year came the *Complaints,* which contained his poem *The Tears of the Muses.* In the latter, nine goddesses bemoan the current state of the arts, despite the fact that a great renaissance of English literature and drama had been taking place, just in time for England's defeat of Spain's attempted invasion in 1588. Now, at the start of a new decade, Spenser was warning that the renaissance had ended.

The English government, having used the wartime services of writers working under de Vere's patronage, promptly forgot them. Burghley began to pressure the earl financially. As a result, many of the writers who depended upon him fell to the wayside. Lyly was out of a job; Kyd was tortured to death on the rack; Watson died in 1590; Greene died in 1592; Marlowe was murdered in 1593; Lodge left England. Future scholars would conclude that "Shakespeare," arriving onto the printed page in 1593, "had the field all to himself."

One of Spenser's laments in *Tears* is delivered by the goddess Thalia, Muse of Comedy, who wails over the public withdrawal of a particular poet-dramatist who, while being "learning's treasure," has been delivering "comic sock" to audiences with his plays:

> Where be the sweete delights of Learning's treasure,
> That wont with comick sock to beautefie
> The painted theaters, and fill with pleasure
> The listners eyes, and eares with melodie,
> In which I late was wont to raine as queene,
> And maske in mirth with graces well beseene?
> O, all is gone! and all that goodly glee,
> Which wont to be the glorie of gay wits,
> Is layd abed, and no where now to see;
> And in her roome unseemly Sorrow sits,
> With hollow browes and greisly countenaunce
> Marring my joyous gentle dalliance.

Spenser certainly knew in 1590 that de Vere had abruptly withdrawn from public life; in that sense, as well as financially, the earl was "dead of late." Continuing her lament in Spenser's poem, Thalia declares:

> And he, the man whom Nature selfe had made
> To mock her selfe, and truth to imitate
> With kindly counter* under mimick shade,
> Our pleasant Willy, ah! Is dead of late
> With whom all ioy and iolly merriment
> Is also deaded, and in dolour drent.*

> Instead thereof scoffing Scurrility;
> And scornfull Follie with Contempt is crept,
> Rolling in rymes of shameles ribaldry
> Without regard, or due decorum kept;
> Each idle wit at will presumes to make*
> And doth the learneds task upon him take.
> But that same gentle spirit, from whose pen
> Large streames of honnie and sweete nectar flow;
> Scorning the boldnes of such base-borne men,
> Which dare their follies forth so rashlie throw,
> Doth rather choose to sit in idle cell,
> Than so himselfe to mockerie to sell.

[*Counter* = counterfeit, imitate; *drent* = drowned; *make* = write poetry]

Only one man in Elizabethan England held the mirror up to nature with such scathingly accurate imitations of truth that his audiences roared with laughter and swooned with delight. "We should be convinced that by 'our pleasant Willy,' Spenser meant William Shakespeare," Nicholas Rowe writes in his *Some Account of the Life* of the bard (1709), the first attempt at Strafordian biography, explaining that "such a character as he gives could belong to no other dramatist of the time."

But Spenser's description has presented an insurmountable problem, as Shakspere of Stratford had barely begun his alleged career in 1591. In no way could he have withdrawn from writing for the stage, nor could he have been "dead of late" or "sitting in idle cell." But such was precisely the case with forty-year-old de Vere, who had become a virtual recluse by 1591; in the Oxfordian view, he had begun revising his previous stage works to be published under the "Shakespeare" pen name. In that view he was "idle" only in the sense that he was no longer writing many original works for the public; otherwise he was hard at work, alone, transmuting much of his prior work into literary and dramatic masterpieces that would live for all time. Perhaps it was no coincidence that, as a much younger man in 1576, Oxford had published a signed poem in *The Paradise of Dainty Devices* concluding he was "never am less idle, lo, than when I am alone."

And what about Spenser's statement about "our pleasant Willy" that he was "Scorning the boldness of such base-born men," reflecting the attitude of a high-born nobleman who looks down with scorn upon commoners? At a time when class distinctions were rigid, how could the commoner Shakspere have fit that description unless he was scorning the boldness of men such as himself? Otherwise it expresses exactly the view of proud de Vere, the highest-ranking earl of Queen Elizabeth's realm.

One of Spenser's seventeen dedicatory verses to noble individuals in *The Fairie Queen* of 1590 was to Oxford, whom he praised directly and personally as a poet, in language that called attention to "the love which thou dost bear to th' Heliconian imps [Muses] and they to thee, they unto thee, and thou to them, most dear." Writing publicly to de Vere, using his real name and calling him the poet most beloved of the Muses, Spenser added:

Dear as thou art unto thyself, so love
That loves and honors thee; as doth behoove.

Ogburn Jr. translates those lines as Spenser telling Oxford: "As dear as you are to yourself, so are you to me, who loves and honors you, as it behooves me to."

The bafflement over the identity of "our pleasant Willy" disappears once the "experts" realize that Spenser was referring to the great author who was not, after all, Shakspere of Stratford, but that same earl of Oxford who was "most dear" to the Muses and would soon adopt the pen name "William Shakespeare."

Reason 31 – "One Whose Power Floweth Far"

A thick volume printed for the Roxburghe Club of London in 1882 featured an Elizabethan book of two narrative poems, *Cephalus and Procris* and *Narcissus*, translated from Ovid by the otherwise unknown Thomas Edwards. It was registered in 1593 and printed in 1595, just after the "Shakespeare" name had made its debut on the dedications of *Venus and Adonis* of 1593 and *Lucrece* of 1594 to Southampton.

Attached to *Narcissus* was an "envoy" or postscript in several stanzas of verse, identifying major poets by using characters in their works: *Collyn Clout* for Spenser; *Rosamond* for Daniel; *Leander* for Marlowe; and *Adon* for Shakespeare. This was followed immediately by reference to a poet "in purple robes distained . . . whose power floweth far" with his "bewitching pen" and "golden art" that should make him "the only object and the star" of England's writers.

Who was this poet, said to be the best of all? In the Roxburghe appendix, one scholar identified "the star" as de Vere while another said it must be a description of Shakespeare! If these two scholars of the late nineteenth century had been in the same room at the same time, one identifying Oxford and the other pointing to Shakespeare, might it have occurred to them that maybe they were both talking about the same man? If so, they would have solved the authorship question then and there. Here, in modernized English, is the stanza praising Shakespeare as "Adon," followed by those praising the poet who "should have been ... the only object and the star":

> *Adon* deafly masking through
> Stately troupes rich conceited,
> Showed he well deserved to,
> Love's delight on him to gaze,
> And had not love herself entreated,
> Other nymphs had sent him *bays.*
>
> Eke in purple robes distained,
> Amidst the Center of this clime,
> I have heard say doth remain
> One whose power floweth far,

That should have been of our rhyme
The only object and the star.

Well could his bewitching pen
Done the Muses' objects to us;
Although he differs much from men
Tilting under Frieries,
Yet his golden art might woo us
To have honored him with *bays*. (Emphases added)

Note that the first stanza about *Adon*, and the second of the next two stanzas about "one whose power floweth far," conclude with "bays"— perhaps intended as a way for readers to link all three stanzas in their praise of a single poet.

Roxburghe Club editor W.E. Buckley reported how the two scholars reached their conclusions:

> If "purple robes" may mean a Nobleman's robes, it gives some colour to the conjecture of Professor [Edward] Dowden, that Vere, Earl of Oxford, may have been intended, as his reputation stood high as a Poet and Patron of Poets.... Dr. B. Nicholson is of opinion that these two stanza must be connected with the preceding one in which Adon—that is, Shakspere—is described.

Buckley noted that *The Arte of English Poesie* had named Oxford "first among the crew of courtly makers" and that Edmund Spenser had written a dedicatory sonnet to the earl in *The Faerie Queene* of 1590 "in which he speaks of 'the love that thou didst bear to th' Heliconian Nymphs, and they to thee.' His 'power flowed far' as he was Lord High Chamberlain of England. He had contributed to *The Paradise of Dainty Devices*, signing 'E.O.' or 'E. Ox' in 1576, and to *The Phoenix Nest* in 1593. One of his poems is a vision of a Fair Maid ('clad all in color of a Nun and covered with a Vail') who complains of love and gets Echo answers of 'Vere.' In another, Oxford represents himself as 'wearing black and tawny' and having 'no bays.'"

Prior to Looney's identification of de Vere in 1920, orthodox scholars could mention him in a positive light without worrying about giving ground in the authorship debate. Buckley also referred to a statement made by the literary antiquary Thomas Coxeter (1689-1747): "Oxford was said by Coxeter to have translated Ovid, which would connect him with Narcissus, but no one has ever seen his Ovid."

An important contribution to work on the *Narcissus L'Envoy* has been made by Dr. Roger Stritmatter, who introduced new evidence allowing "definitive identification of the phrase 'tilting under Frieries' as referring to a notorious series of Blackfriars street fights (1582-85) involving Oxford's retainers." The fighting, in which Oxford was wounded and lamed for life, "left an indelible impression in the popular imagination of the era," he writes, citing a series of documents (transcribed by Alan Nelson for his Oxford biography *Monstrous Adversary*) confirming that the earl's men were "tilting under friaries" in spring 1582 at Blackfriars. Stritmatter further observes:

> The significance of this finding, identifying Oxford as the poet with the "bewitching pen" who "should have been"—but cannot be—the "only object and the star" of the chorus of the Elizabethan poets, should not be underestimated. Without doubt, the 1582-83 Oxford-Knyvet affair at Blackfriars was the most striking instance of "tilting under Frieries" during the thirty-seven years of Elizabeth's reign that informed the imagery and diction of Edwards' enigmatic poem. Before the fray had ended, a literary peer of the realm had been lamed for life, and followers of both factions wounded or killed. The concealed poet of "bewitching pen" and "golden art"—whose men were in 1582 notoriously "tilting under friaries"—is none other than the still controversial Edward de Vere.

The "Envoy to Narcissus" is an example of how, soon after publication of *Venus and Adonis* and the first appearance of the "Shakespeare" name in print, writers were already dropping hints about the presence of an author—in fact, the "star" among them—who had chosen to withhold his identity. The chatter was growing from the start.

Reason 32 – "Our De Vere"

"Most contemporaries alluded to Shakespeare's famous lines or characters – they did not usually mention his name or give personal information. Even praise for the great author was often indirect, implying that there was something secret about him." – Katherine Chiljan, *Shakespeare Suppressed*, 2011

In 1595, two years after the name "Shakespeare" initially appeared in print on the dedication of *Venus and Adonis* to Southampton and one year after it appeared on the dedication of *Lucrece* to that young nobleman, the University of Cambridge published a book containing one of the first mentions of the new poet. One page features an italicized marginal note *"Lucrecia Sweet Shak-speare"* alongside two lines of text, one with the italicized word "Oxford" and the line, below, with a perfect anagram of OUR DE VERE—A SECRET. To be precise, directly underneath "Oxford" is printed the odd hyphenated phrase "COURT-

DEARE-VERSE" containing letters which, in sequence, spell out OUR DE VERE:

["C**OUR**T-**DE**ARE-**VERSE**"]

Moreover, the remaining seven letters (C-T-E-A-R-E-S) form a perfect anagram of two words: A SECRET. The book is *Polimanteia*. Its publication in 1595 was anonymous, but evidence shows it was written by William Covell, a clergyman who received his M.A. from Cambridge in 1588 and served as a Fellow of Queen's College from 1589 to 1599. The discoverer of this Oxford-Shakespeare reference, which was hiding in plain sight for more than four centuries, is Alexander Waugh, the English writer, critic, journalist, composer, cartoonist, record producer, television producer and outspoken critic of the traditional Shakespeare biography (he is also the grandson of novelist Evelyn Waugh).

The complete marginal note reads: "All praise/ worthy./ Lucrecia/ Sweet Shak-/ speare. / Eloquent Gaveston./ Wanton Adonis/Watsons heyre [heir]." "The spelling 'Shakspeare'—missing the medial 'e'—is here forced by lack of space," Waugh points out. Adding an *e* after the *k* would make it collide with the main text, so that "no other significance should be attached to this spelling."

The note's references to *Lucrecia* and *Adonis* refer to Shakespeare's two narrative poems. As the overall topic covers poets and poetry, "Gaveston" most likely refers to Michael Drayton's historical poem, *The Legend of Piers Gaveston*, published two years earlier; and "Watson" refers to the poet Thomas Watson, who had dedicated *Hekatompathia, or the Passionate Century of Love* (1582) to Oxford, his patron—who, according to Watson's dedication, had reviewed the 100 consecutively numbered sonnets in manuscript.

Covell appears to have been well aware that "Shakespeare" was Oxford's new pen name and that it was a highly sensitive state secret, because he was careful to avoid pointing directly to the earl. On the other hand, he was equally careful to place the words *"Lucrecia Sweet Shakspeare"* in the margin right next to the lines containing "Oxford" and "courte-deare-verse." The crucial aspect of his indirect message, therefore, is the combination of both the marginal note and the text; to comprehend Covell's barely hidden meaning, the reader must view them together.

"The main text of *Polimanteia* is supported by a great many marginal notes," Waugh writes in *The De Vere Society Newsletter*, "all of which have been precisely and meticulously placed by the printer so that there can be no doubt as to which line each is intended to reference.... Given that only a handful of direct allusions to Shakespeare are known to exist from the 1590s, and given that the world has been turned upside-down in search of any information relating to the bard, I find it very strange that no Shakespearean scholar has yet seen fit to investigate the meaning of this little note in relation to the text to which it is supposed to refer."

There is a definite political dimension to this story, however, and it involves the public commitment by "Shakespeare" to Southampton, to whom he pledged in the *Lucrece* dedication: "The love I dedicate to your Lordship is without end.... What I have done is yours, what I have to do is yours, being part in all I have, devoted yours." During these years (1592-1594), there had been an open effort to raise the younger earl in the public eye and even to suggest he was a prince who deserved to succeed Elizabeth I on the throne. It appears that by the end of 1591, Southampton had made clear his refusal of a political marriage to Elizabeth Vere, granddaughter of Burghley and reputed daughter of Oxford (who, at one time, had denied his paternity of her). The younger earl preferred instead to join Essex in breaking away from Burghley and his son Robert Cecil. Now, in 1595, Covell was dedicating *Polimanteia* to Essex, pledging his "deep affection" as well as his "kindnesse and love" in the process of devoting "the full interest of myself to your dispose."

Oxford, Essex and Southampton had all been wards of the queen in Burghley's household; all three were Cambridge graduates, as was Covell, who appears to have published *Polimanteia* as a way of publicly (albeit indirectly) declaring his support for the "Essex faction" in the power struggle to control the succession upon Elizabeth's death.

This growing political battle would culminate six years later in the Essex faction's arranging for the Chamberlain's Men to perform *Richard II* at the Globe (with a scene showing the deposition of a monarch) on the eve of the rebellion of 8 February 1601, aimed at removing Robert Cecil from power. It ended in utter failure, followed by the prompt execution of Essex and the long confinement of Southampton in the Tower until after Elizabeth's death in 1603; by that time Cecil had engineered King James's succession to the English throne.

Turning back to 1595, however, Alexander Waugh raises the question of how to explain Covell's "brazen temerity" in publishing at Cambridge at a time when Burghley himself was Chancellor of the university. That fact, plus the dedication of *Polimanteia* to Essex, leads to a "natural supposition that the release of Covell's secret [about Oxford as Shakespeare] was in some way sanctioned by Essex and/or Burghley."

While the proposed alliance of Southampton with the Cecil family through marriage was in play between 1590 and 1594, Burghley would have been in favor of Oxford's attempt to persuade the younger earl to go along (in *Venus and Adonis* the Goddess of Love has thirty-six lines urging the young god to hurry into fatherhood, using virtually the same words as in the first seventeen sonnets urging Southampton to procreate). Even the Archbishop of Canterbury (who took his orders from Burghley and/or the queen) had signed off on *Venus and Adonis*, the first published offering of "Shakespeare." But the potential Oxford-Elizabeth-Burghley alliance with Southampton had ended before 1595, so that now Oxford was breaking with William and Robert Cecil while using "Shakespeare" to support Southampton alone. In doing so, he was joining the Essex faction, perhaps against his better judgment. It appears, therefore, that Covell must have been quite daring to insert his allusion to Oxford as "Shakespeare," with its implied support of Essex and Southampton against the Cecil faction. Yes, quite daring, in a world where writers were being censored, imprisoned, tortured and even killed. At stake, after all, was the crown.

CHAPTER SIX

THE UNIVERSITY WITS

Reason 33 – Shakespeare's "Predecessors"

Many of Shakespeare's immediate literary "predecessors," cited by scholars as providing source materials for the great author, in fact gained their expertise and honed their skills from the Earl of Oxford. From Shakespeare's works there emerges a clear pattern of de Vere's silent but hugely influential presence; he is akin to a towering, pervasive, ghostly figure who has gone virtually unnoticed, simply because no one has been looking for him. A powerful reason why Oxford was "Shakespeare" is that the identified sources for many of the plays are literary or dramatic works by writers who operated under his patronage and guidance. Here are ten such stage works in alphabetical order:

1. *As You Like It*
The direct and primary source is *Rosalynde, Euphues' Golden Legacy*, a prose romance by Thomas Lodge, written by 1587. Lodge followed the euphuistic literary movement (aimed at refining and enriching the English language) of which Oxford was the leader. The earl's secretary, John Lyly, had published two *Euphues* novels in 1579-1580. *As You Like It* contains several thematic links with Lyly's court plays, such as *Sappho and Phao, Galathea* and *The Woman in the Moon*. In addition the play *James IV* by Robert Greene, another writer in Oxford's orbit ("Greene" may even have been one of Oxford's pen names prior to 1593), contains antecedents of the feminine characters in *As You Like It* and is also notable for using a similar rural setting.

2. *The Comedy of Errors*
Once again, writings attributed to Oxford's secretary are identified as sources used by the Shakespearean dramatist. As Campbell writes, "The rhetorical features of the comedy betray the influence of John Lyly that was strong during the formative years of Shakespeare's art."

3. *Love's Labour's Lost*

This play contains "many features of the euphuistic style made fashionable by the publication of Lyly's *Euphues, the Anatomy of Wit*," Derran Charlton and Kevin Gilvary report; H.R. Woudhuysen observes that parts of the play are "reminiscent of the court comedies and the prose romances of John Lyly."

4. *The Merchant of Venice*

Considered a likely source is *Zelauto, the Fountain of Fame* (1580) by another of Oxford's secretaries, Anthony Munday, who dedicated it to the earl. Details of plot, character and language in Munday's work are paralleled in the Shakespearean play, including the usurer's daughter and her marriage, as well as the two ladies who disguise themselves as lawyers. It appears that Portia's speech about the "quality of mercy" was influenced by the judge's pleas for mercy in the same work by Munday, who referred to himself in the dedication as "Servant to the Right Honourable the Earl of Oxenford."

5. *The* **Merry Wives of Windsor**

According to Philip Johnson, the treatment of Falstaff by the "fairies" in the final scene appears to parallel the episode in *Endymion* (credited to Lyly) in which the soldier Corsites is pinched by fairies. Johnson also notes that some influence on Falstaff "may have been derived" from the character of Captain Crackstone in Munday's *Fedele and Fortunio* (1585), a translation from Luigi Pasqualigo.

6. *A Midsummer Night's Dream*

H.F. Brooks and C.L. Barber agree that this play also reflects the court dramas attributed to Lyly. Geoffrey Bullough believes *Endymion* influenced the Shakespearean play. H.F. Brooks and Nevill Coghill observe that the dramatic structure of *Dream* is similar to a combination of leading features in Munday's play *John a Kent and John a Cumber*.

7. *Much Ado About Nothing*

The English source appears to be *Fedele and Fortunio* (1585) by Oxford's secretary Munday, who apparently adapted it from an Italian play, *Il Fedele*, written in 1579.

8. *The Tempest*

The play *Friar Bacon and Friar Bungay* (c. 1591) by Robert Greene "bears some primitive and remote resemblance to *The Tempest*,"

Campbell writes, "and is one of the earliest examples of the successful interweaving of a subplot with the main story." In addition, Greene's play *The History of Orlando Furioso* (1594) drew from Ariosto's work of that name (1516). In the book *On the Date, Sources and Design of Shakespeare's "The Tempest"* (2013), Roger Stritmatter and Lynne Kositsky show how that Italian epic poem is itself an important source of this Shakespearean play (and also of *Much Ado*).

9. *The Two Gentlemen of Verona*

Bullough notes some common techniques in *Two Gentlemen* and the comedies and romances of Lyly; he believes that Lyly's novel *Euphues, The Anatomy of Wit* (1579), which was inspired (and perhaps dictated to him) by Oxford, his employer, comes closest to this work. "Shakespeare's debt appears in the courtly atmosphere of Lyly's romance plays," Noemi Magri writes; and C. Leech, editor of the Arden edition of *Two Gentlemen*, notes "many incidental echoings" of Lyly. He also suggests that the Launce-Speed dialogue in the first scene of act three contains a major "crib" from Lyly's romantic comedy *Midas*, played in 1591 by the Paul's Boys for Elizabeth at court. The title of *Two Gentlemen* is suggestive of Munday's play *Fidele and Fortunio, the Deceits in Love Discoursed in a Comedy of Two Italian Gentlemen*. R. Hosley, an editor of Munday's work, suggests that *Fidele and Fortunio* was acted before the queen by Oxford's Boys.

10. *The Winter's Tale*

"The source of the main plot is Greene's novel *Pandosto, or the Triumph of Time* (1588)," Campbell writes. The Shakespearean play carries over all the characters in *Pandosto* except one, Mopsa. "There has been considerable disagreement among scholars as to the relationship of Greene and Shakespeare," he observes, adding, "If, as many scholars have believed, Shakespeare began his career by revising other men's plays, then it is probable that some of these plays were at least partly Greene's."

Some Oxfordians, notably Stephanie Hughes and Nina Green, have set forth impressive arguments that "Robert Greene" was an early pen name used by Oxford before "killing him off" in September 1592, shortly before adopting the "Shakespeare" pseudonym the following year. One of Greene's earliest books, *Card of Fancy* (1584), was dedicated to Oxford. Greene called him "a worthy favourer and fosterer of learning" who had "forced many through your excellent virtues to offer the first-fruits of their study at the shrine of your Lordship's courtesy."

The Winter's Tale owes much to the use of Greek Romances. Two contemporary writers linked to Oxford contributed suggested sources: Angel Day, who published an English translation of *Daphnis and Chloe* in 1587; and Thomas Underdowne, who translated *Heliodorus' Aethiopica* in 1569, dedicating it to nineteen-year-old Oxford and writing of the earl's "haughty courage joined with great skill, such sufficiency in learning, so good nature and common sense," among other virtues. Eddi Jolly, noting the influence of *Aethiopica* upon *The Winter's Tale*, observes that "the entire moving force is a king's jealousy."

Reason 34 – John Lyly

John Lyly was the principal court dramatist in the 1580s and a pivotal figure of the English renaissance. Stephen Greenblatt of Harvard makes no mention in *Will in the World* of Lyly's twelve-year literary apprenticeship under Oxford's guidance, paving the way for the court comedies of "Shakespeare" in the 1590s—not a word more about this person who, even to traditional scholars, is so crucial to the story of "how Shakespeare became Shakespeare." But Lyly is offered here as another link in the chain of evidence that de Vere was the writer who used "Shakespeare" as a pen name.

Lyly's extravagant novels and courtly comedies are commonly viewed as having a major influence on Shakespeare's early plays. He was employed as Oxford's secretary and theatrical manager until 1590, when the earl withdrew from public life (after which, in 1593, the name "Shakespeare" appeared in print for the first time). Lyly is credited with having written the first English novels, *Euphues: The Anatomy of Wit* in 1579, and *Euphues and his England* in 1580, both featuring an Italianized Englishman as the main character. He had been recruited in 1577 by Burghley, who introduced him to his son-inlaw, the Italianized English earl; and just a few years later he dedicated *Euphues and His England* to Oxford with strong hints that his master had taken an active part in its writing.

Oxford was the leader of euphuism, the new literary movement focusing on the magic of words and the imagery of sentences, and Lyly was both his personal secretary and euphuism's first practitioner. Merriam-Webster defines euphuism as "an elegant Elizabethan literary style marked by excessive use of balance, antithesis, and alliteration and by frequent use of similes drawn from mythology and nature." Lyly and the other young writers under Oxford's wing, later dubbed the University Wits, all dedicated certain "euphuistic" works to him. Besides Lyly, they included Anthony Munday, who wrote publicly to Oxford about "the day when as conquerors we may peacefully resume our delightful literary discussions"; Robert Greene, who praised the earl as "a worthy favorer and fosterer of learning": and Thomas Watson, who thanked Oxford for having "willingly vouchsafed the acceptance" of his work "and at convenient leisure favorably perused" the work while it was still "in written hand" (i.e., in manuscript).

De Vere was deeply involved with these writers and their works, all of which contained a wealth of metaphor and creative juggling of words and sentences. Such skills are handled with flawless ease by "Shakespeare" in *Love's Labour's Lost, A Midsummer Night's Dream* and other sophisticated works composed originally for the entertainment of Elizabeth and the court. Traditional biography requires a youthful Shakspere to absorb, master and even surpass the "euphuistic" outpourings of the University Wits within just a few years. The glover's son, newly arrived in London, had to quickly become the foremost dramatist of courtly love and genteel romance, a peerless practitioner of elaborate puns, repetitions, alliterations, high-flown rhetorical digressions and fanciful references to classical mythology and natural history. Shakespeare's other comedies of the 1590s, all viewed as indebted to writings attributed to Lyly, include *The Comedy of Errors, The Two Gentlemen of Verona, The Taming of the Shrew, Much Ado About Nothing, As You Like It* and *Twelfth Night*. In his three-volume *Complete Works* of Lyly in 1902, R.W. Bond writes that Lyly was "the first regular English dramatist, the true inventor and introducer of dramatic style, conduct and dialogue. There is no play before Lyly. He wrote eight; and immediately thereafter, England produced some hundreds—produced that marvel and pride of the greatest literature in the world, the Elizabethan Drama."

Bond describes "the immense superiority" of Lyly's work "to anything that preceded it" and cites his "prime importance" as Shakespeare's chief master and exemplar: "In comedy Lyly is Shakespeare's only model. The evidence of Shakespeare's study and imitation of him is abundant, and Lyly's influence is of a far more permanent nature than any exercised on the great poet by other writers." Bond even speculates that Lyly "first received the dramatic impulse" from Oxford, but the extent of de Vere's role was virtually unknown until a decade later, in 1912, when Charles William Wallace reported records showing that Oxford had contributed far more to that "evolution" than scholars had realized.

Wallace focused on the Blackfriars playhouse, where plays were rehearsed in front of aristocrats before being brought to the royal court. The private theatre faced closure in 1583 because of deep legal and financial troubles, but then "Oxford, himself celebrated in his day as a dramatist, came to the rescue. Noted alike as swaggerer, roisterer, brawler, coxcomb, musician, poet, Maecenas, the earl was also the devoted patron of John Lyly, whose book *Euphues* had made a stir in all England during the past three years. He believed in Lyly's literary ability. So he bought the Blackfriars lease [and] made a present of it to Lyly.... Thereafter we hear of John Lyly as presenting two plays at Court in the winter of 1583-84 with the Earl of Oxford's servants . . ."

Later in that decade came another play, *Endymion, The Man in the Moon*, performed for Elizabeth; and this stage work was unmistakably about Oxford and the queen, who was known as Goddess of the Moon. When the text was printed in 1591, Lyly's name did not appear on the title page.

Looney took note of Bond's statements about Lyly having probably "first received the dramatic impulse" from the earl. He also cited *The Arte of English Poesie* of 1589, wherein Oxford was said to be "deserving the highest praise for comedy and interlude," concluding:

> The work of Oxford in drama is therefore recognized as having furnished the generative impulse which produced Lyly's work in this particular domain. Therefore we feel quite entitled to say that it was the plays of Edward de Vere that furnished Lyly's dramatic education, while contact with his master is a recognized force in his personal education.
>
> The dramas of Edward de Vere form the source from which sprang Lyly's dramatic conceptions and enterprises, and Lyly's dramas appear as the chief model, in comedy the "only" model, upon which "Shakespeare" worked. We are therefore entitled to claim that the highest orthodox authorities, in the particular department of literature with which we are dealing, support the view that the dramatic activities of Edward de Vere stand in almost immediate productive or causal relationship of a most distinctive character with the dramatic work of "Shakespeare."

Oxford had been the sun from which Lyly drew his light. The only works for which Lyly is credited were produced during the years he worked for de Vere. After the earl withdrew from public life in 1590, no more writing attributed to Lyly came forth. Isn't it far more logical that "Shakespeare" never had to draw his light from Lyly, but, rather, that de Vere continued to be the same source of light in the 1590s, as he developed ever greater dramatic power under the "Shakespeare" name?

Reason 35 – Anthony Munday

Anthony Munday was an actor-printer-writer-translator and anti-Catholic spy who signed himself "Servant to the Right Honourable the Earl of Oxenford." Oscar Campbell is one of many traditional Shakespeare scholars who note the following points of interest about this writer of whom Oxford was patron:

> Shakespeare contributed an addition to the play *Sir Thomas More* (1592), the first draft of which was written by Munday.
> Shakespeare found incidents and ideas for *A Midsummer Night's Dream* (1594) from Munday's play *John a Kent*.
> Shakespeare wrote parts of *The Merchant of Venice* (1596) by drawing upon Munday's long prose romance *Zelauto, The Fountain of Fame.*
> Shakespeare got his general plot outline for *Much Ado About Nothing* (1598) from *Fidele and Fortunio*, an Italian play adapted by Munday.
> Shakespeare received inspiration for the idyllic green world of the forest in *As You Like It* (1599) from a play about Robin Hood by Munday.

In the traditional view it appears that during the 1590s the Bard grabbed stuff from Munday whenever he wanted; the reality, I suggest, was the other way around. Munday was one of many writers who served as secretaries to Oxford during the 1570s and 1580s and benefited from his reckless generosity (Oxford provided money, work space, inspiration and instruction) as they developed the English renaissance of literature and drama. I suggest that in the next decade Oxford adopted "Shakespeare" as a pen name on works containing those same ideas, plots and characters that he himself had originated and had shared with Munday and other writers under his wing. The son of a London draper, Munday had been an actor, most likely in Oxford's boy company and then in his adult troupe. In 1576 he became an apprentice to John Allde, the stationer whose son, Edward Allde, would later print several Shakespeare quartos. Two years later Munday journeyed to Rome "to see strange countries and learn foreign languages," as he recalls in *English Romayne Lyfe* (1582), but Campbell and others state he was actually a spy sent to report on the English Jesuit College in Rome. He returned to England by 1579, when he "may have become an actor again, with the Earl of Oxford's company," and that year he published *The Mirror of Mutability*, dedicating it to his patron and including the following poem to him:

E xcept I should in friendship seem ingrate,
D enying duty, whereto I am bound;
W ith letting slip your Honour's worthy state,
A t all assays, which I have noble found.
R ight well I might refrain to handle pen:
D enouncing aye the company of men.

D own, dire despair, let courage come in place,
E xalt his fame whom Honour doth embrace

V irtue hath aye adorn'd your valiant heart,
E xampl'd by your deeds of lasting fame:
R egarding such as take God Mars his part
E ach where by proof, in honour and in name.

Munday referred to Oxford's "courteous and gentle perusing" of his writings. As Ward notes, the earl was "no ordinary patron," since he was "willing to give both his time and attention to manuscripts submitted to him, and could be relied on to make suggestions and offer advice." Oxford and his Euphuists aimed to refine and enrich the English language, believing in the magic of words and the power of imagery, while Philip Sidney and the Romanticists wanted to retell old stories of knighthood to make them more accessible.

In 1580 Munday dedicated his novel *Zelauto, The Fountain of Fame* to de Vere ("By A.M., Servant to the Right Honourable the Earle of Oxenford"), praising "the rare virtues of your noble mind" and declaring that "among all the brave books which have been bestowed [upon you], these my little labours contain so much faithful zeal to your welfare as [all] others whatsoever." He also wrote that the book was "Given for a friendly entertainment to Euphues" —revealing, in effect, that the character of Euphues stood for Oxford himself.

Munday was one of the chief witnesses against Edmund Campion, the Jesuit priest who was hanged, drawn and quartered on December 1, 1581; part of Munday's savage tract *A Discoverie of Edmund Campion and his Confederates* was read aloud from the scaffold at Tyburn. His political services against Catholics were rewarded in 1584, when he received the post of Messenger to Her Majesty's Chamber.

In his 1588 dedication of *Palmerin d'Olivia, Pt. 2*, a translation, Munday spoke of Oxford's "special knowledge" of foreign languages and referred to his "precious virtues, which makes him generally beloved" and of "mine own duty, which nothing but death can discharge." (Only the 1616 reprint containing this information is extant.) Oxford died in 1604, but Munday would never forget his master; in 1619 he dedicated all three parts of a new edition of his *Primaleon of Greece* to Oxford's son Henry de Vere, 18th Earl of Oxford, and spoke of "having served that noble Earl your father of famous and desertful memory" and of "your honourable father's matchless virtues."

Reason 36 – Thomas Watson

The poet Thomas Watson is a direct forerunner of the poet of *Venus and Adonis* and the *Sonnets*. A leader in the long procession of Elizabethan sonnet-cycle writers, he is linked to "Shakespeare" through Edward de Vere in some startling ways.

In 1582, Watson published *Hekatompathia or The Passionate Century of Love*, a sequence of 100, or a "century," of numbered eighteen-line sonnets or "passions," with "prose headers" demonstrating his knowledge of works by some fifty classical or renaissance authors in their original languages. He dedicated it to Oxford, testifying that the earl "had willingly vouchsafed the acceptance of this work, and at convenient leisures favorably perused it, being as yet but in written hand." It appears likely the "prose headers" were also written by Oxford, who may well have written *all* of this poetical sequence.

In 1589, soon after the earl sold his London mansion Fisher's Folly to William Cornwallis, Watson became employed in the Cornwallis household. That September, when Christopher Marlowe was attacked by an innkeeper's son, William Bradley, for failure to pay a debt, Watson came to his friend's aid and killed Bradley—an act for which he spent six months in prison. Marlowe served as a spy for the English government and it would seem that Watson did, too. His association with Francis Walsingham, head of the secret service, brings him into probable contact with Oxford from this direction as well. On 21 June 1586 Burghley urged Walsingham to confront the queen about financial assistance to Oxford; five days later Elizabeth awarded de Vere an annual grant of 1,000 pounds, which would be continued by King James in 1603 until the earl's death a year later. The fact that Burghley appealed to Walsingham on Oxford's behalf indicates that the latter's grant was somehow connected to intelligence activities at a high level, perhaps involving Catholics among the English nobility as well as diplomatic contact with foreign rulers and courts.

Watson's *Italian Madrigals* was published in 1593, the year after his death. Most of its contents had been composed originally by Luca Marenzio while Marenzio was in Mantua living with the Gonzaga family from 1568 to 1574. Watson had never traveled to Italy, but Oxford had apparently stayed with the Gonzaga family while visiting Mantua in 1575.

Also in 1593, Watson's posthumous sequence of sixty numbered sonnets (in the later-known "Shakespearean" form of fourteen lines) appeared in print as *The Tears of Fancie, or Love Disdained* (with no author's name on the title page and only *"Finis T.W."* after the final sonnet, which was clearly a version of Oxford's early sonnet *Love Thy Choice*, written in the 1570s to express his devotion to the queen).

When SHAKE-SPEARES SONNETS was printed in 1609, one verse in the so-called dark lady series (No. 130) was clearly a takeoff on one of the sonnets printed under Watson's name (No. 7) in *Hekatompathia* of 1582. For example, Watson wrote, "Her lips more red than any Coral stone," and Shakespeare turned it inside out: "Coral is far more-red than her lips' red." *Hekatompathia, or the Passionate Century of Love* attributed to Watson is often cited as paving the way for the Shakespearean sonnet sequence published twenty-seven years later; the two are related through Oxford himself. In the SHAKE-SPEARE volume there is also a series of exactly 100 verses, or a "century" (Nos. 27-126), between two segments of twenty-six sonnets apiece (Nos. 1-26 and 127-152); this central 100-sonnet sequence contains two sections, of eighty and twenty sonnets, respectively, exactly as Watson's earlier century had been "divided into two parts" (as indicated on the title page) in an eighty-twenty format. Watson's dedication begins:

> To the Right Honorable my *very good Lord* Edward de Vere, *Earle* of Oxenford . . .

> Alexander the Great, passing on a time by the workshop of Apelles, curiously surveyed some of his doings, whose long stay in viewing them brought all the people into so great a good liking of the painter's workmanship, that immediately after they bought up all his pictures, what price 'soever he set them at. And the like good hap (Right Honorable) befell unto me lately concerning these my Love Passions, which then chanced to Apelles for his Portraits. For since the world hath understood (I know not how) that your Honor had willingly vouchsafed the acceptance of this work, and at convenient leisure favorably perused it, being as yet but in written hand, many have oftentimes and earnestly called upon me to put it to the press, that for their money they might but see what your Lordship with some liking had already perused....

Reason 37 – A Diversity of Dedications

As far as I can determine, at least twenty-eight publications can be verified as dedicated to de Vere by name during his lifetime. To that list we might add three more items: in 1592 Nashe apparently dedicates *Strange News* to Oxford, using another name for him; in 1603 Davison includes him in a curious political broadsheet or circular; and in 1619 Munday dedicates a book to Henry de Vere, 18th Earl of Oxford, with warm posthusmous praise for Edward de Vere, 17th Earl of Oxford, his father, this bringing a tentative total to thirty-one. (Franklin B. Williams, in the 1962 edition of his *Index of Dedications and Commendatory Verses in English books before 1641*, notes that the accurate figure for dedications to Oxford by name is probably twenty-eight.)

The dedications appear in works that range from Greek history to English literature, geography, military matters, music, medicine, astrology, translations from Italian and French, the Psalms, and so on—mirroring the wide range of subjects that Shakespeare was interested in. The books present us with an array of diverse topics and genres drawn from the European renaissance; they were very much part of the new age of English literature, of which Oxford was a central—perhaps *the* central—moving force prior to "Shakespeare's" entrance in 1593.

The dedications to Oxford were not merely public bids for patronage; they were not the usual stuff of obsequious praise. On the contrary, they came from writers who worked with Oxford in developing common political and artistic goals. Over and over they thanked him personally for taking time to read their works and give his advice. He was not some lofty noble keeping his distance; instead, he rolled up his sleeves and became involved—personally, artistically and financially—in their varied works that covered so many subjects and forms of literary expression.

Here is a list of authors and their books dedicated to Oxford:

1/ 1564: Arthur Golding, *Histories of Trogus Pompeius* (translation) ["Thabridgment [sic] of the histories of Trogus Pompeius, collected and written in the Laten tonge, by the famous historiographer Justine, and translated into English by Arthur Goldyng..."]

2/ 1569: Thomas Underdowne, *An AEthiopian History Written in Greek by Heliodorus* (translation)

3/ 1570: Edmund Elviden, *Pesistratus and Catanea* (poetry) **4/ 1571: Arthur Golding,** *Psalms of David* (translation) **5/ 1573: Thomas Bedingfield,** *Cardanus' Comforte* (translation) [See **Reasons 8 and 25**]

6/ 1573: Thomas Twyne, *Breviary of Britain*.... (Translation) ["Containing a Learned Discourse of the Variable State and Alteration thereof, under Divers as well as Natural, as Foreign Princes and Conquerors, together with the Geographical Description of the same."]

7/ 1574: George Baker, M.D., *Oleum Magistrale* (medical; translation of **Aparico de Zubia's pamphlet)** ["**The Composition or Making of the Most Excellent and Precious Oil called Oleum Magistrale**" – Baker was family surgeon to Oxford.]

8/ 1577: John Brooke, *The Staff of Christian Faith* (translation of Guido's French work into English) ["...profitable to all Christians ... Gathered out of the Works of the Ancient Doctors of the Church . . ."]

9/ 1578: Gabriel Harvey, *Gratulationum Valdensis* (A book in Latin; see Reason 27) [Celebrating the queen's visit that year to Audley End; includes dedications in the first three parts to Elizabeth, Leicester and Burghley; and in part four to Oxford, Hatton and Sidney.)

10/ 1578 (?): Anthony Munday, *Galien of France* – a book, now lost, that Oxford's servant Munday, in *The Mirror of Mutability* (below), says he had dedicated to Oxford.

11/ 1579: Anthony Munday, *The Mirror of Mutability* (verses) [To serve as a religious companion to "The Mirror of Magistrates" – presenting a series of metrical tragedies "selected out of the sacred Scriptures," illustrating the Seven Deadly Sins with biblical stories.]

12/ 1579: Geoffrey Gates, *The Defence of Military Profession* (A book in English) [An argument for the acceptance of the military man, and the military profession, as an essential and reputable member of society.]

13/ 1580: Anthony Munday, *Zelauto, The Fountain of Fame* (prose fiction) [This is the fifth or sixth Elizabethan novel, three of which are associated with Oxford: *The Adventures of Master F.I.*, anonymous, part of *A Hundredth Sundry Flowres*, 1573; *Euphues, The Anatomy of Wit* (Lyly), 1578, and *Euphues and his England* (Lyly), 1580 (next on this list)].

14/ 1580: John Lyly, *Euphues and His England* (novel) [His first novel, *Euphues: The Anatomy of Wit* (1578) was dedicated to Sir William West; the connection between them is not known.]

15/ 1580: John Hester, *A Short Discourse ... upon Chirurgerie* **(Surgery)** (translation) [Italian medical work by Leonardo Phioravanti (Fioravanti) Bolognese, rendered in English]

16/ 1581: Thomas Stocker, *Diverse Sermons of Calvin* (translation)

17/ 1582: Thomas Watson, *Hekatompathia, or The Passionate Century of Love* (100 sonnets, in English; see Reason 36)

18/ 1584: John Southern, *Pandora* (compilation of verses) [Contains four epitaphs attributed to Oxford's wife, Anne Cecil, written upon the death of their infant son; also one by Queen Elizabeth.]

19/ 1584: Robert Greene, *Gwydonius: The Card of Fancy* (*"wherein the Folly of those carpet Knights is deciphered"*) [Romance novel in English]

20/ 1586: Angel Day, *The English Secretary* (*"wherein is contained a Perfect Method for the inditing of all manner of Epistles and familiar letters"*) [Instructions on how a particular type of letter should be written, followed by sample letters.]

21/ 1588: Anthony Munday, *Palmerin d'Olivia Pt. 1 – The Mirror of Nobility* (translation of a Spanish chivalric romance)

22/ 1588: Anthony Munday, *Palmerin d'Olivia Pt. 2* (translation) [more of his "romances of chivalry" from the Spanish]

23/ 1590: Edmund Spenser, *The Faerie Queene* (book-length narrative poem) [One of the seventeen dedicatory sonnets is to Oxford, with reference to him as a poet.]

24/ 1591: John Farmer, *Plain-song Diverse & Sundry* (songbook) [Full title is "Divers and Sundry Waies of Two Parts in One to the Number of Fortie upon One Playn Song." A collection of forty canonic pieces written by him, plus one poem.]

25/1 592: Thomas Nashe, *Strange News* (polemical pamphlet) [In response to Gabriel Harvey's attack on Greene, dedicated to a prolific poet he calls by the pseudonym "Gentle Master William, *Apis Lapis,*" saying to him, "Verily, verily, all poor scholars acknowledge you as their patron" – with "verily, verily" as an apparent play on Oxford's name "Vere" and describing his unique role as a patron of poets, writers and scholars needing his support.]

26/ 1597: Henry Lok, *The Book of Ecclesiastes* (book of verse) [Published by Richard Field, who had published *Venus and Adonis* in 1593 as by "William Shakespeare"; in this work, Lok addresses a dedicatory sonnet to Oxford—perhaps originally written in manuscript in a gift copy of the book for the Earl.]

27/ 1599: John Farmer, *The First Set of English Madrigals* (songbook)

28/ 1599: Angel Day, *The English Secretary* (new edition, revised)

29/ 1599: George Baker, *The Practice of the New and Old Physic* (medical book) [Originally printed in 1576 under the title *New Jewel of Health*, then dedicated to Oxford's wife, Anne Cecil, who died in 1588; now Baker is one of the Queen's physicians; the dedication to the Countess of Oxford is slightly altered to suit the Earl.]

In addition, these explicit mentions of him:

1603: Francis Davison, *Anagrammata* (broadsheet) [With curious writings in Latin to/about Oxford and Southampton and other nobles, with political overtones, some apparently related to the Essex rebellion of 1601.]

1619: Anthony Munday, *Primaleon of Greece* (translation) ["Describing the knightly deeds of armes, as also the memorable adventures of Prince Edward of England. And continuing the former historie of Palmendos, brother to the fortunate Primaleon"—dedicated to Henry de Vere, the 18th Earl of Oxford, who was Edward's son by Elizabeth Trentham, with warm praise by Munday for the father.]

These authors, and their books dedicated to the Earl of Oxford, have been cited as specific "sources" upon which "Shakespeare" drew. Yet we know of no book or literary work of any kind that was dedicated to Shakespeare.

Reason 38 – A Depth of Dedications

The public dedications to de Vere indicate the depth of his personal relationships with other writers. The person who eventually created the "Shakespeare" works did not develop in a vacuum; on the contrary, he had to be part of a community of fellow authors, poets and playwrights. Oxford was not only part of such a community; the tributes make clear he was their leader.

• Arthur Golding (*Histories of Trogus Pompeius*) wrote to him in 1564: "It is not unknown to others, and I have had experiences thereof myself, how earnest a desire your Honor hath naturally grafted in you to read, peruse, and communicate with others as well the histories of ancient times, and things done long ago, as also of the present estate of things in our days, and that not without a certain pregnancy of wit and ripeness of understanding."

• Thomas Underdowne (*AEthiopian History*) told him in 1569 that "matters of learning" were good for a nobleman, but then warned the earl that "to be too much addicted that way, I think it is not good." In that same year the nineteen-year-old Oxford ordered "a Geneva Bible gilt, a Chaucer, Plutarch's works in French, with other books and papers" as well as "Tully's and Plato's works in folio, with other books." Sounds indeed like a young man "addicted" to learning!

• When Thomas Bedingfield dedicated his translation of *Cardanus' Comforte* to Oxford in 1573, he told him that "I do present the book your Lordship so long desired," confirming that the earl had been personally involved in this publication, to which he contributed both a Letter to the Reader and a poem. He reminds Oxford of "the encouragement of your Lordship, who (as you well remember), unawares to me, found some part of this work and willed me in any wise to proceed therein."

• The distinguished physician Thomas Twyne (*Breviary of Britain*) referred to him in 1573 as being "in your flower and tender age" before inviting him to bestow upon his work "such regard as you are accustomed to do on books of Geography, Histories, and other good learning, wherein I am privy your honor taketh singular delight."

• When Anthony Munday (*Mirror of Mutability*) told Oxford in 1579 that he looked forward to "the day when as conquerors we may peacefully resume our delightful literary discussions," he was apparently referring to the rivalry between the Euphuists under Oxford and the Romanticists, who included Philip Sidney and Gabriel Harvey. His reference to "our delightful literary discussions" offers a glimpse of Oxford personally engaged with other writers who were developing a new English literature and drama leading to "Shakespeare." The works created by members of this circle would become known as "contemporary sources" upon which the great author drew.

• Thomas Watson (*Hekatompathia, or The Passionate Century of Love*) reminded Oxford in 1582 that he had "willingly vouchsafed the acceptance of this work, and at convenient leisure favorably perused it, being as yet but in written hand." He cited de Vere as a literary trendsetter whose approval would draw many readers; because of this influence, the earl's acceptance of the work in manuscript meant that "many have oftentimes and earnestly called upon me to put it to the press."

• Angel Day (*The English Secretary*) wrote to him in 1586 about "the learned view and insight of your Lordship, whose infancy from the beginning was ever sacred to the Muses."

• Robert Greene (*Card of Fancy*) publicly told him in 1584 he was "a worthy favorer and fosterer of learning [who] hath forced many through your excellent virtue to offer the first-fruits of their study at the shrine of your Lordship's courtesy." In other words, Oxford encouraged young writers with their very first works, guiding them to the press.

• In 1591 composer John Farmer, who lived in Oxford's household, dedicated his first songbook (*Plain-song Diverse & Sundry*) to him, saying he was "emboldened" because of "your Lordship's *great affection* to this noble science" (music)—which may be said of

Shakespeare. In his second dedication to Oxford (*First Set of English Madrigals*, 1599), Farmer told him that "using this science as a recreation, your Lordship have over-gone most of them that make it a profession."

Unlike the majority of dedications to patrons, the comments to Oxford are genuine and heartfelt. The earl may have had many faults of character, such as a tendency to be jealous and vengeful (as a number of Shakespearean characters are), but among his fellow writers and other artists he was uniquely spirited and generous.

In his Oxford biography *Monstrous Adversary* (2003), the Stratfordian scholar Alan Nelson concedes that Edward de Vere "attracts the attention of theologians, poets, distillers, and a musician, who have translated works from the Continent, or composed original works in English." Citing the *Index* by Williams, he notes that only Queen Elizabeth and a few more powerful nobles had more dedications: Leicester (114); Burghley (85); Walsingham (47); and Charles Howard, the Admiral and hero of England's victory over the Spanish Armada (46). Nelson, p. 384.]

In her Master of Arts in English thesis of 1999 at the University of Texas, focusing on Oxford's patronage, Jonni Koonce Dunn notes that nearly forty percent of it was "expended on fiction with an Italian flavor." The result, she adds, is that the Earl "provided the late sixteenth century with a body of source works to which the literature of the English Renaissance is sorely indebted." Even from a young age, he preferred "literary work over the devotional or practical," and such works "lent themselves to being models for adaptation for the forerunners of the novel as well as being instrumental in the development of English drama."

His introductions as a young man to works such as *The Courtier* and *Cardanus' Comforte*, she adds, "suggests his desire to be instrumental in shaping what was read by the university student and the courtier, thus in a roundabout way to transform the Elizabethan court into the cultured society depicted at Urbino in Castiglione's work…. It would eventually come to pass that William Shakespeare would benefit from the works de Vere patronized, for his plays came to make use of practically every one of the literary number in some fashion." Without such patronage, many of the sources used by Shakespeare "might not have been available to him for inspiration," and therefore this critical contribution "should ensure Edward de Vere the gratitude of every student of literature."

CHAPTER SEVEN

WRITERS IN WARTIME

Reason 39 – The College of Writers

"I lurk in no corners but converse in a house of credit, as well governed as any college, where there be more rare qualified men and selected good Scholars than in any Nobleman's house that I know in England."— Thomas Nashe, "Strange News," 1592

De Vere was thirty in 1580 when he bought a mansion in Bishopsgate, even though he was virtually broke and already owned Vere House by London Stone, where he lived. The extravagant second house was nicknamed Fisher's Folly after its builder, Jasper Fisher, fell into debt because of its too-costly construction. As Charles Barrell suggests, it appears Oxford acquired the mansion "as headquarters for the school of poets and dramatists who openly acknowledged his patronage and leadership."

"Shakespeare" would not, and could not, have developed without other creative artists. Logically, the Bard would have had an ongoing "college" in a building with many rooms and desks for writers, just as the painter Raphael had a workshop of fifty pupils and assistants, many of whom became significant artists in their own right. Orthodox biographers take it for granted that the author of the Shakespearean plays drew upon the work of several immediate predecessors (who were all connected to Oxford; see Reason 33); but once the earl is identified as the author, we can see that those other writers had drawn from his guidance and support. When Oxford was driven into poverty in 1589-90, the same writers began to fall on hard times and suffered misfortune or death.

De Vere owned Fisher's Folly through the late 1580s, as England prepared for the Spanish invasion. This was a time when many "history" plays (including several with the same plots and scenes as "Shakespeare's" stage histories in the next decade) were originally written and performed. This same period saw the great renaissance of English literature and drama by the so-called University Wits, working under Oxford's patronage and guidance—Nashe, Lyly, Watson, Greene,

Munday, Churchyard, Lodge and others—leading to the first appearance of the Shakespeare name in 1593. In December 1588, not long after the victory over Philip's Armada, Oxford sold Fisher's Folly to William Cornwallis, a descendant of the 11th Earl of Oxford. In 1852 the scholar J.O. Halliwell-Phillipps revealed his discovery of a small book in the handwriting of Cornwallis's daughter Anne, who had transcribed the work of various Elizabethan poets including *Verses Made by the Earl of Oxford,* as well as an anonymous poem that would appear in the poetry volume *The Passionate Pilgrim* (1599), its verses attributed to Shakespeare.

When Anne and her family moved into the house in early 1589, did she wander through its many rooms and find these verses in some corner of Oxford's library? Were they tucked away in a desk that one of the University Wits had used?

Halliwell-Phillipps estimated that Anne had transcribed the poems no later than 1590; but since that date was probably too early for Shakspere of Stratford to have written them, he later changed his estimate to 1595. Barrell countered with reasons why the earlier date is more likely. He also showed that the poem Anne transcribed is textually superior to the one printed later in 1599. Her version is apparently the only surviving handwritten copy of a poem attributed to Shakespeare dating from the sixteenth century.

So we start with the theory that Oxford may have written the works attributed to Shakespeare; then we see that he buys a London mansion, which he uses from 1580 to 1588, and that a woman who moves into the place in 1589 transcribes some verses made by Oxford and other poets, including lines that will appear a decade later under the Shakespeare name!

Final stanza of XVIII in *Passionate Pilgrim*, 1599:

But soft, enough—too much, I fear—
Lest that my mistress hear my song;
She will not stick to round me I' the ear,
To teach my tongue to be so long.
Yet will she blush, here be it said,
To hear her secrets so bewray'd.

Final stanza of earlier anonymous poem transcribed in Cornwallis's book:

Now hoe, enough, too much I fear;
For if my lady hear this song,
She will not stick to ring my ear,

To teach my tongue to be so long;
Yet would she blush, here be it said,
To hear her secrets thus bewray'd.

Reason 40 – "The Famous Victories"

The Famous Victories of Henry the Fifth, although not printed until 1598, was part of the wartime repertoire of the Queen's Men in the 1580s. Written by an obviously youthful (and anonymous) dramatist, the play also serves as a template or blueprint for the later Shakespearean trilogy *1 Henry IV, 2 Henry IV* and *Henry V*. Virtually everything in *Famous Victories* is repeated, in a refined and expanded form, in the Shakespeare plays printed in the latter 1590s. From that, traditional scholars conclude that "Shakespeare" was a shameless plagiarist. But isn't it far more likely that the real "Shakespeare" wrote *Famous Victories* at a younger age, later reworking it to create his *Henry* trilogy?

Dr. Seymour Pitcher, a professor of English literature at the State University of New York, published a book in 1961 entitled *The Case for Shakespeare's Authorship of "The Famous Victories,"* declaring that this youthful work "is not at all unworthy of Shakespeare as a spirited and genial apprentice dramatist." The play is "a clatter of events, its quick narrative interspersed with light and raucous comedy. Comical-historical it surely is, but, in its hybrid form, sufficiently self-consistent in tone. Sketchy and sometimes banal, it is gusty and flaunting. At best, it has poignancy in characterization and phrase. How else should we expect Shakespeare to have begun?" Pitcher suggests this must have been the Bard's first play, written during his early twenties. Many Oxfordians would agree, although Ramon Jiménez has concluded that de Vere may have written *Famous Victories* even earlier, in his teens. Whatever the case, there is no evidence that Shakspere of Stratford could have penned *Famous Victories* in his twenties (or at any other time); but the young Earl of Oxford was uniquely qualified to have written it.

Ward concludes that Oxford wrote *Famous Victories* at age twenty-four in 1574. One reason is that the play comically refers to the involvement of Prince Hal (the future Henry V) in a robbery on Gad's Hill, just a year after Oxford's own men had been involved in such a robbery (or prank) in the very same place (see Reason 20: "The Gad's Hill Caper"). Ward believes that the earl presented the play at court before Queen Elizabeth during the Christmas season of 1574.

"One can scarcely read *The Famous Victories* and not see in the skimpy little prose-play an early, comparatively amateurish exercise on the themes that would later come to magnificent flower in the Shakespearean dramas," Ogburn Jr. writes, citing a speech in *Famous Victories* by the newly crowned Henry the Fifth in response to the belittling gift from the French Dauphin of tennis balls: "My Lord Prince Dauphin is very pleasant with me! But tell him instead of balls of leather we will toss him balls of brass and iron—yea, such balls as never were tossed in France...."

This same early material, reworked in the Shakespeare play *Henry V*, becomes a masterful speech by the king that begins:

> "We are glad the Dauphin is so pleasant with us;
> His present and your pains we thank you for:
> When we have match'd our rackets to these balls,
> We will, in France, by God's grace, play a set
> Shall strike his father's crown into the hazard..." (1.2).

A prominent character in *Famous Victories* is Richard de Vere, 11th Earl of Oxford (1385-1417), but in *1 & 2 Henry IV* and *Henry V* by "Shakespeare" that same earl disappears. Ogburn Jr. notes that this "initial inflation and later eradication of Oxford's part" in the play is a telltale sign of something important. Once the author is viewed as de Vere, the explanation for Richard de Vere's disappearance from the play is clear: to continue to give such prominence to an ancestor would jeopardize Edward de Vere's anonymity.

Reason 41 – "The Policy of Plays"

> *"To this effect, the policy of plays is very necessary, howsoever some shallow-brained censurers (not the deepest searchers into the secrets of government) mightily oppose them."*— Thomas Nashe, "Pierce Penniless—The Defense of Plays," 1592

For centuries it was accepted that Shakespeare had little or no interest in the issues confronting England in his time, but in 1947 a book, *Shakespeare's "Histories"—Mirrors of Elizabethan Policy* by Lily B. Campbell, Professor Emeritus of English at UCLA, put forth the radical idea that the history plays were mirrors in which Elizabethans could perceive contemporary political problems. Professor Campbell came out swinging; her first victim was Mark Van Doren of Columbia University, whom she ridiculed for postulating that Shakespeare "does not seem to call for explanations beyond those which a whole heart and a free mind abundantly supply." It's a "heartening conviction," she quips, "that John Doe has only to reassure himself about the wholeness of his heart and the freedom of his mind to undertake to interpret Shakespeare. Any heart and any mind will do."

Then she held H.H. Furness up for scorn, citing his statement in the *New Variorum Edition* of Shakespeare in 1919: "I cannot reconcile myself to the opinion that Shakespeare ever made use of his dramatic art for the purpose of instructing, or as a means of enforcing his own views, any more than I believe that his poetic inspiration was dependent on his personal experiences." These are comforting thoughts, Campbell wryly notes, for writers and critics alike—that whatever the great author wrote had nothing to do with either his personal experiences or his convictions! And just think, she went on— Shakespeare himself had no personal concerns about the problems of contemporary politics!

But she begs to differ: "I do not believe that a poet exists in a vacuum, or even that he exists solely in the minds and hearts of his interpreters. I do not believe he can write great poetry without conviction and without passion. I do not believe that his reflection of his period is casual and fragmentary and accidental. Rather, it seems to me the poet must be reckoned a man among men, a man who can be understood only against the background of his own time...."

Campbell sees the great author deliberately using history to set forth the dangerous and pressing political problems of his day, such as the prospect of civil war because of Elizabeth's lack of an heir and her refusal to name a successor. Plays like *King John* and *Richard II* revolve around issues of legitimacy and the possible need to depose a weak monarch for the sake of England's health and survival. In this way Campbell was breaking through the traditional image of the author. If she did not know about Looney's 1920 identification of Oxford, her argument is all the more powerful: that in fact the great poet-dramatist was deeply, passionately concerned about the country and particularly about the Tudor dynasty, and that there was, in fact, a "policy" of plays.

When Looney pointed to Oxford he simultaneously identified "Shakespeare" as a high-ranking nobleman and member of the House of Lords, a courtier who, while obviously obsessed with poetry and plays and with the power of the printed word and the stage, was demonstrably involved in crucial affairs of state. If Oxford was the author of *King John, Richard II* and *Henry V* (to name three of the histories covered by Campbell), then "Shakespeare" was not just a concerned observer of the great issues of his day, but, indeed, a participant in them. As G.K. Chesterton noted, "Men can always be blind to a thing, so long as it's big enough." Looney, in identifying Oxford, was pointing to an author whose world was certainly "big enough" to blind us. It was also a world much larger than that of the Stratford man, in every possible way.

The overall implication of de Vere's authorship is so enormous, in fact, that even Oxfordians can be blind to it. We are not talking about switching one name for another, or one writer for another, but, rather, about the seismic shift from a man born in a small market town in the countryside to a man raised by blood to inhabit the palace and be part of the government. It is as if the author of popular political novels in the United States turned out to be a top official of the C.I.A. or the State Department, filling his works with inside, even top secret information that had never gotten into the official record.

In the case of Oxford we have the amazing story of a man who, in the 1570s and 1580s, led a renaissance of English literature and drama, helping to rouse unity in the face of foreign invasion; but who, in the 1590s, found himself adopting the pen name "Shakespeare" in a power struggle against the entrenched Cecilian control over the government and the queen herself. In the 1580s Oxford had been working on the same side as Burghley and spymaster Francis Walsingham; in the final stages during the 1590s, however, he was in a battle behind the scenes with Principal Secretary Robert Cecil to determine who would control the succession.

Here is Oxford as a patriotic young man on 24 November 1569, writing to William Cecil (later Lord Burghley), in reference to the Northern rebellion of Catholic earls: "And at this time I am bold to desire your favor and friendship that you will suffer me to be employed by your means and help in this service that now is in hand ... now you will do me so much honor as that by your purchase of my license I may be called to the service of my prince and country...."

He wrote to Lord Burghley in September 1572 about the recent St. Bartholomew's Day massacre of Protestants in France: "And think if the Admiral in France was an eyesore or beam in the eyes of the Papists, then the Lord Treasurer of England is a block and a cross-bar in their way, whose remove they will never stick to attempt, seeing they have prevailed so well in others. This estate hath depended on you a great while, as all the world doth judge, and now all men's eyes ... are, as it were, on a sudden, bent and fixed on you as a singular hope and pillar ...."

Echoes of these remarks appear throughout the Shakespeare works:

- "...shame to your estate, an eyesore to our solemn festival" (3.2) —*The Taming of the Shrew*

- "His brandished sword did blind men with his beams" (1.1) —*Henry VI*, Pt. 1
- "... who, like a block, hath denied my access to thee" (5.2) — *Coriolanus*
- "Any bar, any cross, any impediment" (2.2) —*Much Ado About Nothing*
- "They will not stick to say you envied him" (2.2) —*Henry VIII*
- "...for on his choice depends the safety and health of this whole state" (1.3) —*Hamlet*
- "...why such unplausive eyes are bent on him" (3.3) —*Troilus and Cressida*

"I am one that counts myself a follower of yours now in all fortunes, and what shall hap to you, I count it hap to myself," Oxford continued to Cecil in the same letter, adding,"Thus my Lord, I humbly desire your Lordship to pardon my youth, but to take in good part my zeal and affection towards your Lordship, as on whom I have builded my foundation, either to stand or fall .... I shall be most willing to be employed on the sea coasts, to be in a readiness with my countrymen against any invasion."

When the Queen and Burghley prevented Oxford from pursuing a military career, his service soon took the form of literature and drama. In the process he created a robust language and cultural identity for England, which helped give its people a new sense of national pride. Campbell notes that "each of the Shakespeare histories serves a special purpose in elucidating a political problem of Elizabeth's day, and in bringing to bear upon this problem the accepted political philosophy of the Tudors."

Reason 42 – The Queen's Men

In 1583, as Philip II of Spain prepared to invade England, the British government created a new acting company as part of secret service activities, which included wartime propaganda to promote patriotic loyalty and unity. This new troupe, the Queen Majesty's Players or Queen Elizabeth's Men, was formed at the express command of the monarch. Drawing the best actors from existing companies, it became the dominant theatrical group in the crucial years leading to England's victory in 1588 over the Spanish Armada.

The Queen's Men performed what were, by all appearances, early versions of royal history plays published later as by Shakespeare. "The plots of no fewer than six of Shakespeare's known plays are closely related to the plots of plays performed by the Queen's Men," McMillin and MacLean write in *The Queen's Men and Their Plays* (1998). These histories include *The Troublesome Reign of King John* (repeated "virtually scene for scene" in the Shakespeare play *King John*); *The True Tragedy of Richard III* and *King Leir* (fully covered by Shakespeare in *Richard III* and *King Lear*); and also *The Famous Victories of Henry the Fifth*, which forms the foundation for the material in *1 Henry IV, 2 Henry IV* and *Henry V*.

There is no evidence that Shakspere of Stratford-upon-Avon was part of this prestigious acting company. The likelihood is that he was still in Warwickshire for the birth of his twins in February 1585, when he was twenty years old. By tradition, the "Lost Years" of that man begin in 1585 and continue until Robert Greene supposedly alludes to him in September 1592. By then, for the traditional story to be plausible, he has somehow firmly established himself as a London actor and as a promising, even prominent playwright able to provoke Greene's jealousy.

None of that has any factual basis.

"Documentary evidence as to Shakespeare's whereabouts and activities from 1585 to 1592 is totally lacking," Oscar Campbell writes, adding that "nothing can be confirmed" about the Stratford man's life in that period. Traditional biographers cannot plausibly explain how "Shakespeare" was anonymously writing early versions of his plays for her Majesty's company in the 1580s. Therefore, some suggest he must have joined the Queen's Men as an actor and *memorized* the anonymous plays, which were written by others; then, they propose, he drew upon his prodigious memory to plunder their plots, characters, scenes and even lines, which would mean the greatest writer of the English language was also the most successful plagiarist in history.

As a mature dramatist in the 1590s, McMillin and MacLean declare, Shakespeare set about "rewriting a sizeable portion" of the repertory of the Queen's Men. "Four of nine extant plays were turned into six Shakespeare plays, in an act of appropriation extensive enough to make us think it could have occurred from the inside." Such is the kind of deduction that can come from an incorrect premise. "Shakespeare knew the plays of this company better than those of any company but his own, and the long-standing speculation that he may have begun his career with the Queen's Men seems to us the most likely possibility."

A few scholars have bravely stated the more realistic conclusion that Shakespeare himself must have written those earlier versions of his own plays, despite the fact that such a claim would rule out the Stratford man. It requires Shakspere to have joined the Crown's prestigious acting company too early to fit his biographical time frame. Fresh from life in the market town ninety miles from London, only twenty years old in 1584, he turns out plays of English royal history about monarchs such as *King John, Richard III, Henry IV* and *Henry V*—a miraculous example of pulling oneself up by the bootstraps if there ever was one.

Evidence within *The True Tragedy of Richard the Third* "reveals the high probability that it was Shakespeare himself who wrote that anonymous play," argues Ramon Jiménez, "and that *Richard III* was his major revision of one of his earliest attempts at playwriting." There are also "significant links" between the anonymous play and de Vere "that add to the evidence that he was the actual author of the Shakespeare canon." Furthermore, Jiménez states, the evidence suggests that the anonymous play "was performed for an aristocratic audience, possibly including Queen Elizabeth herself, in the early 1560s, when de Vere was between thirteen and fifteen years old."

Oxford was thirty-three in 1583, when Elizabeth's company was formed by the direct order of Walsingham, head of the government's intelligence operations, just as the war between England and Spain was becoming official. During the next crucial years, leading up to the victory over Philip's Armada in 1588, the new company would perform at court in winter and divide into two traveling troupes in summer. With its actors wearing the queen's livery representing her, the wartime company staged dozens of anonymous plays of English royal history throughout the country to promote patriotic loyalty and unity.

During the 1580s, the Queen's Men performed works that "Shakespeare" would later turn into mature plays. Moreover, the record shows that Oxford and his secretary Lyly were connected to Elizabeth's company from the outset. These two facts provide strong evidence that the author of the earlier works performed by the Queen's Men was Oxford himself, and, too, that he later revised his own previous plays for which "Shakespeare" would get the credit.

Oxford had returned from Italy in 1576, and it appears he proceeded to write plays brought to court by the Children of St. Paul's and by his great friend and supporter Thomas Radcliffe, 3rd Earl of Sussex. Oxford had served with him in the military campaign of 1570, against the northern Catholic earls in rebellion against the Protestant rule of Elizabeth. Sussex was now Lord Chamberlain of the Queen's Household and patron of the first Lord Chamberlain's acting company. Two examples:

- On New Year's Day 1577 at Hampton Court the Paul's Boys performed *"The historie of Error,"* which may well be an early version of *The Comedy of Errors*.
- In February 1577 at Whitehall Palace the Lord Chamberlain's Men performed *"The Historie of the Solitarie Knight,"* likely an early version of *Timon of Athens*.

In addition to his patronage of writers, Oxford now had charge of two acting companies, one (Oxford's Men) of adults and the other (Oxford's Boys) of choir boys from both Her Majesty's Children and Paul's Boys. He had the full sanction of the government; in the mid-1580s, for example, Burghley and Sussex recommended to Cambridge University that Oxford's Men be allowed to "show their cunning in several plays already practiced by them before the Queen's Majesty." Moreover, Oxford saved the private Blackfriars playhouse from extinction by paying for the lease. This venue was frequented by aristocrats and students, its performances functioning as rehearsals for appearances in front of Elizabeth at court. Then he passed the lease on to Lyly, who acted as director-manager. So Oxford was now at the center— he *was* the center—of the new awakening of English drama leading to "Shakespeare" in the next decade.

Sussex was near death when the order came down on 10 March 1583 to Edmund Tilney, Master of the Revels, that her Majesty's new acting company be formed. In effect the Queen's Men would replace the Chamberlain's Men. Assigned to assemble the personnel was Walsingham, who had no personal interest in theatre, but was nonetheless quite aware of its persuasive power. The formation of the Queen's Men signaled a new awareness by the Privy Council of the potential for combining theatrical activity and espionage, since players frequently traveled, nationally and internationally. This new adult company could serve the Crown in multiple ways, such as collecting information useful to Walsingham's intelligence network. The spymaster assembled the Queen's Men by enlisting the dozen best performers from all the existing companies. These included the Dutton brothers, leading players of Oxford's Men; and the popular clown Richard Tarlton, taken from Sussex's troupe, who quickly became the star of Elizabeth's Men.

"The new Queen's Company made its first appearance at the beginning of the Court season on Dec. 26, 1583," Ward reports. "On Jan. 1, 1584 a performance was given by Oxford's Men, and as John Lyly appears in the Chamber Accounts as payee for the company on that date, there is every reason to believe that the play acted was Lyly's *Campaspe*. On March 8, 1584 both Oxford's and the Queen's Men performed; once again Lyly was payee for Oxford's Men...."

"Now, it seems unreasonable to suppose that two plays were presented on this day; the most likely solution, therefore, would be that the two companies [Oxford's and the Queen's] were amalgamated and rehearsed by Lord Oxford's private secretary John Lyly, the author of the play. No other adult companies besides these two appeared at Court during this season."

Oxford was positioned to respond to the Crown's need for patriotic plays of English royal history, and, too, he was involved in the creation and operation of the Queen's Men, whose adult professional actors performed anonymous plays that "Shakespeare" would transform into masterpieces.

Reason 43 – The Thousand-Pound Grant

"But if Her Majesty, in regard of my youth, time, and fortune spent in her Court, and her favors and promises which drew me on without any mistrust, the more to presume in mine own expenses."—Oxford to Robert Cecil, 2 February 1601, describing how he had gone bankrupt in financing his activities (which were not specified) for Queen Elizabeth and the English government.

On 26 June 1586, when England was two years into the official war with Spain and bracing for King Philip's invasion, the queen signed a warrant granting Oxford an extraordinary allowance of 1,000 pounds per year (roughly equivalent to about $400,000 today; also, in Elizabethan times a pound could buy much more than now). The grant was to be paid to him by the Exchequer, by the same formula for payments to Walsingham and his wartime secret service: in quarterly installments with no accounting required. At this time the English government desperately needed all available cash for military defense; moreover, Walsingham required a constant flow of cash to pay foreign and domestic spies. Back in 1582 the Queen had given him 750 pounds; in 1586 she raised it to 2,000 pounds, but that would be the limit for her spymaster, even during the crucial year 1588. Why would Elizabeth, known for being a parsimonious (some would say miserly) monarch, choose to support a "spendthrift" nobleman who had "wasted" the vast bulk of his great inheritance? Why would she do so at this most perilous moment for the nation?

Oxford's grant went unnoticed by historians until two years after Looney published his work on Oxford as "Shakespeare" in 1920. Inspired to conduct further research, B.M. Ward discovered Elizabeth's signature on the Privy Seal Warrant and then looked at surviving records for all other salaries and annuities paid from the Exchequer during her reign. Aside from sums that were paid to King James VI of Scotland for political reasons, Ward found that the grant to Oxford was larger than any other except for the award to Walsingham and an annual 1,200-pound grant to the Master of the Posts for the ongoing expenses of that office.

As Ward noted, there is no hint as to the purpose of the grant except that it was "to be continued unto him during Our pleasure, or until such time as he shall be by us otherwise provided for to be in some manner relieved, at what time our pleasure is that this payment of one thousand pounds yearly to our said cousin in manner above specified shall cease."

By 1586, the thirty-six-year-old de Vere was, in fact, broke; he surely did need "to be in some manner relieved," but the circumstantial evidence clearly suggests he had been working with Walsingham (and Burghley) to serve the government's interests. The evidence points to him playing a multifaceted role behind the scenes that included, but was not limited to, the issuance of his own "comedies" for the stage. Oxford actively patronized two acting companies performing at the private Blackfriars playhouse and at the royal court. He patronized and/or employed many literary men for whom he provided working space, inspiration, guidance and freedom from the wartime suppression of written words and speech. Some of the writers in his service, such as Munday and Watson, operated as secret service agents (as did Christopher Marlowe) while using their artistic activities as public cover. Others working under his wing included Greene, Lyly and Lodge.

"The formation of the Queen's Men in 1583 should be regarded particularly in connection with the intelligence system," McMillin and McLean write in *The Queen's Men and their Plays* (1998). "The point is not that the Queen's Men were spies, but that traveling players wearing the Queen's livery would have been useful to Walsingham—perhaps for occasionally bearing messages to the right persons, more obviously for showing that the central government was attending to the nation through its licensed travelers."

With two companies on tour (except during the winter season, when they played at court), the Queen's Men performed plays that would rouse patriotic fervor and encourage unity among Protestants and Catholics in the face of the coming Spanish invasion. To call this "propaganda" would be true, but not the whole of it. Oxford had spent much of his fortune on helping to bring the European Renaissance to England—a result of his travels in 1575-1576 through France, Germany and Italy, and his employment of various artists who would create the great surge of English literature and drama in the 1580s, leading to the emergence of "Shakespeare" in the following decade.

The writers in Oxford's orbit were creating a new English language, culture and national identity; these were weapons as important as ships and guns in building up England's ability and will to withstand attack. We cannot expect, however, to find these matters written down in the Queen's Privy Seal Warrant authorizing his grant.

In the early 1660s, the Rev. John Ward, vicar of Stratford Parish in Warwickshire, recorded local rumors in his diary that "Shakespeare" had "supplied the stage with two plays every year and for that had an allowance so large that he spent at the rate of a thousand pounds a year." In fact, Oxford received his annual 1,000 pounds during the rest of the Anglo-Spanish War, from 1586 through the death of Elizabeth in 1603 and the succession of James, until his own death in 1604. That amounts to eighteen years, and, of course, two plays per year equals thirty-six, the number of works published in the First Folio of Shakespeare plays in 1623. There is no record that Will Shakspere of Stratford-upon-Avon ever received any allowance from the government or from anyone else.

It looks as though Rev. Ward had come into some accurate information about England's greatest writer, even though, by that time, the author's identity had been paved over and sealed by official history.

Reason 44 – The Tilbury Speech

Queen Elizabeth gave her famous speech to the troops at Tilbury, a village on the Thames, on 19 August 1588, when she and everyone else still believed that the Great Enterprise of Phillip II of Spain—the Armada—was about to land on English soil. A ruthless military force, convinced of God's will for it to succeed, was about to conquer England; but in this moment of terror Gloriana appeared in their midst, riding from rank to rank and smiling as the soldiers cheered, before delivering an address to be remembered for all time. (Let us allow for the possibility that the whole event at Tilbury is a fiction developed well after the event. Meanwhile we forge ahead, based on what most historians have been able to tell us.)

The speech, preserved in at least three versions, has long been studied for its rhetorical structure, simplicity and nobility, as well as for its power to inspire and motivate. It has been likened to the St. Crispin's Day speech in *Henry V*, when the king rallies his troops at Agincourt before heading into battle against overwhelming odds. (Elizabeth would have known the play in the earlier stages of its development; the likelihood is that, while she certainly inspired Oxford in both positive and negative ways, he inspired her as well.)

Oxford was with the fifty-five-year-old queen at Whitehall not long before her visit to Tilbury. The earl had been commanding his own ship the *Edward Bonaventure*, as part of the English fleet led by Lord Admiral Charles Howard, his longtime supporter and close friend, during some of the early fighting against the Armada; the *Bonaventure* had been put out of commission, however, so Oxford left the fleet and arrived on 27 July at the Tilbury camp, reporting to his long-time enemy Leicester, whom her Majesty had appointed supreme commander of the army.

The next day Leicester wrote to Walsingham that Oxford had set off to retrieve his "armor and furniture," so he wondered where on land to assign him. "I would know from you what I should do," he wrote. "I trust he be free to go to the enemy [engage in close combat], for he seems most willing to hazard his life in this quarrel."

When Oxford returned, Leicester put him in charge of 2,000 men at Harwich, a peninsula that promised little if any military action. Leicester wrote again to Walsingham on 1 August, reporting that Oxford "seemed at the first to like well of it," but then "came to me and told me he thought the place of no service or credit." We can only imagine the face-to-face confrontation between these two men, whose mutual enmity had finally erupted. Emotions were already running high; there was a very real fear that their country might be taken over by the king of Spain and the pope of Rome, and the resulting tension (along with de Vere's hatred of Leicester) may have driven him to an act of insubordination.

"Clearly Oxford's motivation was pique rather than cowardice or subversion," Nelson scolds, "but pique cannot excuse a refusal to obey a superior officer in time of war."

Rather than accept such an order from this man he viewed as a "villain, villain, smiling, damned villain," as Hamlet called his uncle, Claudius, he scoffed at it and hurried away. Oxford returned to London, exclaiming he "would to the court and understand her Majesty's further pleasure."

So Oxford went to Whitehall to be with Elizabeth, who was now within a week of making her dramatic speech to the troops at Tilbury. The historical record tells no more of de Vere until the victory procession to St. Paul's on 24 November 1588; but, if he actually met with Elizabeth as he intended, what was the substance of the meeting? How long was he with her? From what they knew at the time, the landing of Spanish troops was imminent; in this dire situation, what would they have talked about?

Did they decide that the queen needed to go to Tilbury to plead for unity and loyalty?

Elizabeth had been de Vere's legal mother from the time he became a royal ward; he had been in Her Majesty's highest favor all during the 1570s and even through his second triumph in the tiltyard, at the great tournament of 22 January 1581. That had been just a few months before his steep fall from grace when his mistress, Anne Vavasour, one of the queen's maids of honor, gave birth to his illegitimate son. Even so, he had alerted Elizabeth and Burghley to the treasonous plots of his erstwhile Catholic associates, proving yet again that his loyalty to her had never wavered.

Now, in the midst of the nation's greatest military crisis, when Elizabeth felt herself in the gravest of dangers, she and Oxford would have dropped all petty concerns and shared their old ties and feelings in the words and phrases we should expect to find from the pen of the great dramatist known as Shakespeare. Just two years before, in 1586, the earl had been cited by Webbe as "the most excellent" of poets at court; in the coming year, he will be cited in *The Arte of English Poesie* as one of the courtiers "who have written excellently well as it would appear if their doings could be found out and made public with the rest."

Elizabeth and Oxford would have understood this might be their final meeting. In these highly charged circumstances, could they avoid the subject of how to rally her troops in the face of the Spanish fury? How could Oxford fail to suggest the kind of speech she might make? No other candidate for the authorship of Shakespeare was in a position to inspire the queen to make a thrilling "Shakespearean" speech to the army!

- When Henry V in Shakespeare's play addresses his soldiers at Agincourt (4.3), he descends to their level as one of them: "We few, we happy few, we band of brothers," he says, adding, *"For he today that sheds his blood with me* shall be my brother!" (4.3)

- Elizabeth does the same, telling her troops: "I am come amongst you, as you see, at this time, not for my recreation and disport, but being resolved, in the midst and heat of the battle, *to live and die amongst you all."*

- Henry at Agincourt reminds his men of the honor they will gain: "And Crispin Crispian shall ne'er go by, from this day to the ending of the world, but *we in it shall be remembered."*

- Elizabeth at Tilbury makes a similar promise: "I myself will be your general, judge, and rewarder of every one of your virtues in the field ... I know already, for your forwardness you have deserved rewards and crowns; and We do assure you in the word of a prince, they shall be duly paid to you; [and] *we* shall shortly have a *famous* victory."

It can be no coincidence that her promise of a "famous victory" echoes the much earlier play *The Famous Victories of Henry the Fifth*, which many Oxfordians believe was written by a young de Vere, and which obviously forms the basis of *1 Henry IV, 2 Henry IV* and *Henry V* by Shakespeare. Inevitably, we should expect to find within Elizabeth's address at Tilbury some phrases to be found in the Shakespeare works:

- Elizabeth: "Let tyrants fear! I have always so behaved myself that, under God, I have placed my chiefest strength and safeguard in the loyal *hearts and goodwill* of my subjects."
- *The Comedy of Errors*: "Money by me! *Heart and goodwill* you might." (4.4)

  Elizabeth: "And think *foul scorn* that Parma or Spain, or any prince of Europe, should dare to invade the borders of my realm."
- *Henry VI (Pt. 1)*: "I owe him little duty, and less love; and take *foul scorn* to fawn on him by sending." (4.4)

- The queen's most famous statement is her ringing declaration: "I know *I have the body of a weak, feeble woman; but I have the heart and stomach of a king!*"
- In *Julius Caesar* there is Portia, wife of Brutus: "*I grant I am a woman; but,* withal, a woman well-reputed, Cato's daughter. *Think you I am no stronger than my sex …?*" (2.1)

Did the Earl of Oxford help or influence Queen Elizabeth's speech at Tilbury? A case can be made that "Shakespeare" surely did!

CHAPTER EIGHT

THE ITALIAN CONNECTION

Reason 45 – Shakespeare in Love …. With Italy

When the case for de Vere as "Shakespeare" finally gains popular acceptance, not the least reason will be the overwhelming evidence that the author (no matter who he was) had traveled in Italy and must have lived in Venice for a time. Such was the experience of twenty-five-year-old Oxford in 1575, when he was welcomed in one place after another as an illustrious dignitary from the English court—a young, high-born nobleman absorbing this land and its people and the Italian renaissance.

In fact, it was a play set in Italy that inspired Looney's search for "Shakespeare": "For several years in succession I had been called upon to go through repeated courses of reading in one particular play of Shakespeare's, namely *The Merchant of Venice*. This long continued familiarity with the contents of one play induced a peculiar sense of intimacy with the mind and disposition of its author and his outlook upon life. The personality which seemed to run through the pages of the drama I felt to be altogether out of relationship with what was taught of the reputed author and the ascertained facts of his career."

He continues:

> For example, the Stratford Shakspere was untraveled, having moved from his native place to London when a young man, and then as a successful middle-aged man of business he had returned to Stratford to attend to his lands and houses. This particular play on the contrary bespeaks a writer who knew Italy at first hand and was touched with the life and spirit of the country. Again the play suggested an author with no great respect for money and business methods, but rather one to whom material possessions would be in the nature of an encumbrance to be easily and lightly disposed of: at any rate one who was by no means of an acquisitive disposition.

Now, nearly a century later, another book, *The Shakespeare Guide to Italy* by Richard Paul Roe (2012), is finally breaking down the rigid walls of Stratfordian tradition as readers demand better explanations. Roe died in 2010 at eighty-eight, having spent the last quarter-century of his life traveling the length and breadth of Italy on what the publisher aptly describes as "a literary quest of unparalleled significance." Here is a beautiful paragraph from Roe, speaking of "Shakespeare" in relation to Venice and *The Merchant*:

> In the latter part of the sixteenth century, the gifted English playwright arrived in the beating heart of this Venetian empire: the legendary city of Venice. He moved about noting its structured society, its centuries-old government of laws, its traditions, its culture, and its disciplines. He carefully considered and investigated its engines of banking and commerce. He explored its harbors and canals, and its streets and squares. He saw the flash of its pageants, its parties and celebrations; and he looked deeply into the Venetian soul. Then, with a skill that has never been equaled, he wrote a story that has a happy ending for all its characters save one, about whom a grief endures and always will: a deathless tragedy.

If Roe's description of the dramatist's activities is at all accurate, how can the authorship continue to be attributed to William of Stratford?

When de Vere traveled through Italy during 1575, he and his retinue skirted Spanish-controlled Milan before navigating by canal and a network of rivers on a 120-mile journey to Verona. His travels took him to Padua, Venice, Mantua, Pisa, Florence, Siena, Naples, Florence, Messina, Palermo and elsewhere, with his home base in Venice.

Aside from three stage works set in ancient Rome (*Coriolanus, Titus Andronicus* and *Julius Caesar*), ten of Shakespeare's fictional plays are set in whole or in part in Italy: *Romeo and Juliet, The Two Gentlemen of Verona, The Taming of the Shrew, The Merchant of Venice, Othello, A Midsummer Night's Dream, All's Well That Ends Well, Much Ado About Nothing, The Winter's Tale* and *The Tempest* (which opens aboard a ship in the Mediterranean between North Africa and Italy).

Only one play of fiction (*The Merry Wives of Windsor*) is set in England— an astounding ten-to-one ratio! Why? The logical answer is that "Shakespeare" (whoever he was) must have fallen in love with Italy. It would be pretty hard to fall in love with a country without ever visiting it!

Oxfordians believe that de Vere "brought the European Renaissance back to England" when he returned in 1576 after fifteen months of travel through France, Germany and, most extensively, Italy. He became the quintessential "Italianate Englishman," wearing "new-fangled" clothes of the latest styles. He brought back richly embroidered, perfumed gloves for Queen Elizabeth, who delighted in them. Such gloves became all the rage among the great ladies of the time; and, for example, he brought back his perfumed leather jerkin (a close-fitting, sleeveless jacket) and "sweet bags" with costly washes and perfumes.

Soon enough Lyly, his secretary and stage manager, issued two novels about an Italian traveler: *Euphues: The Anatomy of Wit* (1578) and *Euphues and his England* (1580), the latter dedicated to de Vere, who apparently supervised the writing of both books. Together they are said to comprise "the first English novel" and in the following decade "Shakespeare" would demonstrate Lyly's influence upon his plays.

"There is a secret Italy hidden in the plays of Shakespeare," Roe begins the introduction to his groundbreaking book. "It is an ingeniously-described Italy that has neither been recognized, nor even suspected—not in four hundred years—save by a curious few. It is exact; it is detailed; and it is brilliant." The descriptions of Italy in the plays are in "challenging detail" and "nearly all their locations" can be found to this day. Whoever wrote them "had a personal interest in that country equal to the interest in his own." The places and things in Italy which Shakespeare alludes to or describes "reveal themselves to be singularly unique to that one country." His familiarity with Italy's sites and sights— "specific details, history, geography, unique cultural aspects, places and things, practices and propensities" and so on—"is, quite simply, astonishing."

Roe never mentions Oxford; instead he takes us right away to Verona, the setting for *Romeo and Juliet,* and recounts making one trip to search for ... sycamore! Roe went to find sycamore trees, which would have to be located in one specific spot, "just outside the western wall" as "remnants of a grove that had flourished in that one place for centuries." The trees are described in the very opening scene –

Where, underneath the grove of sycamore
That westward rooteth from the city's side (1.1.120-121)

There are no sycamore trees in any of the known source materials for the play; they were deliberately put in by the great author himself. So Roe, our intrepid detective-explorer, arrives in the old city of Verona: "My driver took me across the city, then to its edge on the Viale Cristoforo Colombo. Turning south onto the Viale Colonnello Galliano, he began to slow. This was the boulevard where, long before and rushing to the airport at Milan, I had glimpsed trees, but had no idea what kind." His car creeps along the *Viale* and comes to a halt. Are there sycamores at the very same spot where "Shakespeare" said they were? Did the playwright, who is said to be ignorant of Italy, know this "unnoted and unimportant but literal truth" about Verona? Had he deliberately "dropped an odd little stone about a real grove of trees into the pool of his powerful drama"?

Yes, he did!

"No one has ever thought that the English genius who wrote the play could have been telling the truth: that there were such trees, growing exactly where he said in Verona," writes Roe, whose discoveries all demonstrate Shakespeare's depth of knowledge and personal experience of Italy. They comprise yet another solid reason to conclude that Oxford was the great poet-dramatist.

Reason 46 – "Commedia dell'arte"

Scholars identify at least a dozen Shakespeare plays influenced by the Italian dramatic art form known as *Commedia dell'arte*, with its stock characters and improvised skits that were often bawdy and satiric: the list includes *Love's Labour's Lost, The Comedy of Errors, The Taming of the Shrew, Twelfth Night* and *Much Ado About Nothing*. The same scholars, however, cannot plausibly explain how "Shakespeare" became so familiar with this "comedy of art" performed by troupes of traveling players in Italy, since it was virtually unknown in England when he was supposedly writing the plays. The traditional author never set foot in Italy, while de Vere had made his home base in Venice during 1575 and 1576, when the *Commedia dell'arte* was at the peak of its popularity. Early on, supporters of Oxford's authorship predicted they would find evidence that the earl attended *Commedia dell'arte* performances in Venice during his several months there. In 1956, Julia Cooley Altrocchi discovered a "clincher" for that long-held prediction. At the Biblioteca Marciana in Venice she came upon a book called *Dell'Arte Rappresentativa Premeditata ed all'Improviso* or *Dramatic Art by Rote and Extemporaneous Performance* (1699) and subsequently reported:

> A long section is devoted to the stock character of Graziano, the talkative Bolognese "doctor" who tells long tales and never stops for breath. With little schooling and without a medical degree, he blabs endlessly, often in Latin, impressing everyone until he is always shown to be a quack. One of his famous recitals is the so-called "Tirade of the Tournament" (*Tirata della Giostra*) in which the actor rattles off the names of twenty or thirty knights and ladies, their titles and countries of origin, the color and trappings of their horses, the color and devices of their garments and shields, and the events that befell each one on the field of tourney. Even the ladies took part in this hypothetical tournament.

The book included an example of such a long and hilarious "tirade":

"I found myself ambassador of my illustrious country of Bologna at the court of the Emperor Polidor of Trebizond, and attending the great tournament celebrating his marriage to Irene, Empress of Constantinople. Present were many great worthies: Basil, King of Zelconda; Doralba, Princess of Dacia; Arcont, vaivode of Moldavia; Arileus, heir of Denmark; Isuf, Pasha of Aleppo; Fatima, Sultan of Persia; Elmond, *Milord of Oxfort...*" (Emphasis added)

Here in a book published in Naples at the end of the seventeenth century was an apparent reference to Edward de Vere, mentioned by his earldom title as "Milord of Oxfort," within the speech of a stock character in a performed skit of the *Commedia dell'arte!* Altrocchi continues:

> With his outgoing nature, his innate acting ability which would later manifest itself so impressively before the Queen, would he have consorted in friendly fashion with the finest improvisators in the world? Otherwise, why was he given a place in the Doctor's exuberant oration? Wouldn't it have been known that he was a tournament champion in 1571 in England at the young age of twenty-one? Wasn't Graziano paying him a form of personal tribute as an honored guest?

The "Doctor" in his *tirade* says that "Milord of Oxfort" rode a faun-colored horse named *Oltramarin* ("Beyond the Sea") and wore a violet-colored costume while carrying a large sword.

"In this *Tirata*," Altrocchi reported, "Milord of Oxfort, amusingly enough, tilted against Alvilda, Countess of Edemburg, who was mounted on a dapplegray, and was armed with a Frankish lance while robed in lemon color. In the end, Edward and Alvilda, alas, threw one another simultaneously off their horses, both landing face down in the dust!"

She concludes that Oxford was "well and very companionably known" at presentations of the *Commedia dell'arte* while in Venice for many weeks during 1575. He was "recognized as being a good sport as a well as a good sportsman," not to mention having "so resilient a sense of humor that he could be introduced into a skit and, with impunity, be described as meeting a woman in tilt and being un-horsed and rolled to the ground with her in the encounter!"

Oxford undoubtedly witnessed many *Commedia* performances. He may have watched this skit in which the actor playing Doctor Graziano, knowing he was in the audience, suddenly paid him a public tribute by improvising a *"tirade"* that included him by name. How fitting it was for such a compliment to be made, directly and openly, to the great playwright and comic genius who, nearly two decades later in 1593, would adopt the pen name "Shakespeare" as the author of at least a dozen plays bursting with influences from that same *Commedia dell'arte*!

In *Othello ... Annotated from an Oxfordian Perspective*, editors Ren Draya and Richard Whalen comment on the surprising evidence that even this painful tragedy is strongly influenced by *Commedia dell'arte*. They indicate, for example, how the opening of the play can be "played for laughs and probably should be"—with Iago (the scheming *Zanni* of the *Commedia* skits) and Roderigo (the witless, rejected suitor) waking up Brabantio (the foolish, old *Pantalone*) to taunt him with lewd suggestions that his daughter, Desdemona (the innocent), is having sex with Othello in a bestial way after they have eloped. A slice of raucous, obscene comedy, opening a tragic drama of jealousy and rage!

Reason 47 – Titian of Venice

> He sees her coming and begins to glow . . .
> *And with his bonnet hides his angry brow . . .*
> *For all askance he holds her in his eye . . .*
> Now was she just before him as he sat,
> And like a lowly lover down she kneels . . .
> *O what a war of looks was then between them!*
> (Venus and Adonis, 337, 339, 342, 349-350, 355 [emphasis added])

The author of *Venus and Adonis* by "William Shakespeare" in 1593 is describing a painting by Tiziano Vecellio, or Titian, in which Adonis wears a bonnet or cap. Although several copies of the Titian painting existed, the *only* one depicting a bonneted Adonis that could have been seen during Shakespeare's time *was at Titian's home in Venice*. William of Stratford never left England, but Edward de Vere had traveled throughout Italy during 1575-1576, making his home base in Venice, where Titian worked until his death on 27 August 1576.

Dr. Noemi Magri was the first to report that "Shakespeare" based his poem on the only autographed replica in which Adonis wears a bonnet or hat: "Titian's painting was his source of inspiration, the thing that stimulated him to write a poem about this subject though he also had a thorough knowledge of Ovid .... Shakespeare describes the painting in detail: he portrays the painting in words and the description is too faithful to ascribe it to mere coincidence.... It is evident that Shakespeare's Adonis is wearing a hat, a bonnet. The mention of the bonnet is not coincidental."

> With one fair hand she heaveth up his hat (351)
>
> Bonnet nor veil henceforth no creature wear (1081)
>
> And therefore would he put his bonnet on" (1087)

Princes, cardinals, ambassadors and top literary figures "never failed to pay Titian a visit" when they came to Venice, Magri notes. His home was a kind of cultural center and such notables felt they could not leave without going to see the greatest living painter of sixteenth-century Venice, the first to have a predominantly international clientele. To be received into his house was an honor that brought high prestige.

"Considering de Vere's desire for learning and his love for Italian culture, he must have felt the wish to meet him and admire his collection," writes Magri, who provides evidence to confirm that the autographed copy with Adonis wearing a hat, now held in the National Gallery of Palazzo Barberini in Rome, was in fact at Titian's house when Oxford lived in Venice. Anyone who studies even a little of the earl's life will conclude that he could not have failed to pay such a visit.

Shakespeare writes that Adonis looks at Venus "all askance," which, Magri observes, "is a faithful and precise description of Adonis's posture in the painting." Moreover, the two figures' *glances* are "the central motif of the painting" and Shakespeare "has retained the dramatic pictorial element" in his description of their eyes as in "Her eyes petitioners to his eyes suing." Also Shakespeare's reference to "this dumb play" is an accurate description: the *play* they have performed "is a *dumb* one since their words are not to be heard." The two protagonists, Venus and Adonis, "are not acting on a stage: they are painted on the canvas."

Magri even notes how Venus, reacting angrily to Adonis's resistance, bursts out a clear reference to the painted image of him:

Fie, lifeless picture, cold and senseless stone
Well-painted idol . . . (211-212)

Reason 48 – Portia's House

"In Belmont is a lady richly left; and she is fair, and, fairer than that word, of wondrous virtues: sometimes from her eyes I did receive fair speechless messages: her name is Portia"—Bassanio in *The Merchant of Venice* (1.1)

"Belmont ... the estate of Portia ... apparently located on the mainland near Venice ... a fictitious place" – Charles Boyce, *Shakespeare A to Z*, 1990

"Belmont is a real place, though called differently in Italian: its identification has been made possible by the precise geographical information and a specific historical reference given in the play."—Dr. Noemi Magri, *The De Vere Society Newsletter*, 2003; reprinted in *Great Oxford*, 2004

119

Portia's home is a grand palace where trumpets sound as each new member of the nobility is received in its richly decorated Great Hall, where musicians serenade, aristocrats dance and players perform. Shakespeare took the name "Belmont" from his main Italian source, *Il Pecorone*, a novella composed about 1380 and printed in Italian in 1558, wherein the character Gianetto travels a long distance from Venice to see the Lady of Belmont.

The Belmont in that story was a port on the Adriatic coast. To simplify things for his play, Shakespeare puts Belmont much closer to Venice; but no real place by that name actually existed (or exists) at the location he specifies or anywhere near it. As Boyce indicates, scholars have universally viewed Belmont as a fictitious place that Shakespeare created as a vivid contrast to the crass commercial world of Venice.

But the author takes great pains to precisely locate and identify Portia's estate. We learn that the mansion is on a riverbank in the scene with Lorenzo and Jessica outside the great house in the evening, gazing at the water, when Lorenzo exclaims: "How sweet the moonlight sleeps upon this bank!" (5.1). In the third act, Portia makes plans to go to Venice with Nerissa, both disguised as men (Portia will appear as a lawyer acting as judge at Antonio's trial), and then to return straightaway to Belmont. She tells Nerissa to "haste away, for we must measure twenty miles today" (3.4). So the round trip is twenty miles, ten miles to Venice and ten miles back to Belmont.

Now the author inserts another clue. To conceal her true plan, Portia tells Lorenzo and Jessica a fake story about where they're going: "There is a monastery two miles off," she says, and "there we will abide" until the trial in Venice is concluded (3.4).

Thus, we know Belmont is (a) on the bank of a river, (b) ten miles from Venice and (c) two miles from a monastery. It just so happens there was, and still is, a grand mansion on the bank of the River Brenta: the Villa Foscari La Malcontenta, the country residence of the illustrious Foscari family in Venice, exactly ten miles from Venice and precisely two miles from the monastery Ca' delle Monache, the Nun's House.

These clues from "Shakespeare" thus identify Belmont as Villa Foscari, the architectural masterpiece designed by Andrea Palladio and constructed before 1560. This grand villa on the River Brenta, with its richly decorated interior rooms and Great Hall, was known for receiving the nobility (and royalty, such as Henry III of France, in 1574) with trumpets and for entertaining guests with music, dance and plays. It was an unforgettable place the author saw firsthand, later changing its name.

"Though now the central seat of the University of Venice, the Villa-Foscari La Malcontenta can be visited today," writes Roe, who independently came to the same conclusion as Magri. "It was an easy reach to Venice and a fitting 'Belmont' for an heiress, such as Portia, whose hand was sought by princes far and wide," just as princes came from everywhere to seek the hand of Queen Elizabeth.

But the man who wrote *The Merchant* supplied even more specifics, such as when Portia sends her servant Balthasar to Padua for "notes and garments" she needs, telling him to then continue in haste "unto the *tranect*, to the common ferry which trades to Venice" (3.4), where she will be waiting with Nerissa in her coach. The two women will go from the *tranect* by ferry to Venice.

According to Roe, scholars have been wide of the mark trying to identify the *tranect*, unaware it was a narrow strip of land where boats were pulled across dry land by machine from the River Brenta to the canal to Venice.

Travelers like Portia and Nerissa could also travel by coach to the tranect, where they would board the ferry to Venice. Their rendezvous at the *tranect* "would have to have been in Fusina," Roe concludes, because it is five miles by river from Belmont to Fusina, and from there across the water it is "exactly five miles to the landing place called 'il Molo,' which sits in front of the Ducal Palace and Courts of Justice," where Antonio's trial was being held.

The ten-mile journey was in two segments of five miles each. Portia and Nerissa would return from Venice by ferrying the five miles back across the water to the *tranect* at Fusina, then travel by coach beside the River Brenta for the next five miles back to the Villa Foscari (Belmont). The round trip is the "twenty miles" that Portia states so emphatically. In other words, the great dramatist of *The Merchant* described not only the various lengths of the journey, but also the practical means by which the two women would make the trip.

Turning to the "specific historical reference" noted above in the opening quote by Dr. Magri, an event mentioned in *The Merchant* as having occurred at Belmont actually did happen at Villa Foscari. The reference is made by Nerissa, asking Portia if she remembers Bassanio's visit to Belmont: "Do you not remember, lady, in your father's time, a Venetian, a scholar and a soldier that came hither in company of the Marquis of Montferrat?" (1.2).

"Yes, yes, it was Bassanio, as I think, so he was called," Portia replies, ignoring Nerissa's recollection of the Marquis of Montferrat, who is neither one of Portia's suitors nor one of the play's characters (this is the only time he is mentioned). Traditional scholars have never found any good reason for the playwright to make such a gratuitous allusion, but Dr. Magri found the reason in the historical record of the visit to Venice in July 1574 by Henry III of France, who traveled with his party up the River Brenta and stopped at Villa Foscari, where he had been invited for dinner. Accompanying the French king on that visit was Guglielmo Gonzaga, who held the titles of Duke of Mantua and Marquis of Montferrat!

Just eight months later, in March 1575, the twenty-five-year-old earl of Oxford arrived at the royal court in Paris and met King Henry III, who was fond of expressing his admiration for Villa Foscari and its charming location. Oxford continued his journey to Italy and stopped in Mantua, where, Mark Anderson writes, the earl's "probable host" was Guglielmo Gonzaga, Marquis of Montferrat, who surely would have told Oxford about his experiences during that historic visit of the French king.

Oxford's trip from Padua to Venice by *traghetto* (horse-drawn ferry) along the River Brenta lasted seven hours. His ride passed "the classically inspired Villa Foscari," Anderson writes, "as the *traghetto* slowed down to round a wide curve on the riverbank." Magri concludes that Oxford "intended to describe Villa Foscari and had in mind the Brenta with its villas" and "wished to remember the Marquis of Montferrat, Guglielmo Gonzaga Duke of Mantua, the ruler of one of the greatest centers of learning in Renaissance times."

What does it matter who wrote the Shakespeare plays? I'd say that Belmont = Villa Foscari is one good reason.

CHAPTER NINE

THE MARLOWE ENIGMA

Reason 49 – Christopher Marlowe

We now confront the shadowy figure of Christopher Marlowe, the Cambridge student and government spy who was stabbed to death at age twenty-nine on 30 May 1593, just when the initial copies of *Venus and Adonis*, carrying the first appearance of the printed name "William Shakespeare," were on their way to the London bookstalls.

Tamburlaine the Great (in two separate parts) had drawn great crowds to the Rose playhouse from 1587 onward, but Marlowe's name never appeared on any published work during his lifetime. (As audiences seemed uninterested in who wrote the plays they attended, a common assumption that he was "the toast of the town" as a popular playwright may well be a fantasy.) Ironically, however, upon his death the "Shakespeare" name was launched—the name of a previously unknown writer whose highly cultured narrative poem was an instant bestseller. In fact, the name of Shakespeare quickly did become the toast of the town, at least among those who could buy books.

The relationship of "Marlowe" and "Shakespeare" has generated much uncertainty and perplexity among academics. Scholars and biographers have pondered and dissected the inextricable entanglement of those two famous names, and of the works attributed to them, without consensus. Campbell notes the confusion:

> Because the chronology of the composition of Marlowe's plays and those of Shakespeare is uncertain, and because of the dearth of information about Shakespeare's activities during the "seven lost years" [1586 through 1592], it is impossible to discuss with precision the literary interrelationship of these two playwrights … Whatever their personal relationship, it is demonstrable that Shakespeare knew Marlowe's plays and poetry. There are hundreds of verbal echoes and dozens of comparable scenes and situations in the works attributed to the two different men. Frequently it is difficult to guess who is echoing or borrowing from whom….

The tradition is that Will of Stratford, being the same age as Marlowe but newly arrived in London, was so inspired by *Tamburlaine*'s commanding eloquence and unrelenting violence that he began to write *Henry VI* (all three parts) and then his own blood-gushing play *Titus Andronicus*. Exactly how Shakspere found the time to write such plays while engaged in his acting career and moneylending is never explained.

Stephen Greenblatt in *Will in the World* has no trouble comprehending the miracle. He imagines—with no supporting evidence—that just when Shakspere was "finding his feet in London," he noticed the hoopla over *Tamburlaine,* which "may indeed have been one of the first performances he ever saw in a playhouse—perhaps the first." That experience "appears to have had upon him an intense, visceral, indeed life-transforming impact."

The transformation would have been from a young man who had never been inside a London playhouse to a dramatist who not only instantly surpassed Marlowe himself, but also became the greatest playwright of the English language! By 1595 he would have turned out both *Richard II* and *Richard III* and, by 1598, completed no less than twelve plays, including *Love's Labour's Lost, Romeo and Juliet, King John* and *The Merchant of Venice!*

"Shakespeare had never heard anything quite like this before," as Greenblatt imagines the *Tamburlaine* experience, "certainly not in the morality plays or mystery cycles he had watched back in Warwickshire. He must have said to himself something like, 'You are not in Stratford anymore.'" Standing among the groundlings at the Rose and staring up at Edward Alleyn as Tamburlaine, was for Will a "crucial experience" and a "challenge" that "must have been intensified when he learned that Marlowe was in effect his double: born in the same year, 1564 ...."

Let's take our own look at 1593, when *Venus and Adonis*, the sophisticated poem that the author termed "the first heir of my invention," surged to popularity among university students, aristocrats and members of the royal court including young Henry Lord Southampton, to whom it was dedicated. This blockbuster would be joined in 1594 by an even more brilliant poem, *Lucrece*, whose primary source was the story told by Ovid in his *Fasti*, a work not to be translated into English until 1640.

On 28 September 1593, the unfinished manuscript of another narrative poem, *Hero and Leander*, was entered at the Stationers' Register by John Wolf, who described it as "an amorous poem devised by Christopher Marloe." But something happened to stop Wolf from printing it. The first edition was finally published by Edward Blount in

1598, attributed to Marlowe, followed in the same year by another edition from publisher Paul Linley, advertising it as "begun by Christopher Marloe and finished by George Chapman." "Marlowe's *Hero and Leander* is the best of the Ovidian romances," Campbell writes. "It contains the most successful combination of the genre's distinctive characteristics: descriptions of natural beauty, voluptuous development of erotic situations, and an ornate style. These are also the elements of which Shakespeare composed *Venus and Adonis*."

So Marlowe and "Shakespeare" were both writing long, romantic, sensuous, erotic poems based on Ovid; they completed them at virtually the same time—in the year of Marlowe's untimely death—when "Shakespeare" forged ahead by getting his masterful "first heir" into print and taking over the poetical limelight.

Marlowe's name appeared in print for the first time in 1594, when the play *Edward II* was published as by "Chr. Marlow" and another play, *Dido, Queen of Carthage,* was published as by "Christopher Marlow and Thomas Nashe." "No play of Marlowe's is more closely related to one of Shakespeare's than is *Edward II* to *Richard II*," Campbell writes. "For decades scholars assumed that Marlowe's was the first significant English chronicle history play, and that therefore he taught Shakespeare much. Recently, however, it has been established that Shakespeare's *Henry VI* trilogy antedates *Edward II*; in other words, Shakespeare helped Marlowe; the combination of Shakespeare and Marlowe helped Shakespeare in *Richard II*." In classic understatement, he adds: "The intricacies of these interrelationships are detailed and complex."

Marlowe was one of the "University Wits" recruited from Cambridge and Oxford by the Elizabethan government during the 1580s to serve as informants or spies for its wartime intelligence service. These young men also worked as secretaries, scribes and writers under the financial support of Oxford, who provided them with writing space and materials as well as plots, themes, language and even entire works to be published anonymously or under their own or fictitious names.

"During his studies at Cambridge," Daryl Pinksen writes in *Marlowe's Ghost* (2008), "perhaps as early as 1585, Marlowe was recruited into the English secret service headed at that time by Secretary of State Sir Francis Walsingham." Records indicate a "marked increase of spending" as if he "suddenly had a new source of income" and "frequent absences from Cambridge beginning in 1585 for longer and longer periods, also consistent with work as an intelligence agent …. Lord Burghley … was also Chancellor of Cambridge, and worked closely with Walsingham in directing and funding intelligence operations. During Marlowe's years at Cambridge it is likely he made numerous trips, perhaps to the continent, at the behest of Walsingham and Burghley to spy for his country."

"In the fast-expanding arena of Elizabethan espionage, writers were an obvious source of recruits," Charles Nicholl writes in *The Reckoning* (1992). "They were intelligent, educated, observant young men. They knew the international language, Latin, and the literary tastes of the day gave them a good smattering of French and Italian." They were geographically and socially mobile, as well as continually in need of cash, so "it is perhaps not surprising that a number of Elizabethan writers crop up in the files of the intelligence services, both foreign and domestic. They are remembered as poets,

Fig. 10 – A portrait "presmumed" to be Christopher Marlowe

pamphleteers and playwrights, but down there in the reality of their lives they had to profess other skills if they were to survive."

Nicholl mentions writers such as Munday and Lyly, both working from the late 1570s as de Vere's secretaries, and devotes a chapter to "another poet glimpsed in the secret world of the 1580s ... an elusive and engaging figure"—Thomas Watson, who was "a close friend of Marlowe," Lyly and others. Watson is one of many "intermediaries" linking Oxford and Marlowe by just one degree of separation, making it highly likely that de Vere and Marlowe not only knew each other, but worked together on plays such as *Tamburlaine the Great* and on poems such as *Hero and Leander*. But it would not have been an equal relationship; Oxford, fourteen years Marlowe's senior, would have been guiding the younger man.

In 1564, the year of Marlowe's birth, Oxford was already receiving his honorary degree from Cambridge; in 1575, when Marlowe turned eleven, Oxford was twenty-five and spending a year in Italy; and in 1581, when Marlowe entered Cambridge at seventeen, Oxford, at thirty-one, was recruiting young disciples who, during wartime, would help achieve the great renaissance of English literature and drama leading up to "Shakespeare" in the 1590s. The truth about Marlowe becomes clear within the context of this crucial chapter of England's history in which he appears; it begins with Oxford's pivotal role at the center of those young writers who helped create a new language—a new cultural and national identity, leading to a strong sense of English pride and patriotic fervor.

The intention of King Philip's Armada was to not only conquer the island nation, but also to crush the humanistic spirit of the Renaissance in England and overturn the Protestant Reformation. If any single aspect of English life created the immediate, fertile ground from which "Shakespeare" sprang, it was this prolonged expectation of invasion. Once the Anglo-Spanish war became official in 1584, the arrival of enemy ships loomed ever closer; during the next four years, Burghley and Walsingham were determined to employ "the media"—books, pamphlets, ballads, speeches and plays (especially plays of royal history) that promoted unity in the face of internal religious and political conflicts, which threatened to render England too weak to survive.

The phenomenon of "Shakespeare" involves not only the solitary figure of de Vere; it involves an array of others who wrote for him or with him or who lent their names to creations that were entirely his, all contributing to a body of work by Oxford that is much larger than the one "Shakespeare" has been allowed to claim. His labors include a vast body of translation as well as original poetry, prose, plays, dramatic literature, song lyrics, musical compositions and political tracts, presented anonymously or under names of real persons living or dead, not to mention fictitious persons whose "biographies" are skimpy and tentative at best.

Marlowe fits into this picture as one of Oxford's satellite figures who may (or may not) have contributed his own labors to anonymous works such as *Tamburlaine*. (All works later attributed to Marlowe were either unpublished or published anonymously during his brief lifetime.) *Tamburlaine* may have been written earlier by a younger Oxford, who could have given it to Marlowe (age twenty-three in 1587) to work on. Performed on the public stage before the Armada sailed in 1588, its speeches roused audiences to a fever pitch; the character of Tamburlaine, according to Frederick Boas, seemed to Englishmen to embody Philip of Spain himself. He is a tyrant calling himself master of the lands and seas, confident he will conquer "all the ocean by the British shore" and that "by this means, I'll win the world at last!"

Such arrogant confidence and raging, bloodthirsty ambition might well have served to alarm Englishmen over the danger they faced and to further motivate them to join together to defeat the Armada.

Burghley wrote on 21 June 1586 to Walsingham, asking if he had spoken with the queen in support of de Vere. Five days later Her Majesty signed a Privy Seal Warrant authorizing an annual grant to Oxford of 1,000 pounds, an extraordinary figure, especially since England was at war with Spain and desperately needed funds. The grant, to be paid in quarterly installments, expressly stated the earl was not to be called on by the Exchequer to render any account as to its expenditure—a clause which, Ward writes, was "the usual formula made use of in the case of secret service money." (See Reason 43.)

Oxford was playing an important but unpublicized role for Elizabeth, Burghley and Walsingham during these dangerous times. The earl had made extensive sales of land between 1580 and 1585, indicating he had been personally financing writers and play companies, so now the otherwise frugal queen was compensating him for past, as well as future, expenses. In 1585, upon the outbreak of war with Spain in the Netherlands, annual payments to Walsingham rose to 2,000 pounds; it is "at this stage of increased funding and activity," Nicholl writes, "that Marlowe enters the lower ranks of the intelligence world."

Clark notes that the writers known as the University Wits went into high gear during 1586 and 1587. "Play after play flowed from their pens. These were chronicle plays, revenge plays, Senecan plays—mostly plays calculated to keep people at a high pitch of excitement during wartime. Gathering this group of writers together, directing their work, and producing their plays on the stage was the function of the secret service office that Lord Oxford filled and upon which he spent the money that had been granted to him.... In order to keep a heavy program going, he [and Burghley] appealed to recent graduates of Oxford and Cambridge, and even to those on the point of graduation, who gave promise of dramatic ability, to assist in this important work of stage propaganda."

"Lord Oxford, as a prolific writer and scholar, an eclectic, devotee of the theatre, generous patron of literary men and musicians, drew into his orbit the best writers and wits of the day," the Ogburns write. "He was the center and prime inspiration of the University Wits: such men as Lyly, Watson, Kyd and Munday—all of whom he employed—as well as Greene, Peele, Marston, Dekker, Lodge, Nashe and Marlowe. Somewhat older than most of them, infinitely greater than any, he attracted these intellectuals as a magnet attracts steel chips; ... he supported, encouraged, and directed these men, broadening their classics-bound culture through his knowledge of Italian, German, and French literature, as well as of feudal customs and the ways of court-life, while devoting his abundant creative energies to the production of dramas which not only entertained and stimulated the elect but also delighted and edified the intelligent though unschooled."

Oxford had purchased the London mansion known as Fisher's Folly to provide writing space for the younger men, who apparently had been turning out anti-Spanish plays for at least several months before the queen authorized the earl's annual grant. On 20 July 1586 the Venetian ambassador in Spain, Hieronimo Lippomano, wrote to the Doge and Senate that King Philip had been furious over reports about plays being performed at the Elizabethan court: "But what has enraged him more than all else, and has caused him to show a resentment such as he has never displayed in all his life, is the account of the masquerades and comedies which the Queen of England orders to be acted at his expense."

During the second half of 1586, after Walsingham had foiled the Babington Plot to put captive Mary, Queen of Scots on the English throne, Oxford sat on the tribunal at her trial, when she was found guilty of treason. Mary Stuart, mother of twenty-year-old James VI of Scotland, was beheaded on 8 February 1587 at Fortheringhay Castle. Her execution virtually ensured that Philip, with the blessings of the Pope, would soon launch his Armada against England.

On 29 June 1587 the Privy Council sent orders (signed by Burghley and Archbishop Whitgift) to Cambridge authorities that Marlowe should receive his Master's degree, despite frequent absences from the campus amid rumors he was a Catholic traitor—which is what he seems to have pretended to be, as part of secret service work, during visits to the English College at Rheims in Northern France, a key seminary for Catholic defectors. The Council certified that Marlowe had "behaved himself orderly and discreetly whereby he had done her Majesty good service, and deserved to be rewarded for his faithful dealings ... because it was not her Majesty's pleasure that anyone employed as he had been in matters touching the benefit of his Country should be defamed by those that are ignorant in the affairs he went about."

In a letter to Burghley on 2 October 1587, Marlowe was named as a courier in dispatches to Walsingham from Utrecht in Holland, indicating that after leaving Cambridge, his travels for intelligence work were continuing apace. The evidence makes it seem likely that Oxford was giving Marlowe a "cover" in London, according to the needs of Burghley and Walsingham, by taking him under his wing. To what degree Marlowe actually wrote the works for which he is credited is a matter of conjecture; some Oxfordians believe that Oxford wrote all of them.

"Shakespeare" was forged out of the fires of wartime. Because of stage works written or promoted by de Vere, young men from different parts of the country, Protestants and Catholics alike, speaking different dialects that often needed interpretation, descended upon London in the summer of 1588 and volunteered to join together in the face of a common enemy. (That kind of "public relations" effort to foster national unity would be used in the twentieth century by the U.S. government, whose media operations during World War II became a workshop for writers, photographers and filmmakers, enabling them to sharpen their skills.)

England's defeat of the Spanish Armada was, perhaps inevitably, followed by a shameful episode that might be called a "bloodbath" of those same writers. Having utilized their services to help England survive, the authorities no longer had the same need of them and became afraid of their freedom to express themselves and of their power to influence the public. After defeating the enemy without, the government focused on enemies within.

After England destroyed the Armada in the summer of 1588, Oxford played a prominent role in the celebratory procession to St. Paul's Cathedral on 24 November. An observer reported in *A Joyful Ballad of the Royal Entrance of Queen Elizabeth into the City of London*:

> The noble Earl of Oxford then High Chamberlain of England
> Rode right before Her Majesty his bonnet in his hand...
> And afterwards unto Paul's cross she did directly pass,
> There by the Bishop of Salisbury a sermon preached was;
> The Earl of Oxford opening then the windows for her Grace,
> The Children of the Hospital she saw before her face....

This triumphant appearance seemed to mark the end of Oxford's public life. He soon disappeared from court and public view, retiring to the countryside after selling Vere House and Fisher's Folly. His wife, Anne Cecil, had died in June of 1588 and her father, Burghley, as Master of the Court of Wards, instituted procedures against him in early 1589 for debts dating back at least two decades and amounting to a staggering 22,000 pounds, rendering his annuity of a thousand pounds virtually useless.

Oxford had been the central sun around which the writers revolved, so when he could no longer finance their labors they began to fly out of orbit. The result, directly or indirectly, was the loss of nearly all of them within a span of some five years. (See Reason 33.)

The earl's company of child actors, known as Paul's Boys and/or Oxford's Boys, was forced by the government to dissolve in 1590; soon after, writes Clark, "the loud complaints of members of the group are heard; one member dies in poverty; another fails to receive promised preferment; another is killed in a tavern brawl; and others drag on in miserable existence. The goose that laid the Golden Eggs was dead."

Outcries from the writers took various forms that only certain members of the royal court and the aristocracy might have understood. Nashe, in his 1589 preface to Greene's prose work *Menaphon*, entitled "To The Gentlemen Students of Both Universities," referred to an "English Seneca" who had been forced to "die to our stage," that is, to abandon his commitment to theatre: "Yet English Seneca read by candlelight yields many good sentences, as 'Blood is a beggar,' and so forth; and if you entreat him fair in a frosty morning, he will afford you whole Hamlets, I should say handfuls, of tragical speeches. But oh grief! *Tempus edax rerum:* ["Time, the consumer of all things"] what's that will last always? The sea exhaled by drops will in continuance be dry, and Seneca, let blood line by line and page by page, at length must needs die to our stage."

The death of Walsingham in April 1590 sent the world of English espionage into a tailspin, with factions competing for prominence. The strongest was controlled by the father-son team of William and Robert Cecil, the latter determined to gain power over all intelligence-gathering apparatus and, too, over the public stage with its playwrights, play companies and playhouses. Upon the secretary's death some of his spy network fell into the hands of his cousin Thomas Walsingham, who began to lead a kind of rogue operation. Watson and Marlowe both entered into his patronage and Marlowe continued to travel abroad. Nicholl reports that Marlowe was lodging in January 1592 with two other English spies in Flushing, a Dutch seaport town ceded to England in return for support against Spanish invaders. He was arrested as a counterfeiter and deported, a bizarre episode that ended with him returning home as a prisoner to face Burghley in private and answer his questions. Might it be reasonable to ask how Marlowe found time to write? It appears that whatever his literary and dramatic contributions may have been, they had ceased when Oxford gave up Fisher's Folly in 1589 and could no longer support the University Wits. Ogburn Jr. agrees that it was Oxford who had discovered Marlowe's dramatic ability and brought out *Tamburlaine* in 1587, to teach the people what might be expected of a ruthless conqueror like Philip; and later, for publication, he had put Marlowe's name on it.

"The relationship between the two playwrights [Oxford and Marlowe] at this time may be taken to account for the similarities in Shakespeare's early historical dramas to *Edward the Second*, printed in 1594 as Marlowe's," Ogburn also suggests. "The supposition would be that the play was an early one of Oxford's that the earl turned over in draft to Marlowe to make what he would of it."

Dorothy Ogburn writes of "evidence that *Edward II* is a direct forerunner of *Henry IV* and of *Richard II* and is by the same hand, created out of the same consciousness: it is not plagiarized from someone else. There are innumerable correspondences between *Edward II* and these dramas, not only in locutions, imagery and mannerisms, but also in point of view."

On 18 April 1593, the highly cultured and sophisticated narrative poem *Venus and Adonis* was entered at the Stationers' Register in London, without an author's name. On 30 May Marlowe was killed in the company of three other spies. Among them was the most important government agent, Robert Poley, now working for Burghley and Robert Cecil, the latter determined to prevent nobles such as Oxford, Essex and Southampton from choosing a successor to Elizabeth, who was now in her sixtieth year. The only way Cecil could hope to retain power behind the throne beyond the reign of Elizabeth was to become the kingmaker himself.

It appears Cecil had viewed Marlowe as knowing too many secrets to be trusted and as too dangerous to remain alive. By June 1593, virtually at the time of Marlowe's death, *Venus and Adonis* went on sale. No author's name appeared on the title page, but the printed signature beneath the dedication to Southampton carried, for the first time, the name of an otherwise unknown author—William Shakespeare—evoking the image of a warrior-poet shaking the spear of his pen. Oxford had returned.

CHAPTER TEN

OXFORD & ELIZABETH

Reason 50 – Oxford in the Plays

This reason focuses on the author's pervasive presence in the plays. That does not "prove" that Oxford wrote them, but it does add to the overwhelming evidence that he did. A continued gaze through an Oxfordian lens brings a completely different picture into focus, one that feels like truth.

Fig. 11 - Edward de Vere, 17th Earl of Oxford

In a debate in New York City a Stratfordian opponent complained that I was trying to "take away" his personal conception of Hamlet by suggesting the prince is a mirror reflection of Oxford. I replied that knowing who created Hamlet can only enhance our appreciation in every way and certainly can't detract from it!

Of course the character of Hamlet is not strictly auto-biographical. But the author did use various pieces of his own nature and life experiences, then grafted them onto various outside elements including classical sources, some of which served as templates. The mirror image is not literal; after mixing all the elements, he breathed life into a new creature of his imagination. It's no wonder Hamlet seems to be as alive, perhaps more so, as anyone in real life.

Aspects of Oxford's personality and life are depicted in play after play by characters who reveal themselves as creations of the artist. In some cases he splits himself into two separate characters embodying opposite sides of his own nature, such as Valentine and Proteus in *The Two Gentlemen of Verona*. Valentine is virtuous and endowed with noble qualities; Proteus is viewed as "perjured, false and disloyal," according to Silvia, a character who represents Queen Elizabeth. In fact the queen held both views of Oxford, who, as a truth-teller, freely expresses the better and worse sides of himself. Another such splitting can be seen in his portraits in *Measure for Measure* of the noble and kind Duke versus the less than virtuous Angelo. In *As You Like It* we can see Oxford expressing the melancholy side of his nature through Jaques, while Touchstone, the former courtier, is the poet who plays the fool with a scathing wit as well as a profound wisdom: "When a man's verses cannot be understood, nor a man's good wit seconded with the forward child Understanding, it strikes a man more dead than a great reckoning in a little room." (3.3)

Here's a partial list of characters that seem, in various ways, to closely reflect Edward de Vere:

Angelo	*Measure for Measure*
Antonio	*The Merchant of Venice*
Benedick	*Much Ado About Nothing*
Berowne	*Love's Labours Lost*
Bertram	*All's Well That Ends Well*
Duke	*Measure for Measure*
Philip the Bastard	*King John*
Fenton	*The Merry Wives of Windsor*
Feste the Clown	*Twelfth Night*
Hamlet	*Hamlet*
Jaques	*As You Like It*
King Lear	*King Lear*
Othello	*Othello*
Pericles	*Pericles*
Posthumous	*Cymbeline*
Prospero	*The Tempest*
Proteus	*The Two Gentlemen of Verona*
Romeo	*Romeo and Juliet*
Timon	*Timon of Athens*
Touchstone	*As You Like It*
Troilus	*Troilus and Cressida*
Valentine	*The Two Gentlemen of Verona*

Philip the Bastard (Faulconbridge) in *King John* offers a fascinating view of de Vere as a high-spirited young courtier, full of merry mischief and zeal for military combat and glory. Although *King John* is classified as a history play, Philip is the author's own creation. Oxford, who had been called a bastard by his own half-sister when he was thirteen, would have relished the chance to let his Bastard dominate the play and even conclude it with nationalistic gusto:

> This England never did, nor never shall,
> Lie at the proud foot of a conqueror,
> But when it first did help to wound itself.
> Now these her princes are come home again,
> Come the three corners of the world in arms,
> And we shall shock them. Nought shall make us rue,
> If England to itself do rest but true. (5.7)

The word "true" is often a tipoff that Oxford, whose motto was *Nothing Truer than Truth*, is representing some aspect of himself through a character. "But I hope truth is subject to no prescription," he wrote to Robert Cecil, "for truth is truth, though never so old." Consider, for example, this speech by Troilus:

> True swains in love shall in the world to come
> Approve their truths by Troilus: when their rhymes,
> Full of protest, of oath and big compare,
> Want similes, truth tired with iteration,
> As true as steel, as plantage to the moon,
> As sun to day, as turtle to her mate,
> As iron to adamant, as earth to the center,
> Yet, after all comparisons of truth,
> As truth's authentic author to be cited,
> "As true as Troilus" shall crown up the verse,
> And sanctify the numbers. (3.2)

Bringing stage works to the royal court, Oxford played the jester from behind the scenes. Olivia (Elizabeth) in *Twelfth Night* calls Feste (Oxford) a clown or "fool" who is "allowed" (i.e., specifically permitted) to run off at the mouth and make sport of others: "There is no slander in an allowed fool, though he do nothing but rail" (1.5)—the queen's personal playwright can scold or rant all he wants. So long as she shields him with royal protection, no one dares to accuse him of slander. Imagine the ticket she gave him to use his powers, as a master of hilarious, merciless satire and truth-telling, to aim at those who deserved the roast!

In any case, a few characters resembling aspects of de Vere might be deemed a coincidence, but the sheer quantity of them indicates that much more is at work.

Reason 51 – Elizabeth in the Plays

What are the chances of the Stratford man Shakspere creating allegorical portraits of Elizabeth I of England? What are the chances he

135

dared to depict this vain female ruler, an absolute monarch intensely protective of her public image, in accurate and often harshly negative detail? And if he had dared to be so bold, how could he have gotten away with it?

De Vere had known Her Majesty from at least 1561, when he was eleven and she was twenty-eight. The following year she became his legal mother. He reached his majority in 1571, entering the House of Lords, and quickly gained her highest favor at court. He had a front-row seat for one of the most sensational tragic-comedies in world history, the Golden Age of Elizabeth.

Fig. 12 - Queen Elizabeth (Armada Portrait, 1588)

As Oxford was also a poet and dramatist, what are the chances of him creating allegorical portraits of the great Virgin Queen? Scholars of the traditional "Shakespeare" have fleetingly glimpsed such portraits of Elizabeth in the plays, but for them the full picture remains out of focus. Viewing the plays with the wrong author in mind, the images are blurry; on the other hand, knowledge of the true author creates a new lens through which vital aspects of the works emerge as wondrously clear. Much of what was obscure becomes obvious; through that new lens, the Shakespeare plays contain quite a few female characters that appear to reflect Elizabeth.

Once Oxford is viewed as the author, it appears he was actually obsessed with his sovereign Mistress and was constantly grappling with the extremes of her personality. Here are eight of his female characters that appear to represent her:

Cleopatra ....*Antony and Cleopatra*
Cressida ....*Troilus and Cressida*
Gertrude ....*Hamlet*
Olivia ....*Twelfth Night*
Portia ....*The Merchant of Venice*
Rosalind ....*Romeo and Juliet*
Silvia ....*The Two Gentlemen of Verona*
Titania ....*A Midsummer Night's Dream.*

Titania, Queen of the Fairies, is the character most often cited in connection with Elizabeth, mainly because Oberon describes Cupid's attempt to ensnare "a fair vestal throned by the west" (2.1). Many other aspects of Titania reflect Elizabeth, but the point of this "reason" is *the sheer quantity* of such female characters. Taken together they reveal many sides of that extraordinary woman who ruled England for four and a half decades; some of the portraits could have been drawn only by an artist who had experienced those aspects of the queen "up close and personal." For an accurate view of *A Midsummer Night's Dream*, the biographical and historical framework of the earliest versions must be moved back in time from the mid-1590s to the early 1580s. In that perspective, it's possible to see the love affair between Queen Titania and Bottom as depicting the courtship of Queen Elizabeth and the Duke of Alençon.

Other instances where Queen Elizabeth is being depicted include:

In *Twelfth Night*, the portrait of Elizabeth as Olivia stands beside Malvolio as a caricature of Sir Christopher Hatton, Captain of the Queen's Bodyguard.

Elizabeth banished Oxford from court after discovering his affair with Anne Vavasour, who gave birth to his illegitimate child, Edward Vere; we can hear, in *The Two Gentlemen of Verona*, Oxford speaking of his queen as Silvia in Valentine's words:

> And why not death rather than living torment?
> To die is to be banish'd from myself;
> And Silvia is myself: banish'd from her
> Is self from self: a deadly banishment! (3.1)

The vows of constancy made by Troilus to Cressida reflect those Oxford had to make to the queen when his court banishment ended in 1583 and old Roger Manners reported, "The Earl of Oxford came into [the queen's] presence, and after some bitter words and speeches, in the end all sins are forgiven."

To the Elizabethans it would have been obvious that "Shakespeare" modeled Cleopatra on Queen Elizabeth, who sometimes appeared to be modeling herself on the Queen of Egypt.

In the Shakespeare poems and sonnets are more aspects of Elizabeth through the Oxfordian lens. She was the Queen of Love and Beauty, like Venus; she was the "chaste" queen, like Lucrece; she was the Phoenix; and, in my view, the Dark Lady of *The Sonnets*.

Venus ....*Venus and Adonis*
Lucrece ....*Lucrece* (a.k.a. *The Rape of Lucrece*)
Phoenix ....*The Phoenix and the Turtle*
Dark Lady ....*The Sonnets*
Woman ....*A Lover's Complaint*

CHAPTER ELEVEN

THE SONNETS

Reason 52 – Oxford in the Sonnets

Edward de Vere was in the best position of anyone in England to be the author of the sequence of 154 consecutively numbered sonnets published in 1609 as *Shake-speares Sonnets*. The known facts about Oxford's childhood, upbringing, education, and family all interconnect with the sonnets' language and imagery. Oxford was nephew to Henry Howard, Earl of Surrey (1517-1547), who, with Sir Thomas Wyatt, wrote the first English sonnets in the form to be used later by Shakespeare. Oxford himself wrote an early sonnet in that form; entitled *Love Thy Choice*, it expressed his devotion to Queen Elizabeth with the same themes of "constancy" and "truth" that "Shakespeare" would express in the same words:

> *In constant truth to bide so firm and sure* – Oxford's sonnet to Queen Elizabeth
> *Oaths of thy love, thy truth, thy constancy* – Sonnet 152 to the "Dark Lady"

The Shakespeare sonnets are plainly autobiographical, the author using the personal pronoun "I" to refer to himself, telling his own story in his own voice; so it's only natural that he expresses himself with references to the life he experienced since childhood. Much of that experience is captured in Sonnet 91:

> Some glory in their birth, some in their skill,
> Some in their wealth, some in their body's force,
> Some in their garments, though new-fangled ill,
> Some in their Hawks and Hounds, some in their Horse

Oxford was born into England's highest-ranking earldom, inheriting vast wealth in the form of many estates. He was a skilled horseman and champion of two great jousting tournaments at the Whitehall tiltyard. He was the "Italianate Englishman" who wore new-fangled clothing from the Continent. An expert falconer, he wrote poetry comparing women to hawks "that fly from man to man."

And every humor hath his adjunct pleasure,
Wherein it finds a joy above the rest,
But these particulars are not my measure,
All these I better in one general best.
Thy love is better than high birth to me,

Only someone who was of high birth, and was willing to give it up, could make such a declaration to another nobleman of high birth and make it meaningful; if written to Southampton by a man who was not high-born, the statement would be an insulting joke.

Richer than wealth, prouder than garments' cost,
Of more delight than Hawks or Horses be,
And having thee, of all men's pride I boast.
Wretched in this alone, that thou mayst take
All this away, and me most wretched make.

Oxford also left his footprints throughout:

Sonnet 2: *"When forty winters shall besiege thy brow"*
He was forty in 1590, when most commentators believe the opening sonnets were written.

Sonnet 8: *"Music to hear, why hear'st thou music sadly"*
He was an accomplished musician, writing for the lute, and patronized the composer John Farmer, who dedicated two songbooks to him, praising his musical knowledge and skill.

Sonnet 14: *"And yet methinks I have astronomy"*
He was well acquainted with the "astronomy," or astrology, of Dr. John Dee and was praised for his knowledge of the subject.

Sonnet 23: *"As an imperfect actor on the stage"*
He patronized two acting companies, performed in "enterludes" at court and was well known for his "comedies" or stage plays.

Sonnet 33: *"Gilding pale streams with heavenly alchemy"*
He studied with Dee, who experimented with alchemy, and both men invested in the Frobisher voyages.

Sonnet 49: *"To guard the lawful reasons on thy part"*
He studied law at Gray's Inn and served as a judge at the treason trials of Norfolk and Mary Stuart and later at the treason trial of Essex and Southampton; his personal letters are filled with intimate knowledge of the law.

Sonnet 59: *"O that record could with a backward look,*

Even of five hundred courses of the Sunne"
His earldom extended back 500 years to the time of William the Conqueror.

Sonnet 72: *"My name be buried where my body is"*
In his early poetry he wrote, "The only loss of my good name is of these griefs the ground."

Sonnet 89: *"Speak of my lameness, and I straight will halt"*
He was lamed by a sword during a street fight in 1582.

 Sonnet 96: *"As on the finger of a a throned Queen,*
The basest Jewel will be well esteemed"
He gave the queen "a fair jewel of gold" with diamonds in 1580.

Sonnet 98: *"Of different flowers in odor and in hue"*
He was raised amid the great gardens of William Cecil, who imported flowers never seen in England, something that accounts for Shakespeare's vast knowledge of plants.

Sonnet 107: *"And thou in this shalt find thy monument"*
He wrote to Thomas Bedingfield in 1573 that "I shall erect you such a monument. . ."

Sonnet 109: *"My self bring water for my stain"*
He was "water-bearer to the monarch" at the coronation of James on 25 July 1603, in his capacity as Lord Great Chamberlain.

Sonnet 111: *"Potions of Eisel 'gainst my strong infection"*
His surgeon was Dr. George Baker, who dedicated three books to the earl or his wife.

Sonnet 114: *"And to his palate doth prepare the cup"*
His ceremonial role as Lord Great Chamberlain included bringing the "tasting cup" to the monarch.

Sonnet 116: *"O no, it is an **ever**-fixed mark*
*That looks on tempests and is **never** shaken . . . /*
If this be error and upon me proved, /
*I **never** writ nor no man **ever** loved"*
He wrote: "Who was the first that gave the wound whose fear I wear for**ever**? **Vere**." (Emphases added)

Sonnet 121: *"No, I am that I am..."*
He wrote to Burghley using the same words in the same tone (the words of God to Moses in the Bible) to protest his spying on him.

Sonnet 125: *"Were't aught to me I bore the canopy"*
He was reported to have been one of six nobles bearing a "golden canopy" over the queen in the procession on 24 November 1588 celebrating England's recent victory over the Spanish Armada. (But Sonnet 125, I believe, refers to the canopy held over Elizabeth's effigy and coffin in the funeral procession on 28 April 1603.)

Sonnet 128: *"Upon that blessed wood whose motion sounds"*
He was an intimate favorite of the queen, who frequently played music on the virginals.

Sonnet 153: *"I sick withal the help of bath desired"*
He accompanied Elizabeth and her court during her three-day visit in August 1574 to the City of Bath, her only royal visit to that city; and "Shakespeare" is said to write about this visit in the so-called Bath Sonnets 153-154.

The Sonnets of Shakespeare amount to the autobiographical diary of de Vere. The allusions to his life as a high-born nobleman and courtier, appearing throughout the sequence, come forth naturally and spontaneously. In effect, he left his signature for all to see.

Reason 53 – Oxford and Southampton

One of the most compelling reasons to believe de Vere was "Shakespeare" is the central role in the Shakespeare story played by Henry Wriothesley, third earl of Southampton. The grand entrance of "William Shakespeare" onto the published page took place in 1593, as the printed signature on the dedication to Southampton of *Venus and Adonis,* a 1200-line poem that the poet called "the first heir of my invention" in his dedication. The second appearance of "William Shakespeare" in print came a year later, with the publication of an 1800-line poem, *Lucrece*, again dedicated to Southampton. The *Lucrece* dedication was an extraordinary declaration of personal commitment to the twenty-year-old earl: "The love I dedicate to your Lordship is without end .... What I have done is yours, what I have to do is yours, being part in all I have, devoted yours ... Your Lordship's in all duty, William Shakespeare." "There is no other dedication like this in Elizabethan literature," Nichol Smith wrote in 1916, and because the great author never dedicated another work to anyone else, he uniquely linked himself to Southampton for all time. Most scholars agree that the "Fair Youth" of *Shake-speares Sonnets*, the sequence of 154 consecutively numbered poems printed in 1609, is also the Earl of

Southampton, even though he is not identified by name. Most further agree that, in the first seventeen sonnets, the poet is urging Southampton to beget a child to continue his bloodline—demanding it in a way that would ordinarily have been highly offensive: "Make thee another self, for love of me." The trouble is that there's not a scrap of evidence that Shakspere and Henry Wriothesley ever met each other, much less that they might have had any kind of personal relationship allowing the author to command a high-ranking peer of the realm to "make thee another self, for love of me"!

"It is certain that the Earl of Southampton and the poet we know as Shakespeare were on intimate terms," Ogburn Jr. writes, "but Charlotte G. Stopes, Southampton's pioneer biographer (1922), spent seven years or more combing the records of the Earl and his family without turning up a single indication that the fashionable young lord had ever had any contact with a Shakespeare, and for that reason deemed the great work of her life a failure." "Oxford was a nobleman of the same high rank as Southampton and just a generation older," Looney writes, adding that "the peculiar circumstances of the youth to whom the Sonnets were addressed were strikingly analogous to his own."

> De Vere became the first royal ward of Elizabeth in 1562, under the guardianship of William Cecil, and in 1571 he entered into an arranged marriage with the chief minister's fifteen-year-old daughter, Anne Cecil.
>
> Henry Wriothesley became the eighth and last child of state as a boy in 1581-82, also in the chief minister's custody, and during 1590-91 he resisted intense pressure to enter into an arranged marriage with Cecil's fifteen-year-old granddaughter, Elizabeth Vere.

The young lady was also Oxford's daughter, making the elder earl, in fact, the prospective father-in-law. Scholars generally agree that in the seventeen "procreation" sonnets Shakespeare's tone sounds much like that of a prospective father-in-law or father urging Southampton to accept Burghley's choice of a wife for him, although the poet never identifies or describes any specific young woman. J. Dover Wilson writes in 1964: "What man in the whole world, except a father or a potential father-in-law, cares whether any other man gets married?" Obviously, de Vere and Wriothesley both had an extremely important personal stake in the outcome of this marriage proposal coming from the most powerful man in England, who must have had the full blessing of his sovereign Mistress.

Looney noted that both Oxford and Southampton "had been left orphans and royal wards at an early age, both had been brought up under the same guardian, both had the same kind of literary tastes and interests, and later the young man followed exactly the same course as the elder as a patron of literature and drama." The separate entries for Oxford and Southampton in the *Dictionary of National Biography*, written before the twentieth century, revealed that "in many of its leading features the life of the younger man is a reproduction of the life of the elder," Looney noted, adding it was "difficult to resist the feeling that Wriothesley had made a hero of De Vere, and had attempted to model his life on that of his predecessor as royal ward."

By the time Southampton came to court at age sixteen or seventeen, Oxford had removed himself from active attendance. It seems that the two shared some kind of hidden story that tied them together:

- As royal wards, both Oxford and Southampton had Queen Elizabeth as their official mother. Even though their respective biological mothers were alive when their fathers died, under English law they became wards of the state, and the queen became their mother in a legal sense.
- Tradition has it that Shakespeare wrote *Love's Labour's Lost* in the early 1590s for Southampton to entertain college friends at his country house, but given the sophisticated wordplay of this court comedy and its intended aristocratic audience, it is difficult to see how Will of Stratford could have written it.
- Oxford in the early 1590s was Southampton's prospective father-in-law.
- After the failed Essex Rebellion in February 1601, Oxford sat as highest-ranking earl on the tribunal for the treason trial of Essex and Southampton.
- The peers had no choice but to render a unanimous guilty verdict; there is evidence that Oxford then worked behind the scenes to save Southampton's life and gain his eventual liberation, as in Sonnet 35: "Thy adverse party is thy Advocate."
- On the night of Oxford's reported death on 24 June 1604, agents of the Crown arrested Southampton and returned him to the Tower, where he was interrogated all night until his release the following day.
- Henry Wriothesley and Henry de Vere, eighteenth Earl of Oxford (born in February 1593 to Oxford and his second wife, Elizabeth Trentham) became close friends during the reign of James; the earls were known as the "Two Henries." As members of the House of Lords, they often took sides against the king and were imprisoned for doing so.

On the eve of the failed rebellion led by Essex and Southampton in 1601, some of the conspirators engaged the Lord Chamberlain's Company to perform Shakespeare's royal history play *Richard II* at the Globe; many historians assume, perhaps correctly, that Southampton himself secured permission from "Shakespeare" to use the play with its scene of the deposing of the king. On the other hand, it is possible that Robert Cecil himself arranged for it, so he could then summon Essex to court and trigger the rebellion, which had actually been scheduled for a week later. Once the rebellion failed and Southampton was imprisoned in the Tower on the night of 8 February 1601, all authorized printings of heretofore unpublished Shakespeare plays abruptly ceased for several years.

After Southampton was released on 10 April 1603, the poet "Shake-speare" wrote Sonnet 107 celebrating his liberation after being "supposed as forfeit to a confined doom," that is, subjected to a sentence of life imprisonment. When Oxford reportedly died on 24 June 1604, a complete text of *Hamlet* was published.

As part of Christmas and New Year's celebrations surrounding the wedding of Philip Herbert, Earl of Montgomery and Oxford's daughter Susan Vere in December of 1604, the Court of King James held a veritable Shakespeare festival. In the days before and after the wedding, seven performances of the Bard's plays were given. (The royal performances appear to be a memorial tribute to the playwright, rather than a tribute to a living author). One performance was a revival of *Love's Labour's Lost*, for King James and Queen Anne, hosted by Southampton at his house in London.

After *Hamlet* in 1604 all publications again ceased, for four years. (*King Lear* was printed in 1608; *Troilus and Cressida* was issued in two editions during 1608-1609; and *Pericles* appeared in 1609.) Then the silence resumed, for thirteen more years, until a quarto of *Othello* appeared in 1622; and finally the First Folio of thirty-six Shakespeare plays was published in 1623. Fully half of these stage works were printed for the first time; the folio included none of the Shakespeare poetry, nor any mention of Southampton or the Sonnets.

The connections between Oxford and Southampton are numerous and significant; the link between the two earls is crucial for the quest to determine the real Shakespeare.

CHAPTER TWELVE

KNOWLEDGE

Reason 54 – The French Connection

No less than five Shakespeare plays are set at least partly in France: *King John, Henry V, Henry VI, Pt.1, All's Well That Ends Well* and *Love's Labour's Lost*. Would most playwrights deliberately set several plays in France if they had never been there?

In *Henry V* the entirety of Act 3, scene 4, is set within the French king's palace and consists of French dialogue between Princess Katherine and Alice, the lady attending on her. Some of it is "vulgar" French.

Young Oxford would have learned all about the Vere family and its French origin (the name apparently derived from Ver, near Bayeux) as well as about its founder, Aubrey de Vere, who had come into England with William the Conqueror in 1066, five centuries earlier. Edward would have learned to read, write and speak French at a very early age, perhaps in the household of Sir Thomas Smith, where he apparently was sent at age four.

Following are fragments of recorded information:

—When de Vere had entered Cecil House, the printed "Orders for the Earl of Oxford's Exercises" prescribed a daily routine that included two hours of French studies, one in the morning and one in the afternoon. In a letter dated 23 August 1563, the thirteen-year-old boy wrote a letter to Cecil entirely in French; six years later, Oxford ordered books that included "Plutarch's works in French" as well as works in Italian and English.

—The earl was twenty-four in February 1575 when he and his retinue arrived in Paris, where he was entertained at the French court by the royal family: Henry III, Catherine de Medici (the Queen Mother) and Marguerite de Valois. The English ambassador in Paris, Valentine Dale, wrote Burghley on 7 March of having "presented my Lord of Oxford unto the French King and Queen, who used him honorably." He added that "amongst other talk the King asked whether he was married. I said he had a fair lady. *'Il y a donce ce,'* ditil [he says], *'un beau couple.'"*

—After Oxford had left Paris for Strasburg, the ambassador again wrote to Burghley: "I will assure your Lordship unfeignedly my Lord of Oxford used himself as orderly and moderately as might be desired, and with great commendation, neither is there any appearance of the likelihood of any other." So we have Oxford as a young man at the French royal court, speaking fluent French with the royal family; and in fact, his entire life as a nobleman was involved with matters involving France, such as the tumultuous marriage negotiations during the 1570s and early 1580s, when Elizabeth carried on the public fiction that she would wed Alençon.

—At the end of Sonnet 73, which proceeds from autumn to winter in the poet's life, the final couplet reads (with my emphasis):

> This thou perceiv'st, which makes thy love more strong,
> To love that well which thou must *leave ere* long

The phrase "leave ere" in the last line is the exact sound of *l'hiver,* French for "winter," and simultaneously it plays upon Oxford's own name, Ver – the way *The Winter's Tale,* translated into French, is *L'Compte de L'hiver,"* the account or "tale" of Winter, or Vere. In addition, the similar-sounding French word "Comte" denotes the rank of Count in France, which is the equivalent of the English rank of Earl.

Reason 55 – The Greek Connection

G. Wilson Knight, writing of the magical resurrection scene in the final act of *The Winter's Tale,* when the statue of Hermione comes to life, calls it "the most strikingly conceived and profoundly penetrating moment in English literature." While critics have long regarded the play to be derived from *Pandosto,* Robert Greene's 1588 romance, Dr. Earl Showerman points out that Shakespeare not only upgraded the style of Greene's moral tale but also "transformed it into a Renaissance version of a classic Greek trilogy, enriched with references to a library of ancient sources."

Showerman has been systematically discovering Shakespeare's profound knowledge of the Greek language and of ancient Greek drama. "We can now credibly add Euripides's tragicomedy *Alcestis* (438 BCE) to Shakespeare's portfolio of classical Greek sources," he says. While

Greene took names and themes from second-century Greek romance, Shakespeare "chose to craft his romantic masterpiece in the venerable tradition of fifth-century Greek drama," while drawing from his reading of *Alcestis* in the original Greek language.

This should come as worrisome news to scholars bound by Stratfordian biography. It undoubtedly means that, while the works of Shakespeare will always remain intact, these critics had better go looking for an author who could actually read Greek. Showerman points out that many scholars in the nineteenth century recognized *Alcestis* as a source for the statue scene in *The Winter's Tale*, but "as the twentieth century passed the mid-mark, acknowledgment of the connection faded as scholars began to react to the limits on Shakespeare's knowledge of the Greek canon imposed by the Stratford grammar school education. Since then, contemporary scholars have tended to either ignore *Alcestis* or relegate it to a footnote."

Having found evidence of an alarmingly erudite Shakespeare in the plays, some modern scholars are rather frantically proposing that the canon must have had multiple authors. This would be quite surprising to those who gave us the Folio of Shakespeare plays in 1623, given that they never thought to mention any collaborators. Nonetheless, watch for continued escalation of the collaboration theme— anything to avoid the obvious evidence that there was a different single author!

It's not easy to calculate the damage done by the traditional limitation of vision, but by lifting the curtain on the Greek influences in Shakespeare's plays, Showerman is making it increasingly difficult to ignore the Greek underpinning that extends even to the names of many Shakespearean characters: "By examining the personalities and relationships of the names used for the characters of *The Winter's Tale*, one can more fully appreciate the Greek context out of which Shakespeare built his story. I believe that much of the mystical power of this drama derives from these archetypal Greek sources, from the histories and mythologies embedded in its characters' names."

Andrew Werth contradicts many orthodox scholars by concluding: "Greek plots, names, passages, philosophy, dramatic technique, and, most important, the Greek 'spirit,' enhance and inform Shakespeare's plays and sonnets." Through the research of Stephanie Hopkins Hughes, we have learned much about the influence upon de Vere of Sir Thomas Smith, the philosopher, statesman, humanist and Greek scholar. According to the available evidence, Smith raised and tutored the young earl from the ages of four to twelve, at his own household. Sir Thomas had held the post of Greek Orator at Cambridge, lecturing in Greek on

Homer and the ancient Greek dramatists. Surely he would have transferred his enthusiasm for the Greek language to his young pupil, who spent his ninth year at Smith's former college, Queens', at Cambridge.

During Elizabeth's reign, Smith followed Burghley as the queen's principal secretary in 1572 until his death in 1577. During that time, after Oxford had bolted to the Continent without permission, Burghley wrote to Walsingham for help in mollifying the queen, adding, "I doubt not but Master Secretary Smith will remember his old love towards the earl when he was his scholar." After spending his childhood at Smith's estates (presumably with frequent returns to Hedingham), Oxford spent most of his teens at Cecil House. Burghley, who had studied under Smith in much earlier days, also had Greek editions of Homer, Aeschylus, Sophocles, Euripides and Plato in his vast library. In addition the chief minister's wife, Mildred Cooke Cecil, a major force in that household, was fluent in Latin and Greek. Once more, the biography of de Vere makes a perfect fit with the works of Shakespeare.

Reason 56 – Knowledge of Law

"In Shakespeare's multiple personalities, there is none in which he appears more naturally and to better advantage than in the role of the lawyer. If true that all dramatic writing is but a form of autobiography, then the immortal Shakespeare must, at some time in his life, have studied law."— Commentaries on the Law in Shakespeare, 1911, by Edward J. White

There is not a shred of evidence that Shakspere ever went beyond grammar school (if he attended at all), much less to a university or law school. Oxford was seventeen in 1567 when he entered Gray's Inn to study law. He was steeped in legal matters involving his earldom and the royal court; he sat on the juries at the treason trials of the duke of Norfolk (1572), Mary Queen of Scots (1586), and the earls of Essex and Southampton (1601).

A recent book, *Shakespeare's Legal Language* (2000), contains a detailed discussion of Shakespeare's legal terms and concepts. Authors B.J. and Mary Sokol point out that twenty-five of thirty-seven plays refer to a trial and that thirty-five contain the words "judge" and "justice." "Nothing adorns a king more than justice," Oxford wrote to Robert Cecil in May 1603, referring to the newly proclaimed King James, "nor in anything doth a king more resemble God than in justice."

Traditional scholars usually assert that Shakespeare didn't really demonstrate an exceptional knowledge of the law, at the same time struggling to explain how he could have become so "law-obsessed," as the Sokols put it. Back in 1869, for example, Lord Penzance spoke of Shakespeare's "perfect familiarity with not only the principles, axioms, and maxims, but the technicalities of English law, a knowledge so perfect and intimate that he was never incorrect and never at fault .... At every turn and point at which the author required a metaphor, simile, or illustration, his mind ever turned first to the law. He seems almost to have thought in legal phrases...." "Any intelligent writer can acquire knowledge of a subject and serve it up as required," Ogburn Jr. writes, adding it is "something else to have been so immersed in a subject and to have assimilated it so thoroughly that it has become part of one's nature, shaping one's view of the world, coming forward spontaneously to prompt or complete a thought or supply an image or analogy."

Mark Twain wrote in reference to Shakspere of Stratford that he "couldn't have written Shakespeare's works, for the reason that the man who wrote them was limitlessly familiar with the laws, and the law-courts, and law-proceedings, and lawyer-talk, and lawyer-ways—and if Shakespeare was possessed of the infinitely-divided star-dust that constituted this vast wealth, how did he get it, and where, and when? . . . A man can't handle glibly and easily and comfortably and successfully the argot of a trade at which he has not personally served. He will make mistakes; he will not, and cannot, get the trade-phrasings precisely and exactly right; and the moment he departs, by even a shade, from a common trade-form, the reader who has served that trade will know the writer hasn't."

Following is a small sample of excerpts from Oxford's letters showing his familiarity with the law and with legal terms:

> But now the *ground* whereon I lay my *suit* being so *just* and reasonable ... to conceive of the *just* desire I make of this *suit* ... so by-fold that *justice* could not dispense any farther ... The matter after it had received many crosses, many inventions of delay, yet at length hath been *heard before all the Judges—judges* I say both *unlawful*, and *lawful* ... For *counsel*, I have such *lawyers,* and the best that I can get as are to be had in London, who have advised me for my best course ... [to Queen Elizabeth]: And because your Majesty upon *a bare information* could not be so well satisfied of every particular as *by lawful testimony & examination of credible witnesses upon oath* ... So that now, having *lawfully proved* unto your Majesty. . . .

Oxford attended at the House of Lords on forty-four days during the nine sessions from 1571 to 1601. In the sessions from 1585 onward he was appointed one of the "receivers and triers of petitions from Gascony and other lands beyond the seas and from the islands." In November

1586 he was part of a committee appointed to address Elizabeth on the sentencing of Mary Queen of Scots.

In Sonnet 46, the poet describes a trial by jury:

Mine eye and heart are at a mortal war
How to divide the conquest of thy sight;
Mine eye, my heart thy picture's sight would bar
My heart, mine eye the freedom of that right;
My heart doth plead that thou in him dost lie
(A closet never pierced with crystal eyes),
But the defendant doth that plea deny,
And says in him thy fair appearance lies.
To 'cide this title is impaneled
A quest of thoughts, all tenants to the heart,
And by their verdict is determined
The clear eyes' moiety, and thy dear heart's part:
   As thus, mine eyes' due is thy outward part,
   And my heart's right, their inward love of heart.

Scholars of the Stratfordian tradition have often speculated that "Shakespeare" must have been a lawyer. The fact that Oxford himself was a lawyer does not prove that he was the great author, but it is an important piece of the accumulated evidence in his favor.

Reason 57 – Knowledge of Power

Traditional biographies of Shakespeare necessarily place him far from the royal court. But the dramatist writes consistently from the vantage point of an insider, one who knows how and when the levers of power are used. De Vere lived at the heart of Elizabethan political life from at least age twelve at the London home of William Cecil, the most powerful man in England. In 1571 he entered the House of Lords and immediately became an intimate of the queen, continuing in her highest favor for at least a decade.

In late 1580 he discovered that some of his high-ranking Catholic friends or associates were involved in a plot to overthrow Elizabeth and he accused them (correctly) of conspiracy to commit treason. He knew these men of power—their thoughts and emotions, their fears, as they took him into their confidence and eventually tipped their hand. We might imagine him writing at night, his quill pen scratching the page in the candlelight as the words of Brutus come forth:

Since Cassius first did whet me against Caesar,
I have not slept.

Between the acting of a dreadful thing
And the first motion, all the interim is
Like a phantasma, or a hideous dream:
The genius and the mortal instruments
Are then in council; and the state of man,
Like to a little kingdom, suffers then
The nature of an insurrection. (2.1)

De Vere had close-up knowledge of power and real-life political intrigues of the kind to be found not just in *Julius Caesar,* but also in *King John, Henry V, Richard II, Richard III, Macbeth, King Lear, Hamlet* and many other Shakespeare plays. In 1586, amid heavy wartime spending, Elizabeth granted him a lifetime pension in the extraordinary amount of 1,000 pounds per year. After the 1588 defeat of King Philip's Armada, Oxford left court life and in the next decade poems and plays began appearing by an invisible author named "Shakespeare," someone who possessed a remarkably keen knowledge of the uses of power.

"Oxford had frequent access to court, an insider's experience with Elizabeth, the machinations of foreign heads of states and ambassadors, and fawning courtiers," Mark Alexander writes in his online presentation *Shakespeare and Oxford: 25 Curious Connections.* "He saw power manifested in a variety of corruptions. Furthermore, being raised as a ward in Cecil's household, and given his noble position, Oxford would have been exposed to the absolute center of England's power."

"Of all the major writers in the Western literary tradition, there is none who deals so consistently and so profoundly with political matters as Shakespeare," Alvin B. Kernan states in *Politics, Power, and Shakespeare* (1981). "He wrote almost exclusively of courts and aristocratic life; and matters of state, of law, of kingship, and of dynastic succession are always prominent parts of his dramatic matter. This is true even in his comedies ... but it is even more obviously true in Shakespeare's history plays and in his tragedies, where the political issues are the very substance of the plays, and where crucial matters of state are explored with remarkable precision and in great depth."

"All ten of Shakespeare's English history plays are named after politicians," Tim Spiekerman writes in *Shakespeare's Political Realism* (2001). "And they're all about the same thing: who gets to rule ....The plots are political plots (literally plots) ... assassination, treason, civil war, foreign conquest .... If ambition seems to be a universal aspect of political life, so too does the concept of 'legitimacy,' which is the most salient theme of the English history plays. At stake in these plays is the question not only of who will rule, but of who is supposed to rule ... the proper acquisition and use of political power." "The dominant political question which produced the history plays ... was the terms of obedience," Irving Ribner comments in *The English History Plays in the Age of Shakespeare* (1957). "Under what conditions, if ever, was rebellion against a lawful monarch justified?"

"Shakespeare was anything but a writer of commonplace entertainments or an indifferent recorder of history," notes Professor Daniel Wright. "He was, instead, an informed commentator on the contemporary political scene, an expositor of political conviction and an advocate for policy that, often enough, contravened or challenged government—which is to say 'Cecilian'— philosophy and practice."

Alexander quotes the historian A.L. Rowse: "The 17th Earl of Oxford was, as the numbering shows, immensely aristocratic, and this was the clue to his career. In an Elizabethan society full of new and upcoming men, some of them at the very top, like the Bacons and Cecils—the Boleyns themselves, from whom the Queen descended, were a new family—the Oxford earldom stood out as the oldest in the land. He was the premier earl and, as hereditary Lord Great Chamberlain, took his place on the right hand of the Queen and bore the sword of state before her."

Another testimony comes from Adolf A. Berle, Jr., former ambassador and Assistant Secretary of State under President Franklin Roosevelt: "One wonders what the personal reveries of a Plantagenet or Tudor dictator must have been. Shakespeare probably gives a better analysis than historians...." So how did "Shakespeare" gain his intricate, deep knowledge of power and, too, his insights into the powerful? The answer is that, from the beginning, he was living in the midst of that world as both observer and participant and that he recreated it with imagination based on personal experience.

Reason 58 – Military Knowledge

> *"Warfare is everywhere in Shakespeare, and the military action in many of Shakespeare's plays, and the military imagery in all his plays and poems, show that he possessed an extraordinarily detailed knowledge of warfare, both ancient and modern."*—Charles Edelman, *"Shakespeare's Military Language"* (2000)

Edelman's book provides "a comprehensive account of Shakespeare's portrayal of military life, tactics and technology and explores how the plays comment upon military incidents and personalities of the Elizabethan era." How do orthodox biographers imagine Shakspere of Stratford accumulating such "extraordinarily detailed knowledge" of warfare and military matters? Is it through automatic assimilation, by which all intricacies are miraculously absorbed into the very fiber of his being and translated into the dialogue of characters in his plays?

"Shakespeare expresses the courtier-soldier's point of view too clearly and naturally and displays far too familiar a grasp of military methods, objectives and colloquialisms not to have acquired this knowledge through serious study—plus firsthand experience—of the arts of war," Barrell writes. "No such study and experience can be documented in the career of the Stratford native."

At issue is "information" as opposed to innate genius—the former term defined (by my dictionary) as knowledge "communicated or received concerning particular facts or circumstances," or otherwise "gained through study, research, instruction and experience." The great author's information about military life was not genetically inherited; it was *acquired*. He draws upon his wealth of information not in any calculated way but, rather, spontaneously, during the white heat of composition, and employs it for various purposes the way an artist will mix paints on his canvas. On and on come the military terms in the plays, as in *2 Henry IV*, for example, with words such as *alarum, ancient, archer, beacon, beaver, besonian, blank, bounce, bullet, Caesar's thrasonical brag, caliver, captain, chamber, charge, cavalier, chivalry, coat* and *corporal*.

"In every outstanding instance of specialized knowledge," Barrell notes, "Oxford's personal familiarity with the subject can be categorically documented; and this is particularly true in respect to 'Shakespeare's' fund of military information." The earl unquestionably acquired information about "military life, tactics and technology" in ways such as these:

- Oxford's cousins Horatio and Francis Vere, known as the "Fighting Veres" for their exploits as soldiers, may have been the models for the similarly-named soldiers Horatio and Francisco in *Hamlet*.
- Oxford's brother-in-law Peregrine Bertie, Lord Willoughby d'Eresby, devoted his life to the political and military service of Queen Elizabeth.
- When the Northern Rebellion of powerful Catholic earls began in November 1569, Oxford, then nineteen, requested military service, which was granted in the spring of 1570, when he served under Sussex. The chief action he would have seen was the siege

of Hume Castle, whose defenders surrendered to avoid any further bombardment—an episode that calls to mind the siege of Harfleur by Henry the Fifth.

- Oxford was champion of his first tournament at the Whitehall Tiltyard, in May 1571, performing "far above expectation of the world" in front of Queen Elizabeth and the royal court. He blazed his way "with fiery energy," contemporary Giles Fletcher wrote, summoning "a mimicry of war" as he "controls his foaming steed with a light rein and, armed with a long spear, rides to the encounter .... Bravo, valiant youth! 'Tis thus that martial spirits pass through their apprenticeship in war …The country sees in thee both a leader pre-eminent in war, and a skillful man-at-arms…."

- A decade later, in January 1581, Oxford prevailed as champion of his second and final tournament.

- *The Defence of Militarie Profession* was published in 1579, *"wherein is eloquently shewed the due commendation of Martiall prowess, and plainly proved how necessary the exercise of Armes is for this our age."* It was dedicated by its author, Geoffrey Gates, "To the Right honorable Edward de Vere, Earle of Oxenford." The publisher, John Harrison, would later issue *Venus and Adonis* in 1593 and *Lucrece* in 1594, introducing "William Shakespeare" by way of the dedications to Southampton, with both narrative poems having been personally overseen by the poet.

- On 25 June 1585, Oxford wrote to Burghley asking for a loan to help in his suit for a military command in the Netherlands in England's impending war with Spain. In this letter he launched into a Shakespearean string of military metaphors, writing, "For, being now almost at a point to taste that good which her Majesty shall determine, *yet am I as one that hath long besieged a fort and not able to compass the end or reap the fruit of his travail, being forced to levy his siege for want of munition."* ("Munition" was not a common word at the time, but "Shakespeare" used it more than once, as when Gloucester in *Henry VI, Pt. 1* declares, "I'll to the Tower with all the haste I can to view the artillery and munition" [1.1].)

- Later that summer, Oxford (at age thirty-five) was commissioned to command a company of horse in the Low Countries. "Five or six thousand English soldiers have arrived in Flanders with the Earl of Oxford and Colonel Norris," came one report in

September. A month later, however, the queen commanded Oxford to return home and sent Leicester, who, having maneuvered his way into replacing Oxford, would proceed to disgrace himself by his behavior in Holland.

- Oxford was reported among the many "honorable personages" in the summer of 1588 who "were suddenly embarked, committing themselves unto the present chance of war" when the Spanish Armada arrived on its mission to crush England. Apparently Oxford's ship was disabled, because he went directly home for his armor, and even his enemy Leicester reported that "he seems most willing to hazard his life in this quarrel."

How did "Shakespeare" acquire his military knowledge? The life of Oxford provides the most plausible answer. Immediately inside the cover page of *The Defence of Militarie Profession* is the coat of arms usually used by Oxford, with his earldom motto VERO NIHIL VERIUS ("Nothing Truer than Truth") displayed along the bottom. On the first right-hand page begins the dedication "TO THE RIGHT honorable, Edward de Vere, Earle of Oxenford, Viscount Bulbecke, Lord of Escales and Baldesmere, and Lord great Chamberlaine of England." It continues: "It hath been an old controversy in the opinions of the English nation what profession of life is most honorable in worldly states...."

De Vere not only acted as the writer's patron, but also financed the publication; beyond that, he took great interest in this work and likely contributed a great deal to it behind the scenes. Back in November 1569, when the Northern Rebellion had begun, Oxford wrote to Cecil asking for military service against the powerful Catholic earls of the north. To the nineteen-year-old earl, such service was the most honorable course. He told his guardian that "at this time I am bold to desire your favour and friendship that you will suffer me to be employed by your means and help in this service that now is in hand." He reminded Cecil that "heretofore you have given me your good word to have me see the wars and services in strange and foreign places .... Now you will do me so much honour as that by your purchase of my License I may be called to the service of my prince and country."

In September 1572, after the St. Bartholomew's Day Massacre of Protestants in France, Oxford wrote to Burghley saying he would be eager to serve the queen on the Continent: "I had rather serve there than at home where yet some honor were to be got; if there be any setting forth to sea, to which service I bear most affection, I shall desire your Lordship to give me and get me that favour and credit, that I might make one. Which if there be no such intention, then I shall be most willing to be employed on the sea coasts, to be in a readiness with my countrymen against any invasion."

Oxford never lost his eagerness to serve as a military man, always connecting that activity with honor. It is easy to imagine him composing *Hamlet* and having Ophelia cry out:

> O what a noble mind is here o'erthrown!
> The courtier's, soldier's, scholar's, eye, tongue, sword,
> The expectancy and rose of the fair state!

Edward de Vere was all that and much more.

Reason 59 – Medical Knowledge

In his edition of the Shakespeare sonnets, Stephen Booth reproduces the title page of *The Newe Jewell of Health, wherein is contained the most excellent Secrets of Physic and Philosophy, divided into four Books* by the surgeon George Baker, published in 1576. Booth presents an illustration of the doctor's important book in connection with Sonnet 119, which builds upon metaphors and analogies from alchemy and medicine:

> What potions have I drunk of siren tears,
> Distilled from limbecks foul as hell within . . .

"Shakespeare" knew all about the "distillations" of waters, oils and balms as set forth by Dr. Baker, whose book has been long considered a key source for the Bard's interest in alchemy as well as the full range of medical knowledge at the time. It happens that Baker, who would become surgeon to Queen Elizabeth, was the personal physician of de Vere and dedicated *The New Jewel of Health* to the earl's wife Anne Cecil. Baker had dedicated his first book, *Olenum Magistrale* (1574), to de Vere himself, and in 1599 dedicated his *Practice of the New and Old Physic* to the earl as well. Baker was part of the household of de Vere, whose patronage helped to make it possible for this medical pioneer to write his books in the first place.

This is one example of how "Shakespeare's" remarkable knowledge of medicine is mirrored by Oxford's own connection to the leading medical experts and advances of his time, not only in England but also on the Continent. If Baker had just once treated Shakspere for a cut finger, upholders of the Stratford faith would have devoted entire books to that medical incident and its influences upon Shakespeare's writings. On the other hand, Booth uses a full page to illustrate *The Newe Jewell of Health* in connection with Shakespeare's sonnets, but never indicates that

Baker dedicated that very book to the wife of the leading candidate to replace the Stratford man, nor does he mention that the doctor dedicated two other books to the earl of Oxford himself!

Scholars often try to "dumb down" Shakespeare's works to avoid having to explain how he could have acquired such amazing knowledge. They tell us things like, "Well, see, he really didn't know that much. He wrote about stuff that anyone in England could have picked up, in the tavern or on the street, and of course he made mistakes...." If something is too large to be filled by the Stratford man's pitifully small biography, it must be cut down to fit, even while the miracle of his "genius" is further inflated, to explain the inexplicable.

De Vere requires no such adjustments. As for exposure to medical knowledge, he was tutored during childhood by Sir Thomas Smith, known for his interest in diseases, alchemy and therapeutic botanicals. Then he had access to Cecil's library with some 200 books on alchemy and medical topics. In his twenties Oxford lived next door to Bedlam Hospital, a source of firsthand knowledge about patients suffering from mental illness.

Oxford's life forms a picture that deepens our perceptions of the great plays and poems. And because of the Oxfordian authorship theory, researchers are continually finding new evidence that "Shakespeare" was even more brilliant than we have been able to know and appreciate.

Earl Showerman, M.D., points out that the Shakespeare plays contain "over 700 medical references to practically all the diseases and drugs" that were known by the year 1600, along with "knowledge of anatomy, physiology, surgery, obstetrics, public health, aging, forensics, neurology and mental disorders," not to mention "detailed knowledge of syphilis." He quotes from *Shakespeare and Medicine* (1962) by R.R. Simpson, who reports that the poet-dramatist demonstrates "not only an astute knowledge of medical affairs, but also a keen sense of the correct use of that knowledge"—a sign that he was well acquainted with the medical literature of his day. Another work is *The Medical Mind of Shakespeare* (1986) by Aubrey Kail, who writes that the Bard's plays "bear witness to profound knowledge of contemporary physiology and psychology" and that he "employed medical terms in a manner which would have been beyond the powers of any ordinary playwright or physician."

Another Oxfordian researcher, Frank M. Davis, M.D., writes that in Shakespeare's time "true medical literature, like medicine itself, was still in its infancy," so he could not have absorbed much from reading whatever was available in English: "The vast majority of medical works were published in Latin or Greek."

Davis finds it "remarkable" that Shakespeare refers in three plays to the *pia mater*,, the inner lining of the covering of the brain and spinal cord: "Knowledge of this relatively obscure part of anatomy could only mean that Shakespeare had either studied anatomy or read medical literature ... Even more striking to me as a neurosurgeon is his acquaintance with the relationship of the third ventricle with memory," he adds, noting a possible source was Thomas Vicary's *Anatomy of the Body of Man* (1548), which refers to the third ventricle as the "ventricle of memory"—a phrase used in *Love's Labour's Lost*, when the pedant Holofernes states that his various gifts of the mind "are begot in the ventricle of memory, nourished in the womb of the pia mater ..." (4.2).

While the discovery of the circulation of the blood is assigned to William Harvey, who announced it in 1616, "Shakespeare" was likely aware of it long before then. There are at least "nine significant references to the circulation or flowing of blood in Shakespeare plays," Davis writes.

England was far behind the advances in medical technology taking place on the Continent. Most of the great doctors and teachers were based at the University of Padua, then the center for medical learning; others studied there before returning to their hometowns to practice medicine. Oxford, touring the cities of Europe during 1575 at age twenty-five, visited Padua at least once, probably twice. "With the background in pharmacology gained from his years with Sir Thomas Smith," writes Davis, "it seems unlikely that Oxford would have visited Padua without attempting to discover the latest developments in 'physic.'"

In the previous year, the Renaissance doctor Fabricius had discovered "the valves in veins responsible for keeping the blood flowing in one direction toward the heart," Davis notes, adding that Fabricius was "the first to bring this important discovery to light." Even if Oxford had never met Fabricius in person, it is "easy to imagine" that the great teacher's 1574 discovery of those valves, along with other topics related to the circulation of the blood, "would have been an ongoing staple of conversation among the students and faculty at the time of Oxford's visit the following year."

Reason 60 – The Sea and Seamanship

Lieutenant Commander Alexander Falconer, a naval officer during World War II and a professional sailor steeped in the history of seamanship and navigation, published two books that were largely ignored at the time: *Shakespeare and the Sea* (1964) and *A Glossary of Shakespeare's Sea and Naval Terms including Gunnery* (1965). Falconer brings firsthand knowledge and experience to an investigation of Shakespeare's use of seafaring terms and situations involving the sea. He concludes that the poet-dramatist possessed detailed, accurate knowledge of naval matters and was well informed about storms, shipwrecks, pirates, voyages of exploration, and navigation:

> The manning and running of royal ships … duties of officers and seamen … strategy and the principles of sea warfare, gunnery, grappling and boarding are all known to him; so, too, are the main types of ship, their build, rigging, masts, sails, anchors and cables. The sea itself in its varied working, tides, waves, currents, storms and calms, never goes out of his work.

Falconer notes that in the opening scene of *The Tempest*, when the ship is wrecked in a storm, Shakespeare took care for details. He "worked out a series of maneuvers" and "made exact use of the professional language of seamanship."

When the Royal Shakespeare Company presented a "shipwreck trilogy" of Shakespeare plays (*The Tempest, Twelfth Night* and *The Comedy of Errors*), Charles Spencer of *The Telegraph* observed that "although there were books on navigation in Shakespeare's time, nothing on seamanship was published until later." Indeed, Falconer believed the Bard's knowledge in this area could not have come from books alone.

"Most current scholarship fails to note the sophistication of Shakespeare's maritime imagination," writes Dan Brayton in *Shakespeare's Ocean* (2012), noting "the extraordinary degree [in the poems and plays] to which human lives are connected with the sea, or the remarkable specificity of his descriptions of marine phenomena."

The author's exact use of naval and maritime language, along with his intimate knowledge of the sea and seamanship, cannot be explained by anything in the documented life of the man from Stratford. It is sheer fantasy to think he might have been a sailor during his "lost" years, and the same goes for supposing he was a schoolteacher or a law clerk. Meanwhile, scholars generally fail to notice the Bard's experience at sea because they know that the Stratford man never once left dry land. When one assumes it's impossible for something to exist, it becomes quite easy—even necessary—to ignore it.

"Closed minds automatically blockade new information which conflicts with their own beliefs, preventing highly persuasive evidence from entering their brains for evaluation," writes Paul Altrocchi, adding, "Oxfordians believe with conviction that Stratfordianism represents a classic example of the common human tendency to stick tenaciously with conventional wisdom, preventing much more logical and coherent newer theories and facts from being given a fair hearing." When we turn to the life of de Vere, there is no need to "imagine" his experience with the sea and, importantly, there is no longer any reason to ignore the vast knowledge of the sea to be found in the poems and plays.

Oxford was twenty-two in September 1572 when he wrote to Burghley, in reaction to the St. Bartholomew's Day Massacre of Protestants in France, offering to help defend England in any way he could. "If there be any setting forth to sea, to which service I bear most affection," he wrote, "I shall desire your Lordship to give me and get me that favor...." Eventually the earl traveled extensively by ship or boat. He crossed the Channel to France in 1575 and took many trips on canals and other waterways between Italian cities, with Venice as his home base.

In the autumn of 1575, it was reported that Oxford had hurt his knee in a Venetian galley. While returning to England in April 1576, he was captured by pirates in the Channel and nearly killed.

In 1585 he crossed by ship to the Netherlands on a military mission; this time pirates stopped the vessel that was returning his belongings to England and apparently stole everything on board. Earlier, the earl had invested (disastrously) in Martin Frobisher's voyages to discover the Northwest Passage to China, which involved varied and challenging aspects of navigation. He was well acquainted with Dr. John Dee, who was intimately involved in developing Frobisher's navigational routes.

Moreover, Oxford had his own ship, the *Edward Bonaventure*, which he contributed to Captain Edward Fenton's expedition to the Spanish Main in 1582. (The Spanish rebuffed the little fleet, so the earl's investment did not pay off.) Then in June 1588, with the Armada on its way, Oxford prepared to take the *Bonaventure* into battle; although the English defeated the great fleet, it appears his ship became disabled.

In the following year, a poem, apparently by Oxford's secretary Lyly, envisioned the earl standing on the hatch-cover of the *Bonaventure*, literally breathing fire instilled within him by Pallas, the spear-shaker:

De Vere ... like warlike Mars upon the hatches stands.
His tusked Boar 'gan foam for inward ire
While Pallas filled his breast with fire

Shakespeare and the Sea was reviewed in the autumn 1965 edition of the *Shakesperean Authorship Review* by I.L.M. McGeoch, who writes:

Professor Falconer points out that whereas many educated Elizabethans understood the art of navigation—in those happy days art was science, and science was art—only those who actually served at sea could acquire a profound knowledge of the practice of seamanship and the correct meaning and use of the terms proper to the working of ships. That Shakespeare possessed such a profound knowledge is instanced many times.

As an example of "inspired accuracy of allusion seasoned with wit," he offers a line from *King John* (4.2): "And like a shifted wind unto a sail, it makes the course of thoughts to fetch about," and further observes:

> Tacking is to bring a ship's head to lie the other way. True. And "to fetch about" is synonymous with "to tack"; but subtler still is the reference to "course," which is not only the direction in which a ship is heading, but also the name given to the principal sail on any mast of a square-rigged ship. The essence of tacking, therefore, is to bring the wind onto the other side of the sail, or "course," and the necessary re-trimming of the sail is assisted by the wind blowing upon it from the side appropriate to the new tack.

"Not knowing that de Vere wrote the great plays of Shakespeare makes it impossible to understand many of the allusions and subtleties within every play," Dr. Altrocchi writes, adding that this impossibility "deprives the audience of much of a play's texture."

Reason 61 – "Methinks I Have Astronomy"

Among our well renowned men,
Dever merits a silver pen
Eternally to write his honour,
And I in a well-polished verse,
Can set up in our universe
A fame to endure for ever…
For who marketh better than he
The seven turning flames of the sky?

The above lines, published in 1584, come from a Frenchman writing under the pen name John Soothern (or "Southern"; see Reason 37), then living in the household of "Dever" (Edward de Vere) and referring to the "seven turning flames of the sky" to indicate the sun, the moon and the five known planets. According to Soothern, who knew Oxford well, the earl was an expert in the exciting but politically dangerous field of astronomy, which was threatening to overturn the old conception of the cosmos and even upend the old relationships of man to himself, to the world and to God.

Not from the stars do I my judgment pluck,

And yet methinks I have Astronomy

That was "Shakespeare" starting off his Sonnet 14, but right away he announces that he is not speaking of astrological fortune-telling or superstitions. He is not writing about the making of predictions such as that used by Queen Elizabeth to choose the luckiest and most balmy date of her coronation:

But not to tell of good or evil luck...
Of plagues, of dearths, or seasons' quality;
Or say with Princes if it shall go well.
By oft predict that I in heaven find...

On the contrary, by "astronomy" he was referring to revolutionary science in sixteenth-century England that was being studied in secret, notably by the group (later called the School of Night) whose members included Raleigh, Marlowe, Chapman, the mathematician Harriot and de Vere himself. He had studied astronomy from boyhood in the 1550s with his tutor, Smith, and in the 1560s with John Dee. The latter was not only the queen's astrologer, but also a serious mathematician and geographer; because of the book *De Revolutionibus* (1543) by Polish mathematician-astronomer Nicholas Copernicus, these English scholars were well aware that a great change of paradigm was underway. The perception of the universe was in the process of drastic change, but also undergoing upheaval was the social-religious-political order itself, which even Hamlet is reluctant to mention aloud:

There are more things in heaven and earth, Horatio,
Than are dreamt of in your philosophy. (1.4)

Such free-thinking men were moving from the old Ptolemaic model of the earth at the center of the universe to the revolutionary Copernican model, by which the Sun is at rest (motionless) near the center of the Universe, and the Earth, spinning on its axis once daily, revolves annually around the Sun.

Doubt thou the stars are fire,
Doubt that the sun doth move,
Doubt truth to be a liar,
But never doubt I love –
        The prince in *Hamlet* (2.2)

When Oxford was twenty-three in 1573, the English scientist Thomas Digges published a treatise on a supernova, or exploding star, seen in the sky the year before. In this work, dedicated to Burghley, the earl's father-in-law, Digges includes warm praise for the Copernican hypothesis. Burghley and Walsingham, who made it their business to develop intelligence in defense of the realm, were keenly interested in a new-fangled device called a "perspective" glass or trunk, which enabled astronomers to see farther into space. In fact, such new devices would help to quickly spot the warships of the Spanish Armada upon their arrival, playing a significant role in England's victory in 1588.

Digges published another key work, *A Perfect Description of the Celestial Orbs*, in 1576, using allegory to simultaneously set forth and disguise his agreement with Copernicus. He also communicated his heretical view that the Sun is just one star among an infinity of stars in an unending universe.

> "O God, I could be bounded in a nutshell and count myself a king of infinite space" – The prince in *Hamlet* (2.2)

In 1582, when Watson dedicated *Hekatompathia* to Oxford, thanking him for his help editing the manuscript and getting it into print, his sequence of 100 consecutively numbered "passions" or sonnets contained the first known description of the Milky Way as a collection of discrete stars rather than a single mass. Watson was preceding Galileo's published discovery in 1610 by nearly thirty years. The prose header for one of the sonnets (Oxford seems to have written all the headers, and may have even written all the Watson sonnets) refers to "Galaxia" as "a White Way or Milky Circle in the heavens," but the opening lines of the poem contain this radical description:

> Who can recount the virtues of my dear
> Or say how far her fame hath taken flight,
> That cannot tell how many stars appear
> In part of heaven, which Galaxia height,
> Or number all the moats in Phoebus' rays,
> Or golden sands, whereon Pactolus plays?
> Watson Sonnet 31, 1582

In the same year Elizabeth sent Oxford's brother-in-law Peregrine Bertie, Lord Willoughby, on a mission to the Danish court; during that extended visit Willoughby met with Danish astronomer Tycho Brahe, who, in 1572, had made precise observations of the inexplicably brilliant star that became known as "Tycho's Supernova"—a celestial phenomenon which traditionally trained scientists could not explain. The playwright "Shakespeare" would describe it in the night sky over Denmark, however:

> Last night of all,
> When yon same star that's westward from the pole

> Had made his course to illume that part of heaven
> Where it now burns…
>> Bernardo, *Hamlet* (1.1)

"Tycho's Supernova" confirmed what Anderson calls "an emerging scientific understanding of a dynamic universe" as opposed to the prevailing Ptolemaic system, which posited that all heavenly bodies were unchanging and firmly fixed in place.

In June of 1583 the Italian philosopher Giordano Bruno appeared in England and delivered lectures at Oxford, contradicting the university's continuing dogma that every object in the universe orbited a centrally positioned earth. The free-thinking Bruno preached in favor of the Copernican solar system and also proposed that the Sun was just another star moving in space. Inevitably, the university academics rebuked him.

"Oxford University and Giordano Bruno were celestial bodies in opposition," Anderson notes. "The university preached the ancient geocentric theories of Aristotle and Ptolemy. Every object in the heavens, it was said, orbited the earth, and the earth occupied the center of the universe." Bruno advanced the heresies that "the stars, contrary to fixed church doctrine, are free-floating objects in a fluid celestial firmament; that the universe is infinite, leaving no room for a physical heaven or hell; and that elements in the universe [called 'monads'] contain a divine spark at the root of life itself. Even the dust from which we are made contains this spark."

> If circumstances lead me, I will find
> Where truth is hid, though it were hid indeed
> Within the center.
>> Polonius, *Hamlet* (2.2)

Oxfordians have made a compelling case that de Vere began to set down the first of many versions of *Hamlet* as early as 1583, creating a fictional world at the Danish court that reflected the real world at the English court, with Hamlet essentially a self-portrait and Claudius representing Elizabeth's former lover, Leicester, who was thought to be a "serial poisoner" as well as Her Majesty's ambitious friend.

He would be launching into *Hamlet* just when discussions of the new ideas about the heavens were accelerating in England. The prince is a student at the University of Wittenberg in Germany, a major center for the Copernican theory; in fact, Giordano Bruno went on to teach at Wittenberg, where he could freely voice his bold ideas. (Later he was imprisoned for seven years before the Roman Inquisition burned him at the stake in 1600 for heresy.) The main storyline of *Hamlet*, of course, is that Claudius has usurped the throne of Denmark, depriving Hamlet of his rightful place. However, according to Peter Usher, Professor Emeritus of Astronomy and Astrophysics at Pennsylvania State University, the play is also "an allegorical description of the competition between two cosmological models." On one side is the heliocentric universe of Copernicus being taught at Wittenberg and personified by Hamlet; on the other is the old geocentric order, personified by Claudius (named for the ancient astronomer Claudius Ptolemy).

> Claudius: How is it that the clouds still hang on you?
> Hamlet: Not so, my lord. I am too much in the Sun. (1.2)

Hamlet deserves to be king, the royal sun at the center. According to the new astronomy of Copernicus and the sun-centered universe of Digges, the prince belongs on the throne at the center of the realm. As such, he is dangerous to the stability of the old hierarchy and, therefore, poses a direct threat to Claudius and Gertrude.

> Horatio: This bodes some strange eruption to our state. (1.1)
> Hamlet: The time is out of joint. O cursed spite
> That ever I was born to set it right! (1.5)

Within the cosmological allegory, the play is full of allusions to this struggle between the old and new structures. "The idea of a rotating and revolving earth was counter-intuitive to most people and contrary to established religious and scientific doctrine," Usher writes. When Claudius and Gertrude express their desire that Hamlet not return to Wittenberg, they do so by saying that such a course is "most *retrograde* to our desire"—an astronomical term for contrary motion, that is, the prince's motion away from them and toward the Copernican cosmology as taught at Wittenberg—the same place where Martin Luther had initiated the Protestant Reformation that was also disrupting the traditional order in England.

Scientists, according to Anderson, have observed that Shakespeare's record of astronomical knowledge, and his references to major celestial events, cease by mid-1604, the year of Oxford's death. The traditionally perceived author, however, would live until 1616—long enough, if he were really "Shakespeare," to continue to record momentous events such as the discovery of sunspots and of Jupiter's moons, or "other significant celestial phenomena and developments in astronomical science." But the great dramatist has nothing to say about any of the astronomical observations between 1604 and 1616.

"The quest for truth and exposure of falsity is a theme that runs through Shakespeare's play," Usher says. "The castle platform (at Elsinore) is the interface between the castle interior and the sky, a contrast that parallels the contrast of reality and appearance, as when Hamlet says, 'Seems, madam? Nay, it is. I know not seems.' The passage from geocentricism to Digges' vision of an infinite universe is a passage from appearances to reality." Oxford's extant letters show that he was keenly alert to this theme. "But the world is so cunning," he wrote Burghley in 1581, "as of a shadow they can make a substance, and of a likelihood a truth." In 1603 he wrote to Robert Cecil, "But I hope truth is subject to no prescription, for truth is truth though never so old, and time cannot make that false which was once true"—another reason why Oxford and "Shakespeare" were one and the same man.

Reason 62 – Musical Knowledge

> *"How sweet the moonlight sleeps upon this bank! Here will we sit and let the sounds of music creep in our ears. Soft stillness and the night become the touches of sweet harmony!"*

Only a writer with music flowing in his veins would give Lorenzo these famous lines to Jessica in *The Merchant of Venice* (5.1). Music is pervasive in Shakespeare's works; some 170 passages include the words "music" or "musical" or "musician." He continues:

Sit, Jessica. Look how the floor of heaven
Is thick inlaid with patens of bright gold!
There's not the smallest orb which thou behold'st
But in his motion like an angel sings,
Still choiring to the young-eyed cherubins.
Such harmony is in immortal souls . . .

Shakespeare uses "sing" in various forms no less than 247 times. Some forty passages deal with musical instruments. Lorenzo continues:

[*Enter Musicians*]
Come, ho, and wake Diana with a hymn!
With sweetest touches pierce your mistress' ear
And draw her home with music ...

He includes or alludes to the texts of well over a hundred songs. In addition to the numerous stage directions for music and sound effects, his dramatic and poetical work is permeated with specific references to more than 300 musical terms. And more in the same speech of Lorenzo in *The Merchant*:

The man that hath no music in himself
Nor is not moved with concord of sweet sounds

Is fit for treasons, stratagems and spoils:
The motions of his spirit are dull as night
And his affections dark as Erebus.
Let no such man be trusted.
Mark the music!

De Vere was associated with music from his teenage years at Cambridge and Oxford, before arriving at court in 1571 and quickly gaining the highest favor of Queen Elizabeth, becoming her dance partner and apparently performing for her on both the lute and the virginals. Early on he had become associated with Richard Edwards, Master of the Children of the Chapel Royal, who is credited with compiling *The Paradise of Dainty Devices* (1576), which includes at least eight of Oxford's early poems that appear to be song lyrics. He also maintained a company of adult actors and one of choir boys, who sang as well as performed stage works, and records of the 1580s indicate he patronized a traveling company known as The Earl of Oxford's Musicians. Oxford was the patron of John Farmer, the celebrated madrigalist, and from about 1572 onward he was involved in musical activities at court with the composer William Byrd, one of the greatest musicians England has produced. It appears he was Byrd's patron as well. The earl's own accomplishments in the field were praised by professional musicians.

In *Shakespeare's England* (1916), W. Barclay Squire reports that Shakespeare "is far in advance of his contemporaries" in terms of musical references, although his education in that field, "wherever it was acquired," had been "strictly on the lines of the polyphonic school"—a teaching that all parts of a composition must fit equally into the whole, as expressed in *Richard II* (5.5.):

Music, do I hear?
Ha, ha! Keep time. How sour sweet music is
When time is broke and no proportion kept!

Such a passage "cannot be understood without some knowledge of the elaborate system of proportions inherited by Elizabethan composers from the earlier English school," Squire observes. He adds it is "remarkable that the musical terms of the plays should be so consistently those of the old school of polyphony." Why is that remarkable? Because, during the last half of the 1590s, a new style of musical arrangement replaced the old one, yet the great dramatist was apparently unaware of it. "This change dates from about the year 1597," Squire writes, unable to conceal his bafflement, "yet in all the plays which Shakespeare produced from then [on], no allusion to the 'new music' can be discovered."

This would be baffling indeed if the author had actually been Shakspere, who, within the traditional time frame, still had the best of his career in front of him. In that case he surely would have incorporated the "new school" of music into his plays. But in the Oxfordian view, de Vere had finished writing the early versions of all his plays by 1589, which easily explains why "Shakespeare" failed to embrace a musical revolution that began almost a decade later. It would be natural that the best writer of that age, who seemed to know everything about music, would have known and worked with the best composer of the same age. And the evidence shows exactly that, although not in the way that orthodox history would have it.

William Byrd was past fifty when he moved from London in about 1593 to the small town of Stondon Massey, Essex, where he lived the rest of his life. But according to the traditional biography, Shakespere was just then getting started, so on that basis alone he and the great composer never even met each other. De Vere, on the other hand, was twenty-two and enjoying the royal favor in 1572, when Byrd was named a gentleman of the Chapel Royal and began work under Queen Elizabeth as organist, singer and composer.

The evidence suggests "an association between Byrd and Oxford of at least ten years," states Sally Mosher (a musician herself), who adds that they "were both at the court of Elizabeth I from about 1572 on .... Both were involved in activities that provided music for the court; and during this period, Oxford saved Byrd from possible bankruptcy by selling a certain property to Byrd's brother."

The Chapel Royal consisted of some twenty-four male singers and organists who provided church music for the royal household. They remained with the queen as part of her entourage, which included Oxford himself, as she traveled from palace to palace. "The likelihood is strong," Mosher writes, "that both Oxford and the queen would have played these pieces [on lute and virginal keyboard] by the composer whom both had patronized." Byrd's *The Earl of Oxford's March* "has been preserved in at least four versions," she reports, and "it was clearly well-known during the period." As a ranking earl, Oxford had his own "tucket" or musical signature announcing his arrival at tournaments. The tune at the heart of *The March* "has all the earmarks of such a tucket," Mosher says, adding, "In deference to [Oxford's] dreams of martial glory perhaps, or else to provide an entertainment at court, at some point during their close association William Byrd worked Oxford's tucket into a musical setting that called up visions of battle."

"The Shakespeare plays are full of tuckets," Mosher observes (*King Lear, Henry V, Henry VIII*, etc.). "In *Othello*, when Iago hears 'Othello's trumpets,' it means that he recognizes Othello by his tucket. The brief and open-ended tune that introduces *Oxford's March* has all the earmarks of this kind of semi-military identification. . . . Oxford, a veteran of real military action by the time he and Byrd met, would have known the military calls in use and could have supplied them to Byrd."

Byrd also composed music for Oxford's poem "If Women Could be Fair," included in a 1588 collection of Byrd's vocal works. Still another example of collaboration involves "My Mind to Me a Kingdom Is," a poem attributed to Oxford and published in Byrd's *Psalms, Sonnets, and Songs of Sadness and Piety* (1588). "This poem is one of the true masterpieces of the Elizabethan era," the *Harper's Magazine* blog notes, adding it is "understandable on many levels: as a sanctuary of conscience, as a statement of Calvinist precepts, as a dissertation on contentment, as a praise of the powers of imagination and invention. William Byrd's setting of the Oxford poem is one of the finest English art songs of the Elizabethan era."

> To shallow rivers, to whose falls
> Melodious birds sing madrigals!
>   Song in *Merry Wives of Windsor* (3.1)

The celebrated madrigalist John Farmer dedicated his most important work, *The First Set of English Madrigals* of 1599, to "my very good Lord and Master, Edward Devere Earle of Oxenford," praising his "judgment in Musicke" and declaring that "using this science as a recreation, your Lordship have over-gone most of them that make it a profession." This is high praise indeed for Oxford, to whom Farmer had also dedicated his previous work, *Plainsong Diverse & Sundry* of 1591, telling the earl he presented it to him because he knew "your Lordship's great affection to this noble science."

"Nothing is more astonishing in the whole history of music than the story of the English school of madrigal composers," writes Michael Delahoyde, noting that the adapter of *The First Set of Italian Madrigals Englished* in 1590 was Thomas Watson, who had dedicated *Hekatompathia, or the Passionate Century of Love* (1582) to de Vere, his patron.

Inserted in that songbook are "two excellent Madrigals of Master William Byrd, composed after the Italian vaine, at the request of the sayd

Thomas Watson." So we have Oxford connected personally and professionally to Farmer, Byrd and Watson, not to mention his company of musicians and that his many youthful poems were lyrics for songs. Clearly he was a driving force behind the sudden rise of the English Madrigal School.

Oxford was an expert in music just as "Shakespeare" shows himself to be, though orthodox scholars, aware that Shakspere was no such expert, tend to play down that facet of "Shakespeare" works. The only way to maintain that the Stratford man was the greatest writer of the English language is to keep "dumbing down" the works themselves! In fact, however, the Bard *was* an expert in the musical field, as Oxford was an expert. In *Shakespeare's England* (published in 1916, before the earl was identified as the great author), we find that "in no author are musical allusions more frequent than in Shakespeare."

The terms, often technical and always accurate, come bursting freely and spontaneously from the pen of the poet-dramatist, flowing from his very being, never inserted as information gleaned from research. The musical terms come cascading forth not to instruct or impress or do anything other than lend greater power, beauty, humor and meaning to a character's speech, mostly by way of metaphor:

> "What, to make thee an *instrument* and *play false strains* upon thee?
> Not to be endured!" – *As You Like It* (4.3; emphasis added)

Reason 63 - Horses and Horsemanship

> *"But if at any time with fiery energy he should call up a mimicry of war, he controls his foaming steed with a light rein; and, armed with a long spear, rides to the encounter. Fearlessly he settles himself in the saddle, gracefully bending his body this way and that. Now he circles round; now with spurred heel he rouses his charger. The gallant animal with fiery energy collects himself together, and flying quicker than the wind, beats the ground with his hoofs, and again is pulled up short as the reins control him. Bravo, valiant youth!"*—Translation of a Latin verse by Giles Fletcher, describing Oxford in a Westminster tournament at age twenty-one in 1571

I saw young Harry, with his beaver on,
His cuisses on his thighs, gallantly armed,
Rise from the ground like feathered Mercury,
And vaulted with such ease into his seat,
As if an angel dropped down from the clouds
To turn and wind a fiery Pegasus
And witch the world with noble horsemanship!
— Vernon, describing Prince Hal in *1 Henry IV* (4.1)

When Looney began his search that led to *"Shakespeare" Identified* in 1920, he listed eighteen characteristics, based on the poems and plays that the great author—whoever he was—must have possessed. Among them were, for example: "an enthusiast for Italy; a follower of sport (including falconry); a lover of music." Much later, after discovering Oxford, he realized "a grave omission" in his list of characteristics was that of horses and horsemanship: "We find there is more in Shakespeare about horses than upon almost any subject outside human nature. Indeed we feel tempted to say that Shakespeare brings them within the sphere of human nature."

Benedick: Sir, your wit ambles well; it goes easily.
                         —*Much Ado About Nothing* (5.1)

Rosalind: Time travels in divers paces, with divers persons: I'll tell you who Time ambles withal, who Time trots withal, who Time gallops withal, and who he stands still withal.
                         —*As You Like It* (3.2)

"There is, of course, his intimate knowledge of different kinds of horses, their physical peculiarities, all the details which go to form a good or a bad specimen of a given variety, almost a veterinary's knowledge of their diseases and their treatment," Looney continues. "But over and above all this there is a peculiar handling of the theme which raises a horse almost to the level of a being with a moral nature .... Not only did Oxford learn to ride, but, in those days when horsemanship was much more in vogue than it will probably ever be again, and when great skill was attained in horse-management, he was among those who excelled, particularly in tilts and tourneys, receiving special marks of royal appreciation of his skill. Horsemanship was, therefore, a very pronounced interest of his."

His father was the owner of valuable horses in the stable of Castle Hedingham; in his first will, of 1552, John de Vere, listed "ten geldings; nags with saddles, bridles and all things pertaining to them." [In *1 Henry IV*: "I prithee lend me thy lantern, to see my gelding in the stable" (2.1).] In his final will (1562) the sixteenth earl bequeathed "one of my great horses" to each of several friends such as Nicholas Bacon and William Cecil.

The Great Horse was the old English war-horse used for tournaments and service, and that particular kind was undoubtedly the model for Antony's horse in *Julius Caesar*:

It is a creature that I teach to fight,
To wind, to stop, to run directly on,

His corporal motion govern'd by my spirit. (4.1)

In September 1562 the boy Edward de Vere "came riding out of Essex" from his father's funeral "with seven score horse all in black; through London and Chepe and Ludgate, and so to Temple Bar," as noted in Machyn's *Diary* (1848). About a dozen distinct breeds of horses were in England during Oxford's lifetime, the most popular riding horses being the Turkey, the Barb, the Neapolitan and the Spanish Jennet. Of all of them, the Barbary horse or Barb "was undoubtedly the great author's favorite," writes A. Forbes Sieverking in *Shakespeare's England*, adding, "With such affection and intimacy does he dwell upon its merits that it is probable that the poet at one time possessed a roan Barb [usually Chestnut colored, sprinkled with white or gray]."

It may well be that the great author owned a roan Barb, especially if he was the earl of Oxford! The Barbary horse was a special breed from northern Africa, an expensive riding horse known for its fiery temperament and stamina. It was highly prized by the Italians, whose noble families established large racing stables—a horse for kings!

Hotspur:	Hath Butler brought those horses from the sheriff?
Servant:	One horse, my lord, he brought even now.
Hotspur:	What horse? A roan, a crop-ear, is it not?
Servant:	It is, my lord.
Hotspur:	That roan shall be my throne.

—1 Henry IV (2.3)

Henry VIII had purchased a number of Barbary horses from Frederico Gonzago of Mantua and elsewhere; private owners in England used the Barbs to develop the Thoroughbred. In the fourteenth century Richard II had owned a roan Barb, as "Shakespeare" wrote in the play bearing that king's name. When he is in prison after his crown has been taken by Bolingbroke, who is now Henry IV, the Groom tells him how the new king actually rode Richard's own horse (which he calls roan Barbary) in the procession for his coronation:

Groom:	O, how it yearned my heart when I beheld
	In London streets, that coronation day,
	When Bolingbroke rode on Roan Barbary,
	That horse that thou so often hast bestrid,
	That horse that I so carefully have dressed! (5.5)

First Bolingbroke took his crown ... now his horse! Richard cannot conceal his suffering:

Richard:	Rode he on Barbary? Tell me, gentle friend,

	How went he under him?
Groom:	So proudly as if he disdained the ground.

This is too, too much; his own horse has betrayed him!

Richard:	So proud that Bolingbroke was on his back!
	That jade hath eat bread from my royal hand –
	This hand hath made him proud with clapping him.
	Would he not stumble? Would he not fall down,
	Since pride must have a fall, and break the neck
	Of that proud man that did usurp his back?

But then, of course, the horse was merely being true to his own nature:

Richard:	Forgiveness, horse! Why do I rail on thee,
	Since thou, created to be awed by man,
	Wast born to bear? I was not made a horse,
	And yet I bear a burden like an ass,
	Spurred, galled and tired by jouncing Bolingbroke.

There are additional passages referencing "Barbary" horses in *Hamlet,* in which the king wagers six Barbary horses against six French rapiers and poniards on the prince's ability to win the fencing match with Laertes, and in *Othello,* when Iago describes Othello as a Barbary horse, rakishly alluding to the Barbary's Moorish origins and, also, to the practice of breeding one to an English mare.

A favorite Shakespearean passage about horses is to be found in *Venus and Adonis* "in which," Looney wrote, "a mere animal instinct is raised in horses to the dignity of a complex and exalted human passion."

A breeding jennet, lusty, young, and proud,
Adonis' trampling courser doth espy,
And forth she rushes, snorts, and neighs aloud.
The strong-necked steed, being tied unto a tree,
Breaketh his rein, and to her straight goes he.

Imperiously he leaps, he neighs, he bounds,
And now his woven girths he breaks asunder.
The bearing earth with his hard hoof he wounds,
Whose hollow womb resounds like heaven's thunder;
The iron bit he crusheth 'tween his teeth,
Controlling what he was controlled with...

The full scene comprises 59 lines (260-318), leaving no doubt that the poet must have been an expert horseman.

Reason 64 – Knowledge of Heraldry

Two books devoted entirely to Shakespeare's knowledge and treatment of heraldry are *The Heraldry of Shakespeare: A Commentary with Annotations* (1930) by Guy Cadogan Rothery and *Shakespeare's Heraldry* (1950) by Charles Wilfred Scott-Giles. They show that the Bard knew a great deal about coats of arms, blazons, charges, fields, escutcheons (shields), crests, badges, hatchments (panels), gules (red markings or tinctures) and much more. But it's not simply that Shakespeare has considerable knowledge about heraldry; it's that such knowledge is an integral part of his thought process. He uses heraldic terms in spontaneous, natural ways, often metaphorically, making his descriptions more vivid while stirring and enriching our emotions. Take, for example, the word *badge*, which in heraldry is an emblem indicating allegiance to some family or property. Shakespeare uses it literally, of course, but also metaphorically: Falstaff in *2 Henry IV* speaks of "the badge of pusillanimity and cowardice" (4.3); Ferdinand *in Love's Labour's Lost* cries out, "Black is the badge of hell" (4.3); Lysander in *A Midsummer Night's Dream* talks about "bearing the badge of faith" (3.2); Tamora in *Titus Andronicus* declares, "Sweet mercy is nobility's true badge" (1.1); and in Sonnet 44 the poet refers to "heavy tears, badges of either's woe." Surely this author was "one of the wolfish earls," as Walt Whitman perceived, a proud nobleman for whom hereditary titles, shields and symbols were everyday aspects of his environment. From early boyhood, de Vere had been steeped in the history of his line dating back 500 years to William the Conqueror; the heraldry of his ancestors, as well as that of other noble families, became interwoven with his vocabulary.

Helena in *A Midsummer Night's Dream* extends the metaphor of two bodies sharing the same heart by presenting the image of a husband and wife's impaled arms: "So, with two seeming bodies, but one heart; two of the first, like coats in heraldry, due but to one and crowned with one crest" (3.2). Another example of "Shakespeare" thinking and writing in heraldic terms occurs in the opening scene of *Henry VI, Pt.1* at the funeral of Henry V at Westminster Abbey. A messenger warns the English against taking recent victories for granted by describing setbacks in France as the cropping (cutting out) of the French quarters in the royal arms of England:

> Awake, awake, English nobility! Let not sloth dim your honors new-begot: cropped are the flower-deluces in your arms! Of England's coat one half is cut away!

England's coat of arms presented flower-de-luces or *fleur-de-lis*, the emblem of French royalty, quartered with Britain's symbolic lions. Cropping the two French quarters would cut away half the English arms—a vivid description of England's losses in France.

"The Vere arms changed repeatedly over many generations," Robert Brazil notes, adding that details of Oxford's arms had "numerous documented precedents" consisting not only of drawings but also the "blazonry" or descriptions of shields in precise heraldic language, using only words. "Through the science of blazon, infinitely complex visual material is described in such a precise way that one can accurately reproduce full color arms with dozens of complex coats, based on the words of the blazon alone." At the Vere seat of Castle Hedingham, the young earl necessarily studied the seals and tombs of his ancestors. He, after all, was a child of the waning feudal aristocracy, set to inherit the title of Lord Great Chamberlain of England. To assert the rights and rankings of his Vere identity, he needed exact knowledge of his family's heraldry and to "blazon" or describe it in words through the five centuries of its history.

"Shakespeare" uses "blazon" just as we might expect it to be employed by de Vere, that is, as a natural enrichment of language. Mistress Quickly in *The Merry Wives of Windsor* employs the word in a burst of heraldic imagery:

> About, about; search Windsor Castle, elves, within and out …
> Each fair installment, coat, and several crest, with loyal blazon, evermore be blest! (5.5)

Oxford knew Windsor Castle well; he is recorded staying there several times. At nineteen he lodged in a hired room in the town of Windsor while recovering from illness.

Mistress Quickly refers to each "installment" in the castle, that is, each place where an individual knight is installed. The knight's "coat" was on a stall-plate nailed to the back of the stall and the "crest" was a figure or device originally borne by a knight on his helmet.

From the same pen we find "blazon" in a variety of metaphorical contexts:

> I'faith, lady, I think your *blazon* to be true.—*Much Ado About Nothing* (2.1)
> Thy tongue, thy face, thy limbs, actions and spirit do give thee five-fold *blazon*. — *Twelfth Night* (1.5)
> But this eternal *blazon* must not be to ears of flesh and blood.—*Hamlet* (1.5)

In Sonnet 106 the poet uses "blazon" in the context of accounts of medieval chivalry, writing of "beauty making beautiful old rhyme,/ In praise of Ladies dead and lovely Knights," followed by: "Then in the *blazon* of sweet beauty's best,/ Of hand, of foot, of lip, of eye, of brow,/ I see their antique Pen would have expressed/ Even such a beauty as you master now."

In *Hamlet* the prince tells the players that a speech he "chiefly loved" was the one that Virgil's Aeneas delivers to Dido, Queen of Carthage, about the fall of Troy. Before the first player can begin to recite it, however, Hamlet delivers thirteen lines from memory—describing how Pyrrhus, son of the Greek hero Achilles, had black arms while hiding inside the Trojan horse, but then his arms became drenched in the red blood of whole families that were slaughtered.

The story would have had even greater impact upon aristocratic members of the audience who knew the bloody tale was being told in the context of heraldic terms, such as "sable arms" (the black device displayed on Pyrrhus's shield); "gules" (red); and "tricked" (decorated), not to mention that Pryrrhus's arms, covered with red blood, are "smeared with heraldry":

> The rugged Pyrrhus, he whose sable arms,
> Black as his purpose, did the night resemble
> When he lay couched in the ominous horse,
> Hath now this dread and black complexion smeared
> With heraldry more dismal. Head to foot
> Now is he total gules, horridly tricked. (*Hamlet*, 2.2)

Even *Lucrece* (1594), the second publication as by "Shakespeare," is filled with heraldic imagery:

> But Beauty, in that white entitled
> From Venus' doves, doth *challenge* that fair *field*...
> This heraldry in Lucrece's face was seen...
> (Stanzas 9 & 10, emphases added)

["Challenge" = lay claim to; "field" = the surface of a heraldic shield on which figures or colors are displayed, but also evoking a battlefield].

Brazil notes that previous earls of Oxford had employed a special greyhound as a heraldic symbol, but that Edward had stopped using it; in the opening scene of *Merry Wives*, which begins and ends with humorous dialogue involving heraldry, there is a line (unrelated to anything else) about a "fallow" greyhound, one that is no longer used:

> Page: I am glad to see you, good Master Slender.
> Slender: How does your *fallow greyhound*, sir?

In this "throwaway" exchange, is de Vere pointing to his own heraldic history?

Reason 65 – Gardens and Gardening

"One occupation, one point of view, above all others, is naturally his, that of a gardener; watching, preserving, tending and caring for growing things, especially flowers and fruit. All through his plays he thinks most easily and readily of human life and action in the terms of a gardener ... it is ever present in Shakespeare's thought and imagination, so that nearly all his characters share in it."—Caroline Spurgeon, *Shakespeare's Imagery* (1935)

Fig. 13 - John Gerard

Edward de Vere was a ward of Elizabeth for nine years, living at the London home of William Cecil. "One of the chief features of Cecil House was its garden," Ward writes. "The grounds in which the house stood must have covered many acres, and were more extensive than those of any of the other private homes in Westminster. John Gerard would become Sir William Cecil's gardener for twenty years (1578-1597); and Sir William himself evidently took a great pride in his garden.... Cecil imbued his sons and the royal wards under his charge with his own keenness in horticulture." We can easily imagine the teenage lord roaming through the great Cecil gardens, examining and smelling the flowers and learning about them.

Referring to Cecil's country seat of Theobalds, Ogburn Jr. writes that gardens "were laid out on three sides of the mansion by the horticulturalist John Gerard ... (author of *The Herball, or General Historie of Plants*, 1597) ....Trees and shrubs seen rarely if at all in Britain were imported from abroad. The gardens were widely known in Europe."

O, what pity is it
That he [the King] had not so trimm'd and dress'd his land
As we this garden! We at time of year
Do wound the bark, the skin of our fruit-trees,
Lest, being over-proud in sap and blood,
With too much riches it confound itself:
Had he done so to great and growing men,
They might have lived to bear and he to taste

Their fruits of duty: superfluous branches
We lop away, that bearing boughs may live:
Had he done so, himself had borne the crown,
Which waste of idle hours hath quite thrown down.
　　—The Gardener in *Richard II* (3.4)

The gardener sows the seeds, whereof flowers do grow,
And others yet do gather them that took less pain I know.
So I the pleasant grape have pulled from the vine,
And yet I languish in great thirst, while others drink the wine.
　　— Oxford, *Paradise of Dainty Devices*, 1576

O thou weed,
Who art so lovely fair and smell'st so sweet
That the sense aches at thee...
When I have plucked the rose,
I cannot give it vital growth again,
It must needs wither: I'll smell it on the tree.
　　—Othello in *Othello* (4.2 & 5.2)

What doth avail the tree unless it yield fruit unto another? What doth avail the rose unless another took pleasure in the smell? Why should this tree be accounted better than that tree, but for the goodness of his fruit? Why should this vine be better than that vine, unless it brought forth a better grape than the other? Why should this rose be better esteemed than that rose, unless in pleasantness of smell it far surpassed the other rose? And so it is in all other things as well as in man
　　—Oxford's prefatory letter to *Cardanus' Comfort*, 1573

The laboring man that tills the fertile soil
And reaps the harvest fruit, hath not indeed
The gain but pain, and if for all his toil
He gets the straw, the Lord will have the seed.
The manchet fine falls not unto his share,
On coarsest cheat, his hungry stomach feeds.
The landlord doth possess the finest fare,
He pulls the flowers, the other plucks but weeds.
　　— Oxford's poem for *Cardanus' Comfort*, 1573

Oxford was uniquely positioned to assume the point of view of the gardener, as well as to acquire the love and knowledge of seeds, plants, flowers and trees exhibited by Shakespeare.

CHAPTER THIRTEEN

THE FRENCH MATCH

Reason 66 – "Monsieur"

Traditional biographies of Shakespeare give no hint that François de Valois, duke of Alençon, a son of Catherine de Medici, may be depicted in any of the plays; his courtship of Queen Elizabeth had ended by 1582, when William of Stratford was just eighteen. On the other hand, de Vere was then thirty-two, having lived at the center of the political storm of the French Match during the previous decade; with him in mind as the author, a curtain is lifted and Alençon may be seen in several of the plays.

Elizabeth was on royal progress in the summer of 1578 when the French envoys arrived to begin negotiations for her marriage to the youngest son of Catherine de Medici, the most powerful woman in Europe. The queen received the French diplomats at Long Melford, where she sent for Oxford, her highly favored courtier, to perform a dancing exhibition for them. Shockingly, however, de Vere refused to obey his sovereign—not once, but twice.

Fig. 14 – Catherine De Medici, Queen of France

Catherine de Medici of Florence had married Henry II of France in 1547 at age fourteen. She became a political force upon his death in 1559, as the mother of three successive kings: Francis II, who died in 1560; Charles IX, who died in 1574; and Henry III, then twenty-three. Catherine had been the regent for young Charles when persecutions of Huguenots, or French Protestants, erupted in the St. Bartholomew's Day Massacre of 1572, in which thousands were killed in Paris and throughout France.

Six years later, in 1578, Catherine was promoting the marriage of her fourth and youngest son to Elizabeth Tudor. Alençon was twenty-three,

Elizabeth forty-five. In boyhood his face had been scarred by smallpox, which also had slightly deformed his spine. Alençon had rebelled against his family, proclaiming himself a protector of the Huguenots; nonetheless, he was still a Catholic and, given that his brother Henry III was childless, the young duke was next in line to the French throne.

The prospect of a French Match had sent Elizabeth's court into a state of turmoil. Leading the heated opposition were Puritans (right-wing Protestants) such as Walsingham and Sidney, not to mention Leicester, who had wanted to wed the queen himself. Many feared that if Elizabeth married Alençon, she might die without a successor by blood, leaving her widowed king consort free to bring England under French control. Walsingham predicted riots would ensue.

It appears, however, that Elizabeth was enacting a role within a grand romantic drama on the world stage, playing her part in the prospective French Match chiefly to prevent an alliance between France and Spain for as long as possible; that is, she was buying time so that England could build up naval strength capable of withstanding a Spanish invasion.

In the following year Oxford would publicly support the French marriage along with his great friend Sussex, a kind of father figure to him. (Oxford had seen military action under Sussex against the Northern Rebellion in 1570; and it was Sussex who, as Lord Chamberlain, brought plays to court.) Also supporting the match was Burghley; he, Sussex and Oxford may have understood that it was all a charade, but Elizabeth would play her part so well that even they could not always be sure of her intentions.

A year earlier, however, Oxford was still able to express his rage against the Alençon marriage, and his refusal to dance for the French envoys made that clear. The day before, Elizabeth had unfairly reprimanded Sussex for failing to furnish enough "pieces of plate" for the French visitors, so Oxford was already angry at the queen, who, he correctly believed, was being influenced against Sussex by Leicester. The Spanish ambassador reported that Elizabeth "sent twice to tell the Earl of Oxford, who is a very gallant lad, to dance before the ambassadors; whereupon he replied that he hoped Her Majesty would not order him to do so, as he did not wish to entertain Frenchmen. When the Lord Steward presented him with the message the second time, he replied that he would not give pleasure to Frenchmen, nor listen to such a message, and with that he left the room. He is a lad who has a great following in the country...."

It's hard to imagine anyone daring to publicly embarrass the queen in such a way, especially in front of the French ambassadors just when critical negotiations were beginning. How he avoided being tossed in prison or worse is a wonder; but it seems he was not even reprimanded, indicating the favorable position he held in her eyes at the time. In any case, he vehemently opposed the Alençon marriage at the time. It appears that he soon wrote the first version of *Cymbeline*, which was performed by none other than Sussex's company on Sunday, 28 December 1578, at Richmond Palace, where it was recorded as *An history of the crueltie of A Stepmother*.

After Oxford's refusal to dance, Eva Turner Clark suggests, he "wrote a new drama in which, disguised as a play of early Britain, he told the story of the French Queen's efforts to get her son married to the English Queen … the arrival of the Spanish ambassador, and the danger of war with Spain and France over the Low Countries."

The Ogburns describe the relevant part of the play this way:

> A wicked Queen [Cymbeline's wife = Catherine de Medici] endeavors to contrive a match between her stupid, villainous son [Cloten = Alençon] and the daughter [Imogen = Elizabeth, in part] of a King of ancient Britain [Cymbeline], whose stepmother she is hoping to advance her cause of making her son King of Britain by the judicious use of poisonous herbs and compounds. The prototype of this wicked Queen was Catherine de Medici, who, while practicing occultism and astrology, was supposed to have poisoned more than one person whom she wished out of the way.

In this view, Oxford was writing about his own political world and trying to influence Elizabeth and her policies. Personally and politically he had much at stake; with this in mind, the play we know as *Cymbeline* is suddenly comprehended in new and dynamic ways, providing just one answer to the question of why the identity of "William Shakespeare" matters. In this early work first staged at court, Oxford can be seen warning Elizabeth about the character of de Medici and her son, Alençon:

> That such a crafty devil as is his mother
> Should yield the world this ass! A woman that
> Bears all down with her brain; and this her son
> Cannot take two from twenty, for his heart,
> And leave eighteen…
> —Second Lord in *Cymbeline* (2.2)

After Looney identified Oxford in 1920 it became possible to see Alençon depicted in the plays. A surge of new research began; Clark's work appeared in the United States in 1931 as *Hidden Allusions in Shakespeare's Plays*, wherein she notices portraits of Alençon in early versions of *Cymbeline, As You Like It, Love's Labour's Lost, The Two Gentlemen of Verona, Henry VI, Pt.2, Antony and Cleopatra* and *A Midsummer Night's Dream* (see below).

Reason 67 – Bottom's Dream

A multifaceted reason to view Oxford as "Shakespeare" involves the time frame within which the works were created. Most, if not all, of the Shakespeare works were originally written ten or more years earlier than generally supposed. Studies of *A Midsummer Night's Dream*, for example, reveal its first version may have been a court masque parodying the farcical French match (1578-1581), when marriage negotiations between Elizabeth (as Queen Titania) and Hercule François de France, the Duke of Alençon (in the character of Bottom, disguised as an ass) were in full swing. But Shakspere was only seventeen in 1581, still very much in Stratford and not yet married, leading most scholars to date the original composition of the *Dream* no earlier than 1594. One result of that myopia is that few, if any, books about Shakespeare have anything to say about a connection between that masterful romantic comedy and the French Match.

The fact that "William Shakespeare" first appeared as a writer in 1593 is a problem for mainstream scholars all by itself. It means the very first publication by the young man from Stratford was a highly sophisticated, cultured narrative poem, one of the best ever written in England.

The orthodox view requires the original writing of *Dream* to fit within the dates of Shakspere's life, forcing most scholars to place the start of its composition in 1594. Really? Was our struggling young playwright creating *A Midsummer Night's Dream* for the public playhouse? No. "The almost universally held belief among critics" is that the play "was written for a private performance, clearly a part of the festivities attendant upon an aristocratic wedding," writes Campbell, who also states:

> The only existing text is the version of the comedy designed to be presented in the great hall of an Elizabethan gentleman's country house, or possibly at the court, on an occasion at which Queen Elizabeth may have been present [Virtually all scholars acknowledge Titania as a portrait of Elizabeth] … Many weddings of the nobility solemnized about the years 1594-1596 have been suggested as the occasion for which the play was written. One

considered most likely by many historians is that of Elizabeth de Vere, the daughter of the earl of Oxford, to the earl of Derby, which took place on January 26, 1595.

Now, let's get this straight: a young man from Stratford-upon-Avon, a commoner near the start of his London career as an actor-playwright, creates a play not for the public theater, but for a private wedding of the nobility. He includes a major female character, Queen Titania, representing Elizabeth Tudor, and has her fall in love with an ass! Moreover, the play is performed in front of that same female monarch, known for her extreme vanity, along with the full court at Greenwich Palace!

If we remove the constricting timeline of the Stratford fellow's life, it becomes possible to look clearly at the evidence of the *Dream* as a masterpiece that was revised two or three times, according to changing circumstances, over more than a dozen years, from the Alençon affair that reached its climax in 1581 to a wedding at court in 1595. "Tips of the iceberg" keep indicating this "hidden history" of the play, and Campbell is honest enough to mention some of these anomalies, as when he writes: "Certain textual inconsistencies *indicate that the play as we have it has been revised,* and that the lines which deal with the fantasy form only one of two textual layers" (emphasis added).

The easiest way to eliminate the mystery is to realize that the first text of *A Midsummer Night's Dream* was an Elizabethan version of a *Saturday Night Live* skit, written by thirty-year-old Oxford in 1580. He was then still in the highest favor of Elizabeth (though not for long); he and Lyly were presenting plays for aristocrats at the private Blackfriars and at court. Eva Turner Clark suggests that the earl produced *Dream* as a masque (probably for the Blackfriars audience, poking fun at both Elizabeth and Alençon) in 1581, before presenting it in a more complete form for the queen during the Christmas season of 1584. Then he would revise the play again in the 1590s, for performance during the Greenwich festivities celebrating his daughter's marriage to the earl of Derby.

Titania courts Bottom while he wears an ass's head. Bottom repeatedly refers to "mounsieur" for "monsieur," a comical (and mispronounced) reference to Alençon, who would not yield to the pressures on him to leave England, just as Bottom complains: "I see their knavery; this is to make an ass of me; to fright me, if they could. But I will not stir from this place ...!" (3.1) And Titania cries: "My Oberon! What visions have I seen! Methought I was enamored of an ass!" (4.1)

When Alençon finally left the country in early 1582, writes Clark, "he realized that his dream of being Elizabeth's consort and sovereign of

England had come to an end, just as Bottom's dream of a life in fairyland had ended."

Reason 68 – "The Two Gentlemen"

A remarkable episode in Elizabethan history occurred during the time of the French Match, when the duke of Alençon sent over an "advance man" in early 1579 to woo the queen before he himself could get there to marry her. The envoy was Alençon's master of the wardrobe and close friend, Jean de Simier, whose smooth tongue and erotic flattery so captivated Elizabeth that her nobles were shocked in addition to being jealous. As contemporary historian Camden put it, the little French aristocrat was "most skilled in love-toys, pleasant conceits, and court dalliances"—transforming the forty-five-year-old queen of England into a radiant, gasping, giggling young woman suddenly appearing half her age.

Elizabeth called Alençon's dark-skinned representative her "monkey" as she basked in his sweet whisperings and refinements of French passion at Richmond Palace. The masterful Simier appeared to be seducing her in front of the entire English court. He and Elizabeth enjoyed intimate suppers and dined together by candlelight when they weren't otherwise jumping in and out of each other's bedrooms. Could it be that, while paving the way for the queen's bridegroom, he had become her lover?

Alençon came over unofficially that August, staying at Greenwich, where Elizabeth swooned over him as well. Calling him her "frog," she treated him with a great show of affection, despite his being more than twenty years younger, and despite the disfigurations of his face and body from childhood smallpox, which had stunted his growth before he could reach five feet.

Imagine that you happened to be the chief comedy writer and stage producer for the rarefied audience of the Elizabethan royal court. How could you resist putting on some satirical skits to set the palace on a roar? What fertile ground it was for a young playwright such as Oxford, who apparently had Elizabeth's approval, and even her encouragement, to have uproarious fun with it!

On 26 December 1579, a play called *A History of the Duke of Milan and the Marquis of Mantua* was presented at Whitehall by the actors of Sussex, the Lord Chamberlain, who was Oxford's great friend and supporter. Clark concludes that this court comedy was one of the earliest versions of *The Two Gentlemen of Verona*. That play—more clearly than most of Shakespeare's plays—appears to reveal various stages of development.

De Vere had spent much time in Italy during 1575-76, sojourning in Verona and Venice. He had ample opportunity to attend Italian plays and the street theatricals of *Commedia dell'arte*—influences apparent in *Two Gentlemen* with which Shakspere of Stratford could not have been familiar. The settings of the play are Verona, Milan and the frontiers of Mantua, which Clark sees as representing Paris, London and Flanders.

Oxford returned home from the Continent in April 1576 after fifteen months, cutting short his stay because of scandalous gossip at court that his wife, Anne Cecil, had committed adultery and given birth to another man's child. In the play, Valentine apparently alludes to this personal episode by saying he had been traveling "some sixteen months, and longer might have stayed if crooked fortune had not thwarted me" (4.1).

It seems that the early version of 1579 was more topical and much shorter than the later one; the play was mentioned by Meres in 1598 (as merely *Gentlemen of Verona*), but withheld from publishers until it appeared in the Folio of 1623 as *The Two Gentlemen of Verona*. The early version for the court presented characters loosely based on participants in the Anglo-French marriage: Elizabeth became Silvia, the beautiful daughter of the duke of Milan; Alençon became Valentine, the gentleman of Verona who travels to the court at Milan and falls in love with Silvia; and Simier became Proteus, the other gentleman of Verona, who sues for Silvia's affections himself. Within *Two Gentlemen* the many allusions to the proposed match (as it stood circa 1579) include one involving Alençon's escape from the Louvre window by means of a rope ladder, which occurred the year before on Valentine's Day. Perhaps Oxford chose the name Valentine for Alençon because of that incident. Indeed, Valentine appears to refer to the episode when he speaks of himself and Silvia: "Ay, we are betrothed: nay, more, our marriage-hour, with all the cunning manner of our flight, determined of: how I must climb her window, strong the ladder made of cords; and all the means plotted and 'greed on for my happiness" (2.4).

Another allusion is the use of the French word "mal-content" in reference to opponents of Catherine de Medici called the Malcontents, of which Alençon was the figurehead. When Valentine asks Speed how he can tell that he is in love, Speed replies: "Marry, by these special marks: first you have learned, like Sir Proteus, to wreathe your arms like a *malecontent* [sic]; to relish a love-song ..." (2.1).

Oxford apparently kept updating the early topical play as the French Match proceeded to its ultimate failure in early 1582, when Alençon finally left England. In the previous December, the French prince was still stubbornly refusing to leave and actually threatened the queen, telling her: "If I cannot get you for my wife by fair means and affection, I must do so by force, for I will not leave this country without you!"

Proteus mirrors that statement in the final scene of the play:

Proteus:	Nay, if the gentle spirit of moving words can no way change you to a milder form, I'll woo you like a soldier, at arms' end, and love you 'gainst the nature of love, force ye.
Silvia:	O heaven!
Proteus:	I'll force thee yield to my desire! (5.4).

The praise of Silvia in *Two Gentlemen* reflects the worshipful flattery lavished upon Elizabeth, as when Valentine says of Silvia: "Yet let her be a principality, sovereign to all the creatures on the earth!" (2.4).

When the play was revised yet again, its new title, *The Two Gentlemen of Verona,* was perhaps an inside joke indicating "The Two Sides of One Ver":

1. Valentine, the idealistic side of Oxford, the courtier setting forth to travel
2. Proteus, his creative side, as an artist who views the world more darkly.

But that possibility is beyond the topic at hand, that the presence of Alençon and Simier in an earlier, shorter, more topical version of *Two Gentlemen* is yet another reason to conclude that Oxford wrote the works attributed to Shakespeare, not William of Stratford, who, in 1579, was only fifteen years old.

Reason 69 – Portia's Suitors

"I am always inclined to believe that Shakespeare has more allusions to particular facts and persons than his readers commonly suppose," observed Dr. Samuel Johnson (1709-1784) in connection with *The Merchant of Venice*, adding, "Perhaps in the enumeration of Portia's suitors there may be some covert allusion to those of Queen Elizabeth."

Johnson was speaking freely without worrying whether his perceptions fell in line with the Stratford man's life. He noticed, for example, that Portia's unflattering descriptions of her suitors reflect characteristics of Elizabeth's actual suitors from different countries, including those of her main suitor, the Duke of Alençon, who visited England in 1579 and 1581 (when Shakspere was fifteen and seventeen). The duke was well known to Oxford and others at the English court as

"Monsieur," and we find Portia's waiting-gentlewoman asking her: "How say you by the French lord, Monsieur le Bon?"

The mocking reply by Portia may reflect what Oxford heard the Queen say privately about Alençon:

> God made him, and therefore let him pass for a man. In truth, I know it is a sin to be a mocker, but he! Why, he hath a horse better than the Neapolitan's, a better bad habit of frowning than the Count Palentine; he is every man in no man. If a thrush sing, he falls straight a-cap'ring. He will fence with his own shadow. If I should marry him, I should marry twenty husbands. If he would despise me, I would forgive him, for if he loves me to madness, I shall never requite him. (1.2)

In a 1579 diatribe against the stage called *School of Abuse*, Stephen Gosson reported he had seen a play (now apparently lost) about "the bloody minds of usurers" called *The Jew*, performed at the Bull inn-yard in preparation for presentation at court. Clark suggests that *The Jew* was also performed for the royal court at Whitehall on 2 February 1580 as *Portio and Demorantes*, and that it was the original version of *The Merchant of Venice*.

In the play attributed to Shakespeare the character Lancelot Gobbo, a clown and servant to Shylock, refers to "Scylla," a sea-monster, and "Charybdis," a violent whirlpool in the strait between Italy and Sicily, invoking the proverbial difficulty of avoiding one danger without falling prey to the other—what today we might call being "caught between a rock and a hard place."

"Truly then I fear you are damned both by father and mother," Lancelot tells Shylock's daughter Jessica. "Thus when I shun Scylla, your father [the monster], I fall into Charybdis, your mother [the whirlpool]."

Remarkably, on 24 February 1580, just three weeks after the Whitehall performance for her Majesty and the court, the queen used the same phrase to describe her dilemma in relation to the French match. According to Mendoza, the Spanish ambassador, Elizabeth was in her chamber with Burghley and the Archbishop of York when she said:

> Here I am between Scylla and Charybdis. Alençon has agreed to all the terms I sent him, and he is asking me to tell him when I wish him to come and marry me. If I do not marry him, I know not whether he [and France] will remain friendly with me; and if I do I shall not be able to govern my country with the freedom and security I have hitherto enjoyed. What shall I do?

Had Elizabeth referred to "Scylla and Charybdis" during a conversation with Oxford? Was the phrase fresh in her mind after attending the recent court performance of *Portio and Demorantes*? Whatever the case, the only use of that phrase within all of "Shakespeare's" works—in a speech by Portia, who is clearly modeled on the queen—appears to have originated at the same time, in the same context, as Elizabeth's own historical use of it.

Portia expresses her dilemma, moreover, in virtually the same way the queen of England expressed hers; she even invokes an image of Elizabeth's father, Henry VIII, who left behind a "will" instructing that Elizabeth "shall not marry, nor take any person to be her husband, without the assent and consent of the Privy-Councilors and others...." "O me," Portia cries out in *The Merchant*, "the word 'choose'! I may neither choose whom I would, nor refuse whom I dislike; so is the will of a living daughter curbed by the will of a dead father" (1.2). Later in the scene she speaks literally as Elizabeth did: "If I live to be as old as Sibylla, I will die as chaste as Diana, unless I be obtained by the manner of my father's will."

The motif of the three caskets comes from an old story, but in the play their contents correspond to the three crowns of England: silver for the French, gold for Irish, and lead for the English kingdom—exactly as depicted at Elizabeth's coronation. Given such topical allusions to the great issue of the French match at the English court *circa* 1579, how can it still be maintained that Shakspere of Stratford wrote *The Merchant of Venice*?

Reason 70 – Philip Sidney

Edmund Spenser's first mention of someone named "Willie" appeared in *The Shepherd's Calendar* attributed to "Immerito," a pen name, in 1579. At that time Oxford was twenty-nine and a recognized poet (but had stopped signing his poems three years earlier), whereas Shakspere was just fifteen years old.

Spenser depicted a "rhyming match" between two poets, "Willie" and "Perigot." It was a thinly disguised spoof on the current rivalry between the leaders of England's two literary factions: Oxford, head of the Euphuists, and Sir Philip Sidney (1554-1586), a defacto leader of a faction that sought to 'standardize' English versifying. The two men were also on opposite sides politically; in general, Oxford was more liberal while Sidney leaned to the Puritan camp. That year they also became embroiled in an infamous "quarrel," or shouting match, on the Greenwich Palace tennis court, where members of the visiting French delegation had front-row seats, watching from the windows of their private galleries. The delegation had come to England to negotiate the marriage of Queen Elizabeth and the Duke of Alençon, which Sidney opposed and Oxford publicly championed, though Oxford apparently knew, along with Burghley, that the French match was a big charade on her Majesty's part.

Fig. 15 - Sir Philip Sidney

Oxford held Sidney in contempt for his plagiarism of other writers' works; for that reason he hated the contemporary praise Sidney received but didn't deserve. On the royal tennis court, the earl scornfully glared at Sidney and shouted: "Puppy!" to which Sidney retorted, "In respect, all the world knows that puppies are gotten by dogs, and children by men!" Oxford stood silent, allowing Sidney's words to resound within the courtyard. The unintended implication was that Sidney, a puppy, was begotten by a dog (a son of a bitch, we might say). Then after some further sharp words, Sir Philip "led the way abruptly out of the Tennis-Court," as Fulke Greville recorded in his adoring homage *Life of the Renowned Sir Philip Sidney* (written 1610-14, but not published until 1652).

Sidney and other Romanticists aimed to "reform" English poetry by instituting "certain laws and rules of quantities of English syllables for English verse," as Spenser wrote to Harvey. Their objective, Ward writes, was to "reclothe the old stories of knighthood and chivalry as to render them more vivid and applicable to their own times."

Oxford and his Euphuists viewed laws and rules of literature as made to be broken (a view "Shakespeare" would share). Their aim was to refine and enrich the English language; as Ward writes, "It was the magic of words and the imagery of sentences that appealed to them."

Ward also observes that, regardless of how much Sidney irked Oxford, "There is nothing essentially antagonistic in these two points of view; neither can live without the other." These men were literary pioneers, with Oxford and Sidney mutually providing each other with "the necessary stimulus without which no human achievement can be attained."

Probably the most notable example of the Oxford-Sidney literary rivalry is their pair of epigrams, Oxford's beginning with "Were I a king I might command content" and Sidney's verse, in reply, beginning with

"Wert thou a king, yet not command content." Spenser opens the contest in his *Shepherd's Calendar* this way:

Willie (Oxford):	Tell me, Perigot, what shall be the game
	Wherefore with mine thou dare thy music match?
	Or been thy bagpipes run far out of frame?
	Or hath the cramp thy joints benumbed with ache?
Perigot (Sidney):	Ah! Willie, when the heart is ill assayed,
	How can bagpipe or joints be well a-apaid?

The exchange continues through a succession of stanzas and grows into a wild volley of contrapuntal rhyming, such as:

Perigot (Sidney):	It fell upon a holy eve,
Willie (Oxford):	Hey, ho, holiday!
Perigot (Sidney):	When holy fathers were wont to shrieve.
Willie (Oxford):	Now 'ginneth the roundelay!
Perigot (Sidney):	Sitting upon a hill so high,
Willie (Oxford):	Hey, ho, the high hill!
Perigot (Sidney):	The while my flock did feed thereby.
Willie (Oxford):	The while the shepherd self did spill!

Here, I submit, we have Spenser describing a significant chapter in the development of the great author who would begin to call himself "Shakespeare" some fourteen years later. The lines he assigned to "Willie" can be described as "pre-Shakespearean," that is, foreshadowing the scene in *Twelfth Night* when Feste the Clown (representing Oxford) sings with the same "hey, ho" and back-and-forth rhyming:

When that I was and a little tiny boy,
With hey, ho, the wind and the rain,
A foolish thing was but a toy,
For the rain it raineth every day.

But this reason also involves the crucial issue of dating, with the example of *Love's Labours Lost,* a "pleasant conceited comedie" first published in 1598, its title page advertising it as "newly corrected and augmented by W. Shakespere." Orthodox scholars (given the Stratford man's chronology) need to have it written *circa* 1592-1596, but the evidence suggests a much earlier date. In January 1579, several months before Spenser introduced "Willie" and "Perigot," the Elizabethan court was entertained by the double bill of *A Maske of Amazones and A Maske of Knights,* which Oxfordians view as the first version of *Love's Labours Lost,* an extremely sophisticated court comedy in which Berowne is an unmistakable self-portrait of de Vere and Boyet is unmistakably Sidney. *Love's Labours Lost* is full of the same contrapuntal jousting in which Oxford and Sidney were engaged during the late 1570s. It appears to be all in fun, but finally the author moves in for the attack upon Boyet/Sidney, accusing him of stealing from the works of others (pecking it up the way pigeons peck up peas):

> This fellow pecks up wit as pigeons peas,
> And utters it again when God doth please… (5.2)

Three centuries later Sir Sidney Lee would point out that "the majority of Sidney's efforts" had been inspired by Petrarch, Ronsard and Desportes, from whose works in French he grabbed "almost verbatim translations" and passed them off as if they were his own. One day, lovers of Shakespeare will be much richer for their ability to learn the true story of Oxford and Sidney within and beneath the lines.

Sidney died in the Battle of Zutphen in the Netherlands, fighting for the Protestant cause against Spanish forces. Shot in the thigh, he suffered from gangrene for twenty-six days until his death on 17 October 1586, after which he became a national hero.

Reason 71 – *Cymbeline*

Cymbeline, King of Britaine was one of the eighteen plays in the Folio of 1623 that had not previously been published. It was placed last in the book. Most orthodox scholars figure that Will Shakspere of Stratford must have written it a few years before 1611, when there exists a record of its performance. Their problem, however, has been trying to explain why *Cymbeline* appears to be the work of a much younger playwright still learning his craft.

"His old skill in uniting a number of narrative strands to form one master plot seems to have deserted him," Campbell writes, but the criticism had begun much earlier; for example, Samuel Johnson blustered in 1765: "To remark the folly of the fiction, the absurdity of the conduct, the confusion of the names and manners of different times, and the impossibility of the events in any system of life, were to waste criticism upon unresisting imbecility, upon faults too evident for detection, and too gross for aggravation." "No one will rank *Cymbeline* with the greater plays," Harley Granville-Barker writes in *Prefaces to Shakespeare, 1927-1947*. "It is not conceived greatly, it is full of imperfections. But it has merits all its own; and one turns to it from *Othello*, or *King Lear*, or *Antony and Cleopatra*, as one turns from a masterly painting to, say, a fine piece of tapestry, from commanding beauty to more recondite charm."

If these gentlemen could have dropped their late dating of *Cymbeline*, they would have recognized that this play *preceded* those masterpieces of literary and dramatic maturity. They would have seen it contains flashes of the greatness to come while providing what is wholly absent in traditional biographies of the Bard: "evidence of youthful endeavor, the elusive juvenilia," Kevin Gilvary writes in *Dating Shakespeare's Plays*.

Clark suggests that *Cymbeline* was the court drama of 28 December 1578, listed on that date in the Court Revels as *The Cruelty of a Stepmother*." [See Reason 66 above.] That takes us back more than thirty years, when de Vere was twenty-eight and becoming even more intensely involved with playwrights, playing companies and plays.

Oxford had returned to England a few years earlier after traveling to Italy. In 1571 he had married the daughter of William Cecil Lord Burghley, the most powerful man in England and the man by whom he had been brought up in his teens. In Italy he learned his wife was pregnant and that there were rumors she had been unfaithful. Upon his return to England in 1576 he angrily refused to acknowledge his wife or the baby girl. In 1581, after some five years of separation, he finally reconciled with his wife.

The Cruelty of a Stepmother of 1578 appears to have been an early version of a play that Oxford revised in 1582 into *Cymbeline* (with final revisions in about 1590). Here is Gilvary's account of the play's tragicomic story of Posthumous:

> *Cymbeline* describes the travels of a youth to Italy; a youth brought up by the most powerful man in the country, whose daughter he married; a youth who, while away in Italy, is persuaded that his wife has been unfaithful and whom he wishes dead; a youth whose spiritual sympathies are with Rome; a youth imprisoned on his return for loyalties to Rome; a youth who later sought and received forgiveness from his maligned wife and his outraged father-in-law.

Sounds familiar! An important source of *Cymbeline* is the romance *Aethiopica* as translated from the Greek of Herliodorus in 1569 by Thomas Underdowne, who dedicated it to de Vere. The earl was then nineteen and apparently going beyond good taste in "matters of learning," as Underdowne put it, explaining that for a nobleman "to be too much addicted that way, I think it is not good." It appears, however, that Oxford was very much addicted to learning.

"Close examination reveals that *Cymbeline* was probably influenced by the *Aethiopica* and was perhaps even a conscious imitation of that romance," writes C. Gesner in *Shakespeare and the Greek Romance* (1970). Underdowne's translation was reprinted in 1577, when Oxford may well have decided to use its story for a play. He also would have used the first edition of Raphael Holinshed's *Chronicles of England, Scotland and Ireland* in 1577, in which all the historical source material for *Cymbeline* was available to him.

CHAPTER FOURTEEN

ASPECTS OF PLAYS

Reason 72 – *King John*

Elizabeth Tudor embarked on her royal progress in the summer of 1561, less than three years after becoming queen at age twenty-five. In early August the court spent a week at Ipswich, where the Queen attended a performance of *King Johan* (*King John*), the first known historical verse drama in English and the first play to depict a king of England onstage. The author, minister-scholar John Bale (1495-1563), had written the first version of the play by 1537 while in the service of Henry VIII's chief minister Thomas Cromwell, who had helped engineer an annulment of the King's marriage to Catherine of Aragon so that Henry could marry Anne Boleyn. An active member of Cromwell's stable of propagandists, Bale managed to turn King John—despised for centuries as a monarch who had surrendered England to the power of the papacy—into a Protestant hero.

A quarter-century later, in 1561, the daughter of Boleyn was on the throne and her own chief minister, William Cecil, was just as eager to use the stage for Reformation propaganda. By now Bale had updated his *King Johan* in time for the arrival of Elizabeth at Ipswich. A crucial link between the old morality plays and the new style of drama to come later in the sixteenth century, Bale's version of John's reign (1199-1216) presented him as a "good" king struggling against the pope and Church of Rome on behalf of England, just as Henry VIII had done and Elizabeth was doing now.

At this point Bale was writing plays for Edward de Vere's father, John de Vere, 16th Earl of Oxford, whose company of actors performed *King Johan* for Elizabeth at Ipswich. In his 1940 biography of Bale, Jesse W. Harris writes that he was "in the service of Oxford, for whom he wrote a series of plays intended for use as Reformation propaganda."

Elizabeth's progress continued to Hedingham for a visit of five nights (14-19 August 1561). In the great hall of the castle, the elder de Vere's players again performed for the royal entourage, most likely with plays Bale had written under the earl's patronage, including his newly revised play about King John. On hand for the royal festivities was eleven-year-old Edward, the future 17th Earl of Oxford, who keenly watched the young queen's reactions to the performances; historians of the future may judge whether this moment marks the true birth of "William Shakespeare"—who, after all, would write plays of English royal history mirroring current political issues. A year later, upon John de Vere's, death, Cecil had Edward brought to London as a ward of the queen. As Master of the Court of Wards, he "took possession of all the young noble's assets," reports Miller, adding: "Cecil, who had standing orders for his agents on the Continent to supply him with copies of books and publications of interest, would not have failed to appreciate the sixteenth Earl of Oxford's collection of Bale's dramatic works, and to move them for safekeeping to Cecil House on the Strand. Even before Bale's death (in 1563), Archbishop Matthew Parker and Cecil were aware of the value of Bale's work, and were involved in efforts to retrieve Bale's manuscripts from various sources. Undoubtedly 'Shakespeare' saw Bale's manuscript plays, and undoubtedly he saw them through the eyes of Edward de Vere, who owned many of them, in the Library at Cecil House."

The next phase of this story begins with the formation of Queen Elizabeth's Men in 1583 at the instigation of secret service head Walsingham, who knew the power of the stage as a means of spreading political propaganda. Edward de Vere contributed some of his adult players to the Queen's Men along with Lyly, his personal secretary, as stage manager. Among the company's history plays (up through 1588, when England defeated the Spanish Armada and the pope) was the anonymous *Troublesome Reign of King John*, printed in 1591 as "publicly acted by the Queen's Majesty's Players."

Then, in late 1598, Francis Meres informed the world in *Palladis Tamia* that "Shakespeare" was not only the poet of *Venus and Adonis* and *Lucrece*, but was also a playwright. Meres listed six comedies and six tragedies. In addition to *King John*, the latter group included *Titus Andronicus* (published 1594); *Romeo and Juliet, Richard II, Richard III* (all 1597), and the first part of *Henry IV* (1598).

When Meres listed *King John*, was he referring to the anonymous *Troublesome Reign of King John* printed in 1591? We might well think so, given that each of the other listed Shakespeare tragedies had also been printed in those recent years without any author's name. But *Troublesome Reign*'s previous existence in the 1580s is too early for Shakspere, the traditional author, to have written it; therefore (in order to force things so they fit) orthodox scholars insist that the *King John* play mentioned by Meres in 1598 was not the one published in 1591, but, rather, was the one printed in the First Folio of 1623 as *The Life and Death of King John*. It's a different text, though virtually all scholars agree (if reluctantly) that Shakespeare based his own *King John* on the earlier anonymous *Troublesome Reign*—which means he was guilty of substantial plagiarism! Ramon Jiménez writes that both the anonymous *Troublesome Reign of King John* and Shakespeare's *Life and Death of King John* "tell the same story in the same sequence of events, with only minor variations…The same characters appear in both plays … [and] Shakespeare's play contains the same scenes in the same order." The simplest conclusion is that both plays were written by the same author, who could not have been the Stratford fellow and must have been Edward de Vere. Jiménez reports that there is "substantial evidence" that "Shakespeare" wrote *Troublesome Reign* "at an early age" and then "rewrote it in his middle years" to complete the text of *King John* printed eventually in the Folio of 1623.

At this point we might be tempted to announce these facts as "smoking gun" evidence of Oxford's authorship of the Shakespeare plays. "No scholar has suggested that Shakespeare depended on or even knew of John Bale's *King Johan*," writes James A. Morey in *The Shakespeare Quarterly* (Autumn 1994), but he points out: "The accounts of the death of John by Shakespeare and Bale are significantly alike" and, for other reasons as well, "Shakespeare" must have had firsthand knowledge of Bale's play performed by John de Vere's players for Elizabeth back in 1561, three years before William of Stratford was born.

[Note: An additional view on Shakespeare's rewriting of *Troublesome Reign* comes from Prof. Daniel Wright who, in his essay "I am I, how e'er I was begot," notes how the anti-Rome propaganda message in the 1580s *Troublesome Reign* (which, as we noted earlier, followed naturally from Bale's *King Johan* version of John as a "good" king struggling against the pope and Church of Rome) now becomes (in Shakespeare's *King John*) a political message about the 1590s succession crisis: "Shakespeare's accusatory finger … is pointed at the Crown."]

Reason 73 – Bertram

The leading male character in *All's Well That Ends Well* is Bertram, Count of Rousillon, a young French nobleman whose callous self-absorption leads to bad behavior toward his wife. In many respects, Bertram is a representation of a young English nobleman, Edward, Earl of Oxford, whose callous self-absorption led to bad behavior toward his wife.

The play is based on a tale by the great Florentine author-poet Giovanni Boccaccio (1313-1375) in *The Decameron*, a collection of one hundred novellas that became the model of Italian prose for writers in the sixteenth century. A now-lost stage work entitled *The Historie of the Rape of the Second Helene*, recorded as performed at Richmond Palace on 6 January 1579, might have been an early version of *All's Well*, which did not appear in print until the 1623 First Folio.

If the play performed at Richmond was in fact an early draft of *All's Well*, observes William Farina, "then perhaps the play reflects de Vere coming to grips with his own bad behavior toward his wife, in which case Bertram would represent Shakespeare's own unvarnished and unflattering self-portrait of the artist as a young man."

The early version would have been written solely for Queen Elizabeth and members of her royal court, who would have quickly understood its contemporary allusions and inside jests. A revised version for the public playhouse in the 1590s may have been the "unknown" Shakespeare comedy to which Meres refers in *Palladis Tamia* (1598) as *Love's Labours Wonne*. (There is no record of *All's Well* being performed until 1741.) Following are some of the ways in which Bertram appears to reflect Oxford:

Royal Ward. When Oxford's father died, he was summoned to London as a ward in subjection to her Majesty the Queen of England. *All's Well* begins when, upon his father's death, young Bertram has been summoned to Paris as a royal ward of the King of France:

> Countess: In delivering my sonne from me, I bury a second husband.
> Bertram: And I in going, Madam, weep o'er my father's death anew; but I must attend his majesty's command, to whom I am now in Ward, evermore in subjection.

Marriage. When de Vere came of age in 1571, a marriage was arranged between him and Cecil's fifteen-year-old daughter, Anne Cecil, whose father was then a commoner. Bertram is leaving behind the young Helena, a commoner's daughter who had fallen in love with him.

> Helena: I am undone. There is no living, none, if Bertram be away. 'Twere all one that I should love a bright particular star and think to wed it, he is so above me. In his bright radiance and collateral light must I be comforted, not in his sphere.

The King promises to elevate Helena's family to the nobility so she and Bertram can marry. In real life, Elizabeth raised up her chief minister from commoner status to become Lord Burghley, so that Anne, who had grown up with Oxford in the same household and undoubtedly loved him, would be of the nobility and able to marry him.

Military Service. Oxford, who had served in the 1570 campaign against the rebelling Catholic earls of the north, nonetheless had hungered for more military service but had been kept behind for being too young. In the fall of 1572, after the St. Bartholomew's Day Massacre of Protestants in France, he begged Burghley to allow him to serve on a ship or abroad "where yet some honor were to be got," adding he was also "most willing to be employed on the sea coasts, to be in readiness with my countrymen against any invasion." He was continually blocked, however, and his complaints are echoed by the Count in the play:

> Bertram: I am commanded here and kept a coil with 'Too young' and 'The next year' and ''Tis too early'.... I shall stay here the forehorse to a smock [a woman's lead horse], creaking my shoes on the plain masonry [palace floors, instead of rough battlefield], till honor be bought up [exhausted], and no sword worn but one to dance with. By heaven, I'll steal away!

Oxford did "steal away" from England without authorization, in the summer of 1574, but he was forced to return three weeks later.

Promise. Oxford finally received permission to travel abroad in early 1575 and spent more than fifteen months in France, Germany and Italy, with his home base in Venice. Back in England, when the earl's wife revealed she was pregnant, Elizabeth "sprung up from the cushions" and said, "I protest to God that next to them that have interest in it, there is nobody can be more joyous of it than I am!" A bit later, however, she repeated the promise Oxford had given her "openly in the presence chamber, that if she [Anne] were with child, it was not his!" (This is described in a letter from Dr. Richard Master, court physician, written to Burghley on 7 March 1575, while Oxford was at the French court in Paris.)

De Vere had promised the queen that he would not sleep with his wife, just as we find the count saying the same in relation to his wife, Helena.

> Bertram: Although before the solemn priest I have sworn, I will not bed her ... O my Parolles, they have married me! I'll go to the Tuscan wars and never bed her ... I have wedded, not bedded her, and sworn to make the 'not' eternal." (And he writes to Helena): "When thou canst ... show me a

child begotten of thy body that I am father to, then call me husband; but in such a 'then' I write a 'never.'

Bed Trick. Bertram fathers a son by means of a "bed trick," a scheme hatched by Helena whereby another woman goes to bed with him and then, in the dark, Helena trades places with her. Oxford was reported to have been the victim of the same scheme in his own life. (See Reason 75 for further discussion.)

Source. *All's Well* includes a backdrop of the wars in the Netherlands between Spain and the Dutch in the 1570s, along with what Farina describes as "enormous amounts of esoteric knowledge regarding the history and geography of France and Italy, as well as Renaissance literature and courtly social customs"—a further link in the chain of evidence pointing to Oxford as author.

Another source of the play is William Painter's English translation of *Decameron*, published in 1566, when de Vere was sixteen and graduating from Oxford University. The Earl knew Italian and undoubtedly also read *Decameron* in its original language, which "Shakespeare" appears to have done – although traditional scholars have been unable to explain how the Stratford man could have read the Italian version.

Reason 74 – Suspicion and Jealousy

When first learning about de Vere and his relationship to "Shakespeare," I was startled to see a letter written by his wife Anne Cecil in December 1581. Oxford had flown into a rage in 1576 over court gossip that he was not the father of the baby girl (Elizabeth Vere) to whom she had given birth the previous year, when he was in Italy. Besieged by doubts, and furious that the scandal had become "the fable of the world," as he wrote angrily to Burghley, he separated from her and refused to acknowledge the child.

Now, five years later, husband and wife had begun to communicate again, and Anne wrote to him from the Westminster home of her father, pleading:

My Lord—In what misery I may account myself to be, that neither can see any end thereof nor yet any hope to diminish it—and now of late having had some hope in my own conceit that your Lordship would have renewed some part of your favor that you began to show me this summer. . . .

What did this remind me of? Where had I heard this before? She continued:

Now after long silence of hearing anything from you, at the length I am informed—but how truly I know not, and yet how uncomfortably I do not seek it—that your Lordship is entered into misliking of me without any cause in deed or thought.

Of course: Desdemona, the suffering wife of Othello. Anne's letter continues:

And therefore, my good Lord, I beseech you in the name of God, which knoweth all my thoughts and love towards you, let me know the truth of your meaning towards me, upon what cause you are moved to continue me in this misery, and what you would have me do in my power to recover your constant favor, so as your Lordship may not be led still to detain me in calamity without some probable cause, whereof, I appeal to God, I am utterly innocent.

I had played the part of Cassio in college, and now the final scenes came back to me with sudden vividness: the way Desdemona was so baffled by Othello's suspicions and accusations; how she begged him to reveal the tortuous contents of his mind; how she was so helpless in the face of his blind rage; how she was left to merely plead her innocence, plaintively telling Iago, the very manipulator who had roused Othello's jealousy in the first place:

O good Iago, what shall I do to win my Lord again? Good friend, go to him; for, by this light of heaven, I know not how I lost him. Here I kneel: If e'er my will did trespass 'gainst his love either in discourse of thought or actual deed . . . comfort forswear me! Unkindness may do much, and his unkindness may defeat my life, but never taint my love. (4.2)

Yes, I thought, Anne could have been saying the same words. If Oxford was Shakespeare, I mused, then his wife's statement "I am utterly innocent" from the depths of her heart echoes in the play when, after Othello strangles Desdemona to death, Iago's wife Emilia shouts at him: "Nay, lay thee down and roar, for thou hast killed the sweetest innocent that e'er did lift up eye!" When Iago stabs Emilia, she cries to Othello again before dying: "Moor, she was chaste! She loved thee, cruel Moor!" (5.2)

Suspicion and jealousy run through other Shakespearean plays such as *Much Ado about Nothing* and *The Winter's Tale*. Hamlet turns on his fiancée Ophelia, distrusting her and complaining that "the power of beauty will sooner transform honesty from what it is to a bawd than the force of honesty can translate beauty into his likeness." The prince is coming unglued, with young Ophelia crying out, "O what a noble mind is here o'erthrown!" (3.1) Anne wrote to her husband again in December 1581:

> Good my Lord, assure yourself it is you whom only I love and fear, and so am desirous above all the world to please you . . .

She died less than seven years later, at thirty-one, having suffered emotional strains we can only imagine. Oxford had had his complaints about Anne siding too much with her father, much as Hamlet reacts to Ophelia's spying on him for her father, but he may well have blamed himself for his wife's early death. Once the earl is understood as the author, he may be seen drawing upon these upheavals in his life, including his remorse, for portrayals of Desdemona's plight and, too, Ophelia's madness and apparent suicide. When Hamlet sees her brother Laertes leap into her grave, he holds nothing back:

> What is he whose grief bears such an emphasis? Whose phrase of sorrow conjures the wand'ring stars and makes them stand like wonder-wounded hearers? This is I, Hamlet the Dane! [He leaps into the grave with Laertes; after they nearly fight] I loved Ophelia! Forty thousand brothers could not, with all their quantity of love, make up my sum! (5.1)

The prince's grief, anger, rage and guilt are all palpable as he challenges Laertes:

> What wilt thou do for her? ... Woo't weep? Woo't fight? Woo't fast? Woo't tear thyself? Woo't drink up eisell? Eat a crocodile? I'll do't! Dost thou come here to whine? To outface me with leaping in her grave? ... Nay ... I'll rant as well as thou! (5.1)

During the final scene of *Othello* I never failed to experience a wave of gutwrenching emotion as the Moor begs for any crumbs of sympathy before taking his own life: "Soft you; a word or two before you go. I have done the state some service, and they know't—no more of that ..." (5.2).

We might well hear Oxford speaking of his own service to the state—as a playwright and patron of writers and acting companies performing around the countryside, rousing national unity against the coming Spanish invasion, which England survived in the summer of 1588, just a few months after Anne's death. The power of the stage was apparent when young men of widely different dialects, religious views and social status came to London to join in common defense of their country. Othello continues:

> I pray you, in your letters, when you shall these unlucky deeds relate, speak of me as I am, nothing extenuate, nor set down aught in malice. Then must

you speak of one that loved not wisely but too well; of one not easily jealous but, being wrought, perplexed in the extreme; of one whose hand, like the base Indian, threw a pearl away richer than all his tribe; of one whose subdued eyes, albeit unused to the melting mood, drop tears as fast as the Arabian trees their medicinable gum.... (5.2)

I believe we are listening to Oxford's own grief over the wreckage of his past—another reason to believe he wrote *Othello*, which was printed for the first time in 1622, a year before publication of the First Folio of thirty-six plays.

Reason 75 – The Bed Trick

"[Oxford] forsook his lady's bed, but the father of the lady Anne, by stratagem, contrived that her husband should, unknowingly, sleep with her, believing her to be another woman, and she bore a son to him in consequence of this meeting." – Thomas Wright, *The History and Topography of Essex*, 1836, discussing Oxford in relation to his wife Anne Cecil and her father, Lord Burghley.

"[T]he last great Earle of Oxford, whose lady was brought to his Bed under the notion of his Mistress, and from such a virtuous deceit she [Susan Vere, Countess of Montgomery, Oxford's third daughter, but probably meaning to identify his first daughter, Elizabeth Vere] is said to proceed." - Francis Osborne, Esq., *Traditional Memoirs of the Reigns of Queen Elizabeth & King James*, 1658.

These two reports, while differing in their particulars, both assert that de Vere was the victim of a "bed-trick" perpetrated by his wife Anne at the bidding of her father, Burghley—the same situation "Shakespeare" immortalized in no less than four of his plays: *All's Well That Ends Well, Measure for Measure, Cymbeline* and *The Two Noble Kinsmen*.

The "bed-trick" was a popular stage convention by the end of the sixteenth century, but the evidence is that "Shakespeare" employed it earlier than any playwright of the English renaissance; when Oxford is viewed as the author, the dates of composition go back even earlier.

Whether the incident actually happened or Oxford merely thought so, the story as told separately by Wright and Osborne probably stems from the royal visit to Hampton Court Palace in October 1574. When the schedule for the queen and her entourage became available, Anne, Countess of Oxford, requested additional lodgings so she might entice her husband to join her. She wrote to Sussex, Lord Chamberlain of the Household:

My good Lord, because I think it long since I saw Her Majesty, and would be glad to do my duty after Her Majesty's coming to Hampton Court, I heartily beseech your good Lordship to show me your favour in your order to the ushers for my lodging; that in consideration that there is but two chambers, it would please you to increase it with a third chamber next to it . . . for the more commodious my lodging is, the willinger I hope my Lord my husband will be to come hither.

Oxford was in Italy the following September when he received a letter from Burghley telling him Anne had given birth to a girl, Elizabeth Vere, in July; later, upon learning of court gossip that he had been cuckolded, he came to doubt he was the father and separated from his wife for five years. Had he really been deceived in a bed-trick according to the "stratagem" devised by his father-in-law? In that case, the girl was his natural child; the other possibility is that Burghley concocted and spread the bed-trick story to cover up the fact that, at his bidding, Anne had become pregnant by some other man, a radical explanation put forth by Ogburn Jr. in 1984:

> I strongly incline [to the explanation] that her father was determined as far as humanly possible to ensure the continuation of the marriage and the status of his descendants as Earls of Oxford. Three years had passed since Anne's and Edward's wedding and still there was no sign of issue, while it had now become impossible any longer to deny his son-in-law a Continental trip from which, given the hazards of travel, he might not return. Thus, exploiting his daughter's uncommon filial submissiveness and the argument that a child would be the surest means of binding her husband to her, he overcame her compunctions and resistance and brought her to accept service by another male and one of proved fertility....
>
> [Note: Oxford may have given voice to the idea of Burghley's involvement in Anne's pregnancy and deception by means of Hamlet's remark to Polonius: "Conception is a blessing, but [not] as your daughter may conceive—friend, look to't." (2.2) – Curiously, the Folio version of *Hamlet* includes the word "not," while the 1604 Quarto omits it.]

Looney saw Bertram in *All's Well* as virtually a self-portrait of de Vere, but it was only after his 1920 book was in manuscript that he discovered Wright's claim that Oxford himself had been deceived by a bed-trick. The excitement he feels is palpable when introducing "what has been the most remarkable piece of evidence met with in the whole course of our investigations: a discovery made a considerable time after this work had been virtually completed." He continues:

> This evidence is concerned with the play *All's Well*. The striking parallelism between the principal personage in the drama and the Earl of

Oxford having led us to adopt it as the chief support of our argument at the particular stage with which we are now occupied . . . [Chapter X: "Early Manhood of Edward de Vere"]. What we have now to state was not discovered until some months later:

In tracing the parallelism between Bertram and Oxford we confined our attention to the incidentals of the play, in the belief that the central idea of the plot—the entrapping of Bertram into marital relationships with his own wife, in order that she might bear him a child unknown to himself—was wholly derived from Boccaccio's story of Bertram. The discovery, therefore, of the following passage in Wright's *History* of Essex furnishes a piece of evidence so totally unexpected, and forms so sensational a climax to an already surprising resemblance that, on first noticing it, we had some difficulty in trusting our own eyes.

"We would willingly be spared the penning of such matter: its importance as evidence does not, however, permit of this," Looney added, with what Ogburn describes as "quaint Victorian delicacy" in the face of scandalous matters. After citing the passage from Wright's *History* quoted above, he continued:

Thus even in the most extraordinary feature of this play; a feature which hardly one person in a million would for a moment have suspected of being anything else but an extravagant invention, the records of Oxford are at one with the representation of Bertram. It is not necessary that we should believe the story to be true, for no authority for it is vouchsafed.... In any case, the connection between the two is now as complete as accumulated evidence can make it.

Marliss C. Desens writes in *The Bed-Trick in English Renaissance Drama* (1994) that this plot device appears in at least forty-four plays of the period, but also that "an examination of English Renaissance dramas shows that bed-tricks were not being used on stage prior to the late 1590s" and, more specifically, that the bed-trick "begins appearing in plays starting around 1598."

So, if Oxford was "Shakespeare," we can say with virtual certainty that in the Elizabethan reign he was the first to incorporate it, and, too, that he did so after being a victim of it in real life, or believing he was. Oxfordians date the original versions of the plays far earlier than the orthodox dates dictated by the life of Shakspere; in the case of the four plays with bed tricks, here are the differences:

All's Well That Ends Well: Traditionally to *circa* 1604; Oxfordians to 1579-1580

Measure for Measure: Traditionally to 1603-05; Oxfordians to 1581-85

Cymbeline: Traditionally to 1610; Oxfordians to 1578-82

The Two Noble Kinsmen: Traditionally to 1612-13; Oxfordians to 1566, revision in 1594

Here is another example of how the Oxfordian context stands previous scholarship on its head. The view of "Shakespeare's" creative process, and its journey over time, is transformed. It's no wonder the academic world has such built-in resistance to seeing, much less accepting, the change of paradigm.

Reason 76 – *Timon of Athens*

Timon of Athens initially appeared in the First Folio of Shakespeare plays in 1623, under the title *The Life of Tymon of Athens*. There is no agreement about when it was written; some scholars studying the mood and style suggest 1605-1609, while others push the date back to 1601-1602. In the view of those who think de Vere was the author, both time frames are about a quarter-century too late.

Oxford was twenty-six in the spring of 1576 when he returned to England after fifteen months on the Continent, having traveled all through Italy with Venice as home base. It may well be that a now lost play, *The Historie of the Solitarie Knight*, performed on 17 February 1577 for Elizabeth and her court, was an early version of *Timon of Athens*.

Timon is a young nobleman so renowned for his liberality and good nature that poets, painters and tradesmen flock to his home seeking his patronage. He is generous and trusting. He joyously entertains his guests, lavishing them with rich gifts and handing out cash even to the servants. His seemingly inexhaustible wealth means little or nothing to him: "I gave it freely ever, and there's none can truly say he gives if he receives . . . Pray sit, more welcome are ye to my fortune than my fortunes to me!" (1.2).

Oxford, too, had inherited great wealth in the form of vast estates; he, too, was a generous friend (as when he gave money to the scholar Gabriel Harvey at Cambridge in the 1560s) and an actively involved patron of actors, writers, musicians and others. Like Timon, he was a trendsetter. And he was accustomed to what the Poet in the play calls "the infinite flatteries that follow youth and money."

Soon, however, Timon discovers he has run out of money and fallen deeply into debt, with servants accosting him for payments owed to their masters—exactly what Oxford had learned about his financial situation while still in Italy. Shocked and distressed by the news of his sudden lack of funds, he wrote to Burghley in January 1576 from Siena:

> My Lord, I am sorry to hear how hard my fortune is in England. . . . I have thus determined that whereas I understand the greatness of my debt and greediness of my creditors grows so dishonorable to me and troublesome unto your Lordship, that that land of mine which in Cornwall I have appointed to be sold [for travel expenses] ... be *gone* through withal. And to stop my creditors' exclamations (or rather defamations, I may call them), I shall desire your Lordship by the virtue of this letter (which doth not err as I take it from any former purpose, which was that always upon my letter to authorize your Lordship to sell any portion of my land) that you will sell one hundred pound a year more of my land where your Lordship shall think fittest, to disburden me of my debts to Her Majesty, my sister, or elsewhere I am exclaimed upon . . . . [Emphasis added]

As Timon puts it, "How goes the world, that I am thus encountered with clamorous demands of debt, broken bonds and the detention of long such due debts against my honor?" (2.2). He questions Flavius, his steward, just as Oxford must have demanded of Burghley to explain how this "dishonorable" situation could have happened without warning: "You make me marvel wherefore ere this time had you not fully laid my state before me, that I might so have rated my expense as I had leave of means . . ." (2.2).

Flavius defends himself as Burghley would have done: "O my good lord, at many times I brought in my accounts, laid them before you; [but] you would throw them off! I did endure not seldom, nor no slight cheques, when I have prompted you in the ebb of your estate and your great flow of debts. My loved lord, though you hear now, too late . . . the greatest of your having lacks a half to pay your present debts" (2.2). [Below, my emphasis again on "gone".]

> Timon: Let all my land be sold!
> Flavius: '   Tis all engaged, some forfeited and *gone*,
> And what remains will hardly stop the mouth
> of present dues (2.2).

Oxford's surprise that "land of mine in Cornwall" that he had "appointed to be sold" was "already *gone* through withal" can be heard here:

> Timon: To Lacedaemon did my land extend!
> Flavius: O my good Lord, the world is but a world:
> Were it all yours to give it in a breath.
> How quickly it were *gone*! (2.2).

Oxford gave Burghley more instructions, adding, "In doing these things your Lordship shall greatly pleasure me, in not doing them you shall as much hinder me, for although to depart with land your Lordship hath advised the contrary, and that your Lordship for the good affection you bear unto me could wish it otherwise, yet you see I have none other remedy. I have no help but of mine own, and mine is made to serve me and myself, not mine." The same thought and virtually the same words are used in the play when one of the usurers instructs his servant: "Get on your cloak, and haste you to Lord Timon. Importune him for my moneys. . . . Tell him my uses cry to me; I must serve my turn out of mine own. . . . Immediate are my needs, and my relief must not be tossed and turned to me in words, but find supply immediate" (2.1.15-27). After all his former friends refuse to loan him money, Timon leaves Athens for the depths of the woods, finds a cave and begins to live as a solitary hermit—which perhaps explains why the play performed in 1577 was called *The Historie of the Solitarie Knight*.

In the forest Timon expects to find "the *unkindest* beast more *kinder* than man*kind*" (4.1.36)—words that will find an echo when Oxford writes to Robert Cecil in May 1601 (after the Secretary had helped to gain Southampton's reprieve from execution): "I do assure you that you shall have no faster friend and well-wisher unto you than myself, either in kindness, which I find beyond mine expectation in you, or in *kindred*," signing off, "in all kindness and kindred, Edward Oxenford."

Timon is "a lover of truth," writes Harold Goddard, and the play "seems to say that such a man, though buried in the wilderness, is a better begetter of peace than all the instrumentalities of law in the hands of men who love neither truth nor justice."

When Oxford was still a royal ward at Cecil House in 1569-70, enrolled at Gray's Inn to study law, one of his book orders included "Plutarch's works in French." As Campbell notes, the Shakespearean author "clearly knew the digression on Timon in Plutarch... He may also have read Lucian's amusing dialogue *Timon Misanthropus*, if not in Greek, then in either a Latin or a French translation." Aside from being fluent in both Latin and French, Oxford had been raised from about age four in the household of Thomas Smith, a Greek scholar, who had tutored him. Both Smith and Burghley had copies of Lucian, and Burghley's wife was also a Greek expert, so it's a given that the very young de Vere had personal access to all the Shakespearean sources. Many researchers have noted the parallels between Edward de Vere and Timon:

Eva Turner Clark:

The play depicts Timon as being just as solitary in the midst of his grandeur as he later became in his cave in the woods. . . . Not even Timon could have lived a life of greater luxury and grandeur than the young Earl of Oxford throughout his youth. Is it to be wondered at that Edward de Vere, seventeenth Earl of Oxford, grew up without the slightest idea of the value of money? . . .

Young Oxford's mind had been filled by his elders with a love of art and scholarship, of excellence in tournament and the field of war, and there was no room in it for the humdrum, workaday world, with its counting of pounds, shillings and pence. Nevertheless, as he pursued the objects for which he had been trained, he was made to feel the sting of financial demands continuously from the time he came of age. It was when he reached a crisis in his affairs, economically and socially, that he wrote the cynical drama of *The Solitary Knight,* or *Timon of Athens. . . .*

Doubtless it was because of this experience that Oxford adopted the idea of exposing his fellow courtiers by satire and burlesque, by the suggestion of warning and threat, which is to be found is many of his plays. In other words, revenge animated him, and, while revenge is not one of the finer impulses, it is a very human instinct to demand satisfaction for an injury done. [Clark adds, however, that as Oxford grew mentally and spiritually, his personal revenge motive widened and matured into an effort to "show up disloyalty of subjects and dishonesty of politicians, for the benefit of his Queen and for the good of his beloved country." *Hidden Allusions*, 1931]

Dorothy and Charlton Ogburn:

One of the hereditary offices of the Earls of Oxford as Lords Great Chamberlain was that of *the Ewry, or Water-Bearer to the Monarch*. It was purely honorary, a formal gesture of presenting water on state occasions when the Monarch sat at meat. There is a direct reference to this [in *Timon*]: 'One of Lord Timon's men! A gift, I warrant. Why, this hits right; I dreamt of *a silver basin and ewer* tonight.' It is recorded that in 1579 'the Queen's New Year's gift to th'earle of Oxfourde [was] *a bason and ewer of our store . . . .*' Timon's bitter jest of serving his false friends and flatterers with covered dishes containing only warm water is thus particularly ironical, expressing, as it does, the scorn of the impoverished Lord Great Chamberlain. [*This Star of England*, 1952]

Charlton Ogburn, Jr.:

I rather think that *Timon of Athens* as we know it owes more to the manifold adversities that overtook its author in the early 1580's, when the sale of thirty tracts of land in five years left him stripped near as bare as Timon. [*The Mysterious William Shakespeare*, 1984]

William Farina:

Reading de Vere's personal connections to the story of Timon, it is not an overstatement to say that Shakespeare's play tells the story of de Vere's life. As the late Anglo-Oxfordian commentator Edward Holmes succinctly put it: 'The play is closest [of all the plays] to autobiography... Timon is too raw, too real, for comfort. It was begun too close to the catastrophe which prompted it. That must be why it was left artistically undigested, incomplete.' Under this scenario, Shakespeare the writer (de Vere) was writing *Timon* not for commercial gain but because, emotionally, he needed to. According to the Oxfordian view, this was a driven author who perhaps could not finish what he started. [*De Vere as Shakespeare*, 2006]

Reason 77 – Campion and Malvolio

"Provide me with ink and paper and I will write!" cried Edmund Campion, the Catholic priest who lived hermit-like in Prague, teaching at the Jesuit college, before returning in 1580 to England, where he was soon imprisoned in the Tower dungeon. Brought out for public disputations with Church officials intending to ridicule him, Campion was refused the means of providing written answers.

Fig. 16 - Edmund Campion

"[T]he old hermit of Prague that never saw pen and ink." So speaks Feste the clown in *Twelfth Night*, disguised as a clergyman ridiculing Malvolio, who, as the result of a prank, is imprisoned in a cellar for being a lunatic. His words are an otherwise "hidden" reference to Campion as well as a bold criticism of the English government's treatment of him in the fall of 1581. *Twelfth Night* is one of eighteen stage works not printed until the First Folio of Shakespeare plays in 1623. Two decades earlier, in 1602, the law student John Manningham attended "a play called Twelve Night, or what you will" at the Middle Temple; most commentators therefore conclude that this rollicking comedy was written in about 1600.

But once de Vere is envisioned writing *Twelfth Night* in the early 1580s, the scenes come alive with an array of allusions to contemporary persons and events; perhaps the most surprising one remained undiscovered until less than twenty years ago, when Richard Desper reported that one entire scene recreates the Crown's unfair actions toward Campion, who was tortured, found guilty of high treason, and was hanged, drawn and quartered in December 1581. (He was canonized by the Roman Catholic Church in 1970.) Desper's discovery of this allusion (within a comedy, no less) could not have been made unless the correct author had been identified. Shakspere was only seventeen in 1581 and still in Warwickshire. Oxford, however, was thirty-one in 1581 and writing "comedies" for private audiences as well as the court; given his known sympathies toward Catholics in England, it is not surprising that he would be angry at officials of the Crown and Church of England for staging mockeries and travesties of justice.

In September 1581 the Elizabethan government led Campion from his dungeon in the Tower for public "conferences" in an attempt to discredit him. Scholars and clergymen were sent to defeat him in religious disputations. In addition, the Crown sought to portray Campion as trying to rouse English Catholics in rebellion against Elizabeth, with the goal of killing her and putting Mary Queen of Scots on the throne.

The sessions were rigged. Campion was deprived of any means of preparing a defense. During the third disputation he asked his opponent, one Master Fulke, to allow him access to books containing the teachings of St. Augustine and St. John Chrysostom.

"If you dare, let me show you Augustine and Chrysostom!" he cried out. "If you dare!"

Fulke replied before he could stop himself: "If you think you can add anything, put it in writing and I will answer it."

Campion seized his opening: "Provide me with ink and paper, and I will answer it!" Fulke realized his tactical error. The government had no intention of permitting Campion to *write out* his answers; after all, much of his public influence had been achieved through his writings. But now the Jesuit had outwitted his Church opponent

"I am not to provide you ink and paper," Fulke replied.

"Procure me, so that I may have liberty to write!"

Fulke offered an excuse that completely undermined his challenge to Campion. "I know not for what cause you are restrained of that liberty," he said, "and therefore I will not take upon me to procure it."

This exchange, embarrassing to the government, would have been fresh in the public memory in 1582, and the "old hermit of Prague that never saw pen and ink" would immediately have been recognized as Edmund Campion. But why in 1600 would any dramatist insert such a scene into a comedy to metaphorically recreate the ordeal of a Jesuit priest that had taken place two decades earlier?

The scene (as it survived and appeared in the 1623 Folio) begins with Malvolio shut up in the cellar (as Campion was confined in the Tower dungeon). Feste the clown agrees to disguise himself as "Sir Topas the Curate," or cleric, to interrogate the prisoner and humiliate him, as in the following dialogue (with key words or phrases emphasized):

Maria (to Feste):	Nay, I pray thee, put on this gown and this beard. Make him believe thou art Sir Topas the Curate. Do it quickly. I'll call Sir Toby the whilst.
Feste:	Well, I'll put it on, and I will dissemble [disguise] myself in it. And I would that I were the first that ever dissembled in such a gown. (4.2)

As Desper suggests, Shakespeare's negative opinion about such proceedings is revealed at the outset. Feste is donning an academic gown to "dissemble," or pretend to have more learning, as the opponents sent to publicly dispute with Campion pretended—when, in fact, none of them had as much learning as the Jesuit priest.

Feste (continued):	I am not tall enough to become the function well, nor lean enough, to be thought a good student; but to be said an honest man and a good housekeeper goes as fairly, as to say, a careful man and *a great scholar.* The competitors [opponents] enter. (Enter Sir Toby)
Toby:	Jove bless thee, Master *Parson.* (4.2)

"Robert Persons was a fellow Jesuit who traveled with Campion from Rome to France," Desper explains. "The two separated to enter England and, for reasons of security, pursued their ministries individually, meeting each other occasionally. Persons, sometimes referred to as 'Parsons' and a former classmate of Campion, was in charge of the Jesuit mission to England."

Feste:	Bonos dies, Sir Toby: for as the old hermit of Prague that never saw pen and ink very wittily said to a Niece of King Gorboduc, "That that is, is," so I, being Master Parson, am Master Parson: for what is "that" but "that"? And "is" but "is"? (4.2)

Feste's speech contains further references. Desper points out that Gorboduc was a mythical King of England, and Queen Elizabeth was the niece of her father's brother, Arthur, who would have been king if he had lived. The phrase "That that is, is" may be taken as "a religious affirmation, just as Campion's mission to England was a religious affirmation," as his goal was "to affirm the truth [from the Catholic viewpoint] in the face of official displeasure" and efforts to force him to deny what, to him, was reality. The phrase also echoes God's words to Moses, "I Am That I Am." Because Campion owed a higher allegiance to God than to the Crown, the phrase "That that is, is" becomes "the essence of his position vis-a-vis his God and his queen," Desper explains.

| Toby: | To him, Sir Topas! |
| Feste: | What ho, I say, peace in this prison. |

In effect, Malvolio is in a prison as Campion was.

| Toby: | The knave counterfeits well: a good knave. |

It's established at the outset that the conference to be held, like those to which Campion was brought, will be a sham with a "knave" posing as a learned man who will act as the examiner. "The tenor of the remainder of the scene, in the context of Campion's imprisonment, becomes apparent," Desper writes. "The clown is seen assuming the role of the learned men to dispute with the prisoner, just as men of learning brought Campion to dispute at the aforementioned conferences."

| Malvolio (from within): | Who calls there? |
| Feste: | Sir Topas the Curate, who comes to visit Malvolio the Lunatic. (4.2) |

Posing as Sir Topas the Curate, Feste "proceeds to deal with Malvolio as a man possessed and in need of exorcism," Desper explains, "even though, as the Clown, he knows full well that Malvolio—whatever his faults might be— is neither insane nor possessed." As the scene goes on, we can feel the underlying power of the playwright's anger at what was done to Campion:

Malvolio:	Sir Topas, Sir Topas, good Sir Topas, go to my Lady [Olivia].
Feste:	Out, hyperbolical fiend! How vext thou this man? Talkest thou nothing but of Ladies?
Malvolio:	Sir Topas, never was man thus wronged. Good Sir Topas, do not think I am mad. They have laid me here in hideous darkness.
Feste:	Fye, thou dishonest Satan! I call thee by the most modest terms, for I am one of those gentle ones that will use the Devil himself with courtesy. Sayst thou that house is dark?
Malvolio:	As hell, Sir Topas.
Feste:	Why, it hath bay windows transparent as baricadoes, and the clear stores toward the south north are as lustrous as ebony. And yet complaineth thou of obstruction?

Malvolio: I am not mad, Sir Topas. I say to you this house is dark.

Feste: Madman, thou errest! I say there is no darkness but ignorance, in which thou art more puzzled than the Egyptians in their fog. [Exodus 10:21]

Malvolio: I say this house is as dark as ignorance, though ignorance were as dark as hell. And I say there was never man thus abused. I am no more mad than you are. Make the trial of it in any confident question.

Feste: What is the opinion of Pythagoras concerning wildfowl?

Malvolio: That the soul of our grandam might happily inhabit a bird.

Feste: What thinkest thou of his opinion?

Malvolio: I think nobly of the soul, and no way approve his opinion.

Feste: Fare thee well. Remain thou still in darkness. Thou shalt hold the opinion of Pythagoras, ere I will allow of thy wits, and fear to kill a woodcock lest thou dispossess the soul of thy grandam. Fare thee well. (4.2)

Feste chides Malvolio for not upholding the pagan view of the transmigration of souls; likewise, as Desper points out, Campion was expected to provide answers that, in his own view, were illogical and false but accorded with the needs of those in power. "The playwright thus demonstrates for us the world turned upside-down," he writes, "with clowns passing themselves off as men of learning, while men of learning such as Campion are pressed to deny what they believe to be true," all because of the need to serve political ends. In this one scene, he suggests, the author expresses "his bitterness over the trial and execution of one he saw as an innocent man." Was the scene actually performed in the early 1580s? Was it enacted for the queen? Was it so skillfully hidden within the play that even Burghley, architect of the Protestant Reformation, or spymaster Walsingham could have missed the allusions to Campion's ordeal, which was their own doing? Isn't this an example of the author's ability to create one reality on the surface while a wholly different world exists within the same work?

I suggest that no writer other than de Vere had the ability to create a scene that was so dangerous and get away with it.

Reason 78 – *The Winter's Tale*

Traditional scholarship offers many examples of what happens when a literary or dramatic work is viewed with the wrong author in mind. Using an incorrect biography as a guide is equivalent to following the wrong road map. In the case of *The Winter's Tale*, first printed in the

Folio of 1623, viewing the play as by Shakspere has led most orthodox scholars to conclude it was written in 1611.

This has led to some farfetched conclusions—for example, Stephen Greenblatt's suggestion in *Will in the World* that Shakspere decided around 1610 to "enact a final, fantastic theatrical experiment." This had nothing to do with acting or writing, but, rather, with entering into "the everyday life of a country gentleman." He would "return to the place from which he had come," perhaps drawn home by a motive that "seems to lie in plain sight" within what are assumed to be among his final plays. This imaginary motive involves a woman twenty years younger than he, the woman "who most intensely appealed to Shakespeare" during his entire lifetime: his daughter Susanna!

"It cannot be an accident," Greenblatt writes, "that three of his last plays—*Pericles, The Winter's Tale* and *The Tempest*—are centered on the father-daughter relationship and are so deeply anxious about incestuous desires." What the author really wanted was "the pleasure of living near his daughter and her husband and their child," even though this pleasure had "a strange, slightly melancholy dimension, a joy intimately braided together with renunciation."

Here is a prominent orthodox scholar trying to link up the author's work with his life (implicitly acknowledging that literary biography is useful), but doing so by means of pure invention. Yes, Shakspere did spend his final years in Stratford, but was he really obsessed with gnawing "incestuous desires" toward his daughter? Does this really help us understand those three plays? I'd say Greenblatt is driving on the wrong road in the wrong territory, heading for the proverbial cliff.

But if we accept de Vere as the author, we can place the initial composition of *The Winter's Tale* back by a quarter century to the years 1584-1586, thereby offering far more plausible motives and connections:

- His jealous rage at his wife Anne and denial of his paternity of the girl Elizabeth Vere, who was born in 1575 while he was on the Continent—mirrored in the play by the jealous rage of King Leontes against his wife Hermione, plus his order that her newborn infant girl, Perdita, be abandoned in "some remote and desert place" to die.

- The Duchess of Suffolk's scheme in 1577 to trick Oxford into seeing two-year-old Elizabeth Vere without first revealing the girl's identity—as Lady Paulina tries to trick Leontes.

- The rise at court of Sir Walter Raleigh and his expeditions in the 1580s to the New World, including the colonization of Virginia, named in honor of Queen Elizabeth, the Virgin Queen—as echoed in repeated allusions in the play to Raleigh and his affairs.

- The treason trial of Mary, Queen of Scots in October 1586, when Oxford sat at the head of the row of peers on the tribunal—as mirrored by the treason trial of Hermione.

Viewing Oxford as the playwright lends personal links to the sources:

- The miracle of a statue coming to life in *The Winter's Tale* is to be found in the story of Pygmalion and Galatea in Ovid's *Metamorphoses*, leading us back yet again to the 1567 translation used by "Shakespeare" credited to Oxford's uncle Golding, but more likely translated by the young earl himself.

- The source of the main plot of *The Winter's Tale* is generally agreed to be the novel *Pandosto, or the Triumph of Time* by Robert Greene, first printed in 1588; once more we are led to de Vere, who was Greene's patron from at least 1580, and so had firsthand knowledge of the novel well before its publication. (Some researchers believe Oxford used "Greene" as a pen name and wrote *Pandosto* himself.)

- The traditional author's biography holds that "Shakespeare" could not have read Greek dramas in their original language, but Oxford definitely had the ability to do so; for example, Euripides's *Alcestis* provides much more emotional depth of the kind the Bard created in *The Winter's Tale*.

The emergence of de Vere as author has also overturned some oft-repeated misstatements about the "ignorance" of Shakespeare and his alleged "mistakes," such as:

- Near the end of *The Winter's Tale* the statue of Hermione is described as "a piece many years in doing and now newly performed by that rare Italian master, Julio Romano, who, had he himself eternity and could put breath into his work, would beguile Nature of her custom, so perfectly he is her ape: he so near to Hermione hath done Hermione, that they say one would speak to her and stand in hope of answer" (5.2). For a long time Romano was better known (especially outside Italy) as a painter than as a sculptor, but Oxford had traveled through northern Italy and almost certainly saw Romano's work in Mantua. The earl would have known that Romano was also famous for statues that he constructed out of powdered marble and painted to be extraordinarily lifelike.

- The third scene of act three opens with Antigonous saying to a mariner, "Thou art perfect, then, our ship hath touched upon the deserts of Bohemia?" Although Ben Jonson and many subsequent critics have accused Shakespeare of being unaware that Bohemia was landlocked, Oxford spent several months in Venice; eager to learn the history of the region, he would have learned that in the thirteenth century the King of Bohemia had ruled over territories stretching to the Adriatic Sea, thus making it possible for someone to sail from Sicily to Bohemia.

[In addition, Mark Anderson writes of evidence that Bohemia during its most prosperous years had two seacoasts. He notes that "the first patch of foreign coastline Edward de Vere encountered on his 1575 trip down the Adriatic Sea out of Venice was land ruled by the then-King of Bohemia."]

In September 1586, after being arrested for sanctioning an attempted assassination of Elizabeth I, the long-held captive Mary, Queen of Scots was brought to Fortheringhay Castle, where she would be put on trial for high treason. At 9 a.m. on October 15th, Mary entered the room directly above the Great Hall and defended herself alone before a tribunal of thirty-six noblemen, all of whom were expected to vote guilty and sentence her to death.

Fig. 17 - Mary Stuart, Queen of Scots

At the head of the line of peers was Oxford. Now in his thirty-seventh year, he had a front row seat for the most dramatic and emotionally wrenching treason trial of the Elizabethan reign. Once Oxford is viewed as writing an early version of *The Winter's Tale* soon afterward, the scene of Queen Hermione's treason trial becomes his own daring cry of compassion for Mary Stuart. It also becomes his equally dangerous protest against governmental authority as exercised by Burghley, who was determined to destroy the Queen of Scots and be rid of the continual plots against Elizabeth that were centered around placing Mary on the English throne.

The similarities of the trials are striking; one, in particular, would seems to comprise convincing evidence that de Vere wrote the "Shakespeare" play: the use of the phrase "great grief," which Oxford heard spoken by the Lord Chancellor as he opened the proceedings against Mary:

The most high and mighty Queen Elizabeth, being not without *great grief* of mind, being advertised that you have conspired the destruction of her and of England.... (Emphasis added)

As act two, scene three, of *The Winter's Tale* begins, King Leontes opens the treason trial of his wife Hermione and uses the same phrase:

This sessions, to our *great grief* we pronounce, even pushes 'gainst our heart.... (Emphasis added)

The phrase by itself would have gained Oxford's attention not just for its alliteration, but because he himself was personally fond of "grief" (or "griefs"), having employed the word in several verses in *The Paradise of Dainty Devices*, first printed a decade earlier:

The only loss of my good name is of these griefs the ground...

Uncomely love, which now lurks in my breast, Should cease my grief...

Bewray thy grief, thou woeful heart with speed...

I, Hannibal that smile for grief...

It is no accident that "great grief" is used at the opening of both trials, both uttered in the same emotionally charged atmosphere and within the same context. And just ten days later "great grief" is used unforgettably by the Queen of England herself. After her second cousin had been pronounced guilty and sentenced to die, Elizabeth addressed the peers (including Oxford) in the Star Chamber at Westminster, telling them they "have brought me to a narrow strait, that I must give order for her death, a princess most nearly allied unto me in blood, and whose practices against me have stricken me into so great grief ...."

There are other strong similarities between the speeches at the historical and fictional treason trials:

Mary Stuart: I am an absolute queen, and will do nothing which may prejudice either mine own royal majesty, or other princes of my place and rank, or my son ... I am a queen by right of birth and have been consort of a king of France; my place should be there, under the dais .... I am the daughter of James the Fifth, King of Scotland, and granddaughter of Henry the Seventh....

(As recorded): "She answered that she was no subject, and rather would she die a thousand deaths than acknowledge herself a subject, considering, that by such an acknowledgment she should both prejudice the height of regal majesty, and withal confess herself to be bound by all the laws of England, even in the matter of religion."

Hermione: For behold me,
                A fellow of the royal bed, which owe
                A moiety of the throne, a great king's daughter,
                The mother to a hopeful prince, here standing
                To prate and talk for life and honor 'fore
                Who please to come and hear. (3.2)

Mary Stuart: Alas! Here are many counselors, but not one for me! ... I am destitute of counselors, and who shall be my peers I am utterly ignorant!

(As recorded): "Nevertheless she was ready to answer to all things in a free and full parliament, for that she knew not whether this meeting and assembly were appointed against her, being already condemned by fore-judging, to give some show and color of a just and legal proceeding."

Hermione: [This] is more than history can pattern, though devised
And played to take spectators...

Mary Stuart (as recorded): "She warned them therefore to look to their consciences ...."

Hermione: I appeal to your own conscience ...

Mary Stuart: My Papers and Notes are taken from me, and no man dareth step forth to be my advocate. . . . To the judgment of mine adversaries, amongst whom I know all defense of mine innocence will be barred flatly, I will not submit myself.

Hermione: Since what I am to say must be but that
Which contradicts my accusation, and
The testimony on my part no other
But what comes from myself, it shall scarce boot me
To say, 'Not guilty.' Mine integrity,
Being counted falsehood, shall, as I express it,
Be so received. But thus, if powers divine
Behold our human actions (as they do),
I doubt not then but innocence shall make
False accusation blush, and tyranny
Tremble at patience...

Queen Elizabeth: For we princes are set as it were upon stages, in the sight and view of all the world ... It behooves us therefore to be careful that our proceedings be just and honorable.

King Leontes: Let us be cleared
Of being tyrannous, since we so openly
Proceed in justice, which shall have due course,
Even to the guilt or the purgation.

Hermione: Now, my liege,
Tell me what blessings I have here alive,
That I should fear to die? Therefore proceed.
But yet hear this: mistake me not: no life,
I prize it not a straw, but for mine honor,
Which I would free: if I shall be condemned
Upon surmises, all proofs sleeping else
But what your jealousies awake, I tell you
'Tis rigor and not law...

> The Emperor of Russia was my father:
> O that he were alive, and here beholding
> His daughter's trial! That he did but see
> The flatness of my misery, yet with eyes of pity, not
> revenge!

Shakespeare's sympathetic portrait of Mary Stuart may have prevented any public performance of *The Winter's Tale* until after Elizabeth's death and the succession of Mary's son, James Stuart, King James VI of Scotland, as James I of England. On the other hand, Isaac Asimov suggests "the original audience might have experienced a sense of 'familiarity' with the trial scene," in that Henry VIII tried Anne Boleyn after flying into an irrational fit of jealousy just as King Leontes loses all rationality in the play. If so, Oxford could have covered himself by telling Elizabeth he was really writing about the unfair trial of Queen Anne, her own mother.

When Edward de Vere returned to England from his Continental journey in April 1576, he angrily separated from his wife Anne Cecil, believing she had been unfaithful to him. While he was in Italy the young countess had given birth to a girl, Elizabeth Vere, but the earl refused to acknowledge his paternity and remained apart from both wife and the child for five years. During this separation, Catherine (Kate) Willoughby, duchess of Suffolk, wrote in December 1577 to Burghley about a scheme hatched with the earl's sister, Mary Vere, who was engaged to her son Peregrine Bertie, Lord Willoughby. The plan was to trick Oxford into finally laying eyes on the child. Reporting on their conversation, the duchess wrote to Cecil that Mary told her Oxford "would very fain [gladly] see the child [but] is loath to send for her."

"Then," the duchess told Mary, "you will keep my counsel [and] we will have some sport with him. I will see if I can get the child hither to me, when you shall come hither, and whilst my Lord your brother is with you I will bring in the child as though it were some other of my friends', and we shall see how Nature will work in him to like it, and tell him it is his own after." There's no record that Catherine's scheme was put into effect, but *The Winter's Tale* contains a scene that's a veritable copy of this otherwise private episode. The extremely jealous King Leontes is convinced that Queen Hermione has been unfaithful to him, and has her arrested. While in prison she gives birth to a daughter, but Leontes refuses to accept paternity, believing the father to be his friend Polixenes, King of Bohemia. Enter the Lady Paulina, who schemes to bring the infant girl to the king in the belief that the sight of the innocent babe will

220

bring him to his senses. At the prison she addresses Emilia, attending Queen Hermione:

> Lady Paulina:
>
> Pray you, Emilia,
> Commend my best obedience to the Queen:
> If she dares trust me with her little babe,
> I'll show it to the King, and undertake to be
> Her advocate to the loudest.
> We do not know
> How he may soften at the sight of the child:
> The silence often of pure innocence
> Persuades, when speaking fails. (2.2)

With de Vere as the author, he can be seen castigating himself for having accused his own wife of infidelity, portraying his own irrational jealousy and hurtful behavior through Leontes. The Ogburns believe that Oxford began to write *The Winter's Tale* during or shortly after the trial of Mary Stuart in October 1586, when he sat at the head of the tribunal that found her guilty of treason and sentenced her to death. They feel this event profoundly affected him, not only "exciting his compassion but also tormenting his conscience" over having to cast his vote along with the others, regardless of whether he thought she was guilty.

Oxford had earlier fought to save his cousin Thomas Howard, fourth duke of Norfolk, who was convicted in January 1572 of participating with Philip II of Spain in the Ridolfi Plot to put Mary on the English throne. The execution of Norfolk on 2 June 1572 at Tower Hill represented Burghley's triumph over the old feudal nobility as well as his tightening hold over the queen. Now, some fourteen years later, Oxford was forced to join the peers once again in carrying out Cecil's designs, this time sealing the destruction of Mary Stuart. "In the performance of his duty—his prime duty to his sovereign, to which honor and the oath of allegiance compelled him—he had been obliged to violate the dictates of his heart, as well as a still deeper code of humanity and of manhood," the Ogburns write, "whereupon he turned upon himself in a savage mood and created the preposterous Leontes in what he conceived to be his own image. For Leontes, while also a symbol of entrenched if not tyrannical power, is of course largely Oxford again, but Oxford in a moment of revulsion, scorning himself for his own iniquities."

As the Ogburns see it, Oxford was "willing to pillory himself" and have it seem he was simply portraying his own former jealousy and personal tyranny, when in fact Leontes also represents English authority in the person of Burghley and the English peers (including himself) who participated in the legalistic formality of a unanimous verdict. Thus,

Leontes accuses Hermione not only of adultery but also of conspiring with Polixenes to murder him— reflecting the accusation by Elizabeth (and Burghley) that Mary Stuart was plotting to kill her.

Leontes declares his own baby girl a bastard and orders Paulina's husband Antigonous to take the child "to some remote and desert place" (2.3) and leave it to perish. After Hermione is presumed dead, Antigonous names his tiny charge Perdita and abandons her on the stormy coast of Bohemia with his own "character," a written account of what happened. Therefore, Antigonous is a writer who has set down the truth and left it for posterity. In the next moment, however, he sees a hideous beast coming toward him and tries to get back to the ship.

"This is the chase! I am gone for ever!" he cries, running off, and the playwright adds his famous stage direction: "Exit, pursued by a bear" (3.3). A shepherd soon arrives, then a clown, who tells the shepherd how the bear caught up to the man and "tore out his shoulder-bone." The man "cried to me for help and said his name was Antigonous, a nobleman." The truth-telling nobleman-writer has been torn apart by the bear. He "roared and the bear mocked him," the clown says, adding the beast has "half dined" on him and is still "at it now." Later the clown reveals that "authority be a stubborn bear"— in other words, the bear is allegorically the figure of authority or officialdom, which has silenced the nobleman-writer.

De Vere can be seen as depicting himself briefly as the truth-telling nobleman who refers to himself in Antigonous's exit line: "I am gone for *ever!*" (Emphasis added)

If Antigonous stands for Oxford, the nobleman-author, does the baby Perdita represent his plays? Has "authority" directed Oxford to abandon any claim to his writings? "Weep I cannot, but my heart bleeds," (3.3) cries Antigonous as he sets down "this poor wretch" in the wilderness, adding that "most accursed am I to be by oath enjoined to this."

Has officialdom—the stubborn bear of authority, in the form of Queen Elizabeth and Lord Burghley—imposed an "oath" of secrecy upon Oxford? If so, he would have taken such an oath when, on 25 June 1586, four months before Mary Stuart's treason trial, Elizabeth signed a Privy Seal Warrant for a grant to Oxford of 1,000 pounds, an extraordinary sum to be paid to him annually by the Exchequer (see Reason 43). My belief is that Oxford had been selling his land and spending his own money on his play companies and to support the writers under his patronage, and that now he was being repaid. The warrant gave no hint of the reason for the grant and expressly stated that the earl was exempt from accounting for its expenditure. In return, however, was Oxford now being mauled and slowly devoured by authority?

And art made tongue-tied by authority – Sonnet 66

Reason 79 – *Troilus and Cressida*

"Conceived out of the fullest heat and pulse of European feudalism— personifying in unparalleled ways the medieval aristocracy, its towering spirit of ruthless and gigantic cast, its own peculiar air and arrogance (no mere imitation)—only one of the 'wolfish earls' so plenteous in the plays themselves, or some born descendent and knower, might seem to be the true author of those amazing works...." Walt Whitman, *November Boughs*, 1888

Another good example of how identifying the correct author can change our perception of the works is *Troilus and Cressida*, in particular the sections with Agamemnon, commander-in-chief of the Greeks during the Trojan War, and the Greek hero Ulysses, King of Ithaca, fighting on his side. Traditional thinking dates the play to circa 1602, but an Oxfordian view reveals two basic stages of composition, the first much earlier:

Accounts of the Office of the Revels
December 27, 1584
"The History of Agamemnon and
Ulysses, Presented and Enacted before
Her Majesty by the Earl of Oxenford his
Boys on St. Johns Day at night in
Greenwich" (Modernized English)

Clark quotes an orthodox critic (Murray) as surmising that "this play may have been written by the Earl of Oxford himself, as he was known as one of the best dramatic writers of the day." She adds that since the earl was "the only dramatic author of note" at the time, it becomes even more likely that the play was his." Mark Anderson notes that the orthodox scholar Albert Feuillerat also thought Oxford might be the author of this "lost" play.

De Vere had endured two years of banishment from court until June 1583, but now, two nights after Christmas Day 1584, at Greenwich Palace, his children's company performed *Agamemnon and Ulysses* for Elizabeth and her court. The historical context provides evidence that *Agamemnon and Ulysses* was the original version of *Troilus and Cressida*, attributed to "William Shakespeare" a quarter century later in its initial printing of 1609.

The Shakespearean text appears to be a melding of two different plays, with two distinct writing styles. The first two scenes, for example, feature Troilus, Pandarus and Cressida, using the rapid, realistic dialogue of a seasoned playwright; but the very next scene, featuring Agamemnon, Ulysses and other commanders, is filled with long speeches of blank verse—powerful and thoughtful, but in a style used much earlier on the English stage. "Careful study of the two kinds of work in *Troilus and Cressida* will perhaps bring home to the reader— more clearly than anything else could—a sense of what took place in the development of drama in Queen Elizabeth's reign," Looney writes. "What we take to be the earl of Oxford's play of *Agamemnon and Ulysses*, forming the original ground-work for the 'Shakespeare' play about Troilus and Cressida, represents the Elizabethan drama in an early simple stage of its evolution—with few speakers and long speeches— and the finished play *Troilus and Cressida* the work of the same pen, when practice had matured his command over the resources of true dramatic dialogue and a multitude of dramatis personae."

During 1583 and 1584, when war between England and Spain seemed inevitable, Protestant leaders in the Netherlands became desperate to keep Philip II from establishing sovereignty over them. The Dutch begged England for men, money, arms and military leaders. They pressed Elizabeth to take the Provinces into her own hands, to claim sovereignty for herself and meet Spain there in open warfare. The danger of a Spanish takeover was growing, but the queen's counselors were divided: Leicester and the Puritans urged the queen to send an army of several thousand, but Burghley apparently felt England would be too vulnerable without more help from within the ranks of the Low Countries, so she refused. As a result, the English government appeared to be losing its focus, breaking into factions and becoming weaker.

Privately, Oxford was angry at Elizabeth for allowing Walter Raleigh, an outsider, to gain influence over her thinking, and for allowing him to take his own place in her high favor. He was also furious that Leicester still held sway with her. The queen was presenting herself as weak and indecisive, allowing discord within her Council to run rampant. In the 1584 play of *Agamemnon and Ulysees*, the Greeks would have represented England's leaders while Troy represented Spain.

When de Vere is viewed as author of the earlier play, the contemporary history becomes conspicuous. "Elizabeth is Agamemnon," the Ogburns suggest, adding that Ulysses's great speech to Agamemnon "is Oxford's warning and reminder to the queen. No one else in

Elizabeth's court could have spoken with such power, eloquence and nobility."

Ulysses: Agamemnon,
             Thou great commander, nerves and bone of Greece,
             Heart of our numbers, soul and only spirit,
             In whom the tempers and the minds of all
             Should be shut up, hear what Ulysses speaks (1.3)

This speech, the Ogburns write, is "the premier earl of England addressing his sovereign …. It is Edward de Vere pointing out to his queen the weaknesses which are afflicting their beloved country."

Ulysses: Troy, yet upon his basis, had been down,
             And the great Hector's sword had lacked a master,
             But for these instances.
             The specialty of rule hath been neglected:
             And look how many Grecian tents do stand
             Hollow upon this plain, so many hollow factions.
             When that the general is not like the hive
             To whom the foragers shall all repair,
             What honey is expected? Degree being vizarded,
             The un-worthiest shows as fairly in the mask. (1.3)

"He administers a stern rebuke to the queen," the Ogburns write. "She has been lax with conspirators and tolerated the Puritans, thus encouraging the 'hollow factions.' She has ignored, masked, overridden 'degree,' making unworthy men, ambitious nobodies, the equals of those whose ancestors' lives as well as their own, have been dedicated in duty to England, who have fought to make England great, who are responsible for her welfare and should be honored as her spokesmen and defenders. They have earned their high position and responsibility."

"The scene as a whole is a discussion of state policy," Looney writes, "from the standpoint of one strongly imbued with aristocratic conceptions, and conscious of the decline of the feudal order upon which social life had hitherto rested. Make, then, the Earl of Oxford the writer, and Elizabeth's court the audience for 'Shakespeare's' representation of *Agamemnon and Ulysses*, and the whole situation becomes much more intelligible than if we try to make the Stratford man the writer."

Ulysses (continued):

                 The heavens themselves, the planets, and this center
                 Observe degree, priority, and place,
                 Insisture, course, proportion, season, form,
                 Office, and custom, in all line of order.

> And therefore is the glorious planet Sol
> In noble eminence enthroned and sphered
> Amidst the other; whose med'cinable eye
> Corrects the influence of evil planets,
> And posts, like the commandment of a King,
> Sans check to good and bad. But when the planets
> In evil mixture to disorder wander,
> What plagues and what portents, what mutiny,
> What raging of the sea, shaking of earth,
> Commotion in the winds, frights, changes, horrors,
> Divert and crack, rend and deracinate
> The unity and married calm of states
> Quite from their fixture? (1.3)

"This speech expresses the essence of Elizabethan philosophy," the Ogburns continue. "It states the sixteenth-century theory of the cosmos: everything in its place and maintaining its peculiar function in a hierarchy stretching from the highest to the lowest, in an ordered universe .... This is a Vere pronouncing an Elizabethan nobleman's creed. This is not merely a poet, his 'eye in a fine frenzy rolling'; it is an English knight addressing his sovereign with the religious fervor of his patriotism."

Ulysses (continued):

> O, when degree is shaked,
> Which is the ladder to all high designs,
> The enterprise is sick!
> How could communities,
> Degrees in schools, and brotherhoods in cities,
> Peaceful commerce from dividable shores,
> The primogenity and due of birth,
> Prerogative of age, crowns, scepters, laurels,
> But by degree, stand in authentic place?
> Take but degree away, untune that string,
> And hark what discord follows. (1.3)

Anderson notes that in 1567, when Oxford was seventeen, he had sent his retainer Thomas Churchyard off to fight for the Protestants in the Netherlands. By 1584 the situation was growing desperate. Elizabeth was urged to support the campaign by William "the Silent" of Orange to overthrow Spanish forces in the Lowlands. "To the maddeningly cautious queen, though," Anderson writes, "such decisions were best handled by procrastination."

In March the German scholar Sturmius, whom Oxford had visited during his travels in 1575, urged Elizabeth to appoint a force led by "some faithful and zealous personage such as the Earl of Oxford, the Earl of Leicester, or Philip Sidney." While the queen continued to stall, William the Silent was assassinated in July; finally, she agreed to send military aid to the Lowlands. But who would lead the English forces? Who would assume the governorship of this possible English colony?

"Leicester was the leading choice," Anderson notes, but "as Sturmius's letter shows, de Vere had become a contender for the job too," and he took it so seriously that "in the Elizabethan court's Christmas revels of 1584, he gave his aspirations voice" in the play *Agamemnon and Ulysses*. In the scenes preserved in *Troilus and Cressida*, Anderson writes, "Agamemnon notes that the Greek campaign against Troy has been going on for seven years; William the Silent's campaign against Spain had lasted [for seven years] since 1577 ....

"In December of 1584, a play staged for Queen Elizabeth about the siege of Troy would readily have been seen as a representation of the siege of the Netherlands ... [and Oxford] would have been arguing not only for military intervention but also for his leadership of the English forces—portraying himself as Ulysses, a paragon of aristocratic and military ideals." Anderson appears to be the first to suggest that Oxford's writing of *Agamemnon and Ulysses* was directly connected to his bid for military command—that is, "for an office of singular importance to the nation ... in step with the overseas threats now facing the country."

Ulysses (continued):

> ...And this neglection of degree it is
> That by a pace goes backward with a purpose
> It hath to climb. The general's disdained
> By him one step below, he by the next,
> That next by him beneath; so every step,
> Exampled by the first pace that is sick
> Of his superior, grows to an envious fever
> Of pale and bloodless emulation:
> And 'tis this fever that keeps Troy on foot,
> Not her own sinews. To end a tale of length,
> Troy in our weakness stands, not in her strength. (1.3)

In that final line we can hear thirty-four-year-old Oxford telling Elizabeth that Spain is strong not because of its own strength, but, rather, because of the weakness of England's state policy and the divided political factions under her indecisive rule.

Oxford's plea for military leadership apparently worked, because the queen appointed him in August 1585 as commander of a large force in the Netherlands. In September a Spanish agent in London reported that "five or six thousand English soldiers ... arrived in Flanders with the Earl of Oxford and Colonel Norris." About a month later, however, Oxford was recalled— brought home, I suggest, to lead the circle of writers later called the University Wits, and to contribute royal history plays to the touring companies of the Queen's Men, inspiring audiences with calls for patriotism and unity in the face of the Spanish threat.

It may well be that the queen so valued his writing, particularly because of the speeches for Ulysses, that she finally realized he was needed most for his literary and dramatic abilities at home. In that case, his ambition for a military command was undercut by the brilliant, passionate words of the very speeches he wrote in trying to fulfill it.

Troilus and Cressida was printed in 1609 without authorization, according to an epistle inserted in the midst of the print run [see Reason 84] (*Pericles* and the Sonnets also appeared that year). The play was almost left out of the Folio of Shakespearean plays in 1623; it is not listed in the table of contents, and seems to have been included at the last moment. The hesitation may well have come from concerns that readers would recognize its subject matter related to events in late 1584, when Oxford's Boys performed *Agamemnon and Ulysses* for Elizabeth.

Reason 80 – *Macbeth*

The official record states that de Vere died in 1604. Was the play *Macbeth* inspired by the Gunpowder Plot against James I and Parliament in 1605? Did it draw from the subsequent treason-and-equivocation trial of Jesuit priest Henry Garnet in 1606, thereby ruling out Oxford as the author? An enormous amount of research on *Macbeth*—all pointing away from such a late dating of the play—has been done by traditional and Oxfordian scholars. Among the latter, Richard Whalen has compiled powerful evidence that it was Oxford who wrote and rewrote *Macbeth*, and that he did so long before James became King of England.

1567: The Darnley Murder

In February 1567, when Oxford was sixteen, the Elizabethan court learned that Henry Stewart Lord Darnley, husband of Mary Queen of Scots and King Consort of Scotland, had been assassinated. Darnley's death at Kirk o' Field was preceded by gunpowder explosions beneath the room where he slept; he and his valet escaped the blasts only to be strangled to death; later their bodies were found in the orchard, mysteriously surrounded by a cloak, a dagger, a chair and a coat.

Oxford, then enrolled at Gray's Inn, was still a royal ward in the custody of Cecil, whose informants in Scotland were sending back streams of intelligence. Young de Vere had a ringside seat as the gruesome details became urgent topics at Cecil House. The chief minister's vision for military security required a peaceful Scotland, but now that country was on the brink of civil war.

Fig. 18 - Henry Stuart, Lord Darnley

Darnley's assassination reportedly had been engineered by Mary's chief adviser and lover, the ambitious Earl of Bothwell. Other intelligence held that she herself was the responsible party, having lured her husband into a vulnerable position on the pretext that the "wholesome air" would be good for his health—a notable detail of *Macbeth*. Cecil's agents sent back a sketch of the crime scene that was being circulated in Scotland. It showed Darnley's body near a gate and a "floating dagger"—again, key features of the Shakespearean play.

Agents reported Mary had been so traumatized by fear and horror that she had fallen into a trance, not unlike that of Lady Macbeth. Then came news she had married Bothwell, the murderer, and many assumed they had planned it together—ready models for Macbeth and Lady Macbeth, who plan the murder of King Duncan. Soon Mary was forced to abdicate. Her infant son by Darnley, born in 1566, was crowned James VI of Scotland.

1568: "The Tragedy of the King of Scots"

On 3 March 1568 an anonymous stage work *The Tragedy of the King of Scots* (now lost) was performed for Elizabeth by the Children of Her Majesty's Chapel, a boys' company of which Oxford would become the patron. The murdered monarch of the stage work might have been the ancient Macbeth or "any other King of Scotland," Charlotte Stopes writes, indicating the play could have been a source of Shakespeare's tragedy and that it "might even have represented the death of Darnley."

1577: Holinshed and his *Chronicles*

The main source for *Macbeth* is the 1577 edition of *Chronicles of England, Scotland and Ireland* by Raphael Holinshed, dedicated to William Cecil. Back in July 1567, when Oxford had killed an under-cook while practicing his fencing, Cecil had called upon one "Randolph Holinshed" to serve on the jury that ruled the victim had run upon the point of Oxford's sword, committing suicide; de Vere's Stratfordian biographer Alan Nelson has no doubt it was Holinshed the chronicler.

Oxford and Raphael Holinshed were both connected to Burghley and would have known each other early on; the young earl's interest in history would have made him extremely curious about the chronicler's work in progress. Oxford's uncle Golding had written to him in 1564 about "how earnest a desire your honor hath naturally grafted in you to read, peruse, and communicate with others as well the histories of ancient times...." So it's likely that he was privy to the Scottish history for *Macbeth* in Holinshed's *Chronicles* while Holinshed himself was writing it.

1570: Experience in Scotland

The author of *Macbeth* knows so much about Scotland that he must be drawing from personal experience. "I must consider the strong evidence of Shakespeare's acquaintance with the scenes he described," Stopes writes. "No Englishman who had not visited Inverness, and experienced the unexpected mildness of its northern climate, would have thought of describing it as pleasant, delicate, or of noting the martins and their nests....

"Nor would he have changed 'the green lawn' of Holinshed and 'the pleasant wood' of other writers into the blasted heath near Forres, as the spot where the witches appeared, unless he had seen some such moors lying gaunt and terrible, as witnesses of past winter storms. I can hardly imagine an Englishman who had not visited Scotland dreaming of using the peculiarly Scottish idiom 'How far is it called to Forres?' It is possible, and even probable that Shakespeare visited Scotland..."

De Vere spent several months in Scotland during 1570, serving under Sussex in the military campaign against the Northern Rebellion of Catholic earls, who had planned to bring their armies down to London to overthrow Elizabeth and replace her with the Catholic Mary Stuart, who became a captive in England after fleeing Scotland in 1568.

1572: Assassination and Massacre in France

Critics have compared Lady Macbeth with Catherine de Medici, who plotted with Catholic noblemen in France to murder her wedding guests in August 1572. This triggered the St. Bartholomew's Day Massacre of Huguenots and the killing of their leader, Admiral Coligny. A note on a website of the University of California states:

It is quite likely that details of the murders by Shakespeare's Macbeth were taken from accounts of this massacre. Like Lady Macbeth, Catherine de Medici was the driving force behind the King of France, her son, when he approved Coligny's assassination, as Lady Macbeth forced Macbeth to kill Duncan .... Catherine de Medici used a church bell as the signal to kill Coligny. In the play, Macbeth has Lady Macbeth ring a bell as a signal to kill Duncan .... The neurotic reactions of King Charles IX after the Massacre resemble Macbeth's neuroses ....

Oxford was on progress with Elizabeth when, in September, they learned the full details of the massacre. Writing to Burghley in a highly emotional state, he pledged his support. He compared the chief minister to the slain Coligny: "And think, if the Admiral in France was an eyesore or beam in the eyes of the Papists, then the Lord Treasurer of England is a block and a crossbar in their way."

1574: Supper with Lady Lennox

Darnley was the eldest surviving son of Mathew Stuart, fourth earl of Lennox and Lady Margaret Douglas, countess of Lennox. When he was assassinated, Lennox was the most ardent pursuant of justice against Bothwell and other lords who had conspired in the murder of Darnley. Although Lord and Lady Lennox are never mentioned by Holinshed, both appear in *Macbeth*. Just as the contemporary Lennox demanded justice for the murder of his son, Lennox in the play is a pivotal character who gradually questions Macbeth's tyrannical rule. Giving voice to the anger felt by other Scottish nobles, he prays that "a swift blessing may soon return to this our suffering country under a hand accursed!"

Lennox was killed in Scotland in 1571, possibly also the victim of assassination. In his diary Burghley recorded that on 19 and 20 September 1574, he held supper parties at his Theobalds estate attended by Oxford and Lady Lennox, who would have had much to say about the killings that took both her son and her husband.

1575: The French Court

Oxford spent most of March 1575 in France, where he was presented to Henry III, the fourth son of Catherine de Medici. Henry had been involved in the massacre plot. Once again Oxford was brought into personal contact with individuals linked to a possible contemporary source for *Macbeth*.

1588-89: Assassinations in France

Henry III assassinated the Duke of Guise on 23 December 1588. He had lured the popular Guise to his Chateau of Blois, while his mother was inside; once Guise entered he was murdered by the royal guard.

Clark observes "many points in common" between the killing of Duncan by Macbeth and the murder of Guise by Henry III, leading her to believe the play was written in 1589, shortly after the king himself was murdered. She cites the "power and influence" of de Medici, who was inside the Chateau of Blois when the murder took place, just as Lady Macbeth is in Macbeth's castle during the murder of Duncan.

The fact that *Macbeth* was not printed until the Folio of Shakespeare plays in 1623 may be a further sign that it was not written to flatter James; many traditional scholars claim, of course, that Shakespeare wrote *Macbeth* to please the new monarch. Given that his father had been strangled to death and that his mother had been beheaded, James was (justifiably) terrified of assassination or of any violent death. He probably would have run out of the theater!

The notion that the play was based on the Gunpowder Plot of 1605 becomes absurd under close examination. As Whalen writes, that event allegedly involved a plan "by a gang of Roman Catholic radicals—none of whom was in any position to take power—to massacre the whole government of Great Britain, including King James, in a gigantic explosion of gunpowder under Parliament during a ceremonial meeting in broad daylight. Thousands might have been killed. In contrast, Macbeth, ambitious to gain the throne, stabs his guest, King Duncan, in the night while he sleeps alone in his bed. The two regicides could hardly have been more different."

What about the charges of "equivocation"—dissembling under oath, to avoid the sin of lying—made against Father Garnet in 1606, and the conspicuous appearance of that term in *Macbeth*?

"Although equivocation and witchcraft certainly influenced the playwright," Whalen writes, "neither was specific to the early 1600s. [The doctrine of] [e]quivocation had been notorious for years .... Similarly, witchcraft and witch hunts were notorious long before James became King of England." Whalen observes that it "strains belief to suggest that an English actor/playwright would celebrate the new Scottish king of England by writing a gloomy, violent, bloody tragedy depicting the assassination of a Scottish king instigated by witches. That's not the way playwrights, especially commoners, celebrate their monarchs. Nor is it credible that the king's own acting company would dare to perform it. There is no documentary evidence that James ever saw the play, read it or even heard about it, much less felt celebrated."

Reason 81 – *The Tempest*

> *"It is almost certain that William Shakespeare modeled the character of Prospero in 'The Tempest' on the career of John Dee, the Elizabethan magus."*—Britannica Online Encyclopedia

> *"Queen Elizabeth's philosopher, the white magician Doctor Dee, is defended in Prospero, the good and learned conjurer, who had managed to transport his valuable library to the island."*— Frances Yates, "The Occult Philosophy in the Elizabethan Age"

The mathematician and astrologer Dr. John Dee (1527-1609) was enlisted by Elizabeth Tudor to determine a day and time for her coronation when the stars would be favorable (15 January 1558/59 was the selected date), after which he became a scientific and medical adviser to the queen. A natural philosopher and student of the occult, his name is also associated with astronomy, alchemy and other forms of "secret" experimentation. He became a celebrated leader of the Elizabethan Renaissance, helping to expand the boundaries of knowledge on all fronts. With degrees from Cambridge and studies under the top cartographers in Europe, Dee led the navigational planning for several English voyages of exploration.

Defending against charges of witchcraft and sorcery, he listed many who had helped him, citing in particular "the honorable the Earl of Oxford, his favorable letters, anno 1570," when twenty-year-old de Vere was about to become the highest-ranking earl at the court of Elizabeth, who would quickly elevate him to the status of royal favorite.

"We may conjecture that it was in 1570 that Oxford studied astrology under Dr. Dee," Ward writes. "We shall meet these two [Dee and Oxford] again later, working together as 'adventurers' or speculators in Martin Frobisher's attempts to find a North-West Passage to China and the East Indies." Oxford's links to Dee, along with his deep interest in all aspects of the astrologer's work, are yet another piece of evidence pointing to his authorship of the works attributed to Shakespeare.

In 1584 a Frenchman and member of Oxford's household, John Soowthern, dedicated to the earl a pamphlet of poems entitled *Pandora*. His tribute asserted that Oxford's knowledge of the "seven turning flames of the sky" (the sun, moon and the visible planets, through astrology) was unrivaled; that his reading of "the antique" (a noun referring to classical and ancient history) was unsurpassed; that he had "greater knowledge" of "the tongues" (languages) than anyone; and that his understanding of "sounds" that help lead students to the love of music was "sooner" (quicker) than anyone else's:

> For who marketh better than he
> The seven turning flames of the sky?
> Or hath read more of the antique;
> Hath greater knowledge of the tongues?
> Or understandeth sooner the sounds
> Of the learner to love music?

This might as well be a description of the man who wrote *The Tempest*. It's a description of an extraordinarily knowledgeable man, which fits "Shakespeare" perfectly; it's no coincidence that scholars have not only seen Prospero as based on Dee, but also viewed Prospero as the dramatist's self-portrait. Once that window opens, however, the evidence leads to Prospero and "Shakespeare" in the person of Edward de Vere.

Oxford's familiarity with "planetary influences" is "probably attributable to acquaintance with Dee," writes Ogburn Jr., "as is likewise the knowledge of astronomy claimed by the poet of *The Sonnets*." In regard to the latter, here are two examples of the poet's easy, personal identification with both astronomy and alchemy:

> Not from the stars do I my judgment pluck,
> And yet methinks I have Astronomy – Sonnet 14

> Or whether shall I say mine eye saith true,
> And that your love taught it this Alchemy? – Sonnet 114

Dee got into trouble when his delving into the supernatural led to necromancy, the magic or "black art" practiced by witches or sorcerers who allegedly communicated with the dead by conjuring their spirits. Stratfordian scholar Alan Nelson, in his deliberately negative biography of Oxford, *Monstrous Adversary*, includes an entire chapter titled "Necromancer" detailing charges by the earl's enemies that he had engaged in various conjurations, such as that he had "copulation with a female spirit in Sir George Howard's house at Greenwich."

The irony of Nelson's charge is that it not only serves to portray Oxford as similar to both Dee and Prospero, but aligns him with the authors of what Nelson himself calls "a long string of necromantic stage-plays" starting in the 1570s. One such play was *John a Kent* by Munday, who was Oxford's servant; another was *Friar Bacon and Friar Bungay* by Greene, who dedicated *Greene's Card of Fancy* in 1584 to Oxford, calling him "a worthy favorer and fosterer of learning" who had "forced many through your excellent virtue to offer the first fruits of their study at the shrine of your Lordship's courtesy."

In 1577 both Oxford and Dee became "adventurers" or financiers of Martin Frobisher's third expedition to find a sea route along the northern coast of America to Cathay (China)—the fabled Northwest Passage. In fact Oxford was the largest single investor, sinking 3,000 pounds, only to lose it all, which may explain Prince Hamlet's metaphor: "I am but mad north-north-west: when the wind is southerly I know a hawk from a handsaw," i.e., he's mad only on certain occasions, the way he was when he invested so much in that expedition to the Northwest. (It may also explain a reference in *The Merchant of Venice*; see Reason 83 below.)

A play before the queen by the Paul's Boys on 9 December 1577 appears to have been a version of *Pericles, Prince of Tyre*, in which the character of Lord Cerimon seems to be a blend of Oxford (one who prefers honor and wisdom to his noble rank and wealth) and Dee (whose "secret arts" included alleged knowledge of properties within metals and stones):

'Tis known I ever
Have studied physic, through which secret art
By turning o'er authorities, I have,
Together with my practice, made familiar
To me and to my aid the blest infusions
That dwells in vegetives, in metals, stones... (3.2)

Through an Oxfordian lens, *The Tempest* probably originated in the bleak period between Christmas 1580 and June 1583, when the queen had banished Oxford from court, in effect exiling him (unfairly, just as Prospero, rightful Duke of Milan, suffers in the play). But Oxford would have revised and added scenes over the next two decades, especially near the end of his life in 1604, when the greatest writer of the English language makes his final exit through Prospero, begging us to *forgive* him for his faults, to *pray* for him and to *set him free* from the prison of his coming oblivion:

Now my charms are all o'erthrown,
And what strength I have's mine own...
But release me from my bands
With the help of your good hands:
Gentle breath of yours my sails
Must fill, or else my project fails,
Which was to please. Now I want
Spirits to enforce, art to enchant,
And my ending is despair,
Unless I be relieved by prayer,
Which pierces so that it assaults

Mercy itself and frees all faults.
As you from crimes would pardon'd be,
Let your indulgence set me free. (Epilogue)

CHAPTER FIFTEEN

FINGERPRINTS

Reason 82 – The Echo

A Lover's Complaint by "William Shake-speare" (the name is hyphenated on the title page) appeared in print at the end of the first and only quarto of the Sonnets in 1609; the "Echo" poem "Sitting Alone upon My Thought" in *Verses Made by the Earl of Oxforde* was written *circa* 1581. The similarities between the two works are unmistakable; if Oxford wrote the *Complaint* attributed to "Shake-speare," he must have written it about the same time he wrote the "Echo" poem, nearly three decades earlier than 1609. Here is how they both begin:

A Lover's Complaint by Shake-speare (1609)
From off a hill whose concave womb re-worded
A plaintful story from a sistering vale,
My spirits to attend this double voice accorded,
And down I laid to list the sad-tuned tale;
Ere long espied a fickle maid full pale,
Tearing of papers, breaking rings a-twain,
Storming her world with sorrows, wind and rain.
Upon her head a platted hive of straw,
Which fortified her visage from the Sunne,
Whereon the thought might think sometime it saw
The carcass of beauty spent and done...

Sitting Alone Upon My Thought by Oxford (before 1581)
Sitting alone upon my thought in melancholy mood,
In sight of sea, and at my back an ancient hoary wood,
I saw a fair young lady come, her secret fears to wail,
Clad all in color of a nun, and covered with a veil;
Yet (for the day was calm and clear) I might discern her face,
As one might see a damask rose hid under crystal glass.
Three times, with her soft hand, full hard on her left side she knocks,
And sigh'd so sore as might have mov'd some pity in the rocks;
From sighs and shedding amber tears into sweet song she brake,
When thus the echo answered her to every word she spake...

Here, too are lines from *Ruins of Time* attributed to Spenser (1591), also with remarkable similarities:

> It chaunced me one day beside the Shore
> Of silver streaming Thamesis to be,
> Nigh where the goodly Verlame stood of yore,
> Of which there now remains no Memory,
> Nor any little Monument to see;
> By which the Traveller, that fares that way,
> This once was she, may warned be to say.
> There, on the other side, I did behold
> A Woman sitting sorrowfully wailing,
> Rending her yellow Locks, like wiry Gold,
> About her Shoulders carelessly down trailing,
> And Streams of Tears from her fair Eyes forth railing:
> In her right Hand a broken Rod she held,
> Which towards Haven she seem'd on high to weld.

Each of the poems centers upon a mysterious maiden sitting alone and weeping. The Stratfordian model dictates that "Shake-speare" must have seen *Ruins of Time* by Spenser before writing his *Complaint;* but Oxford had already written his *Echo* poem far earlier than 1591, so the likelihood is quite the reverse, i.e., that Spenser borrowed from him. And if Oxford had also written *A Lover's Complaint* much earlier, then Spenser must have borrowed from that poem as well!

Reason 83 – "North-North-West!"

> *"I am but mad north-north-west: when the wind is southerly, I know a hawk from a handsaw."* (2.2) – Prince Hamlet

On the surface Hamlet appears to be referring to an Elizabethan notion that melancholy grows worse when the wind comes out of the north; his madness worsens when the wind is northerly, but, when it's southerly, he is clearheaded and can tell one thing from another. On another level, however, if the author is de Vere, he's referring to his own "mad" (disastrous) investment in the 1578 expedition by Martin Frobisher to discover the Northwest Passage to Cathay, or China, an act of financial madness ending in the loss of all 3,000 pounds that he had put into it.

Just days before the eleven Frobisher ships set forth, hoping to find "gold ore" as well as to establish a settlement on the Meta Incognita peninsula, Oxford dispatched a letter to "My Very Loving Friends," the Commissioners for the voyage:

> Understanding of the wise proceeding and orderly dealing for the continuing of the voyage for the discovery of Cathay by the northwest ... as well for the great liking Her Majesty hath to have the same passage discovered ... [I] offer unto you to be an adventurer therein for the sum of 1000 pounds or more, if you like to admit thereof; which sum or sums, upon your certificate of admittance, I will enter into bond.... I bid you heartily farewell. From the Court, the 21st of May 1578. Your loving friend, Edward Oxenford.

The earl's share soon rose to 3,000 pounds. He entered into bond to buy the stock from Michael Lock, a London merchant who also did business in the Mediterranean. The two men may have met in Venice or Genoa during Oxford's 1575-76 travels in Italy. Oxford became the largest investor, the gambler with most at stake. The expedition resulted in no gold, so Oxford got no return at all—a staggering loss of 3,000 pounds, the sum for which he was "in bond" to Lock, just as Antonio in *The Merchant of Venice* is "in bond" to Shylock for the sum of 3,000 ducats.

A mob of furious men attacked Lock, with Frobisher himself calling him "a false accountant to the company, a cozener of my Lord of Oxford, no venturer at all in the voyages, a bankrupt knave." Convicted upon testimony that he had known beforehand that the ore was worthless, Lock wound up in the Fleet prison.

Added to Hamlet's phrase "north-north-west" (for the Northwest Passage) are the repeated references in *The Merchant* to "3,000 ducats" and the "bond," as well as the name "Shylock" and its similarity to the name of Lock. The phrase "3,000 ducats" becomes a kind of insistent drumbeat of three words uttered exactly a dozen times. And the word "bond" is used thirty-nine times, with different meanings but forming another emphatic, persistent drumbeat:

> Three thousand ducats; I think I may take his bond ... I'll seal to such a bond ... You shall not seal to such a bond for me ... I do expect return of thrice three times the value of this bond ... I will seal unto this bond ... let him look to his bond ... let him look to his bond ... let him look to his bond ... Sweet Bassanio, my ships have all miscarried, my creditors grow cruel [as did Oxford's own creditors, as he descended into insolvency], my estate is very low, my bond to the Jew is forfeit ... I'll have my bond; speak not against my bond: I have sworn an oath that I will have my bond ... I'll have my bond ... I'll have my bond ... I will have my bond ... to have the due

and forfeit of my bond ... I would have my bond ... I crave the law, the penalty and forfeit of my bond ...

Michael Lock "may or may not have been a Christianized Anglo Jew," writes Farina. "Add to this the prefix 'Shy' (one meaning of which is 'disreputable'), and it would be an understatement to say that the (otherwise mysterious) origin of Shylock's name is strongly suggested."

On 2 February 1580, a little over a year after the fiasco of the third Frobisher voyage, *The History of Portio and Demorantes* was performed at Whitehall by the Lord Cham-

Fig. 19 - Martin Frobisher

berlain's Men, whose patron Sussex was Oxford's mentor and supporter at court; in Clark's view *Portio and Demorantes* was the early version of de Vere's play *The Merchant of Venice*, to be attributed to "Shakespeare" in 1598.

With Oxford viewed as the author of *The Merchant*, the character of Antonio may be understood as standing in for Oxford himself; Portia quite distinctly becomes Queen Elizabeth, making it a safe bet that "Portio" in *Portio and Demorantes* had been the early Portia-Elizabeth. It has also been suggested that "Demorantes" could have been a misspelling of "the merchants." Antonio's friends appear to voice the concerns and anxieties Oxford must have experienced while the ships were away and there was little to do but wait for the results:

> Salanio: Believe me, sir, had I such venture forth ... The better part of my affections would be with my hopes abroad, I should be still plucking the grass to know where sits the wind. Peering in maps for ports, and piers, and roads ... My wind, cooling my broth, would blow me to an ague [fever] when I thought what harm a wind too great at sea might do ... (1.1)

Orthodox dating of *The Merchant* assigns it to about 1596, but all the major sources for the play were available by 1558, according to Joe Peel and Noemi Magri in *Dating Shakespeare's Plays* (2010). The connections to Oxford, Elizabeth and the English royal court are so strong that this play by itself becomes the next reason to conclude that de Vere was the author known as Shakespeare.

Reason 84 – "Ever or Never"

In 1603 the play *Troilus and Cressida* was mysteriously "blocked" from publication by James Roberts, who had issued a number of other Shakespeare quartos. Then, several years after the publication of *Hamlet* in 1604, came a brief burst of plays printed for the first time.

One of these was *King Lear* in 1608; another was *Pericles* in 1609; and a third was *The Historie of Troylus and Cressida,* also in 1609, five years after its initial blockage. Midway through the printing of *Troilus,* however, the title page was replaced with a new one, and a remarkable epistle to the reader was inserted inside (by someone who had the clout to do so) with the curious heading "A never writer, to an ever reader. Newes." The epistle itself was a sharp and angry warning that other yet-unpublished Shakespeare works also existed, but were in danger of being suppressed by their "grand possessors."

Also published in 1609 was the original quarto of SHAKE-SPEARES SONNETS *Never before Imprinted*, which seems to have vanished from public view for more than a century. Inside was a strange dedication, arranged in the form of three upside-down pyramids, with dots inserted after each word or initial. The dedication referred to the author as OUR EVER-LIVING POET, which usually (if not always) meant he was dead—even though Shakspere of Stratford was still alive and would not die until 1616.

These uses of NEVER and EVER in two Shakespeare works in 1609 are, at the very least, intriguing. No orthodox scholar has been able to explain them, but it appears that the words were consciously and deliberately chosen:

NEVER WRITER ... EVER READER ... EVER-LIVING.

In Oxford's youthful, signed poetry, there is an "echo" poem in which the "fair young lady ... clad all in color of a nun, and covered with a veil," cries out her questions and receives answers from the echo. She plays upon "ever" for *E. Ver* (which is also an anagram of *Vere*), and the echo replies with that name:

Oh heavens! Who was the first that bred in me this fever? Vere.
Who was the first that gave the wound whose fear I wear forever? Vere.
What tyrant, Cupid, to my harm usurps thy golden quiver? Vere.
What wight first caught this heart and can from bondage it deliver? Vere.

It was apparently Oxford who, in 1575, inscribed a Latin poem on a blank page of a Greek New Testament sent to his wife, Anne Cecil, in England while he was in Europe; one line, translated into English, expressed the hope that her motto would be EVER LOVER OF THE TRUTH/VERE.

In 1598 the satirist and playwright John Marston wrote the following lines that seem to point to Edward de Vere (emphases added):

> Fly far thy fame,
> Most, most of me beloved! *whose silent name*
> *One letter bounds*; thy *true* judicial style
> I *ever* honor; and if my love beguile
> Not much my hopes, then thy unvalued worth
> Shall mount fair place when Apes are turned forth

If Oxford was "Shakespeare" then his hidden real name was indeed "silent" as Marston indicated; and, of course, "Edward de Vere" is bounded on either side by one letter: "E".

Also in 1598 the poet Richard Barnfield wrote a verse addressing "Shakespeare thou, whose honey-flowing vein (pleasing the world) thy praises doth obtain":

> Live *ever* you, at least in Fame live *ever*:
> Well may the Body die, but Fame dies *never*...

For certain members of society, notably writers, the issue of the great author's actual "name" was even then in play; it appears they already knew that "ever" and "never" identified him—silently. *Wits Recreation* of 1640 contained an anonymous epigram that began:

> To Mr. William Shake-spear
> Shake-speare, we must be silent in thy praise...

Venus and Adonis was published in 1593 with the name "William Shakespeare" appearing in print for the first time (beneath the dedication to Southampton); *Lucrece* was issued in 1594 with another dedication by "Shakespeare" to the young earl. That year also saw the publication of the poetical work *Willobie His Avisa*, an enigmatic anonymous work, which has been attributed to de Vere by researcher Barb Flues through stylistic tests; this work contains the next printed reference to "Shakespeare" after the two poem dedications:

> Yet Tarquyne pluckt his glistering grape,
> And *Shake-speare*, paints poore Lucrece rape.

This is also the first appearance of the hyphenated "Shake-speare," strongly indicating a pen name. Also of note is that it refers to *Lucrece*, printed the same year, as his work, rather than to *Venus and Adonis*. Who but the author himself would have known, at the time *Willobie His Avisa* was composed, about the second Shakespeare poem and been able to use it as such?

Willobie His Avisa winds up with a long poem, *The Praise of a Contented Mind*, containing a passage about the historical figures of Troilus and Cressida. At the very end is the author's printed signature in large italicized typeface: *Ever or Never*.

It seems we can hear the author's own voice in many of Prince Hamlet's speeches; and at the end of the first act are these famous lines with "ever" and "I" spoken together:

> The time is out of joint. O cursed spite
> That *ever I* was born to set it right!

In two scenes of the play the prince uses "ever" in connection with his "name." Both involve Horatio, the character that appears to be based on Oxford's cousin Horatio Vere (emphases added):

> Hamlet: I am glad to see you well. Horatio – or I do forget myself!
> Horatio: The same, my lord, and your poor servant *ever*.
> Hamlet: Sir, my good friend—*I'll change that name with you.* (1.2)

At the end of the full text of the play, printed in 1604 after Oxford's recorded death that year, the words "ever" and "name" again appear in connection with Horatio, as the dying Hamlet tells him (emphases added):

> O good Horatio, what a wounded *name*!
> (Things standing thus unknown) shall live behind me!
> If thou didst *ever* hold me in thy heart,
> Absent thee from felicity awhile,
> And in this harsh world draw thy breath in pain
> To tell my story. (5.2)

It's in the Sonnets where Oxford speaks in his own voice; here the signature words "ever" and "never" are even more difficult to avoid (emphases added):

> Why write I still all one, *ever* the same,
> And keep invention in a noted weed,
> That *every* word doth *almost tell my name*,
> Showing their birth, and where they did proceed? (Sonnet 76)

In Sonnet 116 the words "ever" and "never" appear to be part of an insistent identification, first speaking of love:

> O no, it is an *ever*-fixed mark,
> That looks on tempests and is *never* shaken...

If this be error and upon me proved,
I *never* writ, nor no man *ever* loved.

While none of this wordplay *proves* that Oxford was "our ever-living poet," it does add to the evidence, and is another reason to believe he was the "Never Writer" (the author who was never acknowledged) addressing the "Ever Reader" (who has been thrilled and moved to laughter and tears by his immortal words).

When a translation of *Cardanus Comforte* appeared in 1573 by the "commandment" of Oxford, who was twenty-three, he also contributed an eloquent prefatory letter and a poem of several stanzas. In the latter, he defied his own social class by complaining that "the laboring man" does all the painful work while "the lord" gets all the benefits of such labor:

The laboring man that tills the fertile soil,
And reaps the harvest fruit, hath not indeed
The gain, but pain; but if for all his toil
He gets the straw, the lord will have the seed...
For he that beats the bush the bird not gets...

In the same year appeared what has been called the first English poetry anthology, *A Hundredth Sundrie Flowres*, with verses attributed to various pen names (such as *Ever or Never*) as well as the real name of Oxford's friend George Gascoigne. One verse echoes lines of Oxford's prefatory poem:

Thy brother *Troilus* eke, that gem of gentle deeds,
To think how abused he was, alas my heart it bleeds:
He beat about the bush, while others caught the birds,
Whom crafty *Cresside* mocked too much, yet fed him still with words...

Two years later *Flowres* was drastically altered and republished as *The Posies of George Gascoigne,* and to this day most scholars attribute both versions to Gascoigne. It was not until Oxford was identified as "Shakespeare" in 1920 that it became possible to see that Queen Elizabeth's government saw fit to have *Flowres* censored and mangled for reprinting. Ward identifies Oxford as editor of *Flowres* and contributor of at least sixteen of its poems. In the years since 1920, much more of the anthology has been seen as coming from his pen, including the eight poems attributed to *Ever or Never*. Such insights have led to even more evidence that *Flowres* was the creation of a young man whose genius would later give the world the great works attributed to William Shakespeare.

In the poems of *Flowres*, Ogburn, Jr., writes, "we read of the ups and downs of the fortunes of love. In them the lover is paired with a gentlewoman explicitly or implicitly of high degree ....I'd settle for most of its being addressed by Oxford to Queen Elizabeth. One is written to a 'Gentlewoman' for whom the poet has been unable to show his affection .... Other verses reflect bitterly on the poet's treatment at the hands of his lady."

In one line by *Ever or Never*, for example, he writes: "My muse is tied in chains" and in another verse of *Flowres* he writes, "My tongue is tied by one constraint"—just as "Shakespeare" will write in Sonnet 85 about his "tongue-tied Muse" and in Sonnet 66 about his art being "tongue-tied by authority." A thread spanning more than three decades connects *Flowres* (1573), when the young Oxford is already likening himself and the queen to the historical images of Troilus and Cressida, to the author named *Ever or Never* making the same identifications in *Willobie his Avisa* (1594) and finally to the "Never Writer" of 1609 who addresses the "Ever Reader" of *Troilus and Cressida*.

Reason 85 – "Truth's Authentic Author"

"Shakespeare" was obsessed with truth. In his works he used the word "truth" at least 309 times and "true" no less than 766 times, with "truer" and "truest" and "truths" about three dozen times—well over a thousand usages of those five word forms. Equally obsessed with truth was Edward de Vere, starting with his earldom motto VERO NIHIL VERIUS or *Nothing Truer than Truth*. So similar are "Shakespeare" and Oxford in this respect that "truth" is another reason to believe they were one and the same.

The similarity is not just in terms of quantity but also in regard to how "truth" is used by "Shakespeare" and by Oxford in writings under his own name. For example, in the Shakespeare plays the phrase *"truth is truth"* appears three times: *King John* (1.1); *Love's Labour's Lost* (4.1); and in *Measure For Measure* (5.1), when Isabella says: "It is not truer he is Angelo than this is all as true as it is strange: Nay, it is ten times true; for truth is truth to the end of reckoning."

Oxford wrote to Robert Cecil on 7 May 1603, several weeks after the death of Queen Elizabeth and the accession of King James: "But I hope truth is subject to no prescription, for truth is truth though never so old, and time cannot make that false which was once true."

In my view, Oxford wrote Shakespeare's Sonnet 123 during the same period, just a few days before Elizabeth's funeral on 28 April 1603, expressing the same theme: "NO! Time, thou shalt not boast that I do change … Thy registers and thee I both defy … For thy records, and what we see, doth lie … This I do vow, and this shall ever be: I will be true, despite thy scythe and thee."

Given such a similarity between the words in Oxford's letter and those of Shakespeare's sonnet, how can we fail to consider that both might have been written by the same man? "Shakespeare" believed that even though the winners of political power struggles would write the history for future generations, the truth will eventually come out. Certainly that was his overall objective for the sonnet sequence. His intention was to create a "monument … which eyes not yet created shall o'er-read." (Sonnet 81).

> *The Merchant of Venice* (2.2): "Give me your blessing; truth will come to light; murder cannot be hid long; a man's son may, but in the end truth will out."

> *The Rape of Lucrece* (stanza 135): "Time's glory is to calm contending kings, to unmask falsehood and bring truth to light."

> Oxford to Robert Cecil in January 1602, in eerily similar words: "But now time and truth have unmasked all difficulties."

> Sonnet 82: "Thou, truly fair, wert truly sympathized in true plain words by thy true-telling friend."

In the Shakespeare play, Troilus echoes Oxford's motto *Nothing Truer than Truth*:

> True swains in love shall in the world to come
> Approve their truths by Troilus: when their rhymes,
> Full of protest, of oath and big compare,
> Want similes, truth tired with iteration,
> As true as steel, as plantage to the moon,
> As sun to day, as turtle to her mate,
> As iron to adamant, as earth to the center,
> Yet, after all comparisons of truth,
> As *truth's authentic author* to be cited,
> "As true as Troilus" shall crown up the verse,
> And sanctify the numbers. (*Troilus and Cressida*, 3.2, emphasis added)

Reason 86 – "I Am That I Am"

And God said unto Moses, I AM THAT I AM': and he said, Thus shalt thou say unto the children of Israel, I AM hath sent me unto you." -- Exodus, 3.14

As far as we know, only two individuals during the Elizabethan age used the biblical phrase "I AM THAT I AM" to describe themselves, and they did so within identical contexts: the author of the Shakespearean sonnets and Edward de Vere. After composing a letter to Burghley on 30 October 1584, Oxford signed off in his own hand. Then he added a postscript bitterly protesting the chief minister's attempts to use his own servants to spy on him. He set forth the facts and continued:

> But I pray, my Lord, leave that course, for I mean not to be your ward nor your child. I serve her Majesty, and *I am that I am*, and by alliance near to your Lordship, but free, and scorn to be offered that injury to think I am so weak of government as to be ruled by servants, or not able to govern myself. If your Lordship take and follow this course, you deceive yourself, and make me take another course than yet I have not thought of. Wherefore these shall be to desire your Lordship, if that I may make account of your friendship, that you will leave that course as hurtful to us both. (Emphasis added)

(When Oxford warns, "If your Lordship take and follow this course, you ... *make me take another course than yet I have not thought of,*" he appears to anticipate King Lear's outburst against his two selfish daughters: "I will do such things—*what they are yet I know not....*")

The other personal use of the biblical phrase occurs in Sonnet 121, in which "Shakespeare" echoes Oxford's complaint to Burghley. Isn't this the same mind at work? The same protest? The same angry, accusing voice?

Sonnet 121
Tis better to be vile than vile esteemed,
When not to be receives reproach of being,
And the just pleasure lost, which is so deemed,
Not by our feeling, but by others' seeing.
For why should others' false adulterate eyes
Give salutation to my sportive blood?
Or on my frailties why are frailer *spies*,
Which in their wills count bad what I think good?
No, *I am that I am,* and they that level
At my abuses reckon up their own.
I may be straight though they themselves be bevel;
By their rank thoughts my deeds must not be shown;
    Unless this general evil they maintain:
    All men are bad and in their badness reign. (Emphasis added)

We can be sure that de Vere was intimately acquainted with those words of God to Moses; both he and "Shakespeare" were Biblical experts—another reason to think they were one and the same.

Reason 87 – "The Quality of Mercy"

The works of "Shakespeare" contain the author's own meditations on justice and mercy, emphasizing the need for kings to carry out lawful remedies and punishments with compassion and forbearance. In Portia's famous speech in *The Merchant of Venice* about "the quality of mercy" being "not strained" (not constrained), she declares that mercy is "mightiest in the mightiest" and "becomes the throned monarch better than his crown." Mercy is above such trappings and is "enthroned in the hearts of kings," she says, adding:

> It is an attribute to God himself;
> And earthly power doth then show likest God's
> When mercy seasons justice (4.1).

On 7 May 1603, six weeks after Queen Elizabeth died and James VI of Scotland was proclaimed James I of England, fifty-three-year-old Oxford wrote a business letter to Secretary Robert Cecil and, in passing, made this comment (printed below in the form of a speech in a Shakespeare play):

> Nothing adorns a King more than justice,
> Nor in anything doth a King more resemble God than in justice,
> Which is the head of all virtue,
> And he that is endued therewith hath all the rest.

There is a remarkable similarity of thinking between Oxford and "Shakespeare" as well as a similarity of words; for example, Portia's statement that when a king combines justice with mercy his "earthly power doth then show likest God's" is reflected in Oxford's remark that "nor in anything doth a King more resemble God than in justice"—by which he clearly meant a kind of justice that contains the "virtue" of mercy, or the capacity for forgiveness.

It's easy to imagine Oxford giving Isabella these words about monarchs in *Measure for Measure*:

> Not the King's Crown nor the deputed sword,
> The Marshall's Truncheon nor the Judge's Robe,
> Become them with one half so good a grace
> As mercy does (2.2).

In his dissertation on the "marginalia" of de Vere's Geneva bible, which the earl had purchased in 1569-70 before age twenty, Roger Stritmatter reports Oxford had marked a series of verses in *Ecclesiasticus* on the theme of mercy. The question of mercy "is central to the unfolding action of *The Tempest*," he notes. "In this fable Prospero, like Hamlet, learns to abandon the lust to punish his enemies and realizes that 'the rarer action is in virtue than in vengeance.' (5.1). In that statement, 'virtue' is a metaphor for 'mercy'." Stritmatter also points out that previous students of Shakespeare and the Bible failed to notice that Prospero's epilogue—"as you from crimes would pardoned be"—derives "direct, unequivocal inspiration" from Ecclesiasticus 28.1-5, which Oxford had marked in his Geneva bible.

"There can be little doubt as to which side Oxford's sympathies would lean" during the treason trial of the Catholic Mary Queen of Scots in October 1586," Looney writes. In other words, the earl, who sat as one of the commissioners at the trial, would have been on Mary's side, and "as we read of her wonderfully brave and dignified bearing, and of her capable and unaided conduct of her own defense, we can quite believe that if the dramatist who wrote *The Merchant of Venice* was present at the trial of the Scottish Queen . . . he had before him a worthy model for the fair Portia. . . ."

Looney quotes Martin Hume: "Mary defended herself with consummate ability before a tribunal almost entirely prejudiced against her. She was deprived of legal aid, without her papers and in ill health. In her argument with [Burghley] she reached a point of touching eloquence which might have moved the hearts, though it did not convince the intellects, of her august judges."

Hume himself quotes a letter in which Burghley says of Mary, "Her intention was to move pity by long, artificial speeches." Looney writes, "With this remark of Burghley's in mind, let the reader weigh carefully the terms of Portia's speech on 'Mercy,' all turning upon conceptions of royal power, with its symbols the crown and the scepter. . . . Now let any one judge whether this speech is not vastly more appropriate to Mary Queen of Scots pleading her own cause before Burghley, Walsingham, and indirectly the English Queen, than to an Italian lady pleading to an old Jew for the life of a merchant she had never seen before. Who, then, could have been better qualified for giving an idealized and poetical rendering of Mary's speeches than Oxford, touted as 'the best of the courtier poets,' who was also a sympathetic listener to her pathetic and dignified appeals?"

Note: Oxford may have written the first version of *Merchant* several years prior to the trial of Mary Stuart—that is, by the early 1580s, having returned in 1576 from fifteen months on the Continent with Venice as his home base.

Reason 88 – "You are not *Ipse*, for I am he!"

One scene in the Shakespeare plays, viewed through the lens of de Vere as the dramatist, is so starkly illuminating that it quickly shatters the myth that the author could have been William Shakspere. This scene opens Act Five of the comedy *As You Like It*. Set in the Forest of Arden, it has no function in the plot and appears to be one of several late additions to the play. In this short scene the courtier-clown Touchstone confronts William, a country fellow (who appears nowhere else in the entire play) and orders him to stop claiming possession of Audrey, a country wench who is betrothed to Touchstone. Orthodox scholars and teachers are constrained to treat the scene seriously, trying to make sense of it in the context of the rest of the comedy. They often come up with interesting explanations, except for the most obvious one, that it represents the author speaking directly about authorship and trying to tell us the truth by means of allegorical fiction. Touchstone the courtier-clown is the playwright, Oxford, the courtier who was praised as "best for comedy" at Queen Elizabeth's royal court; Audrey the country wench stands for the body of Oxford's plays, regarded by the Puritans as immoral; and William the country fellow is William of Stratford-upon-Avon in the Warwickshire countryside.

In this short allegorical scene, Oxford accuses Shakspere of trying to claim credit for the Shakespeare plays (or to gain profit by selling them), and tells him to abandon all pretensions as author: "All your writers do consent that *ipse* is he; now, you are not *ipse*, for I am he." (5.1) ["All the writers who worked under my patronage know that I am the man himself, the master writer. Now, you, William, are not *he himself*, because I am!"]

Touchstone is one of Oxford's clearest self-portraits. Just as in the 1570s and 1580s he had enjoyed the queen's license to write and produce plays satirizing members of her court, Touchstone is an "allowed fool" (as Olivia calls Feste in *Twelfth Night*) who can say what he wants and get away with it. He is brilliant, insightful, witty and argumentative. He can laugh at the madness of the world and at himself. Above all, he is a "touchstone" or identifier of truth and true value (or the lack of it) beneath the surface appearances.

We are prepared in Act Three to recognize Touchstone as the dramatist. In the forest with Audrey (who represents the plays), he tells her: "I am here with thee and thy goats, as the most capricious poet, honest Ovid, was among the Goths" (3.3). Ovid, the ancient Roman poet and Shakespeare's favorite source, was banished to the land of the Goths, just as Oxford was prevented from taking credit as author. Touchstone then sets up the truth as told best by "feigning" or being deceptive:

> Touchstone: When a man's verses cannot be understood, nor a man's good wit seconded with [acknowledged by] the forward child, understanding, it strikes a man more dead than a great reckoning in a little room. Truly, I would the gods had made thee poetical.
>
> Audrey: I do not know what poetical is. Is it honest in deed and word? Is it a true thing?
>
> Touchstone: No, truly; for the truest poetry is the most feigning ...

The best (or only) way for Oxford to tell the truth is by means of symbolism and allegory in his dramatic works, which are otherwise fictional; but, he warns, if you fail to understand my "hidden" meanings you will be denying my existence; you might as well kill me in the little room of a torture chamber.

Here is Act Five, Scene 1 with some of my comments inserted. The Forest of Arden [which, in real life, lay between Stratford-upon-Avon and one of Oxford's estates on the Avon known as Bilton]; Touchstone [Oxford] and Audrey [the plays] are onstage. Enter William [of Stratford]:

> William: Good even, Audrey.
>
> Audrey: God ye good even, William.
>
> William: And good even to you, sir.
>
> Touchstone: Good even, gentle friend. Cover thy head, cover thy head; nay, prithee, be covered. How old are you, friend?
>
> William: Five and twenty, sir.
>
> [Note: William of Stratford was twenty-five in 1589. By then Oxford would have completed the original versions of all the plays, but he would have written this scene no earlier than 1599, when the "Shakespeare" name had just begun to be printed on the plays, and possibly as late as 1603.]
>
> Touchstone: A ripe age. Is thy name William?
>
> William: William, sir. [If the playwright's first name was William, would he decide to give that name to this country bumpkin?]

251

Touchstone: A fair name. Wast born i' the forest here?

William: Ay, sir, I thank God.

Touchstone: "Thank God;" A good answer. Art rich?

William: Faith, sir, so-so.

Touchstone: "So-so" is good, very good, very excellent good; and yet it is not, it is but so-so. Art thou wise?

William: Ay, sir, I have a pretty wit.

Touchstone: Why, thou sayest well. I do now remember a saying, "The fool doth think he is wise, but the wise man knows himself to be a fool." The heathen philosopher, when he had a desire to eat a grape, would open his lips when he put it into his mouth; meaning thereby that grapes were made to eat and lips to open. You do love this maid?

William: I do, sir. [William wants to marry the plays, i.e., claim them for himself.]

Touchstone: Give me your hand. Art thou *learned*?

William: No, sir. [William is uneducated, perhaps illiterate.]

Touchstone: Then learn this of me: to have, is to have; for it is a figure in rhetoric that drink, being poured out of a cup into a glass, by filling the one doth empty the other; [By transferring to Shakspere credit for the plays, Oxford is being emptied of credit] for all your writers do consent that *ipse* is he: now, you are not *ipse*, for I am he.

William: Which he, sir?

Touchstone: He, sir, that must marry this woman. [Oxford is the one who deserves to be associated with the plays.] Therefore, you clown, abandon— which is in the vulgar leave—the society—which in the boorish is company—of this female—which in the common is woman; which together is, abandon the society of this female, or, clown, thou perishest; or, to thy better understanding, diest; or, to wit I kill thee, make thee away, translate thy life into death, thy liberty into bondage: I will deal in poison with thee, or in *bastinado* [beating with sticks], or in steel; I will bandy with thee in faction [engage in controversy with you]; I will o'errun thee with policy [conquer you with cunning strategy]; I will kill thee a hundred and fifty ways: therefore tremble and depart!

Audrey: Do, good William.

William: God rest you merry, sir. (Exit)

Oxford may have written and inserted this gratuitous scene in 1603, after he had agreed to the complete obliteration of his identity as the author of the "Shakespeare" works. Perhaps he inserted it for a private performance at Wilton in December 1603, some nine months after the succession of King James. For those at Court and possibly others who knew the truth about Oxford's authorship, it must have been both wildly funny and profoundly sad. [See Bibliography and citation of Alex McNeil's article on this topic.]

CHAPTER SIXTEEN

FINAL STAGES

Reason 89 – "Best for Comedy"

"We have at least some dramatic material from all twenty-nine authors, except the politician Ferrers and the courtier De Vere." – MacDonald P. Jackson, *Determining the Shakespeare Canon* (2014)

In the late autumn of 1598, a little commonplace book suddenly appeared with some startling news. The author, Francis Meres, was a Master of Arts of Cambridge and Oxford who was also on his way to becoming a rector in Wing, Rutland, in 1602. Meres apparently had inside information to divulge; about three-quarters into *Palladis Tamia: Wits Treasury, Being the Second part of Wits Commonwealth*, after pages of commentaries on an array of topics (God, Angels, Education, etc.), he abruptly launched into "A comparative discourse of our English Poets," listing twelve plays written by William Shakespeare, the poet heretofore known solely for his *Venus and Adonis* (1593) and *Lucrece* (1594).

Meres reported that Shakespeare had written no less than six tragedies and six comedies, some already printed anonymously and others not yet published (although it's likely that most had been performed). One of the comedies, *Love's Labours Won*, remains unknown (at least under that title) even today. Professor Jackson refers to the other English dramatists listed by Meres and points out that for two of them, George Ferrers and Edward de Vere, no plays or even records of their plays are extant—despite the statement in *The Arte of English Poesie*, published back in 1589: "For Tragedy Lord Buckhurst and Master Edward [*sic*] Ferrys [*sic*] do deserve the highest praise; the Earl of Oxford and Master Edwards of Her Majesty's Chapel for Comedy and Enterlude."

In his own list of English playwrights who were "best for comedy," Meres named both Oxford and Shakespeare. A common inference, of course, is that Meres knew they were two different persons; but it's also possible that he merely assumed they were separate people, or, on the contrary, that he knew Oxford and "Shakespeare" were one and the same, but was intentionally misleading his readers.

The publication of *Palladis Tamia* came just months after the death of Lord Burghley, which could have prompted Oxford not only to instigate the disclosures by Meres, but, also, to bring about the sudden rush of play printings with "Shakespeare" on them; and in that case, Oxford was making sure to publicly separate himself from his own pen name.

Although Meres named "Master Edward Ferris," he actually meant *George* Ferrers, citing him for the poetry collection *Mirror for Magistrates*; in any case Ferrers was not a playwright, which leaves Oxford as the one and only bona fide dramatist on the list whose plays are apparently nowhere to be found. Indeed, Oxford's plays had "vanished" no later than 1692, when antiquarian Anthony Wood noted in *Fasti Oxonienses, Vol. I*: "This most noble Earl of Oxon was ... an excellent poet and comedian, as several matters of his composition, which were made public, did show—which, I presume, are now lost and worn out."

If, according to contemporary records, Oxford was highly regarded for writing some of the most popular plays of his time—the 1570s and 1580s— his standing as the sole dramatist on the Meres list without *any* surviving play (or even a record of one) is a glaring anomaly that cries out for explanation.

The answer from here, of course, is that this is just what to expect if all his "comedies and interludes" were originally anonymous, or credited to others, and were later revised for publication under the "Shakespeare" name. This would explain why all his stage works were "lost" or unrecorded and how the author of Sonnet 81 could predict that "I, once gone, to all the world must die."

"In Edward de Vere we have a dramatist, recognized by all contemporary authorities as belonging to the first rank, yet the whole of his dramas are missing," Looney writes in *Shakespeare Pictorial* (November 1935). "'The lost plays of the Earl of Oxford' had become an outstanding reality of dramatic history many a year before the Shakespeare problem had even been thought of. De Vere is the only dramatist in the long list compiled in 1598 by Francis Meres of whose work no trace has been found. On the other hand, we have in the 'Shakespeare' plays a set of dramas of the highest class attributed to a man [Shakspere] whose personal records have been found by modern historical research to be in direct conflict with all the outstanding and indisputable implications of such authorship. We have therefore an evergrowing mass of evidence that he was but a cover for some unnamed dramatist.

"Briefly, then, we have in Edward de Vere the only first-class dramatist the whole of whose plays are missing, and in the Shakespeare plays the only complete set of first-class dramas the author of which, on the strength of probabilities amounting to a practical certainty, is also supposed to be missing. These facts alone, each in its own way so amazingly strange and wholly unique, being contemporary and complementary, would justify, without further proof, a very strong belief that the Shakespeare plays are 'the lost plays of the Earl of Oxford.'"

On the premise that Oxford wrote the "Shakespeare" works, the plays cited by Meres represent mature versions of earlier texts dating as far back as the 1570s (or even earlier), when they were recorded as performed at court under different titles. In those decades Oxford's plays would have been anonymous.

Meres listed these as "Best for Tragedy": "The Lorde Buckhurst, Doctor Leg of Cambridge, Doctor Edes of Oxford, Master Edward Ferris, the author of the Mirror for Magistrates, Marlow, Peele, Watson, Kid, Shakespeare, Drayton, Chapman, Decker, and Beniamin Iohnson."

He listed these as "Best for Comedy": "Edward, Earle of Oxforde, Doctor Gager of Oxforde, Master Rowley, once a rare scholler of learned Pembrooke Hall in Cambridge, Maister Edwardes, one of Her Maiesties Chappell, eloquent and wittie Iohn Lilly, Lodge, Gascoyne, Greene, Shakespeare, Thomas Nash, Thomas Heywood, Anthony Mundye, our best plotter, Chapman, Porter, Wilson, Hathway, and Henry Chettle."

Oxford had been personally connected to many of the writers on each of the lists: Lyly and Munday were his secretaries who dedicated works to him, as did Watson and Greene; he and Edwards were connected through the Children of the Chapel and as fellow poets; Gascoigne was an acquaintance from earlier years; Peele and Lodge, among others on the list, were in his circle of writers during the wartime years of the 1580s; Chapman wrote about meeting him in Europe.

Reason 90 – The New Clown

Oxfordian researcher Abraham Bronson Feldman cites strong evidence that the great stage clown Robert Armin, known as "Shakespeare's Jester," was an avowed servant of Edward de Vere. Moreover, he found Armin journeying to "Hackney" soon after he had joined the Chamberlain's Men and had begun to play Shakespeare's philosophical fools such as Touchstone in *As You Like It* and Feste in *Twelfth Night*.

Feldman discovered the connection between Oxford and Armin in a rare quarto entitled *Quips upon Questions*, written by the famous jester-clown and printed in 1600 without his name on it. In his mock dedication of this work, Armin wrote that he would "take my journey (to wait on the right Honourable good Lord my Master whom I serve) to Hackney."

"There was only one literary nobleman dwelling in Hackney" when Armin was playing Shakespeare's "licensed" or "allowed" fools, Feldman wrote, adding that the "Honourable good Lord" at Hackney had to have been Lord Oxford. The earl had moved from Stoke Newington to King's Place, Hackney, in 1596 with his second wife, Elizabeth Trentham, and their three-year-old son Henry de Vere, the future eighteenth earl. After the victory over the Spanish Armada in 1588, he had become a reclusive figure who, most Oxfordians agree, spent his time revising and transforming his previous stage works for Blackfriars and the court into the plays that began appearing under the Shakespeare name in the 1590s. One of

Fig. 20 - Robert Armin

those revised works was *As You Like It*, with Armin the first actor to play the updated character Touchstone. As Anderson puts it, the "reasonable inference" is that Armin was "workshopping" the role of Touchstone at Hackney with the author himself, de Vere, who, in our view, was the unseen guiding hand of the Chamberlain's Men, a.k.a. Shakespeare's Company, in addition to being its chief playwright. Another reasonable inference is that Oxford was training Armin to create a new kind of clown, more intelligent than the ones previously created by Richard Tarleton and Will Kemp (the latter whom Armin had just replaced), in the spirit of Hamlet's advice to the players:

> And let those that play your clowns speak no more than is set down for them, for there be of them that will themselves laugh, to set on some quantity of barren spectators to laugh too, though in the meantime some necessary question of the play be then to be considered. That's villainous, and shows a most pitiful ambition in the fool that uses it. (3.2)

In the above lines we seem to be hearing the genuine voice of Hamlet's creator, Oxford, instructing his players in the same manner and tone he used when instructing Armin, who was even then becoming

Touchstone. Armin is generally credited with playing all the "licensed fools" in the repertory of the Chamberlain's and King's Men—not only Touchstone and Feste, but also the Fool in *King Lear* and Lavatch in *All's Well That Ends Well*, with the added possibilities of Thersites in *Troilus and Cressida*, the Porter in *Macbeth*, the Fool in *Timon of Athens* and Autolycus in *The Winter's Tale*. In addition, Armin is thought to have originated the role of Iago, the villain in *Othello*, indicating the high quality of acting skills he must have acquired.

"Armin may have played a key role in the development of Shakespearean fools," a Wikipedia entry states, adding that he "explored every aspect of the clown, from the natural idiot to the philosopher-fool, from serving man to retained jester. In study, writing and performance, Armin moved the fool from rustic zany to trained motley. His characters—those he wrote and those he acted—absurdly point out the absurdity of what is otherwise called normal. Instead of appealing to the identity of the English commoner by imitating them, he created a new fool, a high-comic jester for whom wisdom is wit and wit is wisdom."

The Wikipedia writers seem to believe it was Armin who inspired and even taught Shakespeare to create such "allowed fools" rather than the other way around. This notion undoubtedly comes from the traditional view of the Bard as Shakspere, the country fellow who would have required such teaching. He certainly appears to be the model for the unsophisticated "William, a Country Fellow" in *As You Like It*, when Touchstone tells him (in the voice of the author) that "all your writers do consent that *ipse* is he," adding, "Now, you are not *ipse*, for I am he!" (5.1) [See Reason 89.]

When Armin called himself the "servant" of the nobleman at Hackney, he was talking about himself as one of the actor-servants of the Chamberlain's Men; we can imagine Oxford and Armin discussing this scene between William and Touchstone the clown. "It stands to reason that de Vere was consulting with the players who were bringing [the Shakespeare stage works] to the world at large," Anderson writes. "And the Armin example is, so far at least, the closest we have to a gold standard for de Vere's relationship to the public staging of plays we know today as 'Shakespeare's.'"

Reason 91 – Dramatic Literature

And that he
Who casts to write a living line must sweat
(Such as thine are) and strike the second heat

Upon the Muse's anvil: turn the same
(And himself with it) that he thinks to frame;
Or for the laurel he may gain a scorn,
For a good Poet's made as well as born,
And such wert thou.
Ben Jonson's eulogy to Shakespeare, *The Folio*, 1623

This evidence comprises one of the most important, yet among the least noticed, of the reasons why Oxford is Shakespeare. The plays are masterpieces of dramatic literature—they are works the author has written and rewritten, over long stretches of time, not primarily for playgoing audiences, but for carefully attentive readers. Most can be fully appreciated only when, in addition to being seen and heard, they are read and reread. But to comprehend how they were produced in final form requires a viewpoint wholly opposite from that of Stratfordian tradition.

The standard image is that of a man busily engaged in his acting career, with its nonstop pressures of memorizing, rehearsing and performing, while also traveling back and forth to Stratford-upon-Avon, lending money, buying property, dealing in grain and litigating over petty debts. Simultaneously he is writing to produce, one after the other, popular plays earning profits at the box office. He keeps meeting new commercial demands, leaving each work to be printed as it had been delivered or performed.

This traditional conception continues to be promoted by established authorities, even in the face of growing challenges based on huge anomalies. For example, one of the very first plays with Shakespeare's name on it was *Love's Labour's Lost*, first printed in 1598. Yet the title page states that it is *"Newly corrected and augmented,"* indicating strongly that its author had the time necessary to make such revisions. In 1604 the second quarto of *Hamlet* was "Newly imprinted and enlarged to almost as much againe as it was, according to the true and perfect Coppie"—resulting in a playing time of five hours, as opposed to the two-hour limit of the Elizabethan playhouse (because of the need for daylight).

Such anomalies should make it obvious that the author was deliberately expanding his plays into more detailed and deeper works of literature, for current and future readers. Under the Stratfordian view of the author's motivations and activities, however, such careful and loving attention to the printed versions of his plays simply doesn't fit.

Only a difficult "mental revolution" will overturn the popular conception, as Looney wrote in 1920, referring to what Thomas Kuhn

(1962) would famously call a "paradigm shift," whereby the same facts are able to be viewed within a new framework, revealing an entirely different picture. The fact that most Shakespearean plays are towering works of literature (pounded upon the "anvil" that Jonson mentions) is one more example of the proverbial elephant in the room.

It appears that Looney, while examining de Vere's life, experienced his own "mental revolution" that changed the way he viewed the writing of the plays. Below are sections of his book that are usually overlooked, but, I believe, deserve to be highlighted—a view of the final dozen years of Oxford's life until his recorded passing in 1604:

> In 1592 he is placed in comfortable circumstances. He is just 42 years of age and therefore entering upon the period of the true maturity of his powers. He has behind him a poetic and a dramatic record of a most exceptional character. His poems are by far the most Shakespearean in quality and form of any of that time. His dramatic record places him in the forefront of play writers.
>
> Then a silence of 12 years … of comfort and seclusion [which] exactly corresponds to the period of the amazing outpouring of the great Shakespearean dramas. Unless, therefore, we are to imagine the complete stultification of every taste and interest he had hitherto shown, he must have been, on any theory of Shakespearean authorship, one of the most interested spectators of this culmination of Elizabethan literature, and he himself the natural connecting link between it and the past. Yet never for one moment does he appear in it all…. So far as these momentous happenings in his own peculiar domain are concerned, he might have been supposed to have been already dead.

Continuing on this path, Looney starts to change the picture:

> One of the greatest obstacles to the acceptance of our theory of the authorship of Shakespeare's plays will be a certain established conception of the mode in which they were produced and issued; a conception which arose of necessity out of the old theory … [and] demands *a difficult revolution in mental attitude.* [emphasis added]
>
> We need to look at the facts that have been established respecting the issuing of the plays in the light of the quality and content of the work [and] determine whether the work is suggestive of a hasty enforced production amid a multiplicity of other activities, or of painstaking concentration of mind on the part of a writer relieved from material and other anxieties.

The choice is whether the author was "living as it were 'from hand to mouth' in the production of his dramas" or "one who began the issue [printing of quartos] with large reserves [of manuscript texts] already in hand."

No less than a dozen plays were printed for the first time between 1597 and 1604, when Oxford died, Looney notes, adding:

> If he had done nothing more than write the twelve new plays, even supposing they had been mere ephemeral things intended only for the stage, the achievement would have been extraordinary. When, however, we turn from quantity to the consideration of literary quality, it is difficult to understand how such an accomplishment could ever have been credited.... It is much more reasonable, then, to suppose that what was actually happening ... was the speeding up of the finishing-off process, as though the writer were either acting under a premonition that his end was approaching, or the time had now arrived for giving to the world a literature at which he had been working during the whole of his previous life. Everything suggests the rushing out of supplies from a large accumulated stock....
>
> How it could ever have been believed that the finished lines of Shakespeare were the rapid and enforced production of a man immersed in many affairs will probably be one of the wonders of the future. Everything bespeaks the loving and leisurely revision of a writer free from all external pressure; and this, combined with the amazing rapidity of issue, confirms the impression of "a long foreground" ....
>
> The fact is that his matchless lines, crowded with matter and intellectual refinements, demand not only maturity of mind in the auditor, but a willingness to turn again and again to the same passages, the significance of which expands with every enlargement of life's experiences. This is one reason why, in order to enjoy fully the best contents of a play of Shakespeare's on the stage, it is necessary first to have read it; and the more familiar one is with it beforehand the greater becomes the intellectual enjoyment, if the play is at all capably handled....
>
> Though the writer's first aim may have been to produce a perfect drama for stage purposes, in the course of his labors, by dint of infinite pains and the nature of his own genius, he produced a literature which has overshadowed the stage-play....

The overall idea, Looney concluded, is that the best of the dramas "passed through two distinct phases." They originated as stage plays, doubtless of a high literary quality, which were "subsequently transformed into the supreme literature of the nation." Moreover the idea is "that the man who had the capacity to do this had the intelligence to know exactly what he was doing," and having created this literature he was "not likely to have become so indifferent to its fate as he is represented by the Stratfordian tradition."

Reason 92 – Printers and Publishers

Robert Brazil provides one of the strongest pieces of evidence for Oxford's authorship of the Shakespeare poems, plays and sonnets: publicly printed announcements that "Shakespeare" personally edited at least five of his works, in the form of statements on their title pages. In each case the printer stated or implied that the author had altered or enlarged the play for publication, after it had been performed at court or in the playhouse. "The remarkable thing is that these five instances of advertised authorial corrections and additions all occurred during the time span of 1598 to 1604," says Brazil, so there was "a short window of time, six years, within which 'Shakespeare the author' showed an active involvement in improving printed versions of his works.... After 1604, Shakespeare was apparently unavailable for revisions."

Contrary to the traditional teaching that "Shakespeare" had no control over his play texts and no interest in them once they were sold to a publisher, we have in fact a procession of five different title pages, each indicating that the author had taken an active editorial role after the play's initial composition.

Importantly, that procession begins with the very first printing of the Shakespeare name on a play and ends abruptly after Oxford's death in 1604. The five plays were these:

1598: *Love's Labour's Lost*: "As it was presented before her Highness this last Christmas ... Newly corrected and augmented By W. Shakespere .... Imprinted at London by W.W. [William White] for Cuthbert Burby." This is the first play to carry the Shakespeare name, although the second syllable is spelled "spere" instead of "speare."

1599: *1 Henry IV*: "Newly corrected by W. Shake-speare —At London, Printed by S.S. [Simon Stafford] for Andrew Wise." The name is now hyphenated, separating "Shake" and "speare," strongly indicating a pen name.

1599: *Romeo and Juliet*: "Newly corrected, augmented, and amended: As it hath been sundry times publicly acted, by the right Honorable the Lord Chamberlain his Servants .... London, Printed by Thomas Creede, for Cuthbert Burby." Despite the corrections, augmentations and amendments, the author's name is missing, even though Burby, who had published *Love's Labours Lost*, surely knew who he was. The name is missing despite the fact that Shakespeare's two narrative poems, *Venus and Adonis* of 1593 and *Lucrece* of 1594, both carried his name and were bestsellers, having been reprinted by 1599.

1602: *Richard III*: "As it hath been lately Acted by the Right Honorable the Lord Chamberlain his servants. Newly augmented by William Shakespeare. London, Printed by Thomas Creede, for Andrew Wise."

1604: *Hamlet*: "By William Shakespeare. Newly imprinted and enlarged to almost as much again as it was, according to the true and perfect copy. At London, Printed by J.R. [James Roberts] for N.L. [Nicholas Ling]."

"Oxford can be linked to key Elizabethan publishers and printers for over four decades," Brazil informs us. Those relationships began with William Seres, a publisher who was active from the earliest days of Elizabeth in the 1560s until about 1578. Seres printed the original version of Ovid's *Metamorphoses* (1565; 1567) credited to Oxford's uncle Golding; he was also the "stationer" in 1569 from whom Oxford purchased "a Geneva Bible, gilt, a Chaucer, Plutarch's works in French, with other books and papers."

Brazil coined the phrase "Oxford's Books" for publications linked to the earl's patronage and active involvement as writer or co-writer, noting that "Oxford's Books have a robust, hyper-intelligent and even bawdy character," so they comprise "a special collection in publishing history, because they can be shown to be the reading matter and linguistic universe that 'Shake-speare' as poet and wordsmith resided in."

Such works issued between 1571 and 1586 include *The Courtier, Cardanus Comfort, The New Jewel of Health, Zelauto, Hekatompathia, or the Passionate Century of Love, Euphues and his England* and *The English Secretary*. "All are pivotal pieces of the literary renaissance in England and reflected in the themes and language of the Shakespeare plays."

Oxford's name and talent "were either on display or being praised overtly" in more than eighty books (including reprints and revised editions) while the earl was alive, Brazil reports, naming twenty-three printers or publishers associated with "Oxford's Books." Of these, he takes special note of nine who were also printers or sellers of "Shakespeare" quartos: Thomas Creede, Richard Field, Cuthbert Burby, Peter Short, James Roberts, Simon Stafford, Edward White, John Danter and John Harrison.

One of the "peculiar facts" he observes is that Burby, who published *Love's Labour's Lost* in 1598, in the same year also published *Palladis Tamia* by Francis Meres, the book that praises Oxford among those "best for comedy" while announcing that "Shakespeare" was not only a poet, but the author of twelve plays including *Love's Labour's Lost* and *Romeo and Juliet*. So why, when Burby went on to publish *Romeo and Juliet* just a year later, did he fail to give credit to Shakespeare as its author?

The first edition of *Romeo and Juliet*, a "bad" pirated version published in 1597 by John Danter, says nothing about Shakespeare. Burby's edition in 1599 (the second quarto) contains a much better text (perhaps obtained by his printer, Creede, who is also linked to Oxford), but it still carried no Shakespeare name.

"It boggles the mind," Brazil writes. "This is after Cuthbert Burby himself obtained the true text of the play in 1599! If Shakespeare's name had a commercial cachet associated with it, why was his name not used on this publication of *Romeo and Juliet*? If Shaksper of Stratford, the man allegedly eager for fortune and fame, took the time to provide Burby or Creede with his complete manuscript, why was he not paid or at least acknowledged in the publication? It makes no sense, unless someone other than Shakspere or the theater owners was providing real texts to the printers." And that someone, given the evidence, was Oxford.

Thomas Creede is crucial to Brazil's study, because he was connected to Shakespeare material—accepted and apocryphal works—as well as to books linked to Oxford. He printed the 1602 quarto of Shakespeare's *Richard III*; in 1600 he had printed *The Weakest Goeth to the Wall* (an anonymous work) "as it hath been sundry times played by the right honorable Earle of Oxenford, Lord great Chamberlaine of England his servants." This is apparently "the only instance in which Oxford's name ever appears anywhere overtly on the title page of a printed play," Brazil writes.

James Roberts printed five editions of books featuring de Vere in some way: *Gwydonius: The Card of Fancy* by Greene (second quarto, 1587); *Paradise of Dainty Devices* (seventh quarto, 1600), containing some of Oxford's early poetry; *Euphues and his England* (eighth quarto, 1597; ninth quarto, 1601) by Lyly, who dedicated it to Oxford; and *England's Helicon* (1600).

Roberts printed the authentic 1604 version of *Hamlet* (known as the second quarto; the year before a much shorter, and significantly different, version of the play had been published). When he had entered the second edition at the Stationers Register back on 26 July 1602, the wording indicated that what he had was a pre-existing book or manuscript: "James Robertes. Entered for his Copie under the hands of master Pasefield and master Waterson, warden, a booke called *the Revenge of*

Hamlet Prince of Denmark as it was lately acted by the Lord Chamberleyne his servants."

Roberts registered both *Hamlet* and *Troilus and Cressida* in 1602, but the publications of both were delayed. Brazil reasons that if Roberts didn't know the author, but had received the texts in a "straightforward deal with a theatrical person," he would have had no reason to delay publication. He concludes that Roberts knew the author (Oxford) personally and that the earl trusted him. It also appears that Oxford himself asked for the delay. "Everyone agrees that *Hamlet Q2* has a text that came completely from the pen of Shakespeare (whoever he really was)," Brazil writes, and this revision is "the last time the author interacted directly with the printers in the name of Shakespeare." In other words, Roberts and de Vere were dealing personally with each other, regarding *Hamlet Q2* of 1604, perhaps right up until the earl's death on 24 June of that year.

Reason 93 – The "Shrew" Plays

A Pleasant Conceited History—The Taming of a Shrew was printed for the first time in 1594 without any author's name on the title page. The comedy is actually two plays, one within the other. The main story takes place within a "frame" of scenes. The play begins with two of these "frame scenes"; several other such scenes are inserted throughout the main action, and, after the end of the main play, a single "frame scene" completes the structure.

The frame is set in the Elizabethan present, outside an English country pub, where a drunken tinker (mender of pots or jack of all trades) named Sly quickly falls asleep. In comes a lord with his men, fresh from a hunting trip.

Spotting the drunken, sleeping Sly, the lord decides to play a prank on him. He instructs his servants to pick up Sly "and bear him to my house," where he will be treated as a great lord with all the trappings of his own wealth and high rank:

And in my fairest chamber make a fire,
And set a sumptuous banquet on the board,
And put my richest garments on his back…
Let heavenly music play about him still…

The lord also has a company of players, with whom he has an easy relationship much as Prince Hamlet with the players in Denmark, and they wish to perform a comedy called *The Taming of a Shrew*. Delighted, he tells them:

Go see that you make you ready straight,
For you must play before a lord tonight.
Say you are his men and I your fellow...

Soon enough, Sly awakens and believes himself to be a wealthy nobleman with horses and hawks and hounds as well as a company of players. Behaving as a lord, Sly turns to watch and listen to the "taming" farce that is about to be staged.

But who was the anonymous writer of this ingenious farce? When it was performed for the queen, court members might well have suspected it was Oxford, the only nobleman among them who matched the lord in every way. Reinforcing that identification is the setting of the frame scenes in the present-day England of Queen Elizabeth. In the 1580s, Oxford had patronized two companies of actors while leasing one of the earliest private Elizabethan theaters, the Blackfriars. He was well known for his love of horses, hawks, hounds, banquets, costly apparel and music; he was a prankster, a teller of tall tales, acknowledged as among the best of the courtier poets and as one of the few members of the nobility who wrote plays, especially comedies; for his own amusement, he even acted on the stage.

"The Earls of Oxford had their players as far back as 1492," writes E.K. Chambers, noting that John de Vere, the sixteenth earl, had a company of players up to his death in 1562. Chambers notes that Edward de Vere "was clearly interested in things dramatic," adding, "He took part [acted] in a Shrovetide device at Court in 1579, and is recorded to have been himself a playwright and one of 'the best for comedy amongst us.'"

Chambers also writes that in 1580 Burghley and Sussex (who was responsible for the play productions at court) wrote to the vice-chancellor of Cambridge, urging "that Oxford's Men should be allowed to 'show their cunning in several plays already practiced by them before the Queen's majesty.'"

So when members of the elite audience at the royal court saw an Elizabethan lord on stage with his players, they must have roared with laughter during one of the framing scenes in which Sly, reacting to characters in the play as if they were real-life individuals, suddenly shouts that he wants none of them to be sent to prison.

"My Lord," the lord tells Sly, sounding like Hamlet addressing a peer, "this is but the play, they're but in jest."

But Sly, insisting that his command as a lord be obeyed, exclaims: "Am not I Don Christo Vary?"

"Don" is a Spanish title used by a nobleman and "Christo" represents Christ the Lord. Given that "Vere" was pronounced "vair" (as in "fair"), clearly Sly has come to believe that he himself is "Don Christ-O": the Lord Oxford ("Vary" or Vere). The court audience would also know that the nobleman whose place Sly has taken must be that same earl, giving them a "sly" portrait of himself on stage.

Close study of the opening frame "shows that the Lord of the comedy is pure Oxford," Looney writes, "a nobleman with his own company of play-actors, directing their performances and even participating in them; a poet and musician of pronounced esthetic tastes, delighting in objects of art, fine apparel and delicate perfumes; withal a keen sportsman, taking pleasure in various forms of outdoor exercises. Everything fits to the letter, which, taken along with Sly's farcical appropriation of his family name, establishes for good his identity."

Whenever *A Shrew* was staged prior to its printing in 1594, there had been no dramatist "Shakespeare" to take credit, and therefore no "Shakespeare authorship question" to interfere with obvious evidence that Oxford wrote the play. Even today many scholars, operating within the restrictive assumptions of traditional biography, conclude that Shakespeare could not have written *A Shrew*—making it quite possible, one would think, for them to accept it as one of Oxford's "lost" comedies!

Nearly three decades later, in 1623, a much longer and more mature version of the 1594 comedy made its initial appearance in the First Folio of Shakespeare plays, and now it was retitled *The Taming of the Shrew*. The producers of the Folio now included the beginning of the frame, with Sly (now named Christophero Sly) and the lord, but they excised the part in which Sly cries out that he is "Don Christo Vary." They dropped all the later frame scenes, even the final one, in what must have been a deliberate effort to further conceal Oxford's authorship.

The Folio project in 1623 is where the tilt toward Stratford-upon-Avon begins. There is no link to Warwickshire until the Folio, seven years after Shakspere's death. In making that tilt the Folio producers sacrificed the integrity of *The Taming of the Shrew* by cutting out all the "frame scenes" except the opening two, now titled "The Induction." Many directors of *The Shrew* wisely restore the frame scenes from *A Shrew* for their productions.

The full frame not only makes sense, it makes for a better play.

The traditional attribution of authorship has led scholars away from the instinctive, logical view that *A Shrew* and *The Shrew* represent two different stages, perhaps far apart in time, within the career *of a single author*. The result is an inability to comprehend how "Shakespeare" actually worked; that is, he did not only write in a single, feverish whirl of magical genius, but, rather, by laboring over long periods of time, in separate stages of life experience and artistic growth, to achieve his final masterpieces of drama. Ramon Jiménez has demonstrated that many anonymous plays comprise Oxford's early versions of works attributed to Shakespeare. They are the "apprenticeship" plays upon which the master built his masterpieces. Jiménez writes the following about the relationship between *A Shrew* and *The Shrew*:

> An objective review of the evidence ... confirms that the two plays were written in the order in which they appear in the record, *The Shrew* (1623) being a major revision of the earlier play, *A Shrew* (1594). They were by the same author—Edward de Vere, seventeenth Earl of Oxford, whose poetry and plays appeared under the pseudonym 'William Shakespeare' during the last decade of his life. Events in Oxford's sixteenth year and his travels in the 1570s support composition dates before 1580 for both plays.

Even for seasoned Oxfordians the latter statement may be startling. Can it be that two plays published for the first time in 1594 and 1623, respectively, had both been written before 1580, when the true author was thirty? Well ... yes. Jiménez continues: "These conclusions also reveal a unique and hitherto unremarked example of the playwright's progress and development, from a teenager learning to write for the stage to a journeyman dramatist in his twenties. De Vere's exposure to the intricacies and language of the law, and his extended tour of France and Italy [in 1575-76], as well as his maturation as a poet, caused him to rewrite his earlier effort and produce a comedy that continues to entertain centuries later."

Twelve-year-old de Vere rode to London in September 1562, in the company of twenty-seven-year-old George Gascoigne, the soldier-poet. About to become the first ward of Elizabeth I, he was heading for the home of his guardian, William Cecil, of whom Gascoigne was a cousin-in-law. Edward received honorary degrees from the universities, at fourteen and sixteen, before enrolling by 1567 at Gray's Inn—where *The Supposes*, translated from the Italian of Ariosto's *I Suppositi* (1509) and attributed to Gascoigne, was being performed by law students. Years later it would be hailed as the first English prose comedy and viewed as a key source used by Shakespeare for *The Taming of the Shrew*.

Stephanie Caruana and Elisabeth Sears argue in *Oxford's Revenge* (1989) that de Vere himself wrote *The Supposes* as produced at Gray's Inn. The translation is "unlikely" to have been done by Gascoigne, they maintain, citing his biographer Ronald Johnson's statement that it contains "a form of euphuistic dialogue that is remarkable in its grasp of the techniques perfected over a decade later by Lyly," who became Oxford's secretary by the late 1570s.

The fact that *A Shrew* is devoid of legal terms suggests to Jiménez that Oxford wrote it shortly before, or soon after, his studies at Gray's Inn; however, *The Shrew* attributed to Shakespeare contains frequent legal terms, suggesting Oxford completely rewrote the play after studying the law. It also appears he wrote the more mature version after returning from his Italian travels in 1576. *A Shrew*, the shorter and less mature work, is set in Athens, while the revised and longer play is set in Padua, the center of learning and the arts that Oxford visited with relish. Lucentio seems to voice Oxford's own thoughts upon his arrival:

> Tranio, since for the great desire I had
> To see fair Padua, nursery of arts...
> Here let us breathe and haply institute
> A course of learning and ingenious studies...
>
> Tell me thy mind, for I have Pisa left
> And am to Padua come, as he that leaves
> A shallow plash to plunge him in the deep
> And with satiety seeks to quench his thirst! (1.1)

On 1 January 1579, less than three years after Oxford returned to England, Paul's Boys performed a play at Richmond Palace recorded as *A Moral of the Marriage of Mind and Measure*. Clark suggests this title describes *The Taming of the Shrew*, caricaturing the marriage of Oxford's sister Mary Vere and Peregrine Bertie (Lord Willoughby) the previous year. Apparently Mary was considered a shrew, that is, a woman of violent temper and speech. Thomas Cecil, in a letter to his father Burghley in September 1578, several months after the wedding, told him there was now an "unkindness" between the young couple and predicted that Mary "will be beaten with that rod [by her husband] which heretofore she prepared for others." If Oxford was having sport with Petruchio as his new brother-in-law and Katharina as Mary Vere (for the amusement of the court, where she had been a maid of honor), it appears he was depicting how better "measures" might be used to tame the "mind" of his willful sister:

> Petruchio: Say that she rail; why, then I'll tell her plain
> She sings sweetly as a nightingale:
> Say that she frown; I'll say she looks as clear
> As morning roses newly washed with dew:
> Say she be mute, and will not speak a word;

Then I'll commend her volubility,
And say she uttereth piercing eloquence...(2.1)

Kate's father in *The Shrew*, one of the wealthiest men in Padua, is named Baptista Minola. In November 1575, shortly before his arrival in Padua, Oxford wrote to Burghley that he had "taken up of Mr. Baptisto Nigrone 500 crowns." Meanwhile, Burghley had arranged, through an Italian merchant in London named Benedetto Spinola, for some 4,000 pounds to be advanced to Oxford during his trip. Could it be just coincidence that the character name *Baptista Minola* echoes a combination of *Baptisto* and *Spinola*? Moreover, Kate's father is quite willing to use her for his own personal gain—shades of Polonius, father of Hamlet's fiancée Ophelia; and, too, shades of Burghley, the manipulative father of Oxford's wife Anne Cecil.

The two *Shrew* plays open up a possible understanding of the long creative process of "Shakespeare"—starting with what was perhaps his earliest comedy, written sometime after *The Supposes* in 1567, when he was seventeen, its action set in Greece; and then moving on to an expanded version, set in Italy and mostly written by 1579, when he was twenty-nine. Think of the mind-twisting efforts this will require of someone teaching that "Shakespeare" began his playwriting career no earlier than 1590! Think of the unraveling of prior assumptions required to comprehend *The Taming of a Shrew*, printed anonymously in a quarto of 1594, and *The Taming of the Shrew*, printed in the Folio in 1623!

Looney writes in *Shakespeare Pictorial*:

The two stages in dramatic composition were, then, a result of marked division in the career of the dramatist: in the first period concentrating his powers upon invention, and in the second upon development and literary elaboration..... Taking the first *Shrew* as representative of Oxford's early comedies, and comparing it with pre-Oxfordian drama, some estimate may be formed of his great achievement as a pioneer in dramatic construction quite apart from any contribution to living literature. By a creative effort, the magnitude of which we cannot now measure, he called into existence the very instrument which made the Shakespeare literature possible. The full costliness of "first steps" is seldom realized in the presence of later developments, but it is safe to say that as much inventive genius and mental concentration would be required to create the first Shrew as to transform it into the second a decade or more later .... This conception of a twofold elaboration, first dramatic and then literary, is as essential to a right understanding of Shakespeare as it is to sound judgment about authorship. Both studies are inextricably mixed and show how irrational is the supposition that the authorship problem may be set aside while serious literary study continues. It is the peculiar glory of the Oxford hypothesis that for the first time it unites the two harmoniously.

Postscript: The 1594 quarto title page of *A Shrew* advertises the text "as it was sundry times acted by the Right honorable the Earl of Pembroke his servants," and in fact four of the play's characters carry names of actors or sharers in that company: Sly, Simon, Sander and Tom. The names "were clearly added to the manuscript of *A Shrew* at the time that the company performed the play," Jiménez writes, "and remained in the text when it was printed in 1594." It is also likely, he continues, that phrases and lines from plays attributed to Marlowe were also inserted in the early 1590s.

Second Postscript: When were the "frame scenes" of the 1594 *A Shrew* written? When were they revised or rewritten for the "Induction" to *The Shrew* printed in 1623? Is Sly intended to invoke William of Stratford, in the act of taking Oxford's place as author of the "Shakespeare" works? My belief is that Oxford wrote the play early on, based on an old folk tale, and continued to revise it even after 1594, for the longer and more mature version to be printed eventually in 1623. We can imagine, then, the producers of the latter work cutting most of the Sly scenes, to eliminate even the memory of the tinker's conception of himself as "Don Christo Vary" or Lord Oxford Vere.

Reason 94 – The Pivotal Year of 1604

Under the view that Oxford was the true author of the Shakespeare works, a logical prediction is that after his recorded death on 24 June 1604 we should see significant developments in the history of the play printings. In fact, that is precisely what we find:

- *Hamlet Q2* comes off the press after June 1604 in its most nearly full version, evidently from the author's own manuscript.

- After that *Hamlet* printing, the steady issuance of "authoritative" Shakespeare plays (approved by the author and/or the play company) abruptly ends, leaving eighteen plays unpublished for nearly twenty years.

- In the Christmas season of 1604-05, the court of King James holds an unprecedented festival of seven Shakespeare plays performed in the days before and after the marriage of Oxford's daughter Susan de Vere.

- In 1604 the King's Men, formerly the Chamberlain's Men ("Shakespeare's company"), having gone without problems since its inception in 1594, suddenly has trouble with the authorities.

- The businessman William Shakspere lodges in 1604 with Mountjoy, a maker of women's headdresses; this is the last indication of him as living in London.

- Traditional biographies conjecture that Shakespeare's acting career ends in 1604.

Thirteen Shakespearean plays were printed between 1594 and 1600, but the first six (published 1594-97) were anonymous. The name of the playwright first appeared on play quartos in 1598 (after Burghley's death in August), when the great issuance of dramatic works truly began. After 1600, however, there was a temporarily hiatus of about three years. The reason, Looney offers, was that Henry Wriothesley, earl of Southampton, the dedicatee of the 1593 and 1594 poems, was imprisoned starting in early 1601 for his role in the failed Essex Rebellion.

"All publication of proper literary versions of the plays stopped immediately," Looney notes, adding it seems that "the complete issue of the plays had been decided upon and begun," but Southampton's entrance into the Tower "interfered with the plans." He adds: "There is much to support the view that Henry Wriothesley acted as intermediary between the earl of Oxford and those who were staging and publishing the dramas."

After Southampton's release from prison in April 1603, the corrupt *Hamlet Q1* was published; then, upon Oxford's death in 1604, came *Hamlet Q2*, twice as long: "Newly imprinted and enlarged to almost as much again as it was, according to the true and perfect Copy." In 1608-09 a brief flurry of printings included *King Lear*, *Pericles* and *Troilus and Cressida*, but these were probably taken from acting copies, not from original manuscripts. With *Hamlet Q2* in 1604, all "authoritative" printings of yet-unpublished plays ceased for eighteen years until *Othello* (1622) and the First Folio (1623), with exactly half of its thirty-six plays published for the first time. "We have a flood of Shakespearean plays being published authentically right up to the death of Edward de Vere," Looney writes, referring to *Hamlet Q2* of 1604, "then a sudden stop, and nothing more published with any appearance of proper authorization for nearly twenty years, although the reputed author was alive and active during twelve of these years." In November 1604, less than five months after Oxford's death, the court festival of plays began with *Othello* and *The Merry Wives of Windsor*. The wedding of Oxford's daughter and

Philip Herbert took place on 27 December, with *Measure for Measure* performed the day before and *The Comedy of Errors* enacted the day after the wedding. The Shakespeare productions at the royal court continued in January with *Love's Labours Lost* (hosted by Southampton) and *Henry V*, followed in February by two performances of *The Merchant of Venice*.

From an Oxfordian viewpoint, this Shakespeare festival surrounding the marriage of Susan de Vere is a silent tribute to her father, the recently deceased dramatist. Meanwhile, traditional Shakespeare biographies presume that, just at the moment of Oxford's death, the author's conjectured acting career came to an end.

"We suppose Shakespeare to have ceased to act in the summer of 1604," reports the 1913 Irving edition of the *Complete Works*.

Remarkably enough the Irving edition goes on to report a crisis in the affairs of Shakespeare's acting troupe after 1604: "No sooner had our great dramatist ceased to take part in public performances of the King's players, than the company appears to have thrown off the restraint by which it had been unusually controlled ever since its formation, and to have produced plays which were objectionable to the Court.... Shakespeare, from his abilities, station, and experience, must have possessed great influence with the body at large, and due deference, we may readily believe, was shown to his knowledge and judgment in the selection and acceptance of plays." I believe the Irving editors are correct, but with only one possible explanation: that it was de Vere, not Shakspere, who had the "abilities, station, and experience" to guide the company in its choice of plays and protect it from the authorities.

So the great outpouring of Shakespeare publications in quarto culminated in 1604, the year of Oxford's death, with the authentic version of *Hamlet*, the tragedy viewed generally as the author's supreme dramatic achievement; as Looney concludes: "The last words of Hamlet may almost be accepted as Oxford's dying words":

> Horatio, I am dead;
> Thou livest; report me and my cause aright
> To the unsatisfied...
> If thou didst ever hold me in thy heart,
> Absent thee from felicity awhile,
> And in this harsh world draw thy breath in pain
> To tell my story ...
> *The rest is silence.* (5.2)

Reason 95 – *Minerva Britanna* – 1612

If there's a single Elizabethan or Jacobean picture that cries out *"Secret Author,"* it appears on the title page of *Minerva Britanna*, by Henry Peacham, a book of original emblems (accompanied by his own verses) published in London in 1612. Shown on the front is the proscenium arch of a theater, with the curtain drawn back so we can see the right hand and arm of a writer using a quill pen to complete a Latin inscription: MENTE.VIDEBORI ("By the Mind I shall be seen"): The suggestion is that the author, who is behind the curtain, must remain hidden. In 1937, Eva Turner Clark argued that the phrase "MENTE VIDEBORI" is a Latin anagram of "TIBI NOM. DE VERE" or "The Identity of this Author is De Vere." A closer look reveals that the "dot" in the inscription has been placed directly between the "E" and the "V" to create E.V., the initials of Edward Vere.

Oxford's death date is recorded as 24 June 1604, the same year the authorized, full-length version of *Hamlet* was first published, after which no new "authorized" Shakespearean plays were printed for nineteen years. In 1622, just one year before the publication of the First Folio, Peacham published a treatise entitled *The Compleat Gentleman*, in which he looks back at the Elizabethan reign as a "golden age" that produced poets "whose like are hardly to be hoped for in any succeeding age." He lists those "who honored Poesie [poetry] with their pens and practice" in this order: "Edward Earle of Oxford, the Lord Buckhurst, Henry Lord Paget, the noble Sir Philip Sidney, M. Edward Dyer, M. Edmund Spenser, Master Samuel Daniel, with sundry others...." Curiously, Peacham does not list "Shakespeare" (see Reason 98, below). Peacham (1576?-1644?), a graduate of Cambridge, had been interested in the theatrical world early on; a surviving sketch of a scene of *Titus Andronicus*, thought to have been made in 1595, was signed "Henricus Peacham." He would have been a teenager when he drew the sketch. In the scene, Queen Tamora is pleading for the lives of her two sons while Aaron the Moor gestures with his sword.

At age twenty-five in 1603, Peacham became a schoolmaster at Kimbolton Grammar School; his *Minerva* ("Or a Garden of Heroical Devises, furnished and adorned with Emblems and Impresa of sundry natures") contains 206 emblems, each accompanied by a pair of six-line stanzas. Roger Stritmatter reports that it "has long been considered the most sophisticated exemplar of the emblem book tradition ever published in England."

One of the emblems in *Minerva* shows a boar, which plays a crucial role in Ovid's story of *Venus and Adonis* as well as in the one by "Shakespeare" published in 1593. The boar was also Oxford's heraldic symbol. Below the emblem, Peacham writes:

I much did muse why Venus could not brook
The savage Boar and Lion cruel fierce,
Since Kings and Princes have such pleasure took
In hunting: 'cause a Boar did pierce
Her Adon fair, who better liked the sport,
Then spends his days in wanton pleasure's court.
Which fiction though devised by Poet's brain...
Such exercise Love will not entertain,
Who liketh best to live in Idleness:
The foe to virtue, Canker of the Wit,
That brings a thousand miseries with it

The line "Who liketh best to live in Idleness" is a direct reflection of what Oxford had written in 1576: "That never am less idle lo, than when I am alone!" Clearly Peacham was well aware, even in 1612, of an authorship mystery involving the poet of *Venus and Adonis*. With his emblem containing the boar symbol of the Vere earldom and those lines underneath it, he brought together "Shakespeare" and Oxford on the same page, providing the solution for all to see.

Reason 96 – George Chapman – 1612

The scholar-poet-playwright George Chapman (c.1559-1634), translator of Homer, was well acquainted with de Vere, who was about a decade older. Aware that Oxford's creation of the character Hamlet was essentially a self-portrait, the younger man knew the answer to the Shakespeare authorship question; after the earl's recorded death in 1604, when the full *Hamlet* was printed in quarto, Chapman made every attempt to tell the rest of the world. It appears that Chapman was obsessed with de Vere.

Let us begin with his play *The Revenge of Bussy D'Ambois*, written about 1607 and published six years later. Chapman set it in France in the 1570s, modeling his fictional main character, Clermont D'Ambois, after Prince Hamlet. Clermont seeks to avenge the murder of his brother, Bussy, reluctantly and long delaying it. Some of the dialogue is straight out of *Hamlet*, such as in a scene about the appearance of the dead brother's ghost:

Guise: Why stand'st thou still thus, and appliest thine ears and eyes to nothing?

Clermont: Saw you nothing here?

Guise: Thou dream'st awake now; what was here to see?

Clermont: My brother's spirit, urging his revenge.

Guise: Thy brother's spirit! Pray thee mock me not!

Clermont: No, by my love and service.

In one speech Clermont describes the real-life figure of Oxford, virtually tagging him as the author of *Hamlet*. Clermont recalls an event that must have actually occurred in 1576 when a teenage Chapman "overtook" (caught up to) the twenty-six-year-old earl as he was making the journey back to England from the Continent:

> I overtook, coming from Italy,
> In Germany, a great and famous earl
> Of England, the most goodly fashioned man
> I ever saw; from head to foot in form
> Rare and most absolute; he had a face
> Like one of the most ancient honored Romans,
> From whence his noblest family was derived;
> He was beside of spirit passing great,
> Valiant and learned, and liberal as the sun,
> Spoke and writ sweetly, or of learned subjects,
> Or of the discipline of public weals;
> And 'twas the Earl of Oxford ...

It's an amazing homage that bears close reading. Oxford was "the most goodly fashioned man I *ever* saw," indicating Chapman's likely knowledge of the earl's earlier pen name *Ever or Never*. It also echoes Ophelia's description of Hamlet as "the glass of fashion and the mold of form, the observed of all observers," and so on. De Vere was "of spirit passing great" or surpassingly great, as well as "valiant and learned, and liberal as the sun." He was "liberal" because, as the Oxford English Dictionary puts it, he was steeped in the arts and sciences and "directed to general intellectual enlargement and refinement ... free in bestowing; bountiful, generous, open-hearted ... free from restraint, free in speech or action ... free from narrow prejudice ... open-minded." He "spoke and writ sweetly"—that is, Clermont identifies him as not only a talker but a writer, an author who "writ" or wrote "sweetly," which, as Barbara Burris observes, is "wording that brings to mind the 'sugared sonnets' and references to Shakespeare as 'honey tongued.'"

276

Clermont's speech marks an "extremely rare occurrence in which a nobleman is actually named on stage," writes Burris, who also observes, "Chapman made sure that he highlighted the Oxford connection .... By openly describing and naming Oxford in this play, Chapman made it clear that he not only knew who really wrote *Hamlet*, but that the original character of Hamlet was modeled on Oxford himself." But Chapman was also conflicted about him. On the one hand he had a "negative and grudging" attitude toward the noble poet, Burris notes, and on the other hand he admired him. Chapman himself was apparently quite different from the earl in his personality, viewed by some as "of

Fig. 21 - George Chapman

most reverend aspect, religious and temperate, qualities rarely meeting in a poet." And while Clermont's story is based on *Hamlet*, the character is nonetheless the opposite of the prince in his manner: calm, austere, stoical, which was Chapman's preference.

As Clermont continues his speech about de Vere, he switches gears by describing Oxford's refusal to review the army of Duke Casimir, a German Calvinist prince and leader of Huguenot forces against the Catholic troops of Henri III. Oxford had left Venice in March 1576, traveling via Milan and Lyons to Paris on his way home. For the entire month the two opposing armies in France's religious war were camped at Moulin in central France, according to Nina Green, who adds that very likely Oxford passed very near Casimir's 6,000 troops.

> And being offered
> At that time by Duke Casimir the view
> Of his right royal army then in field,
> Refused it, and no foot was moved to stir
> Out of his own free fore-determined course.
> I, wondering at it, asked for it his reason,
> It being an offer so much for his honour.
> He, all acknowledging, said 'twas not fit
> To take those honors that one cannot quit.

"'Twas answered like the man you have described," replies Renel, a marquesse, considering that Oxford's response was appropriate for a proud nobleman who would not accept any honors he did not deserve. But Chapman, again through Clermont, delivers his own negative judgment of Oxford's startling behavior (with four consecutive lines starting with the letter *O*):

> O, 'tis a vexing sight to see a man
> Out of his way, stalk proud, as he were in;
> Out of his way to be officious,
> Observant, wary, serious and grave,
> Fearful and passionate, insulting, raging,
> Labor with iron flails to thresh down feathers
> Flitting in air.

Sounds like the Prince of Denmark!

Chapman's first published poem, *The Shadow of Night* (1594), reflects his membership in the contemporary group that became known as the School of Night, a group that included learned men such as playwright Christopher Marlowe, astronomer-mathematician Thomas Harriott, writer Thomas Nashe, explorer Sir Walter Raleigh and, yes, the poet-playwright Edward de Vere. Regardless of his reputation as a strict moralist, Chapman was known for comedy as well as serious stuff. One of his earliest works, *An Humorous Day's Mirth*, was a huge comedy hit played all during 1597 by the Admiral's Men at the Rose. In that work, Richard Whalen writes, "Chapman seems to be depicting Oxford in the character of Lemot, a witty courtier who controls the action of the play."

"Le mot" is French for "the word," and Whalen suggests that Lemot is a writer as well as a courtier and a wit. A female character addresses Lemot as "Monsieur Verbum" and he replies, "Why, 'tis a green bum, ver is green and you know what a bum is, I am sure of that." Whalen goes on to suggest that the punning on "ver" indicates "Vere" or Oxford as "the punning courtier, sometime jester, and recognized writer at Elizabeth's court."

In 1605, when Chapman collaborated with Ben Jonson and John Marston on the comic drama *Eastward Ho,* that play contained no less than five allusions to *Hamlet.* All three authors were briefly imprisoned in connection with this work, purportedly because of perceived slurs against the Scots who had come to court with King James. One of the characters is "Hamlet, a footman" and another is "William Touchstone," who has a daughter named "Gertrude," the name of Hamlet's mother. Other characters are related to Oxford himself, such as "Golding," the name of de Vere's uncle, Arthur Golding, who is credited with translating Ovid's *Metamorphoses.*

As if all of this were not enough, it appears that the title character in another Chapman play, *Monsieur d'Olive,* also represents Oxford. At least one of d'Olive's speeches seems to represent Chapman's recollection of Oxford's speaking style, from his personal experience:

> D'Olive: Tush, man! I mean at my chamber, where we may take free use of ourselves; that is, drink sack, and talk satire, and let our wits run wild goose chase over court and country. I will have my chamber the rendezvous of all good wits, the shop of good words, the mint of good jests, an ordinary of fine discourse; critics, essayists, linguists, poets, and other professors of that faculty of wit, shall at certain hours I' th' day resort thither; it shall be a second Sorbonne...

Monsieur d'Olive, representing Oxford, slips into Shakespearean references such as his statement: "The weaver, sir, much like the virginal Jack, start nimbly up," which appears to echo Shakespeare's Sonnet 128: "Do I envy those Jacks that nimble leap." As the sonnets were not printed until 1609, Chapman must have seen number 128 in manuscript. Such deliberate attempts to link Oxford with the Shakespeare writings— whether or not the public would have recognized any reference to the private sonnets—bring us "almost into smoking-gun territory," Brazil writes.

Below are some additional facts:

> —Chapman in the early 1580s was in the household of Sir Ralph Sadler, who was employed by both Queen Elizabeth and Oxford's father-in-law Burghley.

> —Chapman was friends with Oxford's daughter Susan de Vere, Countess of Montgomery, wife of one of the "incomparable pair of brethren" to whom the First Folio of Shakespeare plays was dedicated. For his translation of the *Iliad* (1609), Chapman wrote a dedication poem to Susan in the Shakespearean sonnet form.

> —Chapman is linked to Oxford's military cousins Francis and Horatio Vere, who were known as the Fighting Veres. "Early in his career," Whalen writes, he "described in minute detail an incident in Sir Francis Vere's campaign in the Netherlands, while late in his career he urged the rescue of Sir Horace Vere and his troops who were besieged in Germany." The play *Hamlet* includes a soldier named Francis and another soldier, the Prince's trusted friend, named Horatio.

Reason 97 – "The Two Henries" – *circa* 1619

"There were some gallant spirits that aimed at the Public Liberty more than their own interest ... among which the principal were Henry, Earl of

Oxford, Henry, Earl of Southampton ... and divers others, that supported the old English honor and would not let it fall to the ground." – Arthur Wilson, "History of Great Britain" (1653), referring to the earls' opposition to the policies of King James in 1621

Venus and Adonis was recorded in the Stationers Register on 18 April 1593 and published soon after. No author's name appeared on the title page, but the dedication was signed "William Shakespeare." It was the first appearance of that name in print. The dedicatory epistle was addressed to nineteen-year-old Henry Wriothesley, third earl of

Southampton, to whom the poet also dedicated *Lucrece* the following year. Never again would this author dedicate anything to anyone else, thereby uniquely linking Southampton to "Shakespeare" for all time. Less than two months earlier, on 24 February 1593, a son was born to de Vere and his second wife Elizabeth Trentham, a former maid of honor to the queen. The two had married in 1591 and moved to the village of Stoke Newington, just north of Shoreditch, site of the Curtain and Theater playhouses. The boy, destined to be the

Fig. 22- "The two most noble Henries" - Henry de Vere, 18ᵗʰ Earl of Oxford (l) and Henry Wriothesley, 3ʳᵈ Earl of Southampton (r)

eighteenth earl of Oxford, was brought to the Parish Church on 31 March 1593 and christened Henry de Vere—not Edward, after his father, nor after any of the men in the great Vere lineage. "It is curious that the name 'Henry' is unique in the de Vere, Cecil and Trentham families," Ward comments. "There must have been some reason for his being given this name, but if so I have been unable to discover it."

Henry Wriothesley was being sought by Burghley in the early 1590s for the hand of Oxford's eldest daughter, Elizabeth Vere. Oxford had become a royal ward in Burgley's household in 1562; Southampton had followed in 1581; and now, little more than two weeks after the christening of Oxford's male heir as *Henry* de Vere, the new poet "William Shakespeare" was dedicating "the first heir of my invention" to *Henry* Wriothesley. "The metaphor of 'the first heir' would seem to echo the recent birth of Oxford's only son and heir to his earldom," Looney notes, "and as 'Shakespeare' speaks of Southampton as the 'godfather' of 'the first heir of my invention,' it would certainly be interesting to know whether Henry Wriothesley was godfather to Oxford's heir, Henry de Vere."

In the *Lucrece* dedication the author made a unique public promise to Southampton, indicating a close and caring relationship, coupled with an extraordinary vision of future commitment: "The love I dedicate to your Lordship is without end.... What I have done is yours, what I have to do is yours, being part in all I have, devoted yours."

As Henry Wriothesley is the only person to whom "Shakespeare" is known to have written any letters (in the form of the two dedications), he should be regarded as the central individual within the biography of the poet-dramatist. This is especially so when Southampton is perceived—correctly, I believe—as the younger man being memorialized in the Sonnets. The problem, however, is that scholars have never discovered any trace of a relationship between Southampton and Shakspere.

But if the poet was de Vere, dedicating his first published work under a newly invented pen name to Henry Wriothesley, then his promising that "what I have to do is yours" suggests there must be evidence of their continued linkage. Among such possible evidence is the performance of *Richard II* on the eve of the Essex rebellion on 8 February 1601 led by Essex and Southampton. If Oxford was the dramatist, had he given permission to use his play for such a dangerous motive? To help Southampton, had he given his personal approval? These are among the many questions for which the historical record has offered no answers.

Looney points to a "spontaneous affinity of Oxford with the younger earls of Essex and Southampton," all three of whom, having been royal wards in Burghley's custody, were most hostile to the Cecil influence at Court. Many scholars have noted evidence in the "Shakespeare" plays that the author was sympathetic to the Essex faction, which makes sense if Oxford and "Shakespeare" were one and the same.

Oxford was summoned from retirement to act as the senior nobleman on the tribunal at the joint treason trial of Essex and Southampton on 19 February 1601. The peers had no choice but to render a unanimous verdict of guilt and to sentence both to death. It was "the veriest travesty of a trial," Ward comments. Essex was beheaded six days later, but

Southampton was spared. After more than two years in prison, he was ordered released by the newly proclaimed King James.

Oxford is recorded as having died at fifty-four on 24 June 1604. That night agents of the Crown arrived at Southampton's house in London, confiscating his papers and bringing him (and other Essex supporters) back to the Tower, where he was interrogated before being released the following day. This episode is known mainly through reports of foreign ambassadors, not through any official record of English history. Whether Oxford's death and the arrest of Southampton were related remains a matter of conjecture.

According to tradition, Southampton had entertained his university friends in the early 1590s with private performances of *Love's Labours Lost*. Now in January 1605, he hosted a private performance of that Shakespearean comedy for the new monarch's wife, Queen Anne.

In the latter years of James both Henry Wriothesley and Henry de Vere became increasingly opposed to the king's favorite George Villiers, Duke of Buckingham, and the intended marriage of the king's son Prince Charles and Maria Ana of Spain. They feared that Spain would grow even stronger to the point of invading with an armed force, conquering England and turning it back into the repressive Catholic country it had been under Queen Mary. On 14 March 1621, Southampton, aged forty-eight, got into a verbal altercation with Buckingham in the House of Lords; that June he was confined to the Dean of Westminster's house (and later to his own seat of Titchfield) on charges of "mischievous intrigues" with members of the Commons. In July Henry de Vere, aged twenty-eight, spent a few weeks in the Tower for expressing his anger toward the prospective Spanish match.

Southampton was set free in September.

On 20 April 1622, after railing against Buckingham again, Henry de Vere was rearrested and confined in the Tower for twenty months until December 1623, just when the First Folio of Shakespeare plays had become available for purchase. When Henry de Vere volunteered for military service to the Protestant cause in the Low Countries in June 1624, as the colonel of a regiment of footsoldiers, he put forward a "claim of precedency" over his fellow colonel of another regiment, Henry Wriothesley. Eventually the Council of War struck a bargain between the two, with Oxford entitled to precedency in civil capacities and Southampton, "in respect of his former commands in the wars," retaining precedence over military matters.

The colonels of the other two regiments were Robert Devereux, third earl of Essex, the son of Southampton's great friend Essex; and Robert

Bertie, Lord Willoughby, son of Edward de Vere's sister Mary Vere and his brother-in-law Peregrine Bertie, Lord Willoughby.

"There seems to have been no ill will between Southampton and Oxford," Rowse writes. "They were both imbued with conviction and fighting for a cause for which they had long fought politically. It was now a question of carrying their convictions into action, sacrificing their lives."

Southampton and his elder son James (born 1605) sailed for Holland in August 1624; in November, the Earl's regiment in its winter quarters at Roosendaal was afflicted by fever. Father and son both caught the contagion; the son died on 5 November; Southampton, having recovered, began the long journey with his son's body back to England. Five days later, however, he himself died at Bergen-op-Zoom at fifty-one. A contemporary report was that agents of Buckingham had poisoned him to death. King James died on 25 March 1625 and Henry de Vere died at The Hague on 25 July that year, after receiving a bullet wound on his left arm.

Why might the "Two Henries" be another reason to conclude that Edward de Vere was the real author of the Shakespeare works? To begin with, in this story there is not a trace of the Stratford man. More important, however, is the central role in the authorship story that was played by Henry Wriothesley, who went on to embody the spirit of "Shakespeare" and the Elizabethan age—the great spirit of creative energy, of literature and drama, of romance and adventure, of invention and exploration, of curiosity and experimentation, of the Renaissance itself.

Southampton had become a father figure to the sons of Oxford and Essex and Willoughby, the new generation of those "gallant spirits that aimed at the public liberty more than their own interest" and who "supported the Old English honor and would not let it fall to the ground." How these men must have shared a love for "Shakespeare" and his stirring words! How they must have loved speeches such as the one spoken by the Bastard at the close of *King John*: "Nought shall make us rue / If England to itself do rest but true!"

Reason 98 – *The Compleat Gentleman* – 1622

Henry Peacham (1578-c.1644) suggested in *Minerva Britanna* (1612) that de Vere had been a playwright of hidden identity (see Reason 95, above) A decade later, in 1622, he published *The Compleat Gentleman,* in which he stated:

"In the time of our late Queen Elizabeth, which was truly a golden age (for such a world of refined wits, and excellent spirits it produced, whose like are hardly to be hoped for, in any succeeding age) above others, who honored Poesie with their pens and practice (to omit her Majesty, who had a singular gift herein) were *Edward* Earle of *Oxford*, the Lord *Buckhurst,* *Henry* Lord *Paget*; our *Phoenix*, the noble Sir *Philip Sidney*, M. *Edward Dyer*, M. *Edmund Spencer*, M. *Samuel Daniel*, with sundry others: whom (together with those admirable wits, yet living, and so well known) not out of Envy, but to avoid tediousness I overpass."

Eva Turner Clark in *The Man Who Was Shakespeare* (1937) was the first Oxfordian to report on this passage. "Significantly," she writes, "Peacham does not mention Shakespeare, a name he knew to be the *nom de plume* of Oxford." Louis P. Benezet of Dartmouth writes in 1945 that Peacham's testimony is "one of the best keys to the solution of the Shakespeare Mystery....We recall the statement of Sir Sidney Lee [1898] that the Earl of Oxford was the best of the court poets in the early years of Elizabeth's reign, and Webbe's comment [1586] that 'in the rare devices of poetry he (Oxford) may challenge to himself the title of the most excellent among the rest.' Also we remember that *The Arte of English Poesie* [1589] ... states that in Elizabeth's time had sprung up a new group of 'courtly writers, who have written excellently well, if their doings could be found out and made public with the rest, of which number is first that noble gentleman, Edward, Earl of Oxford.'

"Now comes Henry Peacham, confirming all that has been said by others," Benezet continues, noting the date of 1622, when the likes of Chapman and Jonson were "yet living, and so well known," while Shakspere had been dead for six years and therefore should have been on the list—unless "Shakespeare" already headed the list under his real name, Edward de Vere. Peacham "was in a position to know the truth," Benezet writes. He had been the tutor of the three sons of Thomas Howard, Earl of Arundel, Oxford's cousin; living in the family circle, "he knew the secret behind the pen name" under which were printed *Venus and Adonis* and *Lucrece*, poems that, "with *The Fairie Queene* [by the late Spenser, whom Peacham *does* mention], provide the high water mark of Elizabethan rhyming."

Greenwood had noted in 1908 that theatrical manager Philip Henslowe had never entered Shakespeare's name in his diary, Benezet recalls, adding that "still more compelling is the silence of Henry Peacham, for not only does he ignore the Stratford man, but, at the head of his list of the great poets of 'the Golden Age,' where the name of the Bard of Avon should be expected, we encounter instead that of one who is not even mentioned in any of the histories of English literature consulted as 'authority' by my colleagues of the Departments of English—the greatest of the world's unknown greats, Edward de Vere, Earl of Oxford."

In the mid-1590s, as a seventeen-year-old Cambridge graduate, Peacham had created a sketch apparently depicting the rehearsal or performance of a scene from *Titus Andronicus*. As Francis Meres in *Palladis Tamia* of 1598 listed *Titus* as one of Shakespeare's tragedies on the public stage, we can be sure, if Peacham had thought the Bard of Avon and Edward de Vere were two different persons, he would have included "Shakespeare" on his list of the greatest authors of Elizabeth's time who were no longer living. But Peacham knew differently.

Subsequent editions of *The Compleat Gentleman* in 1627 and 1634 also omitted Shakespeare from the list, proving that Peacham, who died in 1643, did not accidentally "forget" to mention him.

Reason 99 – Daughters and Dedications

Only three men received dedications of Shakespeare works. Each man had been engaged to (or was married to) one of Oxford's daughters:

Henry Wriothesley, third earl of Southampton, to whom *Venus and Adonis* (1593) and *Lucrece* (1594) were dedicated, was then engaged to Oxford's eldest daughter Elizabeth de Vere. He refused to marry her despite pressure from William Cecil, the girl's grandfather and his guardian. Elizabeth de Vere married William Stanley, earl of Derby at Greenwich Palace on 26 January 1595, when *A Midsummer Night's Dream*, in the view of many scholars, may have been performed for the guests.

The only other "Shakespeare" work dedicated to a named individual (I thus omit the "Mr. W.H." in the Sonnets of 1609, whom I believe to be Southampton) was the First Folio in 1623, with thirty-six plays in over 900 pages, offered "TO THE MOST NOBLE And INCOMPARABLE PAIRE OF BRETHREN":

William Herbert, earl of Pembroke, who had been engaged in 1597 to Oxford's second daughter, Bridget de Vere; and

Philip Herbert, earl of Montgomery (William's brother), who married Oxford's youngest daughter, Susan de Vere, in 1604.

The Folio of 1623 appeared nineteen years after Oxford's death and seven years after Shakspere's death. The introductory matter, supervised by Ben Jonson (who also wrote its main epistles), never explicitly

identifies the Warwickshire man; instead, it contains one reference to the dramatist as "sweet Swan of Avon" and a separate mention of "thy Stratford moniment," leaving it to readers in the future to conclude that Shakspere of Stratford-upon-Avon was the great author. It is upon this shaky foundation that an entirely fictional "biography" has been built.

Oxfordian researcher Ruth Loyd Miller called the Shakespeare folio "a family affair" that began with the marriage of Susan de Vere and Philip Herbert during the 1604-05 Christmas

Fig. 23 - William Herbert, 3rd Earl of Pembroke

seaon, six months after Oxford's reported death on 24 June 1604. Court festivities for the wedding included performances of seven "Shakespeare" plays, an unspoken tribute to the absent author.

The first two plays were "The Moor of Venice" (*Othello*) and *The Merry Wives of Windsor*. Two more were performed, before and after the main event:

26 December: *Measure for Measure*
27 December: the wedding of Susan de Vere and Philip Herbert
28 December: *The Comedy of Errors*

In January the performances continued with *Love's Labours Lost*, hosted by Southampton, followed by *Henry the Fifth* and *The Merchant of Venice*, the latter presented twice. Also presented was *Masque of Blackness* by Jonson at Whitehall Palace; its performers included the bride and groom, Susan and Philip; Elizabeth de Vere and her husband, Derby; and Bridget de Vere's former fiancé William Herbert, earl of Pembroke.

"This was the beginning of a long and intimate association between the daughters of the Earl of Oxford and their families, and Ben Jonson, climaxed in 1623 with the publication of the First Folio," Miller writes. Jonson remained "particularly close" to Susan de Vere and the two Herbert brothers, Pembroke and Montgomery, with Pembroke bestowing on Jonson twenty pounds every New Year "with which to purchase books." It was also the start of "an active, determined and intense campaign by Pembroke for the position of Lord Chamberlain of the Royal Household," Miller continues, noting the position "had purview over the office and properties of the Revels Office" and those of the Lord Chamberlain's Company, now the King's Men.

Jonson published a folio of his own works (the first of its kind in England) in 1616, listing "Shakespeare" as having acted in two of his plays, *Every Man in His Humour* of 1598 and *Sejanus* of 1603 (without mentioning him as a writer). Jonson's costly folio was dedicated to Pembroke, his patron, who apparently financed it; in addition, Pembroke arranged at that time for Jonson to receive an annual pension of 100 marks. Jonson's folio was issued just a few months after the death of Shakspere in April 1616, an event that occurred without any public comment. The identification by Jonson that year of Shakespeare as an actor would be emphasized in the front matter of the Folio of 1623 in "The Names of the Principall Actors in all these Playes"—a further attempt to emphasize the Bard as strictly a theatrical man. It should be noted that the 1623 Shakespeare folio included only his plays; conspicuously, it contained none of the poems and sonnets, nor any mention of Southampton, to whom the poetry had been dedicated.

In 1621 Pembroke temporarily increased Jonson's pension to 200 pounds. Having become the Lord Chamberlain, now "all [Pembroke] wanted to do was retain" his position, Miller writes, "and under no conditions was he willing to accept more lucrative posts unless he might leave his place to his brother Montgomery." The logical deduction is that Pembroke was fiercely committed to publishing Shakespeare's plays in folio.

The Shakespeare dedications all lead back to Edward de Vere and his daughters and other relatives. To repeat Miller's phrase, what we have here is "a family affair."

Reason 100 – "The Record of a Wasted Genius"

When Looney launched his "systematic search" for the true author, he predicted that this man could not have completely hidden his talent; he would already be "a recognized and recorded genius." Because he was working behind a pen name, however, the same man would also be viewed as wasting his life:

> Although we are obliged, from the nature of our problem, to assume that the true author's contemporaries generally were not aware of his producing the

great works, it is hardly probable that one endowed with so commanding a genius should have been able to conceal the greatness of his powers wholly from those with whom he habitually associated; and therefore we may reasonably expect to find him a man of recognized and recorded genius.

On the other hand, "Between what contemporary records represent him as being, and what he really was, we ought, indeed, to be prepared to find some striking discrepancies .... For example, a man who has produced so large an amount of work of the highest quality, but was not seen doing it, must have passed a considerable part of his life in what would appear to others like doing nothing of any consequence."

The result is that in contemporary accounts of him, we should expect to find "the record of a wasted genius."

Such a man, operating in anonymity, would be seen as "something of an eccentric: his nature, or his circumstances, or probably both, were not

normal." The true genius would be "a man much more akin mentally to Byron or Shelley than to the placid Shakespeare suggested by the Stratford tradition." Given his marvelous insight into human nature, allowing him to see the motives of others, we

Fig. 24 - Castle Hedingham

may expect "to find him giving vent to himself in acts and words which must have seemed extraordinary and inexplicable to other men: for the man who sees most deeply into the inner workings of the human mind must often act upon knowledge of which he may not speak." The Cambridge scholar Gabriel Harvey's conflicted attitude toward Oxford is an example. First he praised him as a writer, in effect calling him a recognized genius: "Your British numbers have been widely sung, while your Epistle [to *The Courtier*, 1572] testifies how much you excel in letters, being more courtly than Castiglione himself, more polished. I have seen your many Latin verses, and more English verses are extant; thou hast drunk deep draughts not only of the Muses of France and Italy, but hast learned the manners of many men, and the arts and laws of foreign countries." Then, however, he called him "a passing singular odd man" and mocked his "little apish hat, couched fast to the pate, like an oyster; French cambric ruffs ... delicate in speech; quaint in array; conceited in all points." Harvey confirms Looney's prediction that the real Shakespeare would be "more or less a man apart, whose very aloofness is provocative of hostility in smaller men" toward whom he would "assume a mask" to conceal his thoughts and emotions.

Contemporaries would have found him "not merely eccentric in his bearing, as they have frequently found the genius whom they could not understand, but even, on occasion, guilty of what seemed to them vagaries of a pronounced type."

In 1567 young Oxford inflicted a fatal wound on an under-cook at Cecil House; Gilbert Talbot referred in 1573 to the earl's high favor with the queen but marveled at his "fickle head"; in 1574 de Vere abruptly bolted without authorization to the Continent; two years later he separated from his wife, refusing to accept paternity of her infant daughter; in 1579 he quarreled on the palace tennis court with Philip Sidney, in front of the French delegation, calling him a "puppy." The following year he (accurately) accused his Catholic friends of treason; in turn, they charged him with a long list of "vagaries of a pronounced type," as Looney predicted, with Charles Arundel calling him a "monstrous adversary."

When the true author's mask is finally penetrated, Looney forecast, the revelation "may necessitate a complete reversal of former judgments—one of the most difficult things to accomplish once such judgment has passed beyond mere individual opinion, and has taken firm root in the social mind.... The work in question being the highest literary product of the age, it cannot be otherwise than that the author, whoever he may have been, when he is discovered must seem in some measure below the requirements of the situation; unequal, that is, to the production of such work. We shall therefore be called upon in his case radically to modify and correct a judgment of three hundred years' standing."

Such radical modifying and correcting still remains to be done.

POSTSCRIPT – A Man and His Life

This final reason for de Vere's authorship of the Shakespeare works is by no means the end; it takes us back to the beginning, to the characteristics and conditions required even by the "genius" of that great author. It takes us back to the "long foreground" of earlier development that "Shakespeare" needed to complete his masterworks such as *Hamlet* and the sequence of 154 sonnets. When Looney came upon a summary of de Vere's life compiled by Shakespeare editor and biographer Sidney Lee in the *Dictionary of National Biography* for 1885-1900, he was amazed and gratified by what he found. To find the true author, Looney had proposed eighteen criteria, which he divided into two groups of nine. In the first group was: (1) a matured man of recognized genius, (2) apparently eccentric and mysterious, (3) of intense sensibility—a man apart, (4) unconventional, (5) not adequately appreciated, (6) of pronounced and known literary tastes, (7) an enthusiast in the world of drama, (8) a lyric poet of recognized talent and (9) of superior education—classical— the habitual associate of educated people. In the second group he listed: (1) a man with feudal connections, (2) a member of the higher aristocracy, (3) someone connected with Lancastrian supporters, (4) an enthusiast for Italy, (5) a follower of sport, including falconry, (7) a lover of music, (8) a man loose and improvident in money matters, (8) a man who was doubtful and somewhat conflicting in his attitude to women, and (9) someone of probable Catholic leanings, but touched with skepticism.

Lee's DNB article on Oxford mentioned that his uncle Golding ("the translator of Ovid," Shakespeare's "favorite classical source") acted as his tutor and receiver of property while the young earl lived at Cecil House as the queen's first ward. Lee noted Oxford's studies at Cambridge and that one of his tutors was Clerke, Latin translator of *The Courtier*, publication of which was sponsored by the earl in 1572, a major source of *Hamlet*. Lee had written of de Vere:

> He was thoroughly grounded in French and Latin, but at the same time learnt to dance, ride, and shoot. While manifesting a natural taste for music and literature, the youth developed a waywardness of temper which led him into every form of extravagance, and into violent quarrels with other members of his guardian's household....
>
> [Burghley] found his perverse humor a source of grave embarrassment [but] found in the earl "more understanding than any stranger to him would think" .... "My Lord of Oxford," wrote Gilbert Talbot to his father, the Earl of Shrewsbury, on 11 May 1573, "is lately grown into great credit, for the

queen's Majesty delighteth more in his personage, and his dancing and valiantness, than any other …. If it were not for his fickle head, he would pass any of them shortly …."

In 1575 Oxford realized his ambition of foreign travel, and … made his way to Italy. In October he reached Venice by way of Milan. He returned home laden with luxurious articles of dress and of the toilet. To him is assigned the credit of first introducing from Italy into this country embroidered gloves, sweet-bags, perfumed leather jerkins, and costly washes or perfumes. He ingratiated himself with the queen by presenting her with a pair of perfumed gloves trimmed with tufts or roses of colored silk…. Oxford's eccentricities and irregularities of temper grew with his years….

In September 1579 he grossly insulted Sir Philip Sidney in the tennis court at Whitehall by calling him a "puppy" …. In 1581 he received from the queen's hand a prize for the prowess that he displayed in a grand tilt at court….

In March 1581 his violence involved him in new difficulties…. He engaged in a duel with Thomas Knyvet, a gentleman of the privy chamber. Both were wounded, the earl dangerously…. In October 1586 he was appointed special commissioner for the trial of Mary Queen of Scots…. In 1588 he joined, as a volunteer, the fleet which repelled the Spanish Armada….

During these years Oxford's continued extravagance involved him in pecuniary difficulties…. He had squandered some part of his fortune upon men of letters whose bohemian mode of life attracted him. He was patron of a company of players….

Oxford, despite his violent and perverse temper, his eccentric taste in dress, and his reckless waste of his substance, evinced a genuine interest in music, and wrote verse of much lyric beauty. Puttenham and Meres reckon him among "the best for comedy" in his day; but, although he was a patron of a company of players, no specimens of his dramatic productions survive. [Note: for Puttenham as author, see Reason 29.]

Lee continued:

A sufficient number of his poems is extant, however, to corroborate Webbe's comment that he was the best of the courtier-poets in the early years of Elizabeth's reign, and that 'in the rare devices of poetry, he may challenge to himself the title of the most excellent among the rest….'

Verses by Oxford "To the Reader," together with a prefatory letter from the earl's pen to the translator, were prefixed to Bedingfield's translation of Cardanus's Comfort, 1573, which was "published by commandment of the right honorable the Earl of Oxenford …."

Among men of letters who acknowledged Oxford's patronage the chief were John Lyly, who dedicated to him *Euphues and his England* (1580), and Edmund Spenser, who addressed a sonnet to him in the opening pages of his *Faerie Queen* (1590). Of books of smaller account that were dedicated to him mention may be made of the translation of Justinus's abridgment of *Trogus Pompeius* by his uncle, Arthur Golding (1564), Underdown's rendering of *Heliodorus* (1569), Thomas Twine's translation of Humphrey Lhuyd's *Breviary of Britain* (1573), Anthony Munday's *Galien of France* (1579? lost), *Zelauto* (1580) and *Palmerin d'Olivia* (1588), Southern's *Diana* (1584) and John Farmer's song-books (1591, 1599).

"I venture to say," Looney writes, "that if only such of those terms as are here used to describe the character and quality of his work were submitted without name or leading epithet, to people who only understood them to apply to some Elizabethan poet, it would be assumed immediately that Shakespeare was meant."

What scientists today are learning about "genius" applies to Oxford:

Let us challenge the basic assumption that the individual creator is the only critical component of the creative process. Indeed, let us consider the possibility that groups play an essential role in creativity.... We concluded that it is problematic and unhelpful to separate the creativity of individual minds from the communities in which they flourish.--*Scientific American*, July/August 2014

For centuries, the myth of the lone genius has towered over us, its shadow obscuring the way creative work really gets done. The Lennon-McCartney partnership reveals just how misleading that myth can be, because John and Paul were so obviously more creative as a pair than as individuals.... The essence of their achievements, it turns out, was relational.--*The Atlantic*, July/August 2014

Oxfordians agree that "Shakespeare" was a genius, but we also know he was bound by the natural laws of humankind. We know that any inherited capacity of intellect or talent, especially on the part of one who writes masterworks, is a seed that requires nurturing soil and other elements to ensure its life and growth to full maturity. From birth, Oxford found himself in circumstances and relationships that "Shakespeare," whoever he was, needed to flourish as he did:

Had access to enormous amounts of information and a vast array of sources.

Placed in extremely competitive situations.

Motivated by the vibrant, complicated, unpredictable female monarch who claimed him as her first royal ward and then as her highest-ranking earl.

Led to built-up resentments over hypocrisies and lies perpetrated by members of the court, fueling his devotion to revealing the truth about them, however indirectly.

Stimulated by collaborative relationships with scholars and musicians, writers and actors.

And much more.

No one emerges from the womb intimately familiar with Italy, music, botany, seamanship and medicine, not to mention Venetian law. Such knowledge cannot be "imagined" out of whole cloth; it must be absorbed by the artist before he or she can adapt and mold it creatively. The author of *Hamlet* used his own vast storehouse of facts with consummate ease, spontaneously, even joyously, as it flowed from his mind and heart in service of higher purpose. That purpose was eventually driven by the knowledge that powerful forces were determined to eradicate him from the record. "My name be buried where my body is," he forecasts in Sonnet 72, writing now as an act of survival, if only for generations in the future. "Your name from hence immortal life shall have," he tells Southampton in Sonnet 81, "though I, once gone, to all the world must die."

Those personal predictions by the great author could never have been made by the man traditionally perceived as "Shakespeare"—a writer's name that is surely among the most popular and enduring the world has known. So, hereby submitted are these hundred reasons why the man behind that illustrious name was instead a proud, eccentric, passionate, misunderstood, complicated, Hamlet-like nobleman who died lamenting his "wounded name" and asking his trusted friend, Horatio, to do what we have hoped to further accomplish, however slightly, in these pages:

"Report me and my cause a-right to the unsatisfied."

BIBLIOGRAPHY / WORKS CITED

Akrigg, G.P.V., *Shakespeare and the Earl of Southampton.* Cambridge (Mass.) : Harvard University Press, 1968

Alexander, Mark. *Sourcetext (website).*
http://www.sourcetext.com/sourcebook/ and also
http://www.sourcetext.com/sourcebook/essays/coincidences/

Allen, Ned B. *Shakespeare and Arthur Brooke.* Newark [Delaware], Delaware Studies, University of Delaware Library (URL: http://udspace.udel.edu/handle/197161/4553), 1944

Altrocchi, Julia Cooley. "Edward de Vere and the Commedia dell'Arte." *Shakespearean Authorship Review*, Autumn 1959.

Altrocchi MD, Paul H. "Ideational Change: Why is it so difficult?" *Shakespeare Oxford Newsletter* 42.4, Fall 2006.
—"Shakespeare, Not Arthur Brooke, Wrote *Tragicall Historye of Romeus & Juliet.*" *Shakespeare Oxford Newsletter* 43.1, Winter 2007.

Anderson, Mark. *Shakespeare by Another Name.* New York: Gotham, 2005.

Asimov, Isaac. *Asimov's Guide to Shakespeare.*, New York: Gramercy Books, 2003.

Baade, Eric C. *Seneca's Tragedies*, [New York] Macmillan, 1969

Barber, C.L. *Shakespeare's Festive Comedy*, Princeton, NJ: Princeton University Press, 1959.

Barrell, C.W. Shakespeare Fellowship (American) 1939-1948; Altrocchi & Whittemore: *Building the Case for Edward de Vere as Shakespeare* (volumes 1-3); also, Mark Alexander's website:
http://www.sourcetext.com/sourcebook/library/barrell/index.htm

Beauclerk, Charles. *Shakespeare's Lost Kingdom*, New York: Grove Press, 2010.

Benezet, Louis P. *Shakespeare Fellowship Quarterly*, October 1945; see Altrocchi and Whittemore, Vol. 3 of *Building the Case...*

Berle, Adolf A. *Power*, New York, Harcourt, Brace & World, 1965

Boas, Frederick. *University Drama in the Tudor Age*, New York: Arno, 1978, 1914 (reprint).

Boccaccio, Giovanni. *The Decameron* (1349 AD); *The Decameron of Giovanni Boccaccio*, English translation by Rigg, J.M., London, George Routledge & Sons,1903, 1921.

Bond, R.W. *Complete Works of John Lyly* (3 volumes). Oxford: Clarendon Press, 1902.

Booth, Stephen. (Editor). *Shakespeare's Sonnets*. New Haven: Yale University Press, 1977

Boyce, Charles. *Shakespeare A to Z,* New York: Facts on File, 1990.

Boyle, Charles. "Bitter Fruit: Troilus and Cressida in the Court of Elizabeth." *Elizabethan Review* 2.2 (Autumn 1994). Reprinted in: Boyle, *A Poet's Rage*, Chapter 9.

Boyle, William, editor. *A Poet's Rage*. Somerville (MA): Forever Press, 2013.

Branaugh, Kenneth. *Henry V* (film), 1989

Brazil, Robert. *Edward de Vere and the Shakespeare Printers*. Seattle, WA: Cortical Output, LLC, 2010

Brazil, Robert. *The True Story of the Shakespeare Publications: Edward de Vere and the Shakespeare printers*. [s.l.]: Robert Brazil, 2000.

Brooks, H.F. (editor) *A Midsummer Night's Dream* (The Arden Shakespeare, 2nd series). London: Methuen, 1979

Buckley, W.E. (editor) Cephalus and Procris. Narcissus. By Thomas Edwards. From the unique copy in the Cathedral Library, Peterborough. London: Roxburghe Club, 1882.

Bullough, Geoffrey. *Narrative and Dramatic Sources of Shakespeare*. London: Routledge & Kegan Paul, 1958

Burris, Barbara. "A Golden Book, Bound Richly Up: comparing Chapman's words with the Ashbourne." *Shakespeare Matters* 1.1 (Fall 2001): 1, 12-17.

Campbell, Lyly B. *Shakespeare's Histories: mirrors of Elizabethan policy*. San Marino, Calif., Huntington Library, 1965, 1947.
    —"Hamlet, A Tragedy of Grief" In*: Shakespeare's Tragic Heroes*. New York: Barnes & Noble, 1968, 1930.

Campbell, Oscar James. *The Reader's Encyclopedia of Shakespeare*. New York: Crowell, 1966.

Caruana, Stephanie, and Sears, Elisabeth. *Oxford's Revenge*. [Place of publication not identified] : [Spear Shaker Press], ©1989.

Cecil, Michael, Lord Burghley. "Nothing is Truer Than Truth" at the Ashland Authorship Conference (2010). See YouTube: https://www.youtube.com/watch?v=6nLIJ53kH0Q

Chambers, Sir Edmund. *The Elizabethan Stage* (4 volumes). Oxford: The Clarendon press, 1923

Charlton, Derran (with Kevin Gilvary). *"Love's Labor's Lost."* In: Gilvary, *Dating Shakespeare's Plays*, Chapter 7.

Charlton, Derran (with Kevin Gilvary). *Titus Andronicus.* In: Gilvary, *Dating Shakespeare's Plays*, Chapter 27.

Chesterton, G.K. "The Story of the Vow." In his: *The Superstition of Divorce.* New York: John Lane, 1920.

Chiljan, Katherine. *Dedication Letters to the Earl of Oxford.* [s.l.]: K. V. Chiljan, 1994.
    —*Shakespeare Suppressed: the uncensored truth about Shakespeare and his works.* San Francisco: Faire Editions, 2011.
    —*Letters and Poems of Edward, Earl of Oxford.* [England]: K. Chiljan, 1998
    — "Palamon and Arcite: an early work by Edward de Vere?" *Shakespeare Oxford Newsletter* 35.1 (Spring 1999): 10-13.

Clark, Eva Turner. *Hidden Allusions in Shakespeare Plays*, Port Washington, NY: Kennikat Press, 1974, 1931.

Coghill, Nevill. *Shakespeare's Professional Skills*, Cambridge (UK): Cambridge University Press, 1964.

Coursen, Herbert R. *Christian Ritual and the World of Shakespeare's Tragedies.* Lewisburg, PA: Bucknell University Press, 1976.

Craig, Hardin. "Hamlet's Book," *Huntington Library Bulletin*, No. 6, pp. 15-37, November 1934

Cutting, Bonner Miller: *Necessary Mischief: Exploring the Shakespeare Authorship Question*, Jennings, LA: Minos Publishing Co., 2018.

Davis, Dr. Frank. "Shakespeare's Medical Knowledge: how did he acquire it?", *The Oxfordian* 3 (2000): 45-58).

Delahoyde, Michael. *Website at Washington State University.* (*http://public.wsu.edu/~delahoyd/shakespeare/*).

Desens, Marliss. *The Bed-Trick in English Renaissance Drama.* Newark: University of Delaware Press; London: Associated University Presses, ©1994.

Desper, C. Richard. "Allusions to Campion in Twelfth Night," *Elizabethan Review* 3.1 (Spring/Summer 1995): 37-47.

Dickinson, Warren. *The Wonderful Shakespeare Mystery.* Nashville, TN: OMNI PublishXpress, 2001.

Douce, Francis. *Illustrations of Shakespeare and Ancient Manners.* London: Printed for T. Tegg, 1839

Dowden, Edward. *The Sonnets of William Shakespeare.* London: Kegan Paul & Co., 1881

Drake, Nathan. *Shakespeare and His Times.* London, T. Cadell and W. Davies, 1817.

Draya, Ren and Whalen, Richard. *Othello, the Moor of Venice: Fully Annotated from an Oxfordian Perspective.* (The Oxfordian Shakespeare Series). Tamarac, FL: Horatio Editions, Llumina Press, 2011.

Edleman, Charles. *Shakespeare's Military Language.* London; New Brunswick, NJ: Athlone Press, 2000.

Erickson, Carolly. *The First Elizabeth.* New York: Summit Books, 1983

Farina, William. *De Vere as Shakespeare.* Jefferson, N.C.: McFarland & Co., 2006.

Feldman, Abraham Bronson. "Shakespeare's Jester—Oxford's Servant." *Shakespeare Fellowship Quarterly* 8.3 (Autumn 1947): 39-43; also in: *Building the Case for Edward de Vere as Shakespeare,* Vol. 4 (Altrocchi-Whittemore, editors).

Fowler, William Plumer. *Shakespeare Revealed in Oxford's Letters.* Portsmouth, NH: Peter E. Randall Publisher, 1986.

French, George Russell. *Shakespeareana Genealogica,* London: Macmillan and Co., 1869

Freud, Sigmund, "Autobiographic Study" in: *The Standard Edition of the Complete Psychological Works of Sigmund Freud.* London: Hogarth Press [1927].

Fripp, Edgar. *Shakespeare, Man and Artist.* London: Oxford University Press, 1938

Furness Jr., H.H. *New Variorum Edition of Shakespeare: The Life and Death of King John,* Philadelphia & London: J.B. Lippincott Company, 1919

Gesner, Carol. *Shakespeare and the Greek Romance.* Lexington: University Press of Kentucky, 1970.

Gilvary, Kevin, editor. *Dating Shakespeare's Plays.* Tunbridge Wells: Parapress, 2010.

Goddard, Harold. *The Meaning of Shakespeare* (2 voilumes). [Chicago]: University of Chicago Press 1951.

Granville-Barker, Harley. *Prefaces to Shakespeare.* Princeton: Princeton Univ. Press, 1946-47.

Green, Nina. Website: *Oxford Authorship Site*, www.oxford-shakespeare.com

Greenblatt, Stephen. *Will in the World.* New York: W.W. Norton, 2004

Greenwood, Sir George. *The Shakespeare Problem Restated.* London: J. Lane, 1908.

Halliwell-Phillips, James O. *Outlines of the Life of Shakespeare,* London: Longmans, Green & Co., 1886.

Hannas, Andrew. "Beowulf, Hamlet, and Edward de Vere." *Shakespeare Oxford Society Newsletter* 26.2 (Spring 1990): 3-6. (originally published under the name "Ignoto.")

Henderson, W. B. Drayton. *Hamlet as a Castiglionean Courtier.* Montreal, 1934 (Note: Extract from the McGill news, Montreal, June 1934).

Hess, Ron. *The Dark Side of Shakespeare* (3 vols.). New York: Writers Club Press, 2002-

Holden, Isabel. *Isabel Holden Papers, 1972-2005.* Available at the Five College Archives & Manuscript Collections: *https://asteria.fivecolleges.edu/findaids/sophiasmith/mnsss437.html)*

Holmes, Edward. *Discovering Shakespeare.* Chester-Le-Street: Mycroft Books, 2001.

Hosley, Richard. (Editor). *The Tragedy of Romeo and Juliet* (The Yale Shakespeare). New Haven: Yale University Press, 1954.

Hughes, Stephanie Hopkins. *Evidence for Oxford's years with Smith.* Available at *politicworm* website: *https://politicworm.com/?s=smith)*

Hume, Martin. *The Love Affairs of Mary Queen of Scots.* New York: McClure, Phillips & Co., 1903.

Hunter, Joseph. *New Illustrations of the Life, Studies and Writing of Shakespeare.* London: Nichols ,1845

Jackson, MacDonald P. *Determining the Shakespeare Canon.* Oxford: Oxford University Press, 2014.

Jimenez, Ramon. *Shakespeare's Apprenticeship: Identifying the Real Playwright's Earliest Works*, Jefferson NC: McFarland & Co, 2018

- "The Famous Victories of Henry the Fifth—Key to the Authorship Question? Part 1." *Shakespeare Oxford newsletter* 37.2 (Summer 2001): 7-10.
- "The Troublesome Raigne of John, King of England: Shakespeare's first version of King John." *The Oxfordian* 12 (2010): 21-55.

- "The true tragedy of Richard III: another early history play by Edward de Vere." *The Oxfordian* 7 (2004): 115-151.
- "Who Was the Author of Five Plays that Shakespeare Rewrote as His Own?" *Shakespeare Oxford newsletter* 44.1 (Winter 2008): 13-20

Johnson, Philip. "Merry Wives of Windsor." In: Gilvary, *Dating Shakespeare's Plays*, Chapter 3.

Johnson, Samuel. *Notes to Shakespeare: vol. 1 : Comedies.* Los Angeles: William Andrews Clark Memorial Library, University of California, 1956 reprint, 1765.

Jolly, Eddi. "The Winter's Tale." In: Gilvary, *Dating Shakespeare's Plays*, Chapter 14.

Kail, Aubrey C. *The Medical Mind of Shakespeare.* Balgowlah, NSW: Williams & Wilkins, ADIS Pty, 1986.

Kaplan, Ken. A comment on "hendiadys" posted under Reason 30 (Part I) on *Hank Whittemore's Shakespeare Blog*, (https://hankwhittemore.wordpress.com/2011/12/20/)

Kenyon, Dr. TK. *"William Shakespeare, Edward de Vere, What's in A Name?"* (February 8, 2009*).* Available at the author's blog: http://tkkenyon.blogspot.com/2009/02/william-shakespeare-edward-de-vere.html)

Kernan, Alvin B. *Politics, Power, and Shakespeare.* Arlington, Tex.: Texas Humanities Resource Center, University of Texas at Arlington Library, 1981.

Knight, G. Wilson. *The Mutual Flame: on Shakespeare's Sonnets and the Phoenix and Turtle.* New York: Barnes, 1955.

Kositsky, Lynne, and Stritmatter, Roger. *On the Date, Sources and Design of Shakespeare's "The Tempest."* Jefferson, North Carolina: McFarland, 2013.

Lee, Sir Sidney. *A Life of William Shakespeare.* London: Smith, Elder and Co., 1898.

Leech, Clifford. (Editor) *The Two Gentlemen of Verona* (Arden Edition). London: Methuen; New York: [Dist.by] Harper & Row, Barnes & Noble Import Div.,1972.

Looney, John Thomas. *"Shakespeare" Identified.* New York: Frederick A. Stokes Co., 1920.

Lotherington, John. (Editor) *The Book of the Courtier*. New York: Barnes & Noble Books, 2005.

Machyn, Henry. *The diary of Henry Machyn: citizen and merchant-taylor of London, from A.D. 1550 to A.D. 1563*. London: Printed for the Camden Society, by J.B. Nichols and Son, 1848.

MacLean, Sally-Beth, and Scott McMillin, *The Queen's Men and their Plays*. Cambridge [UK]; New York: Cambridge University Press, 1998.

Magri, Noemi. *Such Fruits out of Italy: the Italian Renaissance in Shakespeare's plays and poems*. Buchholz, Germany: Laugwitz Verlag, 2014.

—"All's Well That Ends Well" In: Gilvary, *Dating Shakespeare's Plays*, Chapter 12.

—"The Merchant of Venice" (with Joe Peel). In: Gilvary, *Dating Shakespeare's Plays*, Chapter 9.

—"The Tragedie of Othello, the Moore of Venice" In: Gilvary, *Dating Shakespeare's Plays*, Chapter 34.

—"The Two Gentlemen of Verona" In: Gilvary, *Dating Shakespeare's Plays*, Chapter 2.

Malim, Richard. *The Earl of Oxford and the Making of "Shakespeare."* Jefferson, NC; London: McFarland & Company, 2012.

Malone, Edmund. *The plays of William Shakspeare. In ten volumes. With the corrections and illustrations of various commentators ; to which are added notes by S. Johnson and G. Steevens. (An attempt to ascertain the order in which the plays attributed to Shakespeare were written, by E. Malone.) The second edition, revised and augmented*. London: C. Bathurst, etc., 1778-1780.

McMillin, Scott. See MacLean, Sally-Beth and Scott McMillin.

McNeil, Alex. *"Is Touchstone vs. William in* As You Like It *the first authorship story?" Shakespeare Matters* 2.3 (Spring 2003): 14-22.

Miller, Ruth Loyd. *Oxfordian Vistas*. Vol 2 of *Shakespeare Identified in the Seventeenth Earl of Oxford*. Port Washington, N.Y. : Published by Kennikat Press for Minos Pub. Co., 1975. (Ruth Loyd Miller, Editor)

Mosher, Sally. "William Byrd's 'Battle' and the Earl of Oxford." *The Oxfordian* 1 (1998): 43-52.

Neilson, William Allan (Editor). *The Chief Elizabethan Dramatists, excluding Shakespeare*. Boston, New York: Houghton Mifflin Co., 1911.

Nelson, Alan. *Monstrous Adversary*. Liverpool: Liverpool University Press, 2003.
Nicholl, Charles. *The Reckoning*. New York: Harcourt Brace,1992.

Ogburn Jr, Charlton. *The Mysterious William Shakespeare*. New York: Dodd, Mead, 1984.
Ogburn, Dorothy and Charlton. *This Star of England*. New York, Coward-McCann 1952.
Osborne, Francis. *Historical Memoires on the Reigns of Queen Elizabeth and King James*. London: J. Grismond, 1658.

Peck, Francis. *Desiderata Curiosa*, Vol. 1 (1732), London: Printed for Thomas Evans in the Strand, 1779.
Peel, Joe. "The Merchant of Venice" (with Noemi Magri). In: Gilvary, *Dating Shakespeare's Plays*. Chapter 9.
Pinksen, Daryl. *Marlowe's Ghost*. New York: iUniverse, 2008.
Pitcher, Seymour. *The Case for Shakespeare's Authorship of "The Famous Victories."* [New York] : State University of New York, 1961.

Raffel, Burton, translator. *Beowulf*. Amherst: University of Massachusetts Press, 1971 [©1963]
Roe, Richard Paul. *The Shakespeare Guide to Italy*. New York: Harper Perennial, ©2011.
Rowse, A.L. *Shakespeare the Man*. New York: Harper & Row ,1973.

Sears, Elisabeth (Betty), and Stephanie Caruana. *Oxford's Revenge*. [s.l.] : [Spear Shaker Press], ©1989 .
Shahan, John (Editor). *Shakespeare Beyond Doubt?* [Claremont, Calif.] : Shakespeare Authorship Coalition; Tamarac, FL : Llumina Press, 2013.
Shapiro, James. *Contested Will*. New York: Simon & Schuster, 2010.
Sieveking, A. Forbes. "Horsemanship, with Farriery." In: *Shakespeare's England, Vol. 2*. London: Clarendon Press, 1916.
Showerman, Dr. Earl. "How did Shakespeare Learn the Art of Medicine?" In: Shahan, *Shakespeare Beyond Doubt?* (Chapter 9)
"Shakespeare's Greater Greek." *Brief Chronicles* 3 (Fall 2011): 37-70.

Simpson, Robert Ritchie. *Shakespeare and Medicine*, Edinburgh: E. & S. Livingstone, 1962.
Singleton, Esther. *Shakespearian Fantasias: Adventures in the Fourth Dimension*. Norwood, Mass.: Privately printed, 1929.

Squire, W. Barclay. "Music." In: *Shakespeare's England, Vol. 2*, London: Clarendon Press, 1916.

Steffanson, Jan. "Shakespeare at Elsinore." In: *Contemporary Review.* London. (January 1896).

Stopes, Charlotte. *Shakespeare's Industry.* London, G. Bell and Sons, 1916.

Stritmatter, Roger. *The Marginalia of Edward de Vere's Geneva Bible.* Northampton, MA: Oxenford Press, [2001], ©2000.

Stritmatter, Roger, and Wildenthal, Bryan. *The Poems of Edward de Vere, 17ᵗʰ Earl of Oxford ... and the Shakespeare Authorship Question: He that Takes the Pain to Pen the Book.* CreateSpace Independent Publishing Platform, 2019

Stritmatter, Roger and Kositsky, Lynne. *On the Date, Sources and Design of Shakespeare's "The Tempest."* Jefferson, North Carolina : McFarland, 2013.

Usher, Peter. "Review of *Hamlet's Universe*." *The Oxfordian* 10 (2007): 157-158.

Wallace, Charles W. *The Evolution of the English Drama Up to Shakespeare.* Port Washington, N.Y.: Kennikat Press, 1968, 1912.

Ward, B.M. *The Seventeenth Earl of Oxford.* London, J. Murray [1928].

Ward, Rev. John. *Diary of the Rev. John Ward, A.M., vicar of Stratford-upon-Avon, extending from 1648-1679.* London, H. Colburn, 1839.

Warren, James A., editor. *Shakespeare Identified by J. Thomas Looney, Centenary Edition.* Cary, North Carolina, Veritas Publications, 2019

Warren, James A., author. *Shakespeare Revolutionized: The First Hundred Years of J. Thomas Looney's "Shakespeare" Identified.* Cary, North Carolina, Veritas Publications, 2021

Waugaman, Richard. "*The Arte of English Poesie*: The Case for Edward de Vere's Authorship." In: *Brief Chronicles*, Vol. III, 2010.
—THE OXFREUDIAN (website) at www.oxfreudian.com
Newly Discovered Works by "William Shakespeare," a.k.a, Edward de Vere, Earl of Oxford, Oxfreudian Press, 2017

Waugh, Alexander. "A Secret Revealed: William Covell and his Polimanteia (1595)." *De Vere Society Newsletter* 20.3 (Oct. 2013): 7-10.

Werth, Andrew. "Shakespeare's 'Lesse Greek.'" *The Oxfordian* 5 (2002): 11-29.

Whalen, Richard. "Shakespeare in Scotland: What Did the Author of Macbeth Know and When Did He Know It?" *The Oxfordian* 6 (2003): 55-70.

—"On Looking into Chapman's Oxford: A Personality Profile of the Seventeenth Earl." *The Oxfordian* 5 (2002): 119-131.

Whalen, Richard and Draya, Ren. *Othello, the Moor of Venice: Fully Annotated from an Oxfordian Perspective* (The Oxfordian Shakespeare Series). Tamarac, FL: Horatio Editions, Llumina Press, 2011.

White, Edward Joseph. *Commentaries on the Law in Shakespeare.* St. Louis, Mo: F.H. Thomas Law Book Co., St. Louis, Mo: Nixon-Jones Printing Co., ©1911.

Whitman, Walt. *November Boughs.* Philadelphia: David McKay, 1888.

Whittemore, Hank. *The Monument: Shakespeare's Sonnets by Edward de Vere, 17th Earl of Oxford.* Marshfield Hills, MA: Meadow Geese Press, 2005.

—*Hank Whittemore's Shakespeare Blog*, https://hankwhittemore.wordpress.com

Wilde, Oscar. *The Critic as Artist.* Girard, KA: Haldeman-Julius, 1920. (Originally published in 1891).

Wildenthal, Bryan H. *Early Shakespeare Authorship Doubts.* San Diego, CA: Zindabad Press, 2019.

(See Stritmatter, Roger, *The Poems of Edward de Vere*)

Wilson, Arthur. *History of Great Britain: being the life and reign of King James the first, relating to what passed from his first access to the crown, till his death.* London: Printed for Richard Lownds, 1653.

Wilson, J. Dover. *Shakespeare's Sonnets, An Introduction.* Cambridge: Cambridge university press, 1964.

Winstanley, Lilian. *Hamlet and the Scottish Succession.* Cambridge: The University Press, 1921.

Wood, Anthony. *Fasti Oxonienses, Vol. I, 1692*; in *Athenae Oxonienses, Vol. 2: an exact history of all the writers and bishops who have had their education in the University of Oxford : to which are added the Fasti, or Annals of the said University,* "London: Printed for F.C. and J. Rivington ... [and 11 others]," 1813.

Woudhuysen, H.R. (Editor). *Love's Labour's Lost.* London: Arden Shakespeare, an imprint of Thomson Learning, 1998.

Wright, Daniel. *The Anglican Shakespeare.* Vancouver, Wa.: Pacific-Columbia Books, 1993.

—"I am I, how 'ere I was begot." In: Boyle, *A Poet's Rage*, Chapter 10.

Wright, Thomas. *The History and Topography of Essex.* London, G. Virtue, 1836.

INDEX

Author Biography

Hank Whittemore is a former professional actor who became a journalist, columnist, television writer, contributor to PARADE and other magazines, and book author.

His fourteen books include *The Super Cops*, a bestseller made into an MGM movie; *CNN: The Inside Story*; *So That Others May Live, the Story of Caroline Hebard and her Search & Rescue Dogs*; and a novel, *Feeling It*, which was an Alternate Selection of the Literary Guild book club.

Hank became involved in the authorship question in 1987 and attended his first Shakespeare Oxford Society conference in 1991. Since then, he has contributed many papers at Oxfordian conferences and articles for Oxfordian publications.

His books about Edward de Vere include *The Monument* (2005), explaining a macro-theory of the Sonnets from an Oxfordian perspective; *Shakespeare's Son and His Sonnets* (2010), a synopsis of the foregoing book; *Twelve Years in the Life of Shakespeare* (2012), a compilation of his "A Year in the Life" columns *for Shakespeare Matters*; and his current *100 Reasons Shake-speare was the Earl of Oxford* (2016), a specially edited and arranged compilation of pieces first published on *Hank Whittemore's Shakespeare Blog* during nearly four years. (This is the second edition.)

Whittemore has performed the one-man show *Shake-speare's Treason*, co-written with director Ted Story, at various theatrical venues in the U.S. and England.

Made in United States
North Haven, CT
13 January 2023

31042409R00191